Analysis for Financial Management

The McGraw-Hill Education Series in Finance, Insurance, and Real Estate

FINANCIAL MANAGEMENT

Block, Hirt, and Danielsen
Foundations of Financial Management
Sixteenth Edition

Brealey, Myers, and Allen
Principles of Corporate Finance
Twelfth Edition

Brealey, Myers, and Allen
Principles of Corporate Finance, Concise
Second Edition

Brealey, Myers, and Marcus
Fundamentals of Corporate Finance
Ninth Edition

Brooks
FinGame Online 5.0

Bruner, Eades, and Schill
Case Studies in Finance: Managing for Corporate Value Creation
Eighth Edition

Cornett, Adair, and Nofsinger
Finance: Applications and Theory
Fourth Edition

Cornett, Adair, and Nofsinger
M: Finance
Fourth Edition

DeMello
Cases in Finance
Third Edition

Grinblatt (editor)
Stephen A. Ross, Mentor: Influence through Generations

Grinblatt and Titman
Financial Markets and Corporate Strategy
Second Edition

Higgins, Koski, and Mitton
Analysis for Financial Management
Twelfth Edition

Ross, Westerfield, Jaffe, and Jordan
Corporate Finance
Eleventh Edition

Ross, Westerfield, Jaffe, and Jordan
Corporate Finance: Core Principles and Applications
Fifth Edition

Ross, Westerfield, and Jordan
Essentials of Corporate Finance
Ninth Edition

Ross, Westerfield, and Jordan
Fundamentals of Corporate Finance
Twelfth Edition

Shefrin
Behavioral Corporate Finance: Decisions that Create Value
Second Edition

INVESTMENTS

Bodie, Kane, and Marcus
Essentials of Investments
Tenth Edition

Bodie, Kane, and Marcus
Investments
Eleventh Edition

Hirt and Block
Fundamentals of Investment Management
Tenth Edition

Jordan, Miller, and Dolvin
Fundamentals of Investments: Valuation and Management
Eighth Edition

Stewart, Piros, and Heisler
Running Money: Professional Portfolio Management
First Edition

Sundaram and Das
Derivatives: Principles and Practice
Second Edition

FINANCIAL INSTITUTIONS AND MARKETS

Rose and Hudgins
Bank Management and Financial Services
Ninth Edition

Rose and Marquis
Financial Institutions and Markets
Eleventh Edition

Saunders and Cornett
Financial Institutions Management: A Risk Management Approach
Ninth Edition

Saunders and Cornett
Financial Markets and Institutions
Seventh Edition

INTERNATIONAL FINANCE

Eun and Resnick
International Financial Management
Eighth Edition

REAL ESTATE

Brueggeman and Fisher
Real Estate Finance and Investments
Sixteenth Edition

Ling and Archer
Real Estate Principles: A Value Approach
Fifth Edition

FINANCIAL PLANNING AND INSURANCE

Allen, Melone, Rosenbloom, and Mahoney
Retirement Plans: 401(k)s, IRAs, and Other Deferred Compensation Approaches
Twelfth Edition

Altfest
Personal Financial Planning
Second Edition

Harrington and Niehaus
Risk Management and Insurance
Second Edition

Kapoor, Dlabay, Hughes, and Hart
Focus on Personal Finance: An active approach to help you achieve financial literacy
Sixth Edition

Kapoor, Dlabay, Hughes, and Hart
Personal Finance
Twelfth Edition

Walker and Walker
Personal Finance: Building Your Future
Second Edition

Analysis for Financial Management

Twelfth Edition

ROBERT C. HIGGINS
Marguerite Reimers
  Emeritus Professor of Finance
The University of Washington

with

JENNIFER L. KOSKI
Kirby L. Cramer Endowed Chair
  in Finance
Associate Professor of Finance
The University of Washington

and

TODD MITTON
Ned C. Hill Professor of Finance
Brigham Young University

Mc
Graw
Hill
Education

ANALYSIS FOR FINANCIAL MANAGEMENT

Published by McGraw-Hill Education, 2 Penn Plaza, New York, NY 10121. Copyright © 2019 by McGraw-Hill Education. All rights reserved. Printed in the United States of America. No part of this publication may be reproduced or distributed in any form or by any means, or stored in a database or retrieval system, without the prior written consent of McGraw-Hill Education, including, but not limited to, in any network or other electronic storage or transmission, or broadcast for distance learning.

Some ancillaries, including electronic and print components, may not be available to customers outside the United States.

This book is printed on acid-free paper.

1 2 3 4 5 6 7 8 9 LCR 21 20 19 18

ISBN 978-1-260-09191-5
MHID 1-260-09191-0

Cover Image: © *Oleg Podzorov/Shutterstock*

mheducation.com/highered

Brief Contents

Contents

Preface

Like its predecessors, the twelfth edition of *Analysis for Financial Management* is for nonfinancial executives and business students interested in the practice of financial management. It introduces standard techniques and recent advances in a practical, intuitive way. The book assumes no prior background beyond a rudimentary and perhaps rusty familiarity with financial statements—although a healthy curiosity about what makes business tick is also useful. Emphasis throughout is on the managerial implications of financial analysis.

Analysis for Financial Management should prove valuable to individuals interested in sharpening their managerial skills and to executive program participants. The book has also found a home in university classrooms as the sole text in Executive MBA and applied finance courses, as a companion text in case-oriented courses, and as a supplementary reading in more theoretical courses.

Analysis for Financial Management is our attempt to translate into another medium the enjoyment and stimulation we have received over many years working with executives and college students. This experience has convinced us that financial techniques and concepts need not be abstract or obtuse; that significant advances in the field, such as agency theory, market signaling, market efficiency, capital asset pricing, and real options analysis, are important to practitioners; and that finance has much to say about the broader aspects of company management. We are also convinced that any activity in which so much money changes hands so quickly cannot fail to be interesting.

Part One looks at the management of existing resources, including the use of financial statements and ratio analysis to assess a company's financial health, its strengths, weaknesses, recent performance, and future prospects. Emphasis throughout is on the ties between a company's operating activities and its financial performance. A recurring theme is that a business must be viewed as an integrated whole and that effective financial management is possible only within the context of a company's broader operating characteristics and strategies.

The rest of the book deals with the acquisition and management of new resources. Part Two examines financial forecasting and planning, with particular emphasis on managing growth and decline. Part Three considers the financing of company operations, including a review of the principal security types, the markets in which they trade, and the proper choice of security type by the issuing company. The latter requires a close look at financial leverage and its effects on the firm and its shareholders.

Part Four addresses the use of discounted cash flow techniques, such as the net present value and the internal rate of return, to evaluate investment opportunities. It also deals with the difficult task of incorporating risk into investment appraisal. The book concludes with an examination of business valuation and company restructuring within the context of the ongoing debate over the proper roles of shareholders, boards of directors, and incumbent managers in governing America's public corporations.

An extensive glossary of financial terms and suggested answers to odd-numbered, end-of-chapter problems follow the last chapter.

Changes in the Twelfth Edition

Readers familiar with earlier editions of *Analysis for Financial Management* will notice the book now has three authors with Jennifer Koski and Todd Mitton joining long-time author Robert (Rocky) Higgins. We have found this partnership stimulating, and trust you will agree that three heads are, indeed, better than one.

Other noteworthy changes and refinements in the twelfth edition include:

- A complete revision of the appendix to Chapter 5 on financial derivatives and their use in managing risk.

- Expanded coverage in Chapter 2 of "adjusted earnings" in financial reporting.

- Inclusion of operating and cash conversion cycles as part of evaluating financial performance, also in Chapter 2.

- Use of Microsoft's recent $26.2 billion acquisition of LinkedIn Corporation in Chapter 9 to illustrate the market for corporate control.

- Expanded discussion of share repurchases and their role in managing growth appearing in Chapter 4.

- A new introduction to discounted cash flow analysis at the start of Chapter 7, emphasizing the topic's pivotal role in the creation of shareholder value. (If you are inclined to begin study of corporate finance with discounted cash flow analysis and value creation, we suggest you consider starting *Analysis for Financial Management* with Chapter 7, followed by 5, 6, 8, and 9.)

- An updated discussion of crowdfunding and its probable future in Chapter 5.

- Use of Hasbro, Inc., a leading toy and game company, as an extended example throughout the book.

McGraw-Hill's *Connect* (connect.mheducation.com)

connect McGraw-Hill's *Connect®* is an online assessment solution that connects students with the tools and resources they'll need to achieve success. *Connect* allows faculty to create and deliver assignments from the end of chapter material and exams easily with selectable test bank items. Instructors can also build their own questions into the system for homework or practice.

Readers have access to McGraw-Hill's adaptive self-study technology in LearnSmart and SmartBook through their instructor's course URL in *Connect,* and can also access the Excel Spreadsheets that accompany this text through the Student Resources link. For students not enrolled in a course using *Connect,* the Excel Spreadsheets can be accessed at **mhhe.com/Higgins12e.**

Intended primarily for instructor use, the *Connect* Instructor Library houses, among other things:

- A test bank.

- PowerPoint presentations.

- An annotated list of suggested cases to accompany the book.

- Suggested answers to even-numbered problems.

To access the Instructor Library, log in to your *Connect* course, select the "Library" tab, and then select "Instructor Resources."

For more information about *Connect,* LearnSmart, or SmartBook, go to **connect.mheducation.com**, or contact a McGraw-Hill sales representative. For 24-hour support, you can e-mail a Product Specialist or search Frequently Asked Questions at **mhhe.com/support**. Or for a human, call **800-331-5094**.

A word of caution: *Analysis for Financial Management* emphasizes the application and interpretation of analytic techniques in decision making. These techniques have proved useful for putting financial problems into perspective and for helping managers anticipate the consequences of their actions. However, techniques can never substitute for thought. Even with the best technique, it is still necessary to define and prioritize issues, to modify analysis to fit specific circumstances, to strike the proper balance between quantitative analysis and more qualitative considerations, and to evaluate alternatives insightfully and creatively. Mastery of technique is only the necessary first step toward effective management.

We are indebted to Andy Halula of Standard & Poor's for providing timely updates to Research Insight. The ability to access current Compustat data continues to be a great help in providing timely examples of current practice. We also owe a large thank you to the following people for their insightful reviews of the twelfth edition and their constructive advice. They did an excellent job. Any remaining shortcomings are ours, not theirs.

Onur Arugaslan, Western Michigan University

Buleny Aybar, Southern New Hampshire University

Aaron Butler, Warner Pacific College

Ekaterina Emm, Seattle University

Matthew Giguere, University of Wisconsin-Stout

Jaemin Kim, San Diego State University

Mbodja Mougoue, Wayne State University

Ryan Smith, Columbia College

Andy Terry, University of Arkansas

Hongxia Wang, Ashland University

Arthur Wilson, George Washington University

Devrim Yaman, Western Michigan University

Jaime Zender, University of Colorado

We appreciate the exceptional direction provided by Noelle Bathurst, Chuck Synovec, Trina Maurer, and Heather Ervolino of McGraw-Hill on the development, design, and editing of the book. David Beim, Dave Dubofsky, Jack McDonald, George Parker, Megan Partch, and Alan Shapiro have our continuing gratitude for their insightful help and support throughout the book's evolution. Finally, we want to express our appreciation to students and colleagues at the University of Washington, Brigham Young University, Stanford University, IMD, The Darden School, The Pacific Coast Banking School, The Koblenz Graduate School of Management, The Gordon Institute of Business Science, Boeing, and Microsoft, among others, for stimulating our continuing interest in the practice and teaching of financial management.

We envy you learning this material for the first time. It's a stimulating intellectual adventure.

Robert C. (Rocky) Higgins
Marguerite Reimers Emeritus Professor of Finance
Foster School of Business
University of Washington
rhiggins@uw.edu

Jennifer L. Koski
Kirby L. Cramer Endowed Chair in Finance
Associate Professor of Finance
Foster School of Business
University of Washington
jkoski@uw.edu

Todd Mitton
Ned C. Hill Professor of Finance
Marriott School of Business
Brigham Young University
todd.mitton@byu.edu

PART ONE

Assessing the Financial Health of the Firm

Interpreting Financial Statements

Financial statements are like fine perfume; to be sniffed but not swallowed.

Abraham Brilloff

Accounting is the scorecard of business. It translates a company's diverse activities into a set of objective numbers that provide information about the firm's performance, problems, and prospects. Finance involves the interpretation of these accounting numbers for assessing performance and planning future actions.

The skills of financial analysis are important to a wide range of people, including investors, creditors, and regulators. But nowhere are they more important than within the company. Regardless of functional specialty or company size, managers who possess these skills are able to diagnose their firm's ills, prescribe useful remedies, and anticipate the financial consequences of their actions. Like a ballplayer who cannot keep score, an operating manager who does not fully understand accounting and finance works under an unnecessary handicap.

This and the following chapter look at the use of accounting information to assess financial health. We begin with an overview of the accounting principles governing financial statements and a discussion of one of the most abused and confusing notions in finance: cash flow. Two recurring themes will be that defining and measuring profits is more challenging than one might expect, and that profitability alone does not guarantee success, or even survival. In Chapter 2, we look at measures of financial performance and ratio analysis.

The Cash Flow Cycle

Finance can seem arcane and complex to the uninitiated. However, a comparatively few basic principles should guide your thinking. One is that *a company's finances and operations are integrally connected.* A company's

FIGURE 1.1 **The Cash Flow–Production Cycle**

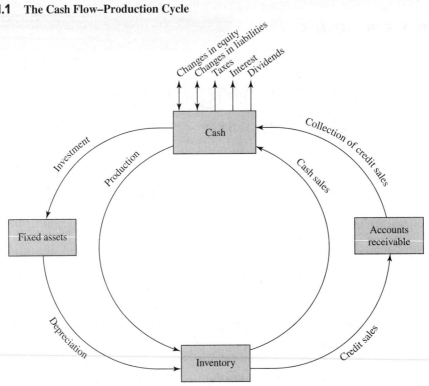

activities, method of operation, and competitive strategy all fundamentally shape the firm's financial structure. The reverse is also true: Decisions that appear to be primarily financial in nature can significantly affect company operations. For example, the way a company finances its assets can affect the nature of the investments it is able to undertake in future years.

The cash flow–production cycle shown in Figure 1.1 illustrates the close interplay between company operations and finances. For simplicity, suppose the company shown is a new one that has raised money from owners and creditors, has purchased productive assets, and is now ready to begin operations. To do so, the company uses cash to purchase raw materials and hire workers; with these inputs, it makes the product and stores it temporarily in inventory. Thus, what began as cash is now physical inventory. When the company sells an item, the physical inventory changes back into cash. If the sale is for cash, this occurs immediately; otherwise, cash is not realized until some later time when the account receivable is collected. This simple movement of cash to inventory, to accounts receivable, and back to cash is the firm's *operating,* or *working capital, cycle.*

Another ongoing activity represented in Figure 1.1 is investment. Over a period of time, the company's fixed assets are consumed, or worn out, in the creation of products. It is as though every item passing through the business takes with it a small portion of the value of fixed assets. The accountant recognizes this process by continually reducing the accounting value of fixed assets and increasing the value of merchandise flowing into inventory by an amount known as *depreciation.* To maintain productive capacity and to finance additional growth, the company must invest part of its newly received cash in new fixed assets. The object of this whole exercise, of course, is to ensure that the cash returning from the working capital cycle and the investment cycle exceeds the amount that started the journey.

We could complicate Figure 1.1 further by including accounts payable and expanding on the use of debt and equity to generate cash, but the figure already demonstrates two basic principles. First, *financial statements are an important window on reality.* A company's operating policies, production techniques, and inventory and credit-control systems fundamentally determine the firm's financial profile. If, for example, a company requires payment on credit sales to be more prompt, its financial statements will reveal a reduced investment in accounts receivable and possibly a change in its revenues and profits. This linkage between a company's operations and its finances is our rationale for studying financial statements. We seek to understand company operations and predict the financial consequences of changing them.

The second principle illustrated in Figure 1.1 is that *profits do not equal cash flow.* Cash—and the timely conversion of cash into inventories, accounts receivable, and back into cash—is the lifeblood of any company. If this cash flow is severed or significantly interrupted, insolvency can occur. Yet the fact that a company is profitable is no assurance that its cash flow will be sufficient to maintain solvency. To illustrate, suppose a company loses control of its accounts receivable by allowing customers more and more time to pay, or suppose the company consistently makes more merchandise than it sells. Then, even though the company is selling merchandise at a profit in the eyes of an accountant, its sales may not be generating sufficient cash soon enough to replenish the cash outflows required for production and investment. When a company has insufficient cash to pay its maturing obligations, it is insolvent. As another example, suppose the company is managing its inventory and receivables carefully, but rapid sales growth is necessitating an ever-larger investment in these assets. Then, even though the company is profitable, it may have too little cash to meet its obligations. The company will literally be "growing broke." These brief examples illustrate why a manager must be concerned at least as much with cash flows as with profits.

To explore these themes in more detail and to sharpen your skills in using accounting information to assess performance, we need to review the basics of financial statements. If this is your first look at financial accounting, buckle up because we will be moving quickly. If the pace is too quick, take a look at one of the accounting texts recommended at the end of the chapter.

The Balance Sheet

The most important source of information for evaluating the financial health of a company is its financial statements, consisting principally of a balance sheet, an income statement, and a cash flow statement. Although these statements can appear complex at times, they all rest on a very simple foundation. To understand this foundation and to see the ties among the three statements, let us look briefly at each.

A *balance sheet* is a financial snapshot, taken at a point in time, of all the assets the company owns and all the claims against those assets. The basic relationship, and indeed the foundation for all of accounting, is

$$\text{Assets} = \text{Liabilities} + \text{Shareholders' equity}$$

It is as if a herd (flock? column?) of accountants runs through the business on the appointed day, making a list of everything the company owns, and assigning each item a value. After tabulating the firm's assets, the accountants list all outstanding company liabilities, where a liability is simply an obligation to deliver something of value in the future—or more colloquially, some form of an "IOU." Having thus totaled up what the company *owns* and what it *owes,* the accountants call the difference between the two *shareholders' equity.* Shareholders' equity is the accountant's estimate of the value of the shareholders' investment in the firm, just as the value of a homeowner's equity is the value of the home (the asset), less the mortgage outstanding against it (the liability). Shareholders' equity is also known variously as *owners' equity, stockholders' equity, net worth,* or simply *equity.*

It is important to realize that the basic accounting equation holds for individual transactions, as well as for the firm as a whole. When a firm pays $1 million in wages, cash declines $1 million and shareholders' equity falls by the same amount. Similarly, when a company borrows $100,000, cash rises $100,000, as does a liability named something like *loans outstanding.* And when a company receives a $10,000 payment from a customer, cash rises while another asset, accounts receivable, falls by the same figure. In each instance, the double-entry nature of accounting guarantees that the basic accounting equation holds for each transaction, and when summed across all transactions, it holds for the company as a whole.

To see how the repeated application of this single formula underlies the creation of company financial statements, consider Worldwide Sports (WWS), a newly founded retailer of value-priced sporting goods. In January 2017, the founder invested $150,000 of his personal savings and added another $100,000 borrowed from relatives to start the business. After buying furniture and display fixtures for $60,000 and merchandise for $80,000, WWS was ready to open its doors.

The following six transactions summarize WWS's activities over the course of its first year.

- Sold $900,000 of sports equipment, receiving $875,000 in cash, with $25,000 still to be paid.

- Paid $190,000 in wages, including the owner's salary.

- Purchased $380,000 of merchandise at wholesale, with $20,000 still owed to suppliers, and $30,000 worth of product still in WWS's inventory at year-end.

- Spent $210,000 on other expenses, such as utilities and rent.

- Depreciated furniture and fixtures by $15,000.

- Paid $10,000 interest on WWS's loan from relatives and another $40,000 in income taxes to the government.

Table 1.1 shows how an accountant would record these transactions. WWS's beginning balance, the first line in the table, shows cash of $250,000, a loan of $100,000, and equity of $150,000. But these numbers change quickly as the company buys fixtures and an initial inventory of merchandise. And they change further as each of the listed transactions occurs.

TABLE 1.1 Worldwide Sports Financial Transactions 2017 ($ thousands)

		Assets			=	Liabilities		+	Equity
	Cash	Accounts Receivable	Inventory	Fixed Assets	=	Accounts Payable	Loan from Relatives		Owners' Equity
Beginning Balance 1/1/17	$ 250				=		$100		$ 150
Initial purchases	(140)		80	60	=				
Sales	875	25			=				900
Wages	(190)				=				(190)
Merchandise purchases	(360)		30		=	20			(350)
Other expenses	(210)				=				(210)
Depreciation				(15)	=				(15)
Interest payment	(10)				=				(10)
Income tax payment	(40)				=				(40)
Ending Balance 12/31/17	$ 175	$25	$110	$45	=	$20	$100		$ 235

Abstracting from the accounting details, there are two important things to note here. First, the basic accounting equation holds for each transaction. For every line in the table, assets equal liabilities plus owners' equity. Second, WWS's year-end balance sheet across the bottom of the table is just its beginning balance sheet plus the cumulative effect of the individual transactions. For example, ending cash on December 31, 2017 is the beginning cash of $250,000 plus or minus the cash involved in each transaction. Incidentally, WWS's first year appears to have been a decent one: Owner's equity is up $85,000 over the year, on top of whatever the owner paid himself in salary.

To further convince you that the bottom row of Table 1.1 really is a balance sheet, the following table presents the same information in a more conventional format.

Worldwide Sports Balance Sheet, December 31, 2017 ($ thousands)

Cash	$175	Accounts payable	$ 20
Accounts receivable	25	**Total current liabilities**	20
Inventory	110	Loan from relatives	100
Total current assets	310	Equity	235
Fixed assets	45	**Total liabilities and**	
Total assets	$355	**Shareholders' equity**	$355

If a balance sheet is a snapshot in time, the income statement and the cash flow statement are videos, highlighting changes in two especially important balance sheet accounts over time. Business owners are naturally interested in how company operations have affected the value of their investment. The income statement addresses this question by partitioning the recorded changes in owners' equity into revenues and expenses, where revenues increase owners' equity and expenses reduce it. The difference between revenues and expenses is earnings, or net income.

Looking at the right-most column in Table 1.1, WWS's 2017 income statement looks like this. Note that the $85,000 net income appearing at the bottom of the statement equals the change in shareholders' equity over the year.

Worldwide Sports Income Statement, 2017 ($ thousands)

Sales	$900
Wages	190
Merchandise purchases	350
Depreciation	15
Gross profit	$345
Other expenses	210
Interest expense	10
Income before tax	$125
Income taxes	40
Net income	$ 85

FIGURE 1.2   **Ties among Financial Statements**

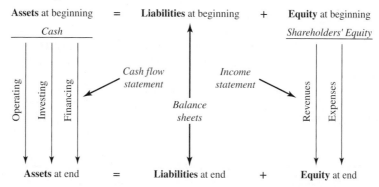

The focus of the cash flow statement is solvency, having enough cash in the bank to pay bills as they come due. The cash flow statement provides a detailed look at changes in the company's cash balance over time. As an organizing principle, the statement segregates changes in cash into three broad categories: cash provided, or consumed, by operating activities, by investing activities, and by financing activities. Figure 1.2 is a simple schematic diagram showing the close conceptual ties among the three principal financial statements.

To illustrate the techniques and concepts presented throughout the book, I will refer whenever possible to Hasbro, Inc. Hasbro is a leading toy and game company whose products and brands, such as Monopoly, Nerf, and Play-Doh, bring back vivid memories of childhood. Hasbro also develops toys and games for partners, including for the Marvel and Star Wars franchises. In 2016, it began a licensing agreement with Walt Disney Company to market Disney Princess and Frozen dolls. Hasbro sells toys and games in over 120 countries and has offices in 35 countries. The company focus is on having fun, or as they describe it, "Creating the World's Best Play Experience."

Headquartered in Pawtucket, Rhode Island, with annual sales of $5 billion, Hasbro trades on the NASDAQ stock market. The firm was founded in 1923 by Henry and Hillel Hassenfeld as Hassenfeld Brothers, later shortened to Hasbro Inc.. The company started off selling textile remnants and school supplies, and in the 1940s expanded its product line to include its first toys. During the next couple of decades, Hasbro introduced some iconic brands such as Mr. Potato Head and G.I. Joe. In the 1990s, Hasbro successfully adapted its product line to embrace digital games and videos. By 2016, 46 percent of Hasbro's sales came from its own brands. Partner Brands contributed 28 percent of sales, with the remainder coming from the Hasbro Gaming and Emerging Brands product lines.

See **hasbro.com**. Follow Corporate > Investors > Financials & Filings for financial statements.

TABLE 1.2 Hasbro Inc. Balance Sheets ($ millions)*

Source: Data from Hasbro 2016 annual report and Compustat

	December 31		Change in Account
	2015	2016	
Assets			
Cash and cash equivalents	$ 977	$1,282	$ 306
Accounts receivable, less reserve for possible losses	1,218	1,320	102
Inventories	384	388	3
Other current assets	287	238	(49)
Total current assets	2,866	3,228	
Gross property, plant, and equipment	601	651	50
Less accumulated depreciation and amortization	364	384	20
Net property, plant, and equipment	238	267	30
Goodwill and other intangible assets, net	874	817	(57)
Other assets	744	780	36
Total assets	$4,721	$5,091	
Liabilities and Shareholders' Equity			
Debt due in one year	165	522	358
Accounts payable	241	320	79
Accrued liabilities	659	776	117
Total current liabilities	1,065	1,618	
Long-term debt	1,547	1,199	(348)
Other long-term liabilities	445	411	(34)
Total liabilities	3,057	3,228	
Common stock	105	105	
Additional paid-in capital	894	985	
Retained earnings	3,706	3,954	
Treasury stock	(3,041)	(3,182)	
Total shareholders' equity	1,664	1,863	199
Total liabilities and shareholders' equity	$4,721	$5,091	

*Totals may not add due to rounding.

Tables 1.2 and 1.3 present Hasbro's balance sheets and income statements for 2015 and 2016. If the precise meaning of every asset and liability category in Table 1.2 is not immediately apparent, be patient. We will discuss many of them in the following text. In addition, all of the accounting terms used appear in the glossary at the end of the book.

Hasbro Inc.'s balance sheet equation for 2016 is

$$\text{Assets} = \text{Liabilities} + \text{Shareholders' equity}$$
$$\$5{,}091 \text{ million} = \$3{,}228 \text{ million} + \$1{,}863 \text{ million}$$

TABLE 1.3 Hasbro Inc. Income Statements ($ millions)*

Source: Data from Hasbro 2016 annual report and Compustat

	January 1 to December 31	
	2015	2016
Net sales	$4,448	$5,020
Cost of goods sold	1,987	2,231
Gross profit	2,460	2,789
Selling, general, and administrative expenses	1,616	1,813
Depreciation and amortization	155	154
Total operating expenses	1,772	1,968
Operating income	689	821
Interest expense	97	97
Other nonoperating expense (income)	(17)	14
Total nonoperating expenses	80	111
Income before income taxes	609	710
Provision for income taxes	157	159
Net income	$ 452	$ 551

*Totals may not add due to rounding.

Current Assets and Liabilities

By convention, U.S. accountants list assets and liabilities on the balance sheet in order of decreasing liquidity, where liquidity refers to the speed with which an item can be converted to cash. Thus, cash, marketable securities, and accounts receivable appear at the top, while land, plant, and equipment are toward the bottom. Similarly on the liabilities side, short-term loans and accounts payable are toward the top, while shareholders' equity is at the bottom.

Accountants also arbitrarily define any asset or liability that is expected to turn into cash within one year as *current* and all others assets and liabilities as *long term.* Inventory is a current asset because there is reason to believe it will be sold and will generate cash within one year. Accounts payable are short-term liabilities because they must be paid within one year. Note that over half of Hasbro's assets are current, a fact we will say more about in the next chapter.

A Word to the Unwary

Nothing puts a damper on a good financial discussion (if such exists) faster than the suggestion that if a company is short of cash, it can always spend some of its shareholders' equity. Equity is on the liabilities side of the balance sheet, not the asset side. It represents owners' claims against existing assets. In other words, that money has already been spent.

Shareholders' Equity

A common source of confusion is the large number of accounts appearing in the shareholders' equity portion of the balance sheet. Hasbro has four, beginning with common stock and ending with treasury stock (see Table 1.2). Unless forced to do otherwise, my advice is to forget these distinctions. They keep accountants and attorneys employed, but seldom make much practical difference. As a first cut, just add up everything that is not an IOU and call it shareholders' equity.

The Income Statement

Looking at Hasbro's operating performance in 2016, the basic income statement relation appearing in Table 1.3 is

Revenues	−			Expenses					=	Net income
Net sales	−	Cost of goods sold	−	Operating expenses	−	Nonoperating expenses	−	Taxes	=	Net income
$5,020	−	$2,231	−	$1,968	−	$111	−	$159	=	$551

Net income records the extent to which net sales generated during the accounting period exceeded expenses incurred in producing the sales. For variety, net income is also commonly referred to as *earnings* or *profits,* frequently with the word *net* stuck in front of them; net sales are often called *revenues* or *net revenues;* and cost of goods sold is labeled *cost of sales.* I have never found a meaningful distinction between these terms. Why so many words to say the same thing? My personal belief is that accountants are so rule-bound in their calculations of the various amounts that their creativity runs a bit amok when it comes to naming them.

Income statements are commonly divided into operating and nonoperating segments. As the names imply, the operating segment reports the results of the company's major, ongoing activities, while the nonoperating segment summarizes all ancillary activities. In 2016, Hasbro reported operating income of $821 million and nonoperating expenses of $111 million, consisting largely of interest expense.

Measuring Earnings

This is not the place for a detailed discussion of accounting. But because earnings, or lack of same, are a critical indicator of financial health, several technical details of earnings measurement deserve mention.

Accrual Accounting

The measurement of accounting earnings involves two steps: (1) identifying revenues for the period and (2) matching the corresponding costs to revenues.

Looking at the first step, it is important to recognize that revenue is not the same as cash received. According to the *accrual principle* (a cruel principle?) of accounting, revenue is recognized as soon as "the effort required to generate the sale is substantially complete and there is a reasonable certainty that payment will be received." The accountant sees the timing of the actual cash receipts as a mere technicality. For credit sales, the accrual principle means that revenue is recognized at the time of sale, not when the customer pays. This can result in a significant time lag between the generation of revenue and the receipt of cash. Looking at Hasbro, we see that revenue in 2016 was $5,020 million, but accounts receivable increased $102 million. We conclude that cash received from sales during 2016 was only $4,918 million ($5,020 – $102 million). The other $102 million still awaits collection.

Depreciation

Fixed assets and their associated depreciation present the accountant with a particularly challenging problem in matching. Suppose that in 2018, a company constructs, for $50 million, a new facility that has an expected productive life of 10 years. If the accountant assigns the entire cost of the facility to expenses in 2018, some weird results follow. Income in 2018 will appear depressed due to the $50 million expense, while income in the following nine years will look that much better as the new facility contributes to revenue but not to expenses. Thus, charging the full cost of a long-term asset to one year clearly distorts reported income.

The preferred approach is to spread the cost of the facility over its expected useful life in the form of depreciation. Because the only cash outlay associated with the facility occurs in 2018, the annual depreciation listed as a cost on the company's income statement is not a cash outflow. It is a *noncash charge* used to match the 2018 expenditure with resulting revenue. Said differently, depreciation is the allocation of past expenditures to future time periods to match revenues and expenses. A glance at Hasbro's income statement reveals that, in 2016, the company included a $154 million noncash charge for depreciation and amortization among their operating expenses. Further along in the text, we will see that during the same year, the company spent $155 million acquiring new property, plant, and equipment.

To determine the amount of depreciation to take on a particular asset, three estimates are required: the asset's useful life, its salvage value, and the method of allocation to be employed. These estimates should be based on economic and engineering information, experience, and any other objective data about the asset's likely performance. Broadly speaking, there are two methods of allocating an asset's cost over its useful life. Under the *straight-line* method, the accountant depreciates the asset by a uniform amount each year. If an asset costs $50 million, has an expected useful life of 10 years, and has an estimated salvage value of $10 million, straight-line depreciation will be $4 million per year ([$50 million – $10 million]/10).

The second method of cost allocation is really a family of methods known as *accelerated depreciation*. Each technique charges more depreciation in the early years of the asset's life and correspondingly less in later years. Accelerated depreciation does not enable a company to take more depreciation in total; rather, it alters the timing of the recognition. While the specifics of the various accelerated techniques need not detain us here, you should recognize that the life expectancy, the salvage value, and the allocation method a company uses can fundamentally affect reported earnings. In general, if a company is conservative and depreciates its assets rapidly, it will tend to understate current earnings, and vice versa.

Taxes

A second noteworthy feature of depreciation accounting involves taxes. Most U.S. companies, except very small ones, keep at least two sets of financial records: one for managing the company and reporting to shareholders, and another for determining the firm's tax bill. The objective of the first set is, or should be, to accurately portray the company's financial performance. The objective of the second set is much simpler: to minimize taxes. Forget objectivity and minimize taxes. These differing objectives mean the accounting principles used to construct the two sets of books differ substantially. Depreciation accounting is a case in point. Regardless of the method used to report to shareholders, company tax books will minimize current taxes by employing the most rapid method of depreciation over the shortest useful life the tax authorities allow.

This dual reporting means that actual cash payments to tax authorities usually differ from the provision for income taxes appearing on a company's income statement, sometimes trailing the provision and other times exceeding it. When this happens, the company will report the difference somewhere on its balance sheet. If the company pays less than it owes, it will have a liability with a name like "taxes payable," representing the money it must pay tax authorities in future years. In the meantime, this money can be used to finance the business. Tax deferral techniques create the equivalent of interest-free loans from the government. In Japan and other countries that do not allow the use of separate accounting techniques for tax and reporting purposes, these complications never arise. Hasbro's balance sheet doesn't show a line item for over- or underpaying taxes. Either this number is too small to warrant its own line, or Hasbro is paying the exact amount it owes according to its income statement.

Research and Marketing

Now that you understand how accountants use depreciation to spread the cost of long-lived assets over their useful lives to better match revenues and costs, you may think you also understand how they treat research and marketing expenses. Because research and development (R&D) and marketing outlays promise benefits over a number of future periods, it is only logical that an accountant would show these expenditures as assets when they are incurred and then spread the costs over the assets' expected useful lives in the form of a noncash charge such as depreciation. This may be impeccable logic, but it isn't what accountants do, at least not in the United States. Because the magnitude and duration of the prospective payoffs from R&D and marketing expenditures are difficult to estimate, accountants typically duck the problem by forcing companies to record the entire expenditure as an operating cost in the year incurred. Thus, although a company's research outlays in a given year may have produced technical breakthroughs that will benefit the firm for decades to come, all of the costs must be shown on the income statement in the year incurred. The requirement that companies expense all research and marketing expenditures when incurred commonly understates the profitability of high-tech and high-marketing companies and complicates comparison of American companies with those in other nations that treat such expenditures more liberally.

Defining Earnings

Creditors and investors look to company earnings for help in answering two fundamental questions: How did the company do last period, and how might it do in the future? To answer the first question, it is important to use a broad-based measure of income that includes everything affecting the company's performance over the accounting period. However, to answer the second question, we want a narrower income measure that abstracts from all unusual, nonrecurring events to focus strictly on the company's steady state, or ongoing, performance.

The accounting profession and the Securities and Exchange Commission obligingly provide two such official measures, known as net income and operating income, and require companies to report them on their financial statements.

Net income, or net profit, is the proverbial "bottom line," defined as total revenue less total expenses.

Operating income is profit realized from day-to-day operations excluding taxes, interest income and expense, and what are known as extraordinary items. An extraordinary item is one that is both unusual in nature and infrequent in occurrence.

Managers and investment professionals often consider several other, unofficial measures of earnings. Here are two of the more popular ones:

EBIT (pronounced E-bit) is earnings before interest and taxes, a useful and widely used measure of a business's income before it is divided among creditors, owners, and the taxman. EBIT is sometimes used interchangeably with operating income.

EBITDA (pronounced E-bit-da) is earnings before interest, taxes, depreciation, and amortization. EBITDA has its uses in some industries, such as broadcasting, where depreciation charges may routinely overstate true economic depreciation. However, as Warren Buffett notes, treating EBITDA as equivalent to earnings is tantamount to saying that a business is the commercial equivalent of the pyramids—forever state-of-the-art, never needing to be replaced, improved, or refurbished. In Buffett's view, EBITDA is a number favored by investment bankers when they cannot justify a deal based on EBIT.

Sources and Uses Statements

Two very basic but valuable things to know about a company are where it gets its cash and how it spends the cash. At first blush, it might appear that the income statement will answer these questions because it records flows of resources over time. But further reflection will convince you that the income statement is deficient in two respects: It includes accruals that are not cash flows, and it lists only cash flows associated with the sale of goods or services during the accounting period. A host of other cash receipts and disbursements do not appear on the income statement. Thus, Hasbro increased its investment in accounts receivable by $102 million in 2016 (Table 1.2) with little or no trace of this buildup on its income statement. Hasbro also decreased long-term debt by almost $350 million with little effect on its income statement.

To gain a more accurate picture of where a company got its money and how it spent it, we need to look more closely at the balance sheet or, more precisely, two balance sheets. Use the following two-step procedure. First, place two balance sheets for different dates side by side, and note all of the changes in accounts that occurred over the period. The changes for Hasbro in 2016 appear in the rightmost column of Table 1.2. Second, segregate the changes into those that generated cash and those that consumed cash. The result is a *sources and uses statement.*

Here are the guidelines for distinguishing between a source and a use of cash:

- *A company generates cash in two ways: by reducing an asset or by increasing a liability.* The sale of used equipment, the liquidation of inventories, and the reduction of accounts receivable are all reductions in asset accounts and are all sources of cash to the company. On the liabilities side of the balance sheet, an increase in a bank loan and the sale of common stock are increases in liabilities, which again generate cash.

- *A company also uses cash in two ways: to increase an asset account or to reduce a liability account.* Adding to inventories or accounts receivable and building a new plant all increase assets and all use cash. Conversely, the repayment of a bank loan, the reduction of accounts payable, and an operating loss all reduce liabilities and all use cash.

Because it is difficult to spend money you don't have, total uses of cash over an accounting period must equal total sources.

Table 1.4 presents a 2016 sources and uses statement for Hasbro Inc. The single largest source for Hasbro is an increase in debt due in one year of $358 million. This amount is almost exactly offset by a decrease in long-term debt. Together, it looks like about $350 million in Hasbro's long-term debt is maturing within the coming year, and the firm's accountants have moved

TABLE 1.4 **Hasbro Inc. Sources and Uses Statement, 2016 ($ millions)**

Source: Data from Hasbro 2016 annual report and Compustat

Sources	
Reduction in other current assets	49
Reduction in goodwill and intangible assets	57
Increase in debt due in one year	358
Increase in accounts payable	79
Increase in accrued liabilities	117
Increase in total shareholders' equity	199
Total sources	**$ 859**
Uses	
Increase in cash and cash equivalents	306
Increase in accounts receivable	102
Increase in inventories	3
Increase in net property, plant, and equipment	30
Increase in other assets	36
Decrease in long-term debt	348
Decrease in other long-term liabilities	34
Total uses	**$ 859**

it from long-term debt into debt due in one year. As we will discuss soon, Hasbro's other major sources and uses relate more directly to operations.

The Two-Finger Approach

I personally do not spend a lot of time constructing sources and uses statements. It might be instructive to go through the exercise once or twice just to convince yourself that sources really do equal uses. But once beyond this point, I recommend using a "two-finger approach." Put the two balance sheets side by side, and quickly run any two fingers down the columns in search of big changes. This should enable you to quickly observe that the largest numbers again show the shift of maturing debt out of long-term and into debt due

How Can an Increase in Cash Be a Use of Cash?

One potential source of confusion in Table 1.4 is that the increase in cash and cash equivalents in 2016 appears as a use of cash. How can an increase in cash be a use of cash? Simple. It is the same as when you deposit money into your checking account. You increase your bank balance but have less cash on hand to spend. Conversely, a withdrawal from your bank account decreases your balance but increases spendable cash in your pocket.

in one year. Otherwise, the majority of Hasbro's cash came from shareholders' equity and increased accrued liabilities and most of it went to increase accounts receivable and build up Hasbro's cash balance. In 30 seconds or less, you have the essence of a sources and uses analysis and are free to move on to more stimulating activities. The other changes are largely window dressing of more interest to accountants than to managers.

The Cash Flow Statement

Identifying a company's principal sources and uses of cash is a useful skill in its own right. It is also an excellent starting point for considering the cash flow statement, the third major component of financial statements along with the income statement and the balance sheet.

In essence, a cash flow statement just expands and rearranges the sources and uses statement, placing each source or use into one of three broad categories. The categories and their values for Hasbro in 2016 are as follows:

Category	Source (or Use) of Cash ($ millions)
1. Cash flows from operating activities	$775
2. Cash flows from investing activities	($138)
3. Cash flows from financing activities	($331)

Double-entry bookkeeping guarantees that the sum of the cash flows in these three categories equals the change in cash balances over the accounting period.

Table 1.5 presents a complete cash flow statement for Hasbro in 2016. The first category, "cash flows from operating activities," can be thought of as a rearrangement of Hasbro's financial statements to eliminate the effects of accrual accounting on net income. First, we add all noncash charges, such as depreciation and amortization, back to net income, recognizing that these charges did not entail any cash outflow. Then, we add the changes in current assets and liabilities to net income, acknowledging, for instance, that some sales did not increase cash because customers had not yet paid, while some expenses did not reduce cash because the company had not yet paid. Changes in other current assets and liabilities, such as inventories, appear here because the accountant, following the matching principle, ignored these cash flows when calculating net income.

If cash flow statements were just a reshuffling of sources and uses statements, as many textbook examples suggest, they would be redundant, for a reader could make his own in a matter of minutes. A chief attraction of cash

TABLE 1.5   Hasbro Inc. Cash Flow Statement, 2016 ($ millions)*

Source: Data from Hasbro 2016 annual report and Compustat

Cash Flows from Operating Activities	
Net income	$ 551
Adjustments to reconcile net income to net cash provided by operating activities:	
Depreciation and amortization	154
Stock-based compensation expense	62
Changes in assets and liabilities:	
Increase in accounts receivables	(150)
Increase in inventories	(12)
Decrease in other current assets	7
Increase in accounts payable and accrued liabilities	204
Other	(41)
Net cash provided by operating activities	775
Cash Flows from Investing Activities	
Capital expenditures	(155)
Other investing activities	17
Net cash used by investing activities	(138)
Cash Flows from Financing Activities	
Proceeds from stock option transactions	42
Repurchase of common stock	(150)
Dividends paid	(249)
Net proceeds from short-term borrowings	9
Other financing activities	17
Net cash provided by financing activities	(331)
Net increase (decrease) in cash	306
Cash at beginning of year	977
Cash and marketable securities at end of year	$1,282

*Totals may not add due to rounding.

flow statements is that companies reorganize their cash flows into new and sometimes revealing categories. To illustrate, Hasbro's cash flow statement in Table 1.5 reveals that during 2016 it paid dividends of $249 million, repurchased $150 million of its common stock, and invested $155 million in new capital expenditures. This is the only place in its financial statements where these basic activities are even mentioned.

A second attraction of a cash flow statement is that it casts a welcome light on firm solvency by highlighting the extent to which operations are generating or consuming cash. Hasbro's cash flow statement in 2016 indicates

---

Why Are the Numbers Different?

Hasbro's sources and uses statement in Table 1.4 tells us that accounts receivable rose $102 million in 2016, yet its cash flow statement in Table 1.5 says that accounts receivable increased $150 million over the same period. Nor is this an isolated example. Many of the apparently identical quantities differ from one statement to the other. Why the difference?

Here are two possible answers. Companies often divide changes in current assets and liabilities into two parts: those attributable to existing activities, and those due to newly acquired businesses, with the first appearing in cash flows from operating activities and the second in cash flows from investing activities. By pushing as much of the increase into investing activities as possible, Hasbro enhances its recorded cash generated by operating activities—an appealing outcome. The second answer involves exchange rates. Hasbro has assets and liabilities of various types scattered all over the world. To construct a consolidated balance sheet, its accountants translate the company's foreign-denominated accounts into U.S. dollars at the then prevailing exchange rates. As a result, the balance sheet changes we observe on their consolidated statements are due at least in part to changing currency values. However, because the currency-induced changes are not cash flows until the assets or liabilities are brought home, Hasbro omits them from the numbers appearing on its cash flow statement.

Are these answers complicated? Yes. Do the manipulations described add to our understanding of Hasbro's performance? I doubt it.

---

that cash flow from operating activities exceeded net income by a hearty 40 percent. One reason for the difference is that the income statement includes a $154 million noncash charge for depreciation. An even larger amount comes from an increase of over $200 million in accounts payable and accrued liabilities. This includes money that Hasbro owes its suppliers (the accounts payable) and various other obligations such as payroll and dividends that have been promised but not yet paid.

Another noteworthy entry on Hasbro's cash flow statement is "stock-based compensation expense," which contributed $62 million to cash flow from operations in 2016. After a long and bitter battle among businesses, Congress, and accounting regulators, employee stock options are finally, and correctly, classified as an expense. However, they are not a cash flow, neither when they are given to the employee nor when she converts them into company stock. So they too must be added back to net income when calculating cash flow from operations. If you are wondering how stock options can be an expense when the firm never seems to have to pay any cash to anyone, the answer is that they are a cost to shareholders, who see their ownership percentage diluted as employees acquire shares without paying full value for them.

Some analysts maintain that net cash provided by operating activities, appearing on the cash flow statement, is a more reliable indicator of firm performance than net income. They argue that because net income depends on myriad estimates, allocations, and approximations, devious managers can easily manipulate it. Numbers appearing on a company's cash flow statement, on the other hand, record the actual movement of cash, and are thus seen to be more objective measures of performance.

What Is Cash Flow?

So many conflicting definitions of *cash flow* exist today that the term has almost lost its meaning. At one level, cash flow is very simple. It is the movement of money into or out of a cash account over a period of time. The problem arises when we try to be more specific. Here are four common types of cash flow you are apt to encounter.

$$\text{Net cash flow} = \text{Net income} + \text{Noncash items}$$

Often known in investment circles as cash earnings, net cash flow is intended to measure the cash a business generates, as distinct from the earnings—a laudable objective. Applying the preceding formula to Hasbro's 2016 figures (Table 1.5), its net cash flow was $803 million, equal to net income plus depreciation, and other noncash charges.

A problem with net cash flow as a measure of cash generation is that it implicitly assumes a business's current assets and liabilities are either unrelated to operations or do not change over time. In Hasbro's case, the cash flow statement reveals that changes in a number of current assets and liabilities consumed $29 million in cash. A more inclusive measure of cash generation is therefore cash flow from operating activities as it appears on the cash flow statement.

$$\text{Case flow from operating activities} = \text{Net cash flow} \pm \text{Changes in current assets and liabilities}$$

A third, even more inclusive measure of cash flow, popular among finance specialists is

$$\text{Free cash flow} = \frac{\text{Total cash available for distribution to owners and creditors}}{\text{after funding all worthwhile investment activities}}$$

Free cash flow extends cash flow from operating activities by recognizing that some of the cash a business generates must be plowed back into the business, in the form of capital expenditures, to support growth. Abstracting from a few technical details, free cash flow is essentially cash flow from operating activities less capital expenditures. As we will see in Chapter 9, free cash flow is a fundamental determinant of the value of a business. Indeed, one can argue that the principal means by which a company creates value for its owners is to increase free cash flow.

Yet another widely used cash flow is

$$\text{Discounted cash flow} = \frac{\text{A sum of money today having the same value}}{\text{as a future stream of cash receipts and disbursements}}$$

Discounted cash flow refers to a family of techniques for analyzing investment opportunities that take into account the time value of money. A standard approach to valuing investments and businesses uses discounted cash flow techniques to calculate the present value of projected free cash flows. This is the focus of the last three chapters of this book.

My advice when tossing cash flow terms about is to either use the phrase broadly to refer to a general movement of cash or to define your terms carefully.

There is certainly some merit to this view, but also two problems. First, low or even negative net cash provided by operating activities does not necessarily indicate poor performance. Rapidly growing businesses in particular must customarily invest in current assets, such as accounts receivable and inventories, to support increasing sales. And although such investments reduce net cash provided by operating activities, they do not in any way suggest poor performance. Second, cash flow statements turn out to be less objective, and thus less immune to manipulation than might be supposed. Here's a simple example. Suppose two companies are identical except that one sells its product on a simple open account, while the other loans its customers money enabling them to pay cash for the product. In both cases, the customer has the product and owes the seller money. But the increase in accounts receivable recorded by the first company on each sale will lower its cash flows from operating activities relative to the second, which can report the customer loan as part of investing activities. Because the criteria for apportioning cash flows among operating, investing, and financing activities are ambiguous, subjective judgment must be used in the preparation of cash flow statements.

Much of the information contained in a cash flow statement can be gleaned from careful study of a company's income statement and balance sheet. Nonetheless, the statement has three principal virtues. First, accounting neophytes and those who do not trust accrual accounting have at least some hope of understanding it. Second, the statement provides more accurate information about certain activities, such as share repurchases and employee stock options than one can infer from income statements and balance sheets alone. Third, it casts a welcome light on cash generation and solvency.

Financial Statements and the Value Problem

To this point, we have reviewed the basics of financial statements and grappled with the distinction between earnings and cash flow. This is a valuable start, but if we are to use financial statements to make informed business decisions, we must go further. We must understand the extent to which accounting numbers reflect economic reality. When the accountant tells us that Hasbro's total assets were worth $5,091 million on December 31, 2016, is this literally true, or is the number just an artificial accounting construct? To gain perspective on this issue, and in anticipation of later discussions, I want to conclude by examining a recurring problem in the use of accounting information for financial decision making.

Market Value vs. Book Value

Part of what I will call the *value problem* involves the distinction between the market value and the book value of shareholders' equity. Hasbro's 2016 balance sheet states that the value of shareholders' equity is $1,863 million. This is known as the *book value* of Hasbro's equity. However, Hasbro is not worth $1,863 million to its shareholders or to anyone else, for that matter. There are two reasons. One is that financial statements are largely *transactions-based.* If a company purchased an asset for $1 million in 1950, this transaction provides an objective measure of the asset's value, which the accountant uses to value the asset on the company's balance sheet. Unfortunately, it is a 1950 value that may or may not have much relevance today. To further confound things, the accountant attempts to reflect the gradual deterioration of an asset over time by periodically subtracting depreciation from its balance sheet value. This practice makes sense as far as it goes, but depreciation is the only change in value an American accountant customarily recognizes. The $1 million asset purchased in 1950 may be technologically obsolete and therefore virtually worthless today; or, due to inflation, it may be worth much more than its original purchase price. This is especially true of land, which can be worth several times its original cost.

It is tempting to argue that accountants should forget the original costs of long-term assets and provide more meaningful current values. The problem is that objectively determinable current values of many assets do not exist, and it is probably not wise to rely on incumbent managers to make the necessary adjustments. Faced with a choice between relevant but subjective current values and irrelevant but objective historical costs, accountants opt for irrelevant historical costs. Accountants prefer to be precisely wrong than approximately right. This means it is the user's responsibility to make any adjustments to historical-cost asset values she deems appropriate.

Prodded by regulators and investors, the Financial Accounting Standards Board, accounting's principal rule-making organization, increasingly stresses what is known as *fair value* accounting, according to which certain assets and liabilities must appear on company financial statements at their market values instead of their historical costs. Such "marking to market" applies to selected assets and liabilities that trade actively on financial markets, including many common stocks and bonds. Proponents of fair value accounting acknowledge it will never be possible to eliminate historical-cost accounting entirely, but maintain that market values should be used whenever possible. Skeptics respond that mixing historical costs and market values in the same financial statement only heightens confusion, and that periodically revaluing company accounts to reflect changing market values introduces unwanted subjectivity, distorts reported earnings, and greatly increases earnings volatility. They point out that under fair value accounting, changes in owners' equity no longer mirror the results of company operations but also include potentially large and volatile gains and losses from changes in the market values of certain assets and liabilities. The gradual movement toward fair value accounting was initially greeted with howls of protest, especially from financial institutions concerned that the move would increase apparent earnings volatility and, more menacingly, might reveal that some enterprises are worth less than historical-cost financial statements suggest. To these firms, the appearance of benign stability is apparently more appealing than the hint of an ugly reality.

Adjusted Earnings

For a variety of sometimes-legitimate reasons, corporate executives and business analysts have increasingly argued that official earnings measures are inadequate or inappropriate for their purposes, and have encouraged a whole cottage industry devoted to creating and promoting new and improved earnings measures, collectively known as "adjusted earnings." In 2016, Hasbro highlighted adjusted net earnings of $566 million, some $15 million above its bottom line net income of $551 million.

Adjusted earnings began appearing regularly in the early 1990s, and were controversial from the start. Because they were not constrained to follow accounting guidelines, managers often used adjusted earnings as a way to accentuate the positive or meet earnings targets by sweeping various expenses under the carpet. Initially, companies did not have to disclose how they calculated adjusted earnings, so investors were kept in the dark. As a result, adjusted earnings also became known as "earnings before the bad stuff."

In 2003, the SEC refined its rules: Companies could report adjusted earnings as long as they also reported their official net income and explained any differences between the two. There is no set definition of adjusted earnings, so managers are still free to be creative. But now at least they have to show investors what they are doing.

By 2014, over 70% of companies in the Standard and Poor's 500 reported adjusted earnings, up from just over 50% in 2009.[a] Common adjustments eliminate one-time items such as restructuring charges, litigation expenses, and acquisitions. Some companies also remove recurring items, including investment gains or losses, amortization of goodwill, or stock compensation. The adjustments, on average, make companies' earnings look better. From 2014 to 2015, adjusted earnings for the S&P 500 increased 6.6%, while corresponding net income declined 11%.[b]

Ironically, despite general skepticism, evidence suggests that, on average, adjusted earnings are more valued by investors and more predictive of future earnings and cash flows.[c] Although managers have a lot of discretion as to what goes into adjusted earnings, and some may be abusing this flexibility, as a group they appear to be making adjustments that investors value and cannot make on their own.

Still, as articulated by former SEC Chair Mary Jo White and others, concerns remain.[d] In 2016, the SEC issued new guidelines cracking down on the creative use of adjusted earnings, clarifying what it considers reasonable adjustments and requiring that companies reduce the prominence of adjusted earnings in press releases. The debate, no doubt, will continue.

[a] For more details, see Dirk Black, Theodore Christensen, Jack Ciesielski, and Benjamin Whipple, "Non-GAAP Earnings: A Consistency and Comparability Crisis?" March 2017.

[b] Robert Pozen, "No More Dizzying Earnings Adjustments," *The Wall Street Journal,* June 21, 2016.

[c] See, for example, Mark Bradshaw and Richard Sloan, "GAAP versus The Street: An Empirical Assessment of Two Alternative Definitions of Earnings," *Journal of Accounting Research* 40, 2002, pp. 41–66.

[d] A full transcript of White's keynote address in June 2016 is available at https://www.sec.gov/news/speech/chair-white-icgn-speech.html.

To understand the second, more fundamental reason Hasbro is not worth $1,863 million, recall that equity investors buy shares for the future income they hope to receive, not for the value of the firm's assets. Indeed, if all goes according to plan, most of the firm's existing assets will be consumed in generating future income. The problem with the accountant's measure of shareholders' equity is that it bears little relation to future income. There are two reasons for this. First, because the accountant's numbers are backward-looking and cost-based, they often provide few clues about the future income a company's assets might generate. Second, companies typically have a great many assets and liabilities that do not appear on their balance sheets but affect future income nonetheless. Examples include patents and trademarks, loyal customers, proven mailing lists, superior technology, and, of course, better management. It is said that in many companies, the most valuable assets go home to their spouses in the evening. Examples of unrecorded liabilities include pending lawsuits, inferior management, and obsolete production processes. The accountant's inability to measure assets and liabilities such as these means that book value is customarily a highly inaccurate measure of the value perceived by shareholders.

It is a simple matter to calculate the market value of shareholders' equity when a company's shares are publicly traded: Simply multiply the market price per share by the number of common shares outstanding. On December 31, 2016, Hasbro's common shares closed on the NASDAQ Global Select Market at $77.79. With 124.5 million shares outstanding, this yields a value of $9,685 million, or 5.2 times the book value ($9,685/$1,863 million). This figure is the market value of Hasbro's equity, often known as its market capitalization or market cap.

Table 1.6 presents the market and book values of equity for 15 representative companies. It demonstrates clearly that book value is a poor proxy for market value.

Goodwill

There is one instance in which intangible assets, such as brand names and patents, find their way onto company balance sheets. It occurs when one company buys another at a price above book value. Suppose an acquiring firm pays $100 million for a target firm and the target's assets have a book value of only $40 million and an estimated replacement value of only $60 million. To record the transaction, the accountant will allocate $60 million of the acquisition price to the value of the assets acquired and assign the remaining $40 million to a new asset commonly known as "goodwill." The acquiring company paid a handsome premium over the fair value of the target's recorded assets because it places a high value on its unrecorded, or intangible, assets. But not until the acquisition creates a piece of paper with $100 million written on it is the accountant willing to acknowledge this value.

TABLE 1.6   The Book Value of Equity Is a Poor Surrogate for the Market Value of Equity, December 31, 2016

Company	Value of Equity ($ millions)		Ratio, Market Value to Book Value
	Book	Market	
Aetna Inc.	17,881	43,614	2.4
Alphabet Inc. (Google)	139,036	540,659	3.9
Amgen Inc.	29,875	107,932	3.6
Apache Corp.	6,238	24,083	3.9
Coca-Cola Co.	23,062	177,780	7.7
Delta Air Lines Inc.	12,287	35,945	2.9
Duke Energy Corp.	41,033	54,334	1.3
Facebook Inc.	59,194	332,725	5.6
General Motors Co.	43,836	52,260	1.2
Harley-Davidson Inc.	1,920	10,265	5.3
Hasbro Inc.	1,863	9,685	5.2
Intel Corp.	66,226	171,557	2.6
Tesla Motors Inc.	4,753	34,524	7.3
United States Steel Co.	2,274	5,738	2.5
Wal-Mart Stores Inc.	77,798	203,424	2.6

Looking at Hasbro's balance sheet in Table 1.2 under the heading "goodwill and other intangible assets, net," we see that the company has $817 million, or 16 percent of total assets, in goodwill. To put this number in perspective, the median ratio of goodwill and intangible assets to total assets among Standard & Poor's 500 industrial companies—a diversified group of large firms—was 31 percent in 2016. Tobacco giant Reynolds American topped the list with a ratio of 89 percent.[1]

Economic Income vs. Accounting Income

A second dimension of the value problem is rooted in the accountant's distinction between *realized* and *unrealized* income. To anyone who has not studied too much accounting, income is what you could spend during the period and be as well off at the end as you were at the start. If Mary Siegler's assets, net of liabilities, are worth $100,000 at the start of the year and rise to $120,000 by the end, and if she receives and spends $70,000 in wages during the year, most of us would say her income was $90,000 ($70,000 in wages + $20,000 increase in net assets).

---

[1] For many years, accounting authorities required companies to write goodwill off as a noncash expense against income over a number of years. Now they acknowledge that most goodwill is not necessarily a wasting asset and only requires a write-down when there is evidence the value of goodwill has declined. There is no offsetting provision requiring the write-up of goodwill when values appear to have risen. If this sounds vague and capricious, I agree.

But not the accountant. Unless Mary's investments were in marketable securities with readily observable prices, he would say Mary's income was only $70,000. The $20,000 increase in the value of assets would not qualify as income because the gain was not *realized* by the sale of the assets. Because the value of the assets could fluctuate in either direction before the assets are sold, the gain is only *on paper,* and accountants generally do not recognize paper gains or losses. They consider *realization* the objective evidence necessary to record the gain, despite the fact that Mary is probably just as pleased with the unrealized gain in assets as with another $20,000 in wages.

It is easy to criticize accountants' conservatism when measuring income. Certainly the amount Mary could spend, ignoring inflation, and be as well off as at the start of the year is the commonsense $90,000, not the accountant's $70,000. Moreover, if Mary sold her assets for $120,000 and immediately repurchased them for the same price, the $20,000 gain would become realized and, in the accountant's eyes, become part of income. That income could depend on a sham transaction such as this is enough to raise suspicions about the accountant's definition.

However, we should note three points in the accountant's defense. First, if Mary holds her assets for several years before selling them, the gain or loss the accountant recognized on the sale date will equal the sum of the annual gains and losses we nonaccountants would recognize. So it's really not total income that is at issue here but simply the timing of its recognition. Second, accountants' increasing use of fair value accounting, where at least some assets and liabilities are revalued periodically to reflect changes in market value, reduces the difference between accounting and economic income. Third, even when accountants want to use fair value accounting, it is extremely difficult to measure the periodic change in the value of many assets and liabilities unless they are actively traded. Thus, even if an accountant wanted to include "paper" gains and losses in income, she would often have great difficulty doing so. In the corporate setting, this means the accountants frequently must be content to record realized rather than economic income.

Imputed Costs

A similar but subtler problem exists on the cost side of the income statement. It involves the cost of equity capital. Hasbro's accountants acknowledge that in 2016 the company had use of $1,863 million of shareholders' money, measured at book value. They would further acknowledge that Hasbro could not have operated without this money and that this money is not free. Just as creditors earn interest on loans, equity investors expect a return on their investments. Yet if you look again at Hasbro's income statement (Table 1.3), you will find no mention of the cost of this equity; interest expense appears, but a comparable cost for equity does not.

While acknowledging that equity capital has a cost, the accountant does not record it on the income statement because the cost must be imputed—that is, estimated. Because there is no piece of paper stating the amount of money Hasbro is obligated to pay owners, the accountant refuses to recognize any cost of equity capital. Once again, the accountant would rather be reliably wrong than make a potentially inaccurate estimate. The result has been serious confusion in the minds of less knowledgeable observers and continuing "image" problems for corporations.

Following is the bottom portion of Hasbro's income statement as prepared by its accountant and as an economist might prepare it. Observe that while the accountant shows earnings of $551 million, the economist records a profit of only $365 million. These numbers differ because the economist includes a $186 million charge as a cost of equity capital, while the accountant pretends equity is free. (We will consider ways to estimate a company's cost of equity capital in Chapter 8. Here, for illustrative purposes only, I have assumed a 10 percent annual equity cost and applied it to the book value of Hasbro's equity [$186 million $= 10\% \times \$1,863$ million].)

($ millions)	Accountant	Economist
Operating income	$821	$821
Interest expense	97	97
Other nonoperating expenses	14	14
Cost of equity		186
Income before taxes	710	524
Provision for taxes	159	159
Accounting earnings	$ 551	
Economic earnings		$ 365

The distinction between accounting earnings and economic earnings might be only a curiosity if everyone understood that positive accounting earnings are not necessarily a sign of superior or even commendable performance. But when many labor unions and politicians view accounting profits as evidence that a company can afford higher wages, higher taxes, or more onerous regulation, and when most managements view such profits as justification for distributing handsome performance bonuses, the distinction can be an important one. Keep in mind, therefore, that the right of equity investors to expect a competitive return on their investments is every bit as legitimate as a creditor's right to interest and an employee's right to wages. All voluntarily contribute scarce resources, and all are justified in expecting compensation. Remember too that a company is not shooting par unless its economic profits are zero or

International Financial Reporting Standards

A danger inherent in any cross-country comparison of accounting numbers is that accountants in different countries may not keep score by the same rules. Happily, this problem has diminished greatly over the past decade or so, and what optimists might call international accounting standards are emerging. The European Union took the lead in this initiative as part of its much broader effort to hammer out a common, integrated marketplace among member countries. After some 30 years of study, debate, and political wrangling, the accounting initiative became a reality on January 1, 2005, when all 7,000 publicly traded companies in Europe dumped their national accounting rules in favor of the newly designated International Financial Reporting Standards (IFRS). Today, over 120 countries on six continents have adopted IFRS, either directly or by aligning national rules to the international standards. Conspicuously absent from the earlier adopters have been the United States, Japan, and China. Japan now allows voluntary adoption of IFRS, and both Japan and China are working toward convergence with international standards, although no deadlines have been set. For a while, U.S. accounting regulators were working on a project to converge with the international standards, but these efforts have largely been put on hold, at least for now.

For many years, U.S. accounting authorities viewed American accounting rules as the gold standard to which other countries could only aspire, and their approach to international accounting standards was to invite the rest of the world to adopt theirs. But accounting scandals in the early 2000s and the ensuing collapse of the accounting firm Arthur Andersen have made Americans a bit more humble about their accounting rules and a bit more willing to compromise.

A major barrier to greater transatlantic cooperation on accounting standards has been differing philosophical perspectives on the role such standards should play. The European philosophy is to articulate broad accounting principles and to charge accountants and executives to prepare company accounts consistent with the spirit of those principles. Concerned that principles alone would leave too much room for manipulation, the American approach has been to lay down voluminous, detailed rules defining how each transaction is to be recorded and to demand strict conformance to the letter of those rules. Ironically, this rules-based philosophy seems to have backfired, for rather than limiting manipulation, the American "bright-line" approach appears to have encouraged it by shifting some executives' focus from preparing fair and accurate statements to figuring out how best to beat the rules. The argument "we didn't break any rules, so we must be innocent" appears to have been an enticing one.

One response to the breakdown in U.S. accounting standards was passage of the Sarbanes–Oxley Act of 2002, which among other changes requires chief executives and chief financial officers to personally attest to the appropriateness of their company's financial reports. Another was to take the European, broad-brush approach more seriously. Indeed, there was a time some 15 years ago when it appeared that U.S. regulators and accounting authorities were about to name a definitive date when the United States would adopt IFRS. Today, this no longer appears likely. Instead, U.S. and international accounting authorities appear intent on integrating the two standards on a piecemeal basis over an extended period. Not a single standard perhaps, but at least a workable compromise.

greater. By this criterion, Hasbro still had a decent year in 2016, but not quite as stellar as accounting earnings would suggest. On closer inspection, you will find that many companies reporting apparently large earnings are really performing like weekend duffers when the cost of equity is included.

We will look at the difference between accounting and economic profits again in more detail in Chapter 8 under the rubric of economic value added (EVA). In recent years, EVA has become a popular yardstick for assessing company and managerial performance.

In sum, those of us interested in financial analysis eventually develop a love-hate relationship with accountants. The value problem means that financial statements typically yield distorted information about company earnings and market value. This limits their applicability for many important managerial decisions. Yet financial statements frequently provide the best information available, and if we bear their limitations in mind, they can be a useful starting point for analysis. In the next chapter, we consider the use of accounting data for evaluating financial performance.

SUMMARY

1. The cash flow cycle
   - Describes the flow of cash through a company.
   - Illustrates that profits and cash flow are not the same.
   - Reminds a manager she must be at least as concerned with cash flows as with profits.
2. The balance sheet
   - Is a snapshot at a point in time of what a company owns and what it owes.
   - Rests on the fundamental accounting equation, assets = liabilities + owners' equity, which applies to individual transactions as well as entire balance sheets.
   - Lists assets and liabilities with maturities of less than a year as current.
   - Shows shareholders' equity on the liability side of the balance sheet as the accounting value of owners' claims against existing assets.
3. The income statement
   - Divides changes in owners' equity occurring over a period of time into revenues and expenses, where revenues are increases in equity and expenses are reductions.
   - Defines net income, or earnings, as the difference between revenues and expenses.

- Identifies revenues generated during the period and matches the corresponding costs incurred in generating the revenue.
- Embodies the accrual principle, which records revenues and expenses when there is reasonable certainty that payment will be made, not when cash is received or disbursed.
- Records depreciation as the allocation of past expenditures for long-lived assets to future time periods to match revenues and expenses.

4. The cash flow statement

- Focuses on solvency, having enough cash to pay bills as they come due.
- Is an elaboration of a simple sources and uses statement, according to which increases in asset accounts and reductions in liability accounts are uses of cash, while opposite changes in assets and liabilities are sources of cash.

5. The value problem

- Emphasizes that accounting statements suffer from several limitations when used to assess economic performance or value businesses:
  - Many accounting values are transactions-based and hence backward-looking, while market values are forward-looking.
  - Accounting often creates a false dichotomy between realized and unrealized income.
  - Accountants refuse to assign a cost to equity capital, thereby suggesting to lay observers that positive accounting profit means financial health.
- Is diminished by the use of fair value accounting, according to which the value of widely traded assets and liabilities appear at market price rather than historical cost but at the potential cost of distortions, volatility, complexity, and subjectivity.

ADDITIONAL RESOURCES

Downes, John, and Jordan Elliot Goodman. *Dictionary of Finance and Investment Terms*. 9th ed. New York: Barron's Educational Services, Inc., 2012. 912 pages.

   More than 5,000 terms clearly defined. Available in paperback.

Friedlob, George T., and Ralph E. Welton. *Keys to Reading an Annual Report*. 4th ed. New York: Barron's Educational Services, Inc., 2008. 208 pages.

   A no-nonsense, practical guide to understanding financial reports.

Horngren, Charles T., Gary L. Sundem, John A. Elliott, and Donna Philbrick. *Introduction to Financial Accounting*. 11th ed. Englewood Cliffs, NJ: Prentice Hall, 2013. 648 pages.

   The high-octane stuff—a top-selling college text. Everything you ever wanted to know about the topic and then some.

Libby, Robert, Patricia Libby, and Frank Hodge. *Financial Accounting,* 9th ed., McGraw Hill Education, 2016. 864 pages.

Another best-selling accounting text.

Tracy, John A., and Tage Tracy. *How to Read a Financial Report: Wringing Vital Signs Out of the Numbers.* 8th ed. New York: John Wiley & Sons, 2014. 240 pages.

A lively, accessible look at practical aspects of financial statement analysis. Available in paperback.

e145.stanford.edu/upload/Merrill_Lynch.pdf

From this site you can download a free copy of Merrill Lynch's classic "How to Read a Financial Report" as a PDF file.

duke.edu/~charvey/Classes/wpg/glossary.htm

Duke Professor Campbell Harvey's glossary of finance, with more than 8,000 terms defined and more than 18,000 hyperlinks.

nysscpa.org/glossary

Another exhaustive glossary of accounting terms.

secfilings.com

EDGAR, a Securities and Exchange Commission site, contains virtually all filings of public companies in the United States. It is a treasure trove of financial information, including annual and quarterly reports. The referenced site offers a slick way to access EDGAR, including direct downloading of individual filings in PDF and RTF formats. It's free, and I use it often.

cfo.com

An informative, practitioner-oriented website provided by the publishers of CFO magazine. Offers articles on current issues in accounting and finance.

PROBLEMS

Answers to odd-numbered problems appear at the end of the book. Answers to even-numbered problems and additional exercises are available in the Instructor Resources within McGraw-Hill's *Connect* (see the Preface for more information).

1. a. What does it mean when cash flow from operations on a company's cash flow statement is negative? Is this bad news? Is it dangerous?
   b. What does it mean when cash flow from investing activities on a company's cash flow statement is negative? Is this bad news? Is it dangerous?
   c. What does it mean when cash flow from financing activities on a company's cash flow statement is negative? Is this bad news? Is it dangerous?

2. Braintree Corporation has $5 billion in assets, $4 billion in equity, and earned a profit of $100 million last year as the economy boomed. Senior

management proposes paying themselves a large cash bonus in recognition of their performance. As a member of Braintree's board of directors, how would you respond to this proposal?

3. Answer true or false to each of the following. Briefly explain your reasoning for each answer.

   a. If a company gets into financial difficulty, it can use some of its shareholders' equity to pay its bills for a time.

   b. It is impossible for a firm to have a negative book value of equity without the firm going into bankruptcy.

   c. If a company increases its dividend, its net income will decrease.

   d. You can construct a sources and uses statement for 2017 if you have a company's balance sheets for year-end 2016 and 2017.

   e. The "goodwill" account on the balance sheet is an attempt by accountants to measure the benefits that result from a company's public relations efforts in the community.

   f. A reduction in an asset account is a use of cash, while a reduction in a liability account is a source of cash.

   g. A company's market value of equity must always be higher than its book value of equity.

4. Explain briefly how each of the following transactions would affect a company's balance sheet. (Remember, assets must equal liabilities plus owners' equity before and after the transaction.)

   a. Sale of used equipment with a book value of $300,000 for $500,000 cash.

   b. Purchase of a new $80 million building, financed 40 percent with cash and 60 percent with a bank loan.

   c. Purchase of a new building for $60 million cash.

   d. A $40,000 payment to trade creditors.

   e. A firm's repurchase of 10,000 shares of its own stock at a price of $24 per share.

   f. Sale of merchandise for $80,000 in cash.

   g. Sale of merchandise for $120,000 on credit.

   h. A dividend payment to shareholders of $50,000.

5. Why do you suppose financial statements are constructed on an accrual basis rather than a cash basis when cash accounting is so much easier to understand?

6. Table 3.1 in Chapter 3 presents financial statements over the period 2014–2017 for R&E Supplies, Inc.

   a. Construct a sources and uses statement for the company over this period (one statement for all three years).

   b. What insights, if any, does the sources and uses statement give you about the financial position of R&E Supplies?

7. You are responsible for labor relations in your company. During heated labor negotiations, the General Secretary of your largest union exclaims, "Look, this company has $15 billion in assets, $7.5 billion in equity, and made a profit last year of $300 million—due largely, I might add, to the effort of union employees. So don't tell me you can't afford our wage demands." How would you reply?

8. You manage a real estate investment company. One year ago, the company purchased 10 parcels of land distributed throughout the community for $10 million each. A recent appraisal of the properties indicates that five of the parcels are now worth $8 million each, while the other five are worth $16 million each. Ignoring any income received from the properties and any taxes paid over the year, calculate the investment company's accounting earnings and its economic earnings in each of the following cases:

   a. The company sells all of the properties at their appraised values today.
   b. The company sells none of the properties.
   c. The company sells the properties that have fallen in value and keeps the others.
   d. The company sells the properties that have risen in value and keeps the others.
   e. After returning from a property management seminar, an employee recommends that the company adopt an end-of-year policy of always selling properties that have risen in value since purchase and always retaining properties that have fallen in value. The employee explains that, with this policy, the company will never show a loss on its real estate investment activities. Do you agree with the employee? Why, or why not?

9. Please ignore taxes for this problem. During 2016, Acadia, Inc. earned net income of $500,000. The firm increased its accounts receivable during the year by $150,000. The book value of its assets declined by an amount equal to the year's depreciation charge, or $130,000, and the market value of its assets increased by $25,000. Based only on this information, how much cash did Acadia generate during the year?

10. Jonathan currently is a brew master for Acme Brewery. He really enjoys his job, but is intrigued by the prospect of quitting and starting his own brewery. He currently makes $62,000 at Acme Brewery. Jonathan anticipates that his new brewery will have annual revenues of $230,000, and total annual expenses for operating the brewery, outside of any payments to Jonathan, will be $190,000. Jonathan comes to you with his idea. He believes that he would be equally happy with either option, but that starting his own brewery is the right decision in light of its profitability. Ignoring what might happen beyond the first year, do you agree with him? Why or why not?

11. Selected information for Blake's Restaurant Supply follows.

	($ millions)	
	2016	**2017**
Net sales	694	782
Cost of goods sold	450	502
Depreciation	51	61
Net income	130	142
Finished goods inventory	39	29
Accounts receivable	57	87
Accounts payable	39	44
Net fixed assets	404	482
Year-end cash balance	86	135

a. During 2017, how much cash did Blake's collect from sales?
b. During 2017, what was the cost of goods produced by the company?
c. Assuming the company neither sold nor salvaged any assets during the year, what were the company's capital expenditures during 2017?
d. Assuming there were no financing cash flows during 2017 and basing your answer solely on the information provided, what was Blake's cash flow from operations in 2017?

12. Below are summary cash flow statements for three roughly equal-sized companies.

	($ millions)		
	A	**B**	**C**
Net cash flows from operating activities	(300)	(300)	300
Net cash used in investing activities	(900)	(30)	(90)
Net cash from financing activities	1,200	210	(240)
Cash balance at beginning of year	150	150	150

a. Calculate each company's cash balance at the end of the year.
b. Explain what might cause company C's net cash from financing activities to be negative.
c. Looking at companies A and B, which company would you prefer to own? Why?
d. Is company C's cash flow statement cause for any concern on the part of C's management or shareholders? Why or why not?

13. Starbucks Corporation recently had a market value of equity of $90 billion with 1.5 billion shares outstanding. The book value of its equity is $6 billion.

a. What is Starbucks' stock price per share? What is its book value per share?

b. If the company repurchases 25 million shares in the stock market at their current price, how will this affect the book value of equity if all else remains the same?

c. If there are no taxes or transaction costs, and investors do not change their perceptions of the firm, what should the market value of the firm be after the repurchase?

d. Instead of a share repurchase, the company decides to raise money by selling an additional 25 million shares on the market. If it can issue these additional shares at the current market price, how will this affect the book value of equity if all else remains the same?

e. If there are no taxes or transaction costs, and investors do not change their perception of the firm, what should the market value of the firm be after this stock issuance? What would its price per share be?

14. A spreadsheet containing Whistler Corporation's financial statements is available for download from McGraw-Hill's *Connect* or your course instructor (see the Preface for more information).

a. Prepare a sources and uses statement for Whistler Corp. for fiscal year 2017.

b. Prepare a cash flow statement for Whistler Corp. for fiscal year 2017.

CHAPTER TWO

Evaluating Financial Performance

"... liabilities are always 100 percent good. It's the assets you have to worry about."

Charlie Munger

Source: The Best of Lex, *Financial Times,* Alan Livsey, Feb. 17, 2017.

The cockpit of a 747 jet looks like a three-dimensional video game. It is a sizable room crammed with meters, switches, lights, and dials requiring the full attention of three highly trained pilots. When compared to the cockpit of a single-engine Cessna, it is tempting to conclude that the two planes are different species rather than distant cousins. But at a more fundamental level, the similarities outnumber the differences. Despite the 747's complex technology, the 747 pilot controls the plane in the same way the Cessna pilot does: with a stick, a throttle, and flaps. And to change the altitude of the plane, each pilot makes simultaneous adjustments to the same few levers available for controlling the plane.

Much the same is true of companies. Once you strip away the facade of apparent complexity, the levers with which managers affect their companies' financial performance are comparatively few and are similar from one company to another. The executive's job is to control these levers to ensure a safe and efficient flight. And like the pilot, the executive must remember that the levers are interrelated; one cannot change the business equivalent of the flaps without also adjusting the stick and the throttle.

The Levers of Financial Performance

In this chapter, we analyze financial statements for the purpose of evaluating performance and understanding the levers of management control. We begin by studying the ties between a company's operating decisions, such as how many units to make this month and how to price them, and its financial performance. These operating decisions are the levers by which management controls financial performance. Then, we broaden the discussion to consider the uses and limitations of ratio analysis as a tool for evaluating performance. To keep things practical, we will again use the financial statements for Hasbro Inc., presented in Tables 1.2, 1.3, and 1.5 of the last chapter, to illustrate the techniques. The chapter concludes with an evaluation of Hasbro's financial performance relative to its competition. At the end of the chapter, Table 2.4 presents summary definitions of the principal ratios appearing throughout the chapter.

Return on Equity

By far the most popular yardstick of financial performance among investors and senior managers is the *return on equity (ROE),* defined as

$$\text{Return on equity} = \frac{\text{Net income}}{\text{Shareholders' equity}}$$

Hasbro's ROE for 2016 was

$$\text{ROE} = \frac{\$551}{\$1,863} = 29.6\%$$

It is not an exaggeration to say that the careers of many senior executives rise and fall with their firms' ROEs. ROE is accorded such importance because it is a measure of the *efficiency* with which a company employs owners' capital. It is a measure of earnings per dollar of invested equity capital or, equivalently, of the percentage return to owners on their investment. In short, it measures bang per buck.

Later in this chapter, we will consider some significant problems with ROE as a measure of financial performance. For now, let us accept it provisionally as at least widely used and see what we can learn.

The Three Determinants of ROE

To learn more about what management can do to increase ROE, suppose we rewrite ROE in terms of its three principal components:

$$\text{ROE} = \frac{\text{Net income}}{\text{Sales}} \times \frac{\text{Sales}}{\text{Assets}} \times \frac{\text{Assets}}{\text{Shareholders' equity}}$$

Denoting the last three ratios as the profit margin, asset turnover, and financial leverage, respectively, the expression can be written as

$$\frac{\text{Return on}}{\text{equity}} = \frac{\text{Profit}}{\text{margin}} \times \frac{\text{Asset}}{\text{turnover}} \times \frac{\text{Financial}}{\text{leverage}}$$

This says that management has only three levers for controlling ROE: (1) the earnings squeezed out of each dollar of sales, or the *profit margin;* (2) the sales generated from each dollar of assets employed, or the *asset turnover;* and (3) the amount of equity used to finance the assets, or the *financial leverage.*[1] With few exceptions, whatever management does to increase these ratios increases ROE.

Note, too, the close correspondence between the levers of performance and company financial statements. Thus, the profit margin summarizes a company's income statement performance by showing profit per dollar of sales. The asset turnover ratio summarizes the company's management of the asset side of its balance sheet by showing the resources required to support sales. And the financial leverage ratio summarizes management of the liabilities side of the balance sheet by showing the amount of shareholders' equity used to finance the assets. This is reassuring evidence that, despite their simplicity, the three levers do capture the major elements of a company's financial performance.

We find that Hasbro's 2016 ROE was generated as follows:

$$\frac{\$551}{\$1,863} = \frac{\$551}{\$5,020} \times \frac{\$5,020}{\$5,091} \times \frac{\$5,091}{\$1,863}$$

$$29.6\% = 11.0\% \times 0.986 \times 2.73$$

Table 2.1 presents ROE and its three principal components for 10 highly diverse businesses. It shows quite clearly that there are many paths to heaven: Even for companies with ROEs that are quite similar, the combinations of profit margin, asset turnover, and financial leverage producing these end results vary widely. ROE ranges from a high of 31.7 percent for Unilever, a consumer goods company selling products ranging from shampoo to soup, to a low of 10.1 percent for energy company Southern Co., while the range for the profit margin, to take one example, is from a low of 1.7 percent for online retailer Amazon.com to a high of 23.5 percent for banker JPMorgan Chase. ROE differs by about 3 to 1 high to low, but the profit margin varies by a factor of 14 to 1. Comparable ranges for asset turnover and financial leverage are 46 to 1 and 9 to 1, respectively.

Why are ROEs similar across firms, while profit margins, asset turnovers, and financial leverages differ dramatically? The answer, in a word, is competition. Attainment of an unusually high ROE by one company acts as a magnet to attract rivals anxious to emulate the superior performance. As rivals enter the market, the heightened competition drives the successful company's ROE back toward the average. Conversely, unusually low ROEs repel potential new competitors and drive existing companies out of business so that, over time, survivors' ROEs rise toward the average.

To understand how managerial decisions and a company's competitive environment combine to affect ROE, we will examine each lever of

---

[1] At first glance the ratio of assets to shareholders' equity may not look like a measure of financial leverage, but consider the following:

$$\frac{\text{Assets}}{\text{Equity}} = \frac{\text{Liabilities} + \text{Equity}}{\text{Equity}} = \frac{\text{Liabilities}}{\text{Equity}} + 1$$

And the liabilities-to-equity ratio clearly measures financial leverage.

TABLE 2.1 ROEs and Levers of Performance for 10 Diverse Companies, 2016*

	Return on Equity (ROE) (%)	=	Profit Margin (P) (%)	×	Asset Turnover (A) (times)	×	Financial Leverage (T) (times)
Adobe Systems	15.7	=	20.0	×	0.46	×	1.71
Alphabet Inc. (parent of Google)	14.0	=	21.6	×	0.54	×	1.20
Amazon.com	12.3	=	1.7	×	1.63	×	4.33
Hasbro Inc.	29.6	=	11.0	×	0.99	×	2.73
JPMorgan Chase	10.8	=	23.5	×	0.04	×	10.92
Norfolk Southern	13.4	=	16.9	×	0.28	×	2.81
Southern Co.	10.1	=	12.5	×	0.18	×	4.43
Target Corp.	25.0	=	3.9	×	1.86	×	3.42
Tata Motors	12.6	=	3.6	×	1.03	×	3.43
Unilever PLC	31.7	=	9.8	×	0.93	×	3.45

*Totals may not add due to rounding.

performance in more detail. In anticipation of the discussion of ratio analysis to follow, we will also consider related commonly used financial ratios.

The Profit Margin

The profit margin measures the fraction of each dollar of sales that trickles down through the income statement to profits. This ratio is particularly important to operating managers because it reflects the company's pricing strategy and its ability to control operating costs. As Table 2.1 indicates, profit margins differ greatly among industries depending on the nature of the product sold and the company's competitive strategy.

Note too that profit margin and asset turnover tend to vary inversely. Companies with high profit margins tend to have low asset turns, and vice versa. This is no accident. Companies that add significant value to a product, such as JPMorgan Chase or Alphabet Inc., can demand high profit margins. However, because adding value to a product usually requires lots of assets, these same firms tend to have lower asset turns. At the other extreme, grocery stores and discount retailers, such as Target, bring the product in the store on forklift trucks, sell for cash, and make the customer carry out his own purchases. Because they add little value to the product, they have very low profit margins and correspondingly high asset turns. It should be apparent, therefore, that a high profit margin is not necessarily better or worse than a low one—it all depends on the combined effect of the profit margin and the asset turnover.

Return on Assets

To look at the combined effect of margins and turns, we can calculate the *return on assets (ROA):*

$$\text{ROA} = \frac{\text{Profit}}{\text{margin}} \times \frac{\text{Asset}}{\text{turnover}} = \frac{\text{Net income}}{\text{Assets}}$$

Hasbro's ROA in 2016 was

$$\text{Return on assets} = \frac{\$551}{\$5,091} = 10.8\%$$

This means Hasbro earned an average of 10.8 cents on each dollar tied up in the business.

ROA is a basic measure of the efficiency with which a company allocates and manages its resources. It differs from ROE, in that it measures profit as a percentage of the money provided by owners *and* creditors as opposed to only the money provided by owners.

Some companies, such as Alphabet Inc. and JPMorgan Chase produce their ROAs by combining a high profit margin with a low asset turn; others, such as Target and Amazon.com, adopt the reverse strategy. A high profit margin *and* a high asset turn are ideal, but can be expected to attract considerable competition. Conversely, a low profit margin combined with a low asset turn will attract only bankruptcy lawyers.

Gross Margin

When analyzing profitability, it is often interesting to distinguish between variable costs and fixed costs. Variable costs change as sales vary, while fixed costs remain constant. Companies with a high proportion of fixed costs are more vulnerable to sales declines than other firms, because they cannot reduce fixed costs as sales fall.

Unfortunately, the accountant does not differentiate between fixed and variable costs when constructing an income statement. However, it is usually safe to assume that most expenses in cost of goods sold are variable, while most of the other operating costs are fixed. The gross margin enables us to distinguish, insofar as possible, between fixed and variable costs. It is defined as

$$\text{Gross margin} = \frac{\text{Gross profit}}{\text{Sales}} = \frac{\$2,789}{\$5,020} = 55.6\%$$

where gross profit equals net sales less cost of goods sold. Fifty-six percent of Hasbro's sales dollar is a *contribution to fixed cost and profits:* 56 cents of every sales dollar is available to pay for fixed costs and to add to profits.

One common use of the gross margin is to estimate a company's breakeven sales volume. Hasbro's income statement tells us that total operating expenses in 2016 were $1,968 million. If we assume these expenses are fixed and if 56 cents of each Hasbro sales dollar is available to pay for fixed costs and add to profits, the company's zero-profit sales volume must be $1,968/0.56, or $3,514 million.[2] Assuming operating expenses and the gross margin are independent of sales, Hasbro loses money when sales are below $3,514 million, and makes money when sales are above this figure.

Asset Turnover

Some newcomers to finance believe assets are a good thing: the more the better. The reality is just the opposite: Unless a company is about to go out of business, its value is in the income stream it generates, and its assets are simply a necessary means to this end. Indeed, the ideal company would be one that produced income without any assets; then no investment would be required, and returns would be infinite. Short of this fantasy, our ROE equation tells us that, other things constant, financial performance improves as asset turnover rises. This is the second lever of management performance.

The asset turnover ratio measures the sales generated per dollar of assets. Hasbro's asset turnover of 0.99 means that Hasbro generated 99 cents of sales for each dollar invested in assets. This ratio measures asset intensity, with a low asset turnover signifying an asset-intensive business and a high turnover the reverse.

The nature of a company's products and its competitive strategy strongly influence asset turnover. A steel mill will never have the asset turnover of a grocery store. But this is not the end of the story, because management diligence and creativity in controlling assets are also vital determinants of a company's asset turnover. When product technology is similar among competitors, control of assets is often the margin between success and failure.

Control of current assets is especially critical. You might think the distinction between current and fixed assets based solely on whether the asset will revert to cash within one year is artificial. But more is involved than this. Current assets, especially accounts receivable and inventory, have several unique properties. One is that if something goes wrong—if sales decline unexpectedly, customers delay payment, or a critical part fails to arrive—a company's investment in current assets can balloon very rapidly. When even manufacturing companies routinely invest one-half or more of their money in current assets, it is easy to appreciate that even modest alterations in the management of these assets can significantly affect company finances.

A second distinction is that unlike fixed assets, current assets can become a source of cash during business downturns. As sales decline, a company's investment in accounts receivable and inventory should fall as well, thereby freeing cash for other uses. (Remember, a reduction in an asset account is a

---

[2]Income = Sales − Variable costs − Fixed costs = Sales × Gross margin − Fixed costs. Setting income to zero and solving for sales, Sales = Fixed costs/Gross margin.

source of cash.) The fact that in a well-run company current assets move in an accordion-like fashion with sales is appealing to creditors. They know that during the upswing of a business cycle rising current assets will require loans, while during a downswing, falling current assets will provide the cash to repay the loans. In bankers' jargon, such a loan is said to be *self-liquidating* in the sense that the use to which the money is put creates the source of repayment.

It is often useful to analyze the turnover of each type of asset on a company's balance sheet individually. This gives rise to what are known as *control ratios*. Although the form in which each ratio is expressed may vary, every control ratio is simply an asset turnover for a particular type of asset. In each instance, the firm's investment in the asset is compared to net sales or a closely related figure.

Why compare assets to sales? The fact that a company's investment in, say, accounts receivable has risen over time could be due to two forces: (1) Perhaps sales have risen and simply dragged receivables along, or (2) management may have slackened its collection efforts. Relating receivables to sales in a control ratio adjusts for changes in sales, enabling the analyst to concentrate on the more important effects of changing management control. Thus, the control ratio distinguishes between sales-induced changes in investment and other, perhaps more sinister causes. Following are some standard control ratios and their values for Hasbro in 2016.

Inventory Turnover

Inventory turnover is expressed as

$$\text{Inventory turnover} = \frac{\text{Cost of goods sold}}{\text{Ending inventory}} = \frac{\$2,231}{\$388} = 5.8 \text{ times}$$

An inventory turn of 5.8 times means that items in Hasbro's inventory turn over 5.8 times per year, on average. Said differently, the typical item sits in inventory about 63 days before being sold (365 days/5.8 times = 63 days). This last number is known as *days inventory outstanding* (or *days' sales in inventory*), because Hasbro has enough inventory to support 63 days' worth of sales.

Several alternative definitions of the inventory turnover ratio exist, including sales divided by ending inventory and cost of goods sold divided by average inventory. Cost of goods sold is a more appropriate numerator than sales because sales include a profit markup that is absent from inventory. But beyond this, I see little to choose from among the various definitions.

The Collection Period

The *collection period* highlights a company's management of accounts receivable. For Hasbro

$$\text{Collection period} = \frac{\text{Accounts receivable}}{\text{Credit sales per day}} = \frac{\$1,320}{\$5,020/365} = 96.0 \text{ days}$$

Credit sales appear here rather than net sales because only credit sales generate accounts receivable. As a company outsider, however, I do not know what portion of Hasbro's net sales, if any, are for cash, so I assume they are all on credit. Credit sales per day is defined as credit sales for the accounting period divided by the number of days in the accounting period, which for annual statements is obviously 365 days.

Two interpretations of Hasbro's collection period are possible. We can say that Hasbro has an average of 96 days' worth of credit sales tied up in accounts receivable, or we can say that the average time lag between sale and receipt of cash from the sale is 96 days.

Beware of Seasonal Companies

Interpreting ratios of companies with seasonal sales can be tricky. For example, suppose a company's sales peak sharply at Christmas, resulting in high year-end accounts receivable. A naive collection period calculated by relating year-end accounts receivable to average daily sales for the whole year will produce an apparently very high collection period because the denominator is insensitive to the seasonal peak. To avoid being misled, a better way to calculate the collection period for a seasonal company is to use credit sales per day based only on the prior 60 to 90 days' sales. This matches the accounts receivable to the credit sales actually generating the receivables.

If we like, we can define a simpler asset turnover ratio for accounts receivable as just credit sales/accounts receivable. However, the collection period format is more informative, because it allows us to compare a company's collection period with its terms of sale. Thus, if a company sells on 90-day terms, a collection period of 65 days is excellent, but if the terms of sale were 30 days, our interpretation would be quite different.

Days' Sales in Cash

Hasbro's *days' sales in cash* is

$$\frac{\text{Days' sales}}{\text{in cash}} = \frac{\text{Cash and securities}}{\text{Sales per day}} = \frac{\$1,282}{\$5,020/365} = 93.2 \text{ days}$$

Hasbro has 93.2 days' worth of sales in cash and securities. Whether this is the right amount of cash for Hasbro is difficult to say. On the one hand, cash balances should not be too low. Companies require modest amounts of cash to facilitate transactions and are sometimes required to carry substantially larger amounts as compensating balances for bank loans. In addition, cash and marketable securities can be an important source of liquidity for a firm in an emergency. On the other hand, if cash balances are too high, shareholders may become disappointed that the firm's assets are not put to more productive and profitable uses. So the question of how much cash and securities a company should carry is often closely related to the broader question of how important liquidity is to the company and how best to provide it. The median days' sales in cash for nonfinancial companies in the Standard & Poor's 500 Index in 2016 was 76 days, almost double the figure for 2013. In comparison, Hasbro's 93 days is high. But relative to information technology companies, which often carry notoriously high cash balances, Hasbro's cash looks more modest. The median days' sales in cash in 2016 among the information technology companies in the S&P 500 was 187 days, with Microsoft and Facebook clocking in at 480 and 390 days, respectively.

Alphabet's Levers of Performance

The 2016 levers of performance for Internet titan Alphabet (the parent company of Google) make instructive reading. As shown below, the company combined an attractive profit margin and conservative financial leverage with an abysmally low asset turnover of only 0.54 times to generate a rather ordinary ROE of 14.0 percent. This is mediocre performance for a company selling at over 28 times earnings and perceived by most to be the dominant Internet player.

How can an Internet company generate an asset turnover more like that of a steel mill or a public utility? A look at Alphabet's balance sheet explains the mystery. At year-end 2016, roughly $86 billion, or over half of Alphabet's assets, were in cash and marketable securities, and its days' sales in cash was a whopping 350. It's as if the company had merged with a money market mutual fund. And Alphabet is not alone. It is common practice among leading technology companies to build huge war chests, which they argue are necessary to finance continued growth and to facilitate possible acquisitions—like maybe if Panama or South Dakota ever came up for sale. Others, including Ralph Nader, see a more sinister purpose: to keep the money out of the hands of shareholders and to avoid taxes.

To focus on Alphabet's operating performance apart from its ability to invest excess cash, we can strip cash and marketable securities out of the analysis. To do this, imagine the company returned 90 percent of its cash and securities to shareholders as a giant dividend. Alternatively, imagine Alphabet split into two companies: an operating Internet company and a money market mutual fund charged with investing 90 percent of the firm's cash. This would cut the operating company's assets and shareholders' equity by $77 billion, while leaving the company with a still robust 37.7 days' sales in cash. Assuming a modest 2 percent after-tax return on cash and securities, this would knock $1.54 billion from net income. The resulting revised levers of performance appear in the following summary. Asset turnover is now a more plausible, but still modest, 0.99 times, and ROE is up to a robust 28.8 percent. These numbers more accurately reflect the economics of Alphabet's business.

	Return on Equity	=	Profit Margin	×	Asset Turnover	×	Financial Leverage
As reported	14.0%	=	21.6%	×	0.54	×	1.20
Revised	28.8%	=	19.9%	×	0.99	×	1.46

Payables Period

The *payables period* is a control ratio for a liability. It is simply the collection period applied to accounts payable. For Hasbro

$$\frac{\text{Payables}}{\text{period}} = \frac{\text{Accounts payable}}{\text{Credit purchases per day}} = \frac{\$320}{\$2,231/365} = 52.4 \text{ days}$$

The proper definition of the payables period uses credit purchases, because they are what generate accounts payable. However, an outsider seldom knows credit purchases, so it is frequently necessary to settle for the closest approximation: cost of goods sold. This is what I have done above for Hasbro; $2,231 million is Hasbro's cost of goods sold, not its credit purchases. Cost of goods sold can differ from credit purchases for two reasons. First, the company may be adding to or depleting inventory—that is, purchasing at a different rate than it is selling. Second, all manufacturers add labor to material in the production process, thereby making cost of goods sold larger than purchases. Because of these differences, it is tricky to compare a manufacturing company's payables period, based on cost of goods sold, to its purchase terms. For Hasbro, it is almost certain that cost of goods sold overstates credit purchases per day and that Hasbro's suppliers are waiting a good bit longer than 52.4 days, on average, to receive payment.

Fixed-Asset Turnover

Companies or industries requiring large investments in long-lived assets to produce their goods are said to be capital intensive. Because a preponderance of their costs are fixed, capital-intensive businesses, such as auto manufacturers and airlines, are especially sensitive to the state of the economy, prospering in good times as sales rise relative to costs and suffering in bad as the reverse occurs. Capital intensity, also referred to as operating leverage, is of particular concern to creditors because it magnifies the basic business risks faced by a firm.

Fixed-asset turnover is a measure of capital intensity, with a low turnover implying high intensity. The ratio in 2016 for Hasbro was

$$\frac{\text{Fixed-asset}}{\text{turnover}} = \frac{\text{Sales}}{\text{Net property, plant, and equipment}} = \frac{\$5,020}{\$267}$$

$$= 18.8 \text{ times}$$

where $267 million is the book value of Hasbro's net property, plant, and equipment.

Operating and Cash Conversion Cycles

Several of these working capital control ratios are related, and it often makes sense for managers to recognize the connections. When a company begins its production cycle, it uses cash to acquire inventory. When the company sells an item, inventory changes back into cash once the customer pays for it and the accounts receivable is collected. In Chapter 1, we spoke of this movement of cash in qualitative terms as the firm's operating, or working capital, cycle. Here, we can express the same notion numerically as the sum of the number of days cash is tied up in inventory plus the number of days it takes a customer to pay, or the collection period

Operating cycle = Days inventory outstanding + Collection period

For Hasbro, days inventory outstanding is 63 days and the collection period is 96 days, so the total operating cycle is the sum: 159 days. Hasbro's cash is tied up for an average of 159 days between when it acquires inventory and when its customers pay. So Hasbro must find a source for this cash.

The good news for Hasbro is that suppliers are willing to provide some of this cash by allowing Hasbro some time to pay suppliers for the inventory it acquired. Recognizing this, the cash conversion cycle starts with the operating cycle and nets out the length of time Hasbro uses its suppliers' money:

Cash conversion cycle (CCC) = Operating cycle – Payables period
= Days inventory outstanding
+ Collection period – Payables period

Here is a timeline for the operating and cash conversion cycles.

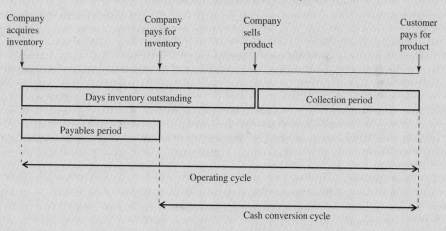

Hasbro's cash conversion cycle is its operating cycle of 159 days minus its payables period of 52 days, for a net of 107 days. Although Hasbro must begin the process by acquiring inventory, it is able to wait 52 days, on average, before paying for this inventory. So the length of time between when cash goes out the door until it comes back in, the cash conversion cycle, is 107 days.

Financial Leverage

The third lever by which management affects ROE is financial leverage. A company increases its financial leverage when it raises the proportion of debt relative to equity used to finance the business. Unlike the profit margin and the asset turnover ratio, where more is generally preferred to less, financial leverage is not something management necessarily wants to maximize, even when doing so increases ROE. Instead, the challenge of financial leverage is to strike a prudent balance between the benefits and costs of debt financing. Later, we will devote all of Chapter 6 to this important financial decision. For now, it is sufficient to recognize that more leverage is not necessarily preferred to less, and that while companies have considerable latitude in their choice of how much financial leverage to employ, there are economic and institutional constraints on their decision.

As Table 2.1 suggests, the nature of a company's business and its assets influence the financial leverage it can employ. In general, businesses with highly predictable and stable operating cash flows, such as Southern Co., an electric utility, can safely undertake more financial leverage than firms facing a high degree of market uncertainty, such as software company Adobe Systems. In addition, businesses such as banks, which usually have diversified portfolios of readily salable, liquid assets, can also safely use more financial leverage than the typical business.

Another pattern evident in Table 2.1 is that ROA and financial leverage tend to be inversely related. Companies with low ROAs generally employ more debt financing, and vice versa. This is consistent with the previous paragraph. Safe, stable, liquid investments tend to generate low returns but substantial borrowing capacity. Banks are extreme examples of this pattern. JPMorgan Chase combines what by manufacturing standards would be a horrible 1.0 percent ROA with an astronomical leverage ratio of 10.92 to generate a modest ROE of 10.8 percent. The key to this pairing is the safe, liquid nature of the bank's assets. (Past loans to Third-World dictators, Texas energy companies, and subprime mortgage borrowers are, of course, another story—one the bank would just as soon forget.)

The following ratios measure financial leverage, or debt capacity, and the related concept of liquidity.

Balance Sheet Ratios

The most common measures of financial leverage compare the book value of a company's liabilities to the book value of its assets or equity. This gives rise to the *debt-to-assets ratio* and the *debt-to-equity ratio,* defined as

$$\text{Debt-to-assets ratio} = \frac{\text{Total liabilities}}{\text{Total assets}} = \frac{\$3,228}{\$5,091} = 63.4\%$$

$$\text{Debt-to-equity ratio} = \frac{\text{Total liabilities}}{\text{Shareholders' equity}} = \frac{\$3,228}{\$1,863} = 173.3\%$$

The first ratio says that money to pay for 63.4 percent of Hasbro's assets, in book value terms, comes from creditors of one type or another. The second ratio says the same thing in a slightly different way: Creditors supply Hasbro with $1.73 for every dollar supplied by shareholders. As footnote 1 demonstrated, the lever of performance introduced earlier, the assets-to-equity ratio, is just the debt-to-equity ratio plus 1.

As many companies have built up large excess balances of cash and marketable securities, analysts have increasingly replaced debt in these equations with "net" debt, defined as total liabilities less cash and marketable securities. The idea is that as safe, interest-bearing assets, excess cash and securities are essentially negative debt and should thus be subtracted from liabilities when measuring aggregate indebtedness. Thought of another way, if a company has excess cash that could, on short notice, be used to pay off outstanding debts, then the company's true level of indebtedness is lower than the standard leverage ratios would suggest. Because, as noted earlier, Hasbro's cash balances are moderately high, calculating their debt ratios using net debt could be enlightening. Indeed, the net debt figures paint a rather different picture of Hasbro's indebtedness, with a debt-to-assets ratio of only 38.2 percent and a debt-to-equity ratio of 104.5 percent.

Coverage Ratios

A number of variations on these balance sheet measures of financial leverage exist. Conceptually, however, there is no reason to prefer one over another, for they all focus on balance sheet values, and hence all suffer from the same weakness. The financial burden a company faces by using debt financing ultimately depends not on the size of its liabilities relative to assets or to equity but on its ability to meet the annual cash payments the debt requires. A simple example will illustrate the distinction. Suppose two companies, A and B, have the same debt-to-assets ratio, but A is very profitable and B is losing money. Chances are that B will have difficulty meeting its annual interest and principal obligations, while A will not. The obvious conclusion is that balance sheet ratios are of primary interest only in liquidation, when the proceeds of asset sales are to be distributed among creditors and owners. In all other instances, we should be more interested in comparing the annual burden the debt imposes to the cash flow available for debt service.

This gives rise to what are known as *coverage ratios,* the most common of which are *times interest earned* and *times burden covered.* Letting EBIT represent earnings before interest and taxes (calculated as earnings before taxes plus interest expense), the ratios are defined as

$$\text{Times interest earned} = \frac{\text{EBIT}}{\text{Interest expense}} = \frac{\$807}{\$97} = 8.3 \text{ times}$$

$$\text{Times burden covered} = \frac{\text{EBIT}}{\text{Interest} + \dfrac{\text{Principal repayment}}{1 - \text{Tax rate}}}$$

$$= \frac{\$807}{\$97 + \dfrac{\$165}{1 - \left(\dfrac{\$159}{\$710}\right)}} = 2.6 \text{ times}$$

Both ratios compare income available for debt service in the numerator to some measure of annual financial obligation. For both ratios, the income available is EBIT. This is the earnings the company generates that can be used to make interest payments. EBIT is before taxes because interest payments are before-tax expenditures, and we want to compare like quantities. Hasbro's times interest earned ratio of 8.3 means the company earned its interest obligation 8.3 times over in 2016; EBIT was 8.3 times as large as interest.

Though dentists may correctly claim that if you ignore your teeth they'll eventually go away, the same cannot be said for principal repayments. If a company fails to make a principal repayment when due, the outcome is the same as if it had failed to make an interest payment. In both cases, the company is in default and creditors can force it into bankruptcy. The times-burden-covered ratio reflects this reality by expanding the definition of annual financial obligations to include debt principal repayments, as well as interest. When including principal repayment as part of a company's financial burden, we must remember to express the figure on a before-tax basis comparable to interest and EBIT. Unlike interest payments, principal repayments are not a tax-deductible expense. This means that if a company is in, say, a 50 percent tax bracket, it must earn $2 before taxes to have $1 after taxes to pay creditors. The other dollar goes to the tax collector. For other tax brackets, the before-tax burden of a principal repayment is found by dividing the repayment by 1 minus the company's tax rate. Adjusting the principal repayment in this manner to its before-tax equivalent is known in the trade as *grossing up* the principal—about as gross as finance ever gets.

An often-asked question is: Which of these coverage ratios is more meaningful? The answer is that both are important. If a company could always roll over its maturing obligations by taking out new loans as it repaid old ones, the *net* burden of the debt would be merely the interest expense, and times interest earned would be the more important ratio. The problem, as we were all vividly reminded during the recent financial panic, is that the replacement of maturing debt with new debt is not an automatic feature of capital markets. In some instances, when capital markets are unsettled or a company's fortunes decline, creditors may refuse to renew maturing obligations. Then, the burden of the debt suddenly becomes interest plus principal payments, and the times-burden-covered ratio assumes paramount importance.

This is what happened beginning in the summer of 2007 when growing defaults on subprime mortgages prompted some short-term lenders to demand immediate payment from a variety of mortgage investment companies. These special purpose companies were issuing short-term debt to finance ownership of complex, long-term mortgage-backed securities. This was a nice business as long as lenders willingly rolled over maturing debts. But the minute they balked, a vicious circle ensued as borrowers sold their securities at cut-rate prices to repay short-term lenders, and short-term lenders, reacting to the falling prices, increasingly refused to roll over maturing obligations.

In sum, it is fair to conclude that the times-burden-covered ratio is too conservative because it assumes the company will pay its existing loans down to zero, but that the times-interest-earned ratio is too liberal because it assumes the company will always roll over all of its obligations as they mature.

Market Value Leverage Ratios

A third family of leverage ratios relates a company's liabilities to the *market value of its equity* or the *market value of its assets.* For Hasbro in 2016,

$$\frac{\text{Market value of debt}}{\text{Market value of equity}} = \frac{\text{Market value of debt}}{\text{Number of shares of stock} \times \text{Price per share}}$$

$$= \frac{\$3,228}{\$9,685} = 33.3\%$$

$$\frac{\text{Market value of debt}}{\text{Market value of assets}} = \frac{\text{Market value of debt}}{\text{Market value of debt} + \text{equity}}$$

$$= \frac{\$3,228}{\$3,228 + \$9,685} = 25.0\%$$

Note that I have assumed the market value of debt equals the book value of debt in both of these ratios. Strictly speaking, this is seldom true, but in most instances, the difference between the two quantities is small. Also, accurately estimating the market value of debt often turns out to be a tedious, time-consuming chore that is best avoided—unless, of course, you are being paid by the hour.

Market value ratios are clearly superior to book value ratios simply because book values are historical, often irrelevant numbers, while market values indicate the true worth of creditors' and owners' stakes in the business. Recalling that market values are based on investors' expectations about future cash flows, market value leverage ratios can be thought of as coverage ratios extended over many future periods. Instead of comparing income to financial burden in a single year as coverage ratios do, market value ratios compare today's value of expected future income to today's value of future financial burdens.

Market value ratios are especially helpful when assessing the financial leverage of rapidly growing, startup businesses. Even when such companies have terrible or nonexistent coverage ratios, lenders may still extend them liberal credit if they believe future cash flows will be sufficient to service the debt. McCaw Communications offers an extreme example of this. At year-end 1990, McCaw had over $5 billion in debt; a debt-to-equity ratio, in book terms, of 330 percent; and annualized interest expenses of *more than 60 percent of net revenues.* Moreover, despite explosive growth, McCaw had never made a meaningful operating profit in its principal cellular telephone business. Why then did otherwise intelligent creditors loan McCaw $5 billion? Because creditors and equity investors believed it was only a matter of time before the company would begin to generate huge cash flows. This optimism was handsomely rewarded in late 1993 when AT&T paid $12.6 billion to acquire McCaw. Including the $5 billion in debt assumed by AT&T, the acquisition ranked as the second largest in corporate history at the time.

Another example is Amazon. In 1998, the company recorded its largest-ever loss of $124 million, had never earned a profit, and had only $139 million left in shareholders' equity. But not to worry: Lenders were still pleased to extend the company $350 million in long-term debt. Apparently, creditors are willing to overlook a number of messy details when a borrower's sales are growing 300 percent a year and the market value of its equity tops $17 billion—especially when the debt is convertible into equity. After all, in market value terms, Amazon's debt-to-equity ratio was only 3 percent. Today, Amazon's equity is worth over $450 billion, and its market-value debt-to-equity ratio is about 12 percent.

Economists like market value leverage ratios because they are accurate indicators of company indebtedness at a point in time. But you should be aware that market value ratios are not without problems. One is that they ignore rollover risks. When creditors take the attitude that debt must be repaid with cash, not promises of future cash, modest market value leverage ratios can be of hollow comfort. Also, despite these ratios' conceptual appeal, few companies use them to set financing policy or to monitor debt levels. This may be due in part to the fact that volatile stock prices can make market value ratios appear somewhat arbitrary and beyond management's control.

Liquidity Ratios

One determinant of a company's debt capacity is the liquidity of its assets. An asset is liquid if it can be readily converted to cash, while a liability is liquid if it must be repaid in the near future. As the subprime mortgage debacle illustrates, it is risky to finance illiquid assets such as fixed plant and equipment with liquid, short-term liabilities, because the liabilities will come due before the assets generate enough cash to pay them. Such "maturity mismatching" forces borrowers to roll over, or refinance, maturing liabilities to avoid insolvency.

Two common ratios intended to measure the liquidity of a company's assets relative to its liabilities are the *current ratio* and the *acid test.* For Hasbro,

$$\text{Current ratio} = \frac{\text{Current assets}}{\text{Current liabilities}}$$

$$= \frac{\$3,228}{\$1,618} = 2.0 \text{ times}$$

$$\text{Acid test} = \frac{\text{Current assets} - \text{Inventory}}{\text{Current liabilities}}$$

$$= \frac{\$3,228 - \$388}{\$1,618} = 1.8 \text{ times}$$

The current ratio compares the assets that will turn into cash within the year to the liabilities that must be paid within the year. A company with a low current ratio lacks liquidity, in the sense that it cannot reduce its current assets for cash to meet maturing obligations. It must rely instead on operating income and outside financing.

The acid-test ratio, sometimes called the *quick ratio,* is a more conservative liquidity measure. It is identical to the current ratio except that the numerator is reduced by the value of inventory. Inventory is subtracted because it is frequently illiquid. Under distress conditions, a company or its creditors may realize little cash from the sale of inventory. In liquidation sales, sellers typically receive 40 percent or less of the book value of inventory.

You should recognize that these ratios are rather crude measures of liquidity, for at least two reasons. First, rolling over some obligations, such as accounts payable, involves virtually no insolvency risk, provided the company is at least marginally profitable. Second, unless a company intends to go out of business, most of the cash generated by liquidating current assets cannot be used to reduce liabilities because it must be plowed back into the business to support continued operations.

Is ROE a Reliable Financial Yardstick?

To this point, we have assumed management wants to increase the company's ROE, and we have studied three important levers of performance by which they can accomplish this: the profit margin, asset turnover, and financial leverage. We concluded that whether a company is IBM or the corner drugstore, careful management of these levers can positively affect ROE. We also saw that determining and maintaining appropriate values of the levers is a challenging managerial task that requires an understanding of the company's business, the way the company competes, and the interdependencies among the levers themselves. Now it is time to ask how reliable ROE is as a measure of financial performance. If company A has a higher ROE than company B, is it necessarily a better company? If company C increases its ROE, is this unequivocal evidence of improved performance?

ROE suffers from three critical deficiencies as a measure of financial performance, which I will refer to as the *timing* problem, the *risk* problem, and the *value* problem. Seen in proper perspective, these problems mean ROE is seldom an unambiguous measure of performance. ROE remains a useful and important indicator, but it must be interpreted in light of its limitations, and no one should automatically assume a higher ROE is always better than a lower one.

The Timing Problem

It is a cliché to say that successful managers must be forward-looking and have a long-term perspective. Yet ROE is precisely the opposite: backward-looking and focused on a single year. So it is little wonder that ROE can at times be a skewed measure of performance. When, for example, a company incurs heavy startup costs to introduce a hot new product, ROE will initially fall. However, rather than indicating worsening financial performance, the fall simply reflects the myopic, one-period nature of the yardstick. Because ROE necessarily includes only one year's earnings, it fails to capture the full impact of multiperiod decisions.

The Risk Problem

Business decisions commonly involve the classic "eat well–sleep well" dilemma. If you want to eat well, you had best be prepared to take risks in search of higher returns. If you want to sleep well, you will likely have to forgo high returns in search of safety. Seldom will you realize both high returns and safety. (And when you do, please give me a call.)

The problem with ROE is that it says nothing about what risks a company has taken to generate it. Here is a simple example. Take-a-Risk, Inc., earns an ROA of 6 percent from wildcat oil exploration in Sudan, which it combines with an assets-to-equity ratio of 5.0 to produce an ROE of 30 percent (6% × 5.0). Never-Dare, Ltd., meanwhile, has an ROA of 10 percent on its investment in government securities, which it finances with equal portions of debt and equity, yielding an ROE of 20 percent (10% × 2.0). Which company is the better performer? My answer is Never-Dare. Take-a-Risk's ROE is high, but its high business risk and extreme financial leverage make it a very uncertain enterprise. I would prefer the more modest but eminently safer ROE of Never-Dare.[3] Security analysts would make the same point by saying that Take-a-Risk's ROE might be higher, but that the number is much lower in quality than Never-Dare's ROE, meaning that it is much riskier. In sum, because ROE looks only at return while ignoring risk, it can be an inaccurate yardstick of financial performance.

Return on Invested Capital

To circumvent the distorting effects of leverage on ROE and ROA, I recommend calculating *return on invested capital (ROIC),* also known as *return on net assets (RONA):*

$$\text{ROIC} = \frac{\text{EBIT}(1 - \text{Tax rate})}{\text{Interest-bearing debt} + \text{Equity}}$$

Hasbro's 2016 ROIC was

$$\frac{\$807(1 - \$159/\$710)}{\$522 + \$1,199 + \$1,863} = 17.5\%$$

The numerator of this ratio is the earnings after tax the company would report if it were all equity financed, and the denominator is the sum of all sources of cash to the company on which a return must be earned. Thus, while accounts payable are a source of cash to the company, they are excluded because they carry no explicit cost. In essence, ROIC is the rate of return earned on the total capital invested in the business without regard for whether it is called debt or equity.[4]

To see the virtue of ROIC, consider the following example. Companies A and B are identical in all respects except that A is highly levered and B is all equity financed. Because the two companies are identical except for capital structure, we would like a return measure that reflects this fundamental similarity. The following table shows that ROE and ROA fail this test. Reflecting

---

[3]Even if I preferred eating well to sleeping well, I would still choose Never-Dare and finance my purchase with a little personal borrowing to lever my return on investment. See the appendix to Chapter 6 for more on the substitution of personal borrowing for company borrowing.

[4] After decades of neglect, companies appear to be rediscovering ROIC. For more, see David Benoit, "The Hottest Metric in Finance: ROIC," *The Wall Street Journal,* May 3, 2016.

the company's extensive use of financial leverage, A's ROE is 18 percent, while B's zero-leverage position generates a lower but better-quality ROE of 7.2 percent. ROA is biased in the other direction, punishing company A for its extensive use of debt and leaving B unaffected. Only ROIC is independent of the different financing schemes the two companies employ, showing a 7.2 percent return for both firms. ROIC thus reflects the company's fundamental earning power before it is confounded by differences in financing strategies.

	Company	
	A	B
Debt @ 10% interest	$ 900	$ 0
Equity	100	1,000
Total assets	$1,000	$1,000
EBIT	$ 120	$ 120
− Interest expense	90	0
Earnings before tax	30	120
− Tax @ 40%	12	48
Earnings after tax	$ 18	$ 72
ROE	18.0%	7.2%
ROA	1.8%	7.2%
ROIC	7.2%	7.2%

The Value Problem

ROE measures the return on shareholders' investment; however, the investment figure used is the *book value* of shareholders' equity, not the *market value*. This distinction is important. Hasbro's ROE in 2016 was 29.6 percent, and indeed this is the return you could have earned had you been able to buy the company's equity for its book value of $1,863 million. But that would have been impossible, for, as noted in the previous chapter, the market value of Hasbro's equity was $9,685 million. At this price, your annual return would have been only 5.7 percent, not 29.6 percent ($551/$9,685 = 5.7%). The market value of equity is more significant to shareholders because it measures the current, realizable worth of the shares, while book value is only history. So even when ROE measures management's financial performance, it may not be synonymous with a high return on investment to shareholders. Thus, it is not enough for investors to find companies capable of generating high ROEs; these companies must be unknown to others, because once they are known, the possibility of high returns to investors will melt away in higher stock prices.

The Earnings Yield and the P/E Ratio

It might appear that we can circumvent the value problem by simply replacing the book value of equity with its market value in the ROE. But the resulting *earnings yield* has problems of its own. For Hasbro,[5]

$$\text{Earning yield} = \frac{\text{Net income}}{\text{Market value of shareholders' equity}}$$

$$= \frac{\text{Earnings per share}}{\text{Price per share}} = \frac{\$4.34}{\$77.79} = 5.6\%$$

Is earnings yield a useful measure of financial performance? No! The problem is that a company's stock price is very sensitive to investor expectations about the future. A share of stock entitles its owner to a portion of *future* earnings, as well as present earnings. Naturally, the higher an investor's expectations of future earnings, the more she will pay for the stock. This means that a bright future, a high stock price, and a *low* earnings yield go together. Clearly, a high earnings yield is not an indicator of superior performance; in fact, it is more the reverse. Said another way, the earnings yield suffers from a severe timing problem of its own that invalidates it as a performance measure.

Turning the earnings yield on its head produces the *price-to-earnings ratio,* or *P/E ratio.* Hasbro's 2016 P/E ratio is

$$\frac{\text{Price per share}}{\text{Earnings per share}} = \frac{\$77.79}{\$4.34} = 17.9 \text{ times}$$

The P/E ratio adds little to our discussion of performance measures, but its wide use among investors deserves comment. The P/E ratio is the price of one dollar of current earnings and is a means of normalizing stock prices for different earnings levels across companies. At year end 2016, investors were paying almost $18 per dollar of Hasbro's earnings. A company's P/E ratio depends principally on two things: its future earnings prospects and the risk associated with those earnings. Stock price, and hence the P/E ratio, rises with improved earnings prospects and falls with increasing risk. A sometimes confusing pattern occurs when a company's earnings are weak but investors believe the weakness is temporary. Then, prices remain buoyant in the face of depressed earnings, and the P/E ratio *rises.* This likely happened to Hasbro as recently as 2013, when its P/E ratio climbed to over 25 despite earnings that dropped 15% from the prior year. In general, the P/E ratio says little about a

---

[5] As is common, Hasbro uses the weighted average number of shares outstanding during the year to calculate its earnings per share. For 2016, this number was 127.0 million shares, versus the 124.5 million shares outstanding as of Dec. 31, 2016, which we used to calculate the total market value of equity. Therefore, the earnings yield of 5.6% here differs slightly from the 5.7% return on market value of equity computed in the last paragraph.

company's current financial performance, but it does indicate what investors believe about future prospects.

ROE or Market Price?

For years, academicians and practitioners have been at odds over the proper measure of financial performance. Academicians criticize ROE for the reasons just cited and argue that the correct measure of financial performance is the firm's stock price. Moreover, they contend that management's goal should be to maximize stock price. Their logic is persuasive: Stock price represents the value of the owners' investment in the firm, and if managers want

---

Can ROE Substitute for Share Price?

Figures 2.1 and 2.2 suggest that the gulf between academicians and practitioners over the proper measure of financial performance may be narrower than supposed. The graphs plot the market value of equity divided by the book value of equity against ROE for two representative groups of companies. The ROE figure is the average ROE over the most recent three years. The solid line in each figure is a regression line indicating the general relation between the two variables. The noticeable positive relationship visible in both graphs suggests that high-ROE companies tend to have high stock prices relative to book value, and vice versa. Hence, working to increase ROE appears to be generally consistent with working to increase stock price.

The proximity of the company dots to the fitted regression line is also interesting. It shows the importance of factors other than ROE in determining a company's market-to-book ratio. As we should expect, these other factors play an important role in determining the market value of a company's shares.

For interest, I have indicated the positions of several companies on the graphs. Note in Figure 2.1 that Hasbro is very close to the regression line, indicating that based purely on historical ROE, Hasbro's stock is fairly priced compared to those of other firms in the toy, gaming, and leisure industries. Many of Hasbro's most direct competitors are also very close to the regression line, but JAKKS Pacific falls fairly far below it and Spin Master is well above. JAKKS has seen steadily declining sales and profits in recent years, which the company attributes to weakness in some key product lines, and the stock price has fallen below $5. Spin Master is a children's toy and game company based in Toronto whose most successful product was the Bakugan characters and stories. Several years ago, as Bakugan approached the end of its life cycle, the company reorganized and strategically refocused on new toy categories. This shift appears to have been successful and the market has responded by rewarding Spin Master's renewed growth.

Figure 2.2 shows the same information for 82 companies in Standard & Poor's 100 Index of the largest U.S. firms. Pepsico takes the prize here for the highest ROE with a figure of over 46 percent, although Amazon.com wins market-to-book honors at over 18 times. Perhaps this has something to do with the fact that Amazon's sales have grown at an average rate of almost 29 percent a year over the past 15 years. At the other end of the spectrum, General Motors and Apple lie well below the regression line.

To summarize, these graphs offer tantalizing evidence that despite its weaknesses, ROE may serve as at least a crude proxy for share price in measuring financial performance.

FIGURE 2.1   Market to Book Value of Equity vs. Return on Equity for 20 Toy, Gaming, and Leisure Products Companies

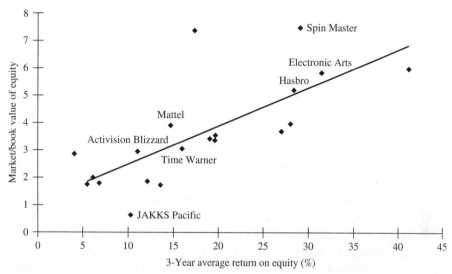

The regression equation is MV/BV = 1.09 + 14.0 ROE, where MV/BV is the market value of equity relative to the book value of equity in December 2016, and ROE is the average return on equity for 2016 and the prior two years. Companies with a negative ROE were eliminated. The adjusted R^2 is 0.51, and the t-statistic for the slope coefficient is 4.6.

FIGURE 2.2   Market to Book Value of Equity vs. Return on Equity for 82 Large Corporations

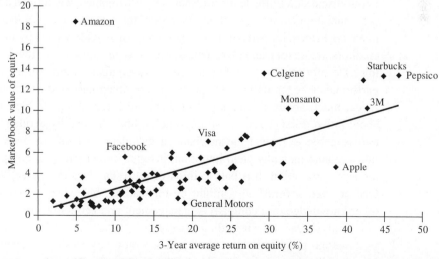

Companies are members of Standard & Poor's 100 Index of largest U.S. corporations. Those with a negative ROE and outliers with ROE above 50 percent were eliminated. The regression equation is MV/BV = 0.33 + 22.0 ROE, where MV/BV is the market value of equity relative to the book value of equity in December 2016, and ROE is the average return on equity for 2016 and the prior two years. The adjusted R^2 is 0.43, and the t-statistic for the slope coefficient is 7.9.

to further the interests of owners, they should take actions that increase value to owners. Indeed, the notion of "value creation" has become a central theme in the writings of many academicians and consultants.

Practitioners acknowledge the logic of this reasoning but question its applicability. One problem is the difficulty of specifying precisely how operating decisions affect stock price. If we are not certain what impact a change in, say, the business strategy of a division will have on the company's stock price, the goal of increasing price cannot guide decision making. A second problem is that managers typically know more about their company than do outside investors, or at least think they do. Why, then, should managers consider the assessments of less-informed investors when making business decisions? A third practical problem with stock price as a performance measure is that it depends on a whole array of factors outside the company's control. One can never be certain whether an increase in stock price reflects improving company performance or an improving external economic environment. For these reasons, many practitioners remain skeptical of stock market–based indicators of performance, even while academicians and consultants continue to work on translating value creation into a practical financial objective. One popular effort along these lines is *economic value added (EVA),* popularized by the consulting firm Stern Stewart Management Services. We will look more closely at EVA in Chapter 8.

Ratio Analysis

In our discussion of the levers of financial performance, we defined a number of financial ratios. It is now time to consider the systematic use of these ratios to analyze financial performance. Ratio analysis is widely used by managers, creditors, regulators, and investors. At root, it is an elementary process involving little more than comparing a number of company ratios to one or more performance benchmarks. Used with care and imagination, the technique can reveal much about a company. But there are a few things to bear in mind about ratios. First, a ratio is simply one number divided by another, so it is unreasonable to expect the mechanical calculation of one or even several ratios to automatically yield important insights into anything as complex as a modern corporation. It is best to think of ratios as clues in a detective story. One or even several ratios might be misleading, but when combined with other knowledge of a company's management and economic circumstances, ratio analysis can tell a revealing story.

A second point to bear in mind is that a ratio has no single correct value. Like Goldilocks and the three bears, the observation that the value of a particular ratio is too high, too low, or just right depends on the perspective of the analyst and on the company's competitive strategy. The current ratio, previously defined as the ratio of current assets to current liabilities, is a case in point. From the perspective of a short-term creditor, a high current ratio is a positive sign, suggesting ample liquidity and a high likelihood of repayment. Yet an owner of the company might look on the same current ratio as a negative sign suggesting that the company's assets are being deployed too conservatively. Moreover, from an operating perspective, a high current ratio could be a sign of conservative management or the natural result of a competitive strategy that emphasizes liberal credit terms and sizable inventories. In this case, the important question is not whether the current ratio is too high but whether the chosen strategy is best for the company.

Using Ratios Effectively

If ratios have no universally correct values, how do you interpret them? How do you decide whether a company is healthy or sick? There are three approaches, each involving a different performance benchmark: Compare the ratios to rules of thumb, compare them to industry averages, or look for changes in the ratios over time. Comparing a company's ratios to rules of thumb has the virtue of simplicity but has little else to recommend it. The appropriate ratio values for a company depend too much on the analyst's perspective and on the company's specific circumstances for rules of thumb to be very helpful. The most positive thing one can say about them is that over the years, companies conforming to these rules of thumb apparently go bankrupt somewhat less frequently than those that do not.

Comparing a company's ratios to industry ratios provides a useful feel for how the company measures up to its competitors, provided you bear in mind that company-specific differences can result in entirely justifiable deviations from industry norms. Also, there is no guarantee that the industry as a whole knows what it is doing. The knowledge that one railroad was much like its competitors was cold comfort in the depression of the 1930s, when virtually all railroads got into financial difficulties.

The most useful way to evaluate ratios involves trend analysis: Calculate ratios for a company over several years, and note how they change over time. Trend analysis avoids the need for cross-company and cross-industry comparisons, enabling the analyst to draw firmer conclusions about the company's financial health and its variation over time.

Moreover, the levers of performance suggest one logical approach to trend analysis: Instead of calculating ratios at random, hoping to stumble across one that might be meaningful, take advantage of the structure implicit in the levers. As Figure 2.3 illustrates, the levers of performance organize ratios into three tiers. At the top, ROE looks at the performance of the enterprise as a whole; in the middle, the levers of performance indicate how three important segments of the business contributed to ROE; and on the bottom, many of the other

FIGURE 2.3   **The Levers of Performance Suggest One Road Map for Ratio Analysis**

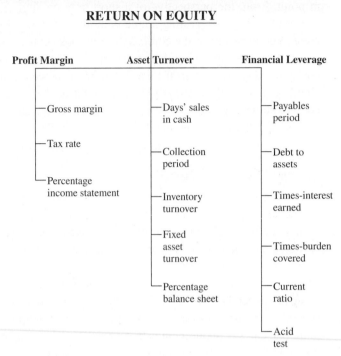

ratios discussed reveal how the management of individual income statement and balance sheet accounts contributed to the observed levers. To take advantage of this structure, begin at the top by noting the trend in ROE over time. Then, narrow your focus and ask what changes in the three levers account for the observed ROE pattern. Finally, get out your microscope and study individual accounts for explanations of the observed changes in the levers. To illustrate, if ROE has plunged while the profit margin and financial leverage have remained constant, examine the control of individual asset accounts in search of the culprit or culprits.

Ratio Analysis of Hasbro Inc.

As a practical demonstration of ratio analysis, let us see what the technique can tell us about Hasbro Inc. Table 2.2 presents previously discussed ratios for Hasbro over the years 2012–2016 and industry average figures for 2016. (For summary definitions of the ratios, see Table 2.4 at the end of the chapter.) The comparison industry consists of seven representative competitors noted at the bottom of the table. (To find similar, readily available data for other companies, see the list of websites at the end of the chapter.)

TABLE 2.2   Ratio Analysis of Hasbro Inc., 2012–2016, and Industry Averages, 2016

Source: Data from Hasbro 2012–2016 annual reports

	2012	2013	2014	2015	2016	Industry Average*
Profitability ratios:						
Return on equity (%)	**22.3**	**17.0**	**28.4**	**27.2**	**29.6**	**14.0**
Return on assets (%)	7.8	6.5	9.2	9.6	10.8	6.4
Return on invested capital (%)	12.9	11.7	14.9	15.5	17.5	10.6
Profit margin (%)	**8.2**	**7.0**	**9.7**	**10.2**	**11.0**	**11.5**
Gross margin (%)	53.2	53.9	54.5	55.3	55.6	53.8
Price-to-earnings ratio (X)	13.8	25.2	16.5	18.6	17.9	29.9
Turnover-control ratios:						
Asset turnover (X)	**0.9**	**0.9**	**0.9**	**0.9**	**1.0**	**0.7**
Fixed-asset turnover (X)	17.7	17.3	18.0	18.7	18.8	13.3
Inventory turnover (X)	6.1	5.4	5.7	5.2	5.8	14.0
Collection period (days)	91.9	97.8	93.4	99.9	96.0	60.0
Days' sales in cash (days)	75.8	61.0	76.2	80.2	93.2	108.3
Payables period (days)	26.7	38.5	39.8	44.3	52.4	58.6
Leverage and liquidity ratios:						
Assets to equity (X)	**2.9**	**2.6**	**3.1**	**2.8**	**2.7**	**2.3**
Debt to assets (%)	65.2	61.8	67.7	64.8	63.4	50.8
Debt to equity (%)	186.9	161.7	209.2	183.7	173.3	128.5
Times interest earned (X)	6.0	4.9	6.8	7.3	8.3	13.5
Times burden covered (X)	1.6	1.2	1.0	1.6	2.6	2.9
Debt to assets (market value, %)	37.8	27.4	30.9	26.7	25.0	34.6
Debt to equity (market value, %)	60.9	37.7	44.8	36.4	33.3	92.8
Current ratio (X)	2.6	1.8	2.5	2.7	2.0	3.1
Acid test (X)	2.3	1.6	2.2	2.3	1.8	2.8

*Industry average of seven firms in the toy and gaming industry: Activision Bilzzard, Electronic Arts, JAKKS Pacific, Mattel, Nintendo, Time Warner and Walt Disney. Nintendo is missing from some of the industry averages, either because of missing data or because its values are outliers.

Beginning with Hasbro's profitability ratios, we see a company that has been on an upward trajectory in recent years. The firm's return on equity, which was as low as 17.0 percent in 2013, has climbed to an impressive 29.6 percent in 2016, over double the industry average of 14.0 percent. Part of the disparity is due to Hasbro's use of higher debt financing than its peers, but a glance at the company's return on invested capital reveals that this is not the whole story. Recall that ROIC abstracts from company financing to reveal the basic earning power of the firm's assets. Hasbro's ROIC has risen steadily from 11.7 percent in 2013 to 17.5 percent in 2016, again well above the industry average. To put these figures into broader perspective, the median ROE chalked up by all nonfinancial firms in the S&P 500 Index in 2016 was 15.5 percent, while the corresponding ROIC was 11.2 percent. By these measures, Hasbro's performance is quite strong.

Hasbro's levers of performance can tell us more about its healthy ROE. Credit for Hasbro's superior performance in 2016 does not go to its profit margin—Hasbro's profit margin of 11.0 percent is actually slightly below the industry average. But, profit margin does deserve a lot of credit for the upward trend, rising noticeably over the period. If Hasbro's 2016 profit margin had remained at its 2013 level of 7.0 percent, ROE in 2016 for Hasbro would have been only 18.9 percent ($7.0\% \times 1.0 \times 2.7 = 18.9\%$), still robust but now much closer to that of its peers. Why the improvement in profit margin? Gross margins are also climbing, although not quite as dramatically as profit margins. This suggests that the rest of the increase is due to decreasing operating expenses, an observation we will be better equipped to explore in a few paragraphs.

Why is Hasbro's ROE so much higher than its peers? Hasbro's strong performance in 2016 can be attributed to both its asset turnover and financial leverage. Asset turnover held steady at 0.9 for several years before increasing slightly to 1.0 in 2016. Compared to the average asset turnover 0.7 for its peers, Hasbro's asset turnover is 43 percent $[0.43 = (1.0 - 0.7)/0.7]$ higher. Financial leverage, measured with Hasbro's assets-to-equity ratio, has varied somewhat, but at 2.7 is 17 percent above the industry average of 2.3.

Digging a little deeper into these broad trends, we see that Hasbro ironically underperforms in the management of several important assets, even though its overall asset turnover ratio is well above the industry average. Hasbro's inventory turnover of 5.8 is less than half of the industry average. Some of Hasbro's competitors, including Electronic Arts and Activision Blizzard, have shifted aggressively away from physical products toward digital gaming—these companies have extremely low levels of inventory and correspondingly high inventory turnover. Hasbro also has a longer collection period and lower payables period, which means that Hasbro is collecting its bills more slowly and paying its suppliers more quickly than competitors. Together, these numbers for Hasbro tell the story of a company that is managing its working capital less efficiently than its peers, a difference that is at least partly attributable to differing lines of business.

So how is Hasbro able to achieve its superior asset turnover? The answer largely falls on fixed-asset turnover which, at 18.8, is well above the industry average. Strong fixed-asset turnover might reflect a less capital-intensive business or more efficient use of property, plant, and equipment. In Hasbro's case, there may be a third explanation. Several of Hasbro's competitors have been actively acquiring other firms. Acquisitions affect the financial statements in sometimes unexpected ways. When a company makes an acquisition, accountants update its balance sheet to reflect the market value of the acquired assets.

This increases asset value above historical cost and, in turn, depresses fixed-asset turnover. As we will see in the next few paragraphs, acquisitions may affect other ratios as well. Hasbro also has slightly lower cash balances, 93 days versus the industry average of 108. Because large cash reserves drag down asset turnover, Hasbro's asset turnover benefits from its lower cash reserves.

Looking at Hasbro's leverage ratios, although there is some year-to-year variation, the company has been fairly consistent in its reliance on other people's money. Book value leverage ratios and the coverage ratios point to greater use of debt compared to industry peers. Market value leverage ratios paint a different picture, though. Hasbro's debt-to-assets ratio in market value terms is slightly lower than peers, and its debt-to-equity ratio at 33 percent is much lower than the industry average of 93 percent. I put more weight on the coverage ratios and conclude that Hasbro uses debt financing more aggressively than its peers. If there is a source of potential concern for Hasbro's leverage, it is the times-burden-covered ratio, which, at 2.6, suggests that Hasbro doesn't have a lot of buffer to pay its interest and maturing debt.

Table 2.3 presents what are known as *common-size financial statements* for Hasbro Inc. over the same period, as well as industry averages for 2016. A common-size balance sheet presents each asset and liability as a percentage of total assets. A common-size income statement is analogous except that all items are scaled in proportion to net sales rather than total assets. The purpose of scaling financial statements in this fashion is to concentrate on underlying trends by abstracting from changes in the dollar figures caused by growth or decline. In addition, common-size statements are useful for removing simple scale effects when comparing companies of different sizes.

Looking first at Hasbro's balance sheet, notice that accounts receivable and inventories are higher than industry averages. Cash and cash equivalents has climbed in recent years, but Hasbro still carries a lower balance than its peers. Overall, short-term assets make up 63.4 percent of Hasbro's total assets, well above the industry average of 46.9 percent. These large balances are another way to quantify potential concerns about Hasbro's working capital and illustrate again the importance of working capital management to most businesses. When a large portion of a company's investment is in assets as volatile as inventory and accounts receivable, that investment bears close watching.

Because the totals must sum to 100 percent and Hasbro's working capital is noticeably higher as a percent of assets than its peers, Hasbro's long-term assets must comprise a smaller fraction of the balance sheet. Thus, Hasbro's percentage investment in net property, plant, and equipment and goodwill and intangible assets is below the industry averages. Again, these ratios for Hasbro's peers may be high because of their relatively greater reliance on acquisitions in recent years. On the liabilities side of the balance sheet, we see a big jump in debt due in one year. We expressed concern earlier that

TABLE 2.3 · Hasbro Inc. Common-Size Financial Statements, 2012–2016, and Industry Averages, 2016

Source: Data from Hasbro 2012–2016 annual reports.

	2012	2013	2014	2015	2016	Industry Average*
Assets						
Cash and cash equivalents	19.6%	15.5%	19.7%	20.7%	25.2%	26.1%
Accounts receivable, less reserve for possible losses	23.8	24.8	24.2	25.8	25.9	12.6
Inventories	7.3	7.9	7.5	8.1	7.6	5.1
Other current assets	7.2	8.1	8.6	6.1	4.7	3.2
Total current assets	58.0	56.3	60.0	60.7	63.4	46.9
Gross property, plant, and equipment	16.5	16.7	16.5	12.7	12.8	24.7
Less accumulated depreciation and amortization	11.1	11.4	11.2	7.7	7.5	15.4
Net property, plant, and equipment	5.3	5.4	5.2	5.0	5.3	9.3
Goodwill and other intangible assets, net	20.6	22.0	20.3	18.5	16.0	32.2
Other assets	16.1	16.2	14.5	15.8	15.3	11.6
Total assets	100.0%	100.0%	100.0%	100.0%	100.0%	100.0%
Liabilities and Shareholders Equity						
Debt due in one year	5.2%	9.9%	5.6%	3.5%	10.3%	2.1%
Accounts payable	3.2	4.5	4.7	5.1	6.3	6.3
Accrued and other current liabilities	13.8	16.5	13.5	14.0	15.2	11.4
Total current liabilities	22.2	31.0	23.7	22.6	31.8	19.8
Long-term debt	32.3	21.8	34.4	32.8	23.5	24.4
Other long-term liabilities	10.7	9.0	9.5	9.4	8.1	7.3
Total liabilities	65.2	61.8	67.7	64.8	63.4	51.5
Total shareholders equity	34.8	38.2	32.3	35.2	36.6	48.5
Total liabilities and shareholders equity	100.0%	100.0%	100.0%	100.0%	100.0%	100.0%
Income Statements						
Net sales	100.0%	100.0%	100.0%	100.0%	100.0%	100.0%
Cost of goods sold	46.8	46.1	45.5	44.7	44.4	46.2
Gross profit	53.2	53.9	54.5	55.3	55.6	53.8
Selling, general, and administrative expenses	34.9	35.3	35.8	36.3	36.1	32.0
Depreciation and amortization	3.7	4.0	3.7	3.5	3.1	5.5
Total operating expenses	38.6	39.2	39.5	39.8	39.2	37.5
Operating income	14.6	14.6	14.9	15.5	16.4	16.3
Interest expense	2.2	2.2	2.2	2.2	1.9	1.9
Other nonoperating expense (income)	1.3	3.7	0.1	(0.4)	0.3	1.0
Total nonoperating expense	3.6	6.0	2.3	1.8	2.2	2.8
Income before income taxes	11.1	8.7	12.7	13.7	14.1	13.5
Provision for income taxes	2.9	1.7	3.0	3.5	3.2	2.0
Net income	8.2%	7.0%	9.7%	10.2%	11.0%	11.5%

*See footnote to Table 2.2 for companies comprising industry sample. Totals may not add due to rounding.

Hasbro's times-burden-covered ratio is only 2.6. Hasbro has a large amount of debt due within the next year, so its times-burden-covered ratio is likely to deteriorate significantly. Hasbro will also need to decide whether to replace the maturing debt or let its leverage ratios decrease once the maturing portion has been repaid.

We are now able to return to the important question of why Hasbro's profit margin has climbed so steadily in recent years. Glancing down the company's common-size income statement reveals that its cost of goods sold has decreased 2.4 percentage points, from 46.8 percent to 44.4 percent. Although the improvement looks modest when compared to sales, relative to Hasbro's profit margin of 11.0 percent, a 2.4 percentage point decrease in cost of goods sold amounts to a 22 percent (2.4/11) improvement in the bottom line. This decrease generates the improving gross margin we saw in Table 2.2, and explains some but not all of the improving profit margin. We expected the rest of the gain to come from improvements in operating expenses, but this turns out not to be the case. Selling, general, and administrative expenses have actually risen faster than sales, wiping out some of the gains in gross margin. These costs have increased from 34.9 percent of sales in 2012 to 36.1 percent in 2016, higher than the industry average of 32.0 percent. The rest of Hasbro's improving profit margin arises from slight declines in several of its other expenses, including depreciation and amortization and nonoperating expenses, which, although small on their own, together add up to economically meaningful gains in profit margin.

Some are prone to think that all operating expenses are fixed—that they shouldn't rise *at all,* much less as a percentage of sales, as in Hasbro's case. Why aren't Hasbro's selling, general, and administrative expenses constant over time, they ask? Where are the economies of scale? The answer is that scale economies are not so simple. If they were, very large companies, like Walmart and Ford, would quickly dominate smaller competitors and eventually monopolize markets. In fact, it appears that while some activities exhibit economies of scale, others are subject to diseconomies of scale, meaning the company becomes less efficient with size. (Imagine how many more meetings are required to coordinate the activities of a 100-person team compared to a 10-person team.) Moreover, many activities exhibit scale economies over only a limited range of activity and then require a large investment to increase capacity. In short, it is natural that Hasbro's selling, general, and administrative expenses will rise as the company grows, but to see them rise even in proportion to sales is concerning, especially because Hasbro's numbers are already higher than its industry peers.

To summarize, our ratio analysis of Hasbro Inc. reveals a stable company with improving profitability, moderate leverage, and strong performance relative to its peers. Despite some potential weaknesses in working capital management, Hasbro is finding efficient uses for its assets. Large amounts of maturing debt pose a short-term challenge, but Hasbro's strong cash position

TABLE 2.4 **Definitions of Principal Ratios Appearing in the Chapter**

Profitability Ratios

Return on equity	= **Net income/Shareholders' equity**
Return on assets	= Net income/Assets
Return on invested capital	$= \dfrac{\text{Earnings before interest and taxes} \times (1 - \text{Tax rate})}{\text{Interest-bearing debt} + \text{Shareholders' equity}}$
Profit margin	= **Net income/Sales**
Gross margin	= Gross profit/Sales
Price to earnings	= Price per share/Earnings per share

Turnover-Control Ratios

Asset turnover	= **Sales/Assets**
Fixed-asset turnover	= Sales/Net property, plant, and equipment
Inventory turnover	= Cost of goods sold/Ending inventory
Collection period	= Accounts receivable/Credit sales per day (If credit sales unavailable, use sales)
Days' sales in cash	= Cash and securities/Sales per day
Payables period	= Accounts payable/Credit purchases per day (If purchases unavailable, use cost of goods sold)

Leverage and Liquidity Ratios

Assets to equity	= **Assets/Shareholders' equity**
Debt to assets	= Total liabilities/Assets (Interest-bearing debt is often substituted for total liabilities)
Debt to equity	= Total liabilities/Shareholders' equity
Times interest earned	= Earnings before interest and taxes/Interest expense
Times burden covered	$= \dfrac{\text{Earnings before interest and taxes}}{\text{Interest exp.} + \text{Prin. pay.}/(1 - \text{Tax rate})}$
Debt to assets (market value)	$= \dfrac{\text{Total liabilities}}{\text{No. equity shares} \times \text{Price/share} + \text{Total liabilities}}$
Debt to equity (market value)	$= \dfrac{\text{Total liabilities}}{\text{No. equity shares} \times \text{Price/share}}$
Current ratio	= Current assets/Current liabilities
Acid test	$= \dfrac{\text{Current assets} - \text{Inventory}}{\text{Current liabilities}}$

should give it ample room to maneuver. Hasbro's recent robust performance has also clearly impressed investors; its stock price jumped 14 percent on February 6, 2017, the day the company announced its 2016 financial results.

Hasbro's rising profitability, combined with relatively modest capital expenditure needs and (at least until 2016) a leisurely growth rate in sales, have left Hasbro in the seemingly luxurious position of having lots of cash. Over the five years ending in 2016, the company's cash flow from operations totaled over $2.7 billion, while its capital expenditures came to only $630 million. The problem: What to do with the other $2 billion? To date, the company's primary answer has been to pay it back to shareholders. Repurchases and dividends came in at a total of $2 billion over the last five years. Yet despite these payouts, Hasbro's cash balance jumped over $300 million in 2016.

Finding ways to spend excess cash might sound like fun, but Hasbro's chief executive Brian Goldner, knows better. He realizes that unless he continues to find productive uses for this cash by maintaining profitable growth, increasing capital expenditures, or returning the money to shareholders, he risks depressing the company's stock price, antagonizing his board and shareholders, and possibly inviting the attention of activist investors. We will have more to say about Hasbro's potential financial challenges and opportunities in coming chapters.

SUMMARY

1. The levers of performance
   - Are the same for all companies from corner stores to multinational corporations.
   - Highlight the means by which managers can influence return on equity.
   - Consist of three ratios:
     - The profit margin.
     - Asset turnover.
     - Financial leverage.
   - Can vary widely across industries depending on the technology and business strategies employed.
2. Return on equity (ROE)
   - Is a widely used measure of company financial performance.
   - Equals the product of the profit margin, asset turnover, and financial leverage.
   - Is broadly similar across industries due to competition.
   - Suffers from three problems as a performance measure:
     - A timing problem because business decisions are forward-looking, while ROE is a backward-looking, one-period measure.
     - A risk problem because financial decisions involve balancing risk against return, while ROE only measures return.
     - A value problem because owners are interested in return on the market value of their investment, while ROE measures return on the accounting book value, a problem that is not solved by measuring the return on the market value of equity.

- Despite its problems can serve as a rough proxy for share price in measuring financial performance.

3. The profit margin
   - Summarizes income statement performance.
   - Measures the fraction of each sales dollar that makes its way to profits.

4. Asset turnover
   - Summarizes asset management performance.
   - Measures the value of sales generated per dollar invested in assets.
   - Is a control ratio, in that it relates sales, or cost of sales, to a specific asset or liability; other control ratios are
     - inventory turnover.
     - collection period.
     - days' sales in cash.
     - payables period.
     - fixed-asset turnover.

5. Financial leverage
   - Summarizes the company's use of debt relative to equity financing.
   - Adds to owners' risk and is thus not something to be maximized.
   - Is best measured in the form of coverage ratios that relate operating earnings to the annual financial burden imposed by the debt.
   - Is also measured using balance sheet ratios that relate debt to assets, measured using book or market values.

6. Ratio analysis
   - Is the systematic use of a number of ratios to analyze financial performance.
   - Involves trend analysis and comparison of company ratios to peer group numbers.
   - Requires considerable judgment because there is no single correct value for any ratio.

ADDITIONAL RESOURCES

Fridson, Martin S., and Fernando Alvarez. *Financial Statement Analysis: A Practitioner's Guide.* 4th ed. John Wiley & Sons, 2011. 400 pages.
   An executive and an academic combine to write a thorough practical overview of the topic.
Jiambalvo, James. *Managerial Accounting.* 6th ed. New York: John Wiley & Sons, 2015. 536 pages.
   A straightforward and concise introduction to the use of managerial accounting in planning, budgeting, management control, and decision making. (Full disclosure: Jim is my dean, but we are still friends and it is a good book.)

Palepu, Krishna G., and Paul M. Healy. *Business Analysis and Valuation: Using Financial Statements.* 5th ed. Cengage Learning, 2015. 336 pages.

> Part finance, part accounting. An innovative look at the use of accounting information to address selected financial questions, especially business valuation. Now available in paperback

All of these sites provide vast amounts of information on publicly traded companies, including overviews, stock quotes, financial statements, ratios, charts, and much more.

> **reuters.com**
> **businessweek.com**
> **google.com/finance**
> **finance.yahoo.com**
> **online.wsj.com**

PROBLEMS

Answers to odd-numbered problems appear at the end of the book. Answers to even-numbered problems and additional exercises are available in the Instructor Resources within McGraw-Hill's *Connect* (see the Preface for more information).

1. The Board of Directors of Collins Entertainment, Inc., has been pressuring its CEO to boost ROE. During a recent interview on CNBC, he announces his plan to improve the firm's financial performance. He will raise prices on all of the company's products by 10%. He justifies the plan by observing that ROE can be decomposed into the product of profit margin, asset turnover, and financial leverage. By raising prices, he will increase the profit margin and thus ROE. Does this plan make sense to you? Why or why not?

2. a. Which company would you expect to have a higher price-to-earnings ratio: Alphabet or railroad company Union Pacific? Why?
   b. Which company would you expect to have the higher debt-to-equity ratio: a financial institution or a high-technology company? Why?
   c. Which company would you expect to have a higher profit margin, an appliance manufacturer or a grocer? Why?
   d. Which company would you expect to have a higher current ratio, a jewelry store or an online bookstore? Why?

3. Answer true or false to each of the following. Briefly explain your reasoning for each answer.
   a. A company's assets-to-equity ratio always equals one plus its liabilities-to-equity ratio.
   b. A company's return on equity will always equal or exceed its return on assets.

    c. A company's collection period should always be less than its payables period.

    d. A company's current ratio must always equal or exceed its acid-test ratio.

    e. All else equal, a firm would prefer to have a higher asset turnover ratio.

    f. Two firms can have the same earnings yield but different price-to-earnings ratios.

    g. Ignoring taxes and transactions costs, unrealized paper gains are less valuable than realized cash earnings.

4. Your firm is considering the acquisition of a very promising technology company. One executive argues against the move, pointing out that because the technology company is presently losing money, the acquisition will cause your firm's return on equity to fall.

    a. Is the executive correct in predicting that ROE will fall?

    b. How important should changes in ROE be in this decision?

5. Selected financial data for Amberjack Corporation follows.

	($ thousands)	
	Year 1	**Year 2**
Sales	271,161	457,977
Cost of goods sold	249,181	341,204
Net income	(155,034)	(403,509)
Cash flow from operations	(58,405)	(20,437)
Cash	341,180	268,872
Marketable securities	341,762	36,900
Accounts receivable	21,011	35,298
Inventories	6,473	72,106
Total current assets	710,427	413,176
Accounts payable	28,908	22,758
Accrued liabilities	44,310	124,851
Total current liabilities	73,218	147,610

    a. Calculate the current and quick ratio at the end of each year. How has the company's short-term liquidity changed over this period?

    b. Assuming a 365-day year for all calculations, compute the following:

        i. The collection period each year based on sales.

        ii. The inventory turnover and the payables period each year based on cost of goods sold.

      iii. The days' sales in cash each year.

      iv. The gross margin and profit margin each year.

   c. What do these calculations suggest about the company's performance?

6. Top management measures your division's performance by calculating the division's return on investment (ROI), defined as division operating income divided by division assets. Your division has done quite well recently; its ROI is 30 percent. You believe the division should invest in a new production process, but a colleague disagrees, pointing out that because the new investment's first-year ROI is only 25 percent, it will hurt performance. How would you respond?

7. Answer the following questions based on the information in the table. The tax rate is 40 percent and all dollars are in millions. For simplicity, assume that the companies have no other liabilities other than the debt shown next.

	Atlantic Corp.	Pacific Corp.
Earnings before interest and taxes	$450	$ 470
Debt (at 8% interest)	$290	$1,490
Equity	$910	$ 370

   a. Calculate each company's ROE, ROA, and ROIC.

   b. Why is Pacific's ROE so much higher than Atlantic's? Does this mean Pacific is a better company? Why or why not?

   c. Why is Atlantic's ROA higher than Pacific's? What does this tell you about the two companies?

   d. How do the two companies' ROICs compare? What does this suggest about the two companies?

8. Table 3.1 in Chapter 3 presents financial statements over the period 2014 through 2017 for R&E Supplies, Inc.

   a. Use these statements to calculate as many of the ratios in Table 2.2 as you can.

   b. What insights do these ratios provide about R&E's financial performance? What problems, if any, does the company appear to have?

9. You are trying to prepare financial statements for Bartlett Pickle Company, but seem to be missing its balance sheet. You have Bartlett's income statement, which shows sales last year were $420 million with a gross profit margin of 40 percent. You also know that credit sales equaled three-quarters of Bartlett's total revenues last year. In addition, Bartlett had a collection period of 55 days, a payables period of 40 days, and an inventory turnover of 8 times based on cost of goods sold. Calculate Bartlett's year-ending balance for accounts receivable, inventory, and accounts payable.

10. In 2016, Natural Selection, a nationwide computer dating service, had $500 million of assets and $200 million of liabilities. Earnings before interest and taxes were $120 million, interest expense was $28 million, the tax rate was 40 percent, principal repayment requirements were $24 million, and annual dividends were 30 cents per share on 20 million shares outstanding.
    a. Calculate the following for Natural Selection:
        i. Liabilities-to-equity ratio
        ii. Times-interest-earned ratio
        iii. Times burden covered
    b. What percentage decline in earnings before interest and taxes could Natural Selection have sustained before failing to cover:
        i. Interest payment requirements?
        ii. Principal and interest requirements?
        iii. Principal, interest, and common dividend payments?

11. Given the following information, complete the balance sheet shown next.

Collection period	71 days
Days' sales in cash	34 days
Current ratio	2.6
Inventory turnover	5 times
Liabilities to assets	75%
Payables period	36 days

(All sales are on credit. All calculations assume a 365-day year. Payables period is based on cost of goods sold.)

Assets

Current assets:	
Cash	$1,100,000
Accounts receivable	
Inventory	1,900,000
Total current assets	
Net fixed assets	
Total assets	8,000,000

Liabilities and shareholders' equity

Current liabilities:	
Accounts payable	
Short-term debt	
Total current liabilities	
Long-term debt	
Shareholders' equity	
Total liabilities and equity	

12. The following data present key ratios for six well-known U.S. corporations: Apple, Boeing, Citigroup, Facebook, McDonald's, and Walmart. However, the companies are not listed in order, and their names have been removed from the column headings. Using only your understanding of the ratios and the nature of each company listed, match each of the sets of ratios with the appropriate company.

	A	B	C	D	E	F
Return on equity (%)	17.23	136.80	19.70	6.64	45.43	36.90
Return on assets (%)	6.85	5.31	17.82	0.77	12.54	14.93
Profit margin (%)	2.81	5.17	36.86	19.52	17.82	21.19
Gross margin (%)	25.65	14.57	86.29	NA	38.52	39.08
Price to earnings (X)	17.15	22.51	38.08	12.59	26.00	18.24
Asset turnover (X)	2.44	1.03	0.48	0.04	0.71	0.70
Collection period (days)	4.30	30.49	43.24	NA	20.55	27.59
Inventory turnover (X)	8.26	1.79	NA	NA	181.35	58.64
Debt to equity (X)	1.56	109.15	0.10	6.96	3.40	1.51
Times interest earned (X)	9.66	19.20	NA	1.64	8.76	43.15
Current ratio (X)	0.86	1.25	11.97	0.37	1.39	1.35
Acid test (X)	0.19	0.38	11.63	0.37	0.78	1.22
(NA = Not applicable)						

13. The following table presents selected 2016 annual income statement items and balance sheet items for Toyota Motor and Apple. All dollars are in millions. Use the information to answer the questions that follow.

	Toyota	Apple
Sales	$252,708	$ 215,369
Cost of goods sold	201,125	131,376
Accounts receivable	83,027	29,299
Inventory	18,342	2,132
Accounts payable	48,570	59,321

a. Calculate and interpret the length of the operating cycle for Toyota and Apple.

b. Calculate and interpret the length of the cash conversion cycle for Toyota and Apple.

c. What are the advantages and disadvantages of Apple's way of running operations compared to Toyota's way?

14. A spreadsheet containing financial statements for Men's Wearhouse, Inc., for fiscal years 2006–2010 is available for download from McGraw-Hill's *Connect* or your course instructor (see the Preface for more information).

    a. Use the spreadsheet to calculate as many of the company's profitability, turnover-control, and leverage and liquidity ratios as you can for these years (see Table 2.4).

    b. What do these ratios suggest about the company's performance over this period?

15. To answer the following questions, use Boeing Company's financial statements available for download from McGraw-Hill's *Connect* or your course instructor (see the Preface for more information).

    a. For the years 2005–2009, calculate the following for Boeing:
       i. Debt-to-equity ratio
      ii. Times-interest-earned ratio
     iii. Times-burden-covered ratio

    b. What percentage decline in earnings before interest and taxes could Boeing have sustained in these years before failing to cover:
       i. Interest payments?
      ii. Interest and principal payments?

    c. What do these calculations suggest about Boeing's financial leverage during this period?

PART TWO

Planning Future Financial Performance

Financial Forecasting

Planning is the substitution of error for chaos.
Anonymous

To this point, we have looked at the past, evaluating existing financial statements and assessing past performance. It is now time to look to the future. We begin in this chapter with an examination of the principal techniques of financial forecasting. In the following chapter, we look at planning problems unique to the management of company growth. Throughout this chapter, our emphasis will be on the techniques of forecasting and planning, so as a counterweight, it will be important that you bear in mind that proper technique is only a part of effective planning. At least as critical is the development of creative market strategies and operating policies that underlie the financial plans.

Pro Forma Statements

Finance is central to a company's planning activities for at least two reasons. First, much of the language of forecasting and planning is financial. Plans are stated in terms of financial statements, and many of the measures used to evaluate plans are financial. Second, and more important, the financial executive is responsible for a critical resource: money. Because virtually every corporate action has financial implications, a vital part of any plan is determining whether the plan is attainable given the company's limited resources.

Companies typically prepare a wide array of plans and budgets. Some, such as production plans and staff budgets, focus on a particular aspect of the firm, while others, such as pro forma statements, are much broader in scope. Our focus here is on the broader techniques that are a key part of planning in large corporations.

Pro forma financial statements are the most widely used vehicles for financial forecasting. A pro forma statement is simply a prediction of what the company's financial statements will look like at the end of the forecast period. These predictions may be the culmination of intensive, detailed operating plans and budgets or nothing more than rough, back-of-the-envelope projections. Either way, the pro forma format displays the information in a logical, internally consistent manner.

A major purpose of pro forma forecasts is to estimate a company's future need for external funding, a critical first step in financial planning. The process is a simple one. If the forecast says a company's assets will rise next year to $100, but liabilities and owners' equity will total only $80, the obvious conclusion is that $20 in external funding will be required. The forecast is silent about what form this new financing should take—whether trade credit, bank borrowing, new equity, or whatever—but one way or another a fresh $20 is necessary. Conversely, if the forecast says assets will fall below projected liabilities and owners' equity, the obvious implication is that the company will generate more cash than necessary to run the business. And management faces the pleasant task of deciding how best to deploy the excess. In equation form,

$$\begin{array}{c} \text{External} \\ \text{funding required} \end{array} = \begin{array}{c} \text{Total} \\ \text{assets} \end{array} - \left(\text{Liabilities} + \begin{array}{c} \text{Owners'} \\ \text{equity} \end{array} \right)$$

Practitioners often refer to external funding required as the "plug" because it is the amount that must be plugged into the balance sheet to make it balance.

Percent-of-Sales Forecasting

To paraphrase an old Danish proverb, "Forecasting is always difficult, especially with regard to the future." One straightforward yet effective way to simplify the challenge is to tie many of the income statement and balance sheet figures to future sales. The rationale for this *percent-of-sales* approach is the tendency, noted in Chapter 2, for all variable costs and most current assets and current liabilities to vary directly with sales. Obviously, this will not be true for all of the entries in a company's financial statements, and certainly, some independent forecasts of individual items, such as plant and equipment, will be required. Nonetheless, the percent-of-sales method does provide simple, logical estimates of many important variables.

The first step in a percent-of-sales forecast should be an examination of historical data to determine which financial statement items have varied in proportion to sales in the past. This will enable the forecaster to decide which items can safely be estimated as a percentage of sales and which must be forecast using other information. The second step is to forecast sales. Because so many other items will be linked mechanically to the sales forecast, it is critical to estimate sales as accurately as possible. Also, once the pro forma statements are completed, it is a good idea to test the sensitivity of the results to reasonable variations in the sales forecast. The final step in the percent-of-sales forecast is to estimate individual financial statement items by extrapolating the historical

patterns to the newly estimated sales. For instance, if inventories have historically been about 20 percent of sales and next year's sales are forecast to be
$10 million, we would expect inventories to be $2 million. It's that simple.

To illustrate the use of the percent-of-sales method, consider the problem
faced by Suburban National Bank. R&E Supplies, Inc., a modest-sized whole-
saler of plumbing and electrical supplies, has been a customer of the bank for
a number of years. The company has maintained average deposits of approximately $30,000 and has had a $50,000 short-term, renewable loan for five
years. The company has prospered, and the loan has been renewed annually
with only cursory analysis.

In late 2017, the president of R&E Supplies, Inc. visited the bank and
requested an increase in the short-term loan for 2018 to $500,000. The president
explained that despite the company's growth, accounts payable had increased
steadily and cash balances had declined. A number of suppliers had recently
threatened to put the company on COD for future purchases unless they received
payments more promptly. When asked why he was requesting $500,000, the
president replied that this amount seemed "about right" and would enable him
to pay off his most insistent creditors and rebuild his cash balances.

Knowing that the bank's credit committee would never approve a loan
request of this magnitude without careful financial projections, the lending
officer suggested that he and the president prepare pro forma financial statements for 2018. He explained that these statements would provide a more
accurate indication of R&E's credit needs.

The first step in preparing the pro forma projections was to examine the
company's financial statements for the years 2014 through 2017, shown in
Table 3.1, in search of stable patterns. The results of this ratio analysis appear
in Table 3.2. The president's concern about declining liquidity and increasing
trade payables is well founded; cash and securities have fallen from 22 days'
sales to 7 days' sales, while accounts payable have risen from a payables
period of 39 days to 66 days.[1] Another worrisome trend is the increase in cost
of goods sold and general, selling, and administrative expenses in proportion
to sales. Earnings clearly are not keeping pace with sales.

The last column in Table 3.2 contains the 2018 projections agreed to by
R&E's president and the lending officer. In line with recent experience,
sales are predicted to increase 25 percent over 2017. General, selling, and
administrative expenses will continue to rise as a result of an unfavorable labor settlement. After comparing R&E's cash balances to historical
levels and to those of competitors, the president believes cash and securities should rise to at least 18 days' sales. Because cash and securities are

---

[1] See Table 2.4 in Chapter 2 for definitions of the ratios used in this chapter.

TABLE 3.1 **Financial Statements for R&E Supplies, Inc., December 31, 2014–2017 ($ thousands)**

Income Statements				
	2014	**2015**	**2016**	**2017***
Net sales	$11,190	$13,764	$16,104	$20,613
Cost of goods sold	9,400	11,699	13,688	17,727
Gross profit	1,790	2,065	2,416	2,886
Expenses:				
General, selling, and administrative expenses	1,019	1,239	1,610	2,267
Net interest expense	100	103	110	90
Earnings before tax	671	723	696	529
Tax	302	325	313	238
Earnings after tax	$ 369	$ 398	$ 383	$ 291
Balance Sheets				
Assets				
Current assets:				
Cash and securities	$ 671	$ 551	$ 644	$ 412
Accounts receivable	1,343	1,789	2,094	2,886
Inventories	1,119	1,376	1,932	2,267
Prepaid expenses	14	12	15	18
Total current assets	3,147	3,728	4,685	5,583
Net fixed assets	128	124	295	287
Total assets	$ 3,275	$ 3,852	$ 4,980	$ 5,870
Liabilities and Owners' Equity				
Current liabilities:				
Bank loan	$ 50	$ 50	$ 50	$ 50
Accounts payable	1,007	1,443	2,426	3,212
Current portion long-term debt	60	50	50	100
Accrued wages	5	7	10	18
Total current liabilities	1,122	1,550	2,536	3,380
Long-term debt	960	910	860	760
Common stock	150	150	150	150
Retained earnings	1,043	1,242	1,434	1,580
Total liabilities and owners' equity	$ 3,275	$ 3,852	$ 4,980	$ 5,870

*Estimate.

generally low return assets, this figure represents the minimum amount the president believes is necessary to operate the business efficiently. This reasoning is reinforced by the fact that any cash or securities balances above this minimum will just add to the loan amount and thus cost the company more money. Because much of R&E's cash balances will sit in his bank, the lending officer readily agrees to the projected increase in cash.

TABLE 3.2 Selected Historical Financial Ratios for R&E Supplies, Inc., 2014–2017

	History				Forecast
	2014	2015	2016	2017E	2018F
Annual growth rate in sales	—	23%	17%	28%	25%
	Ratios Tied to Sales				
Cost of goods sold (% of sales)	84	85	85	86	86
General, selling, and administrative expenses (% of sales)	9	9	10	11	12
Cash and securities (days sales in cash)	22	15	15	7	18
Accounts receivable (collection period)	44	47	47	51	51
Inventories (inventory turnover)	8	9	7	8	9
Accounts payable (payables period)	39	45	65	66	59
	Other Ratios in Percent				
Tax/earnings before tax*	45	45	45	45	45
Dividends/earnings after tax	50	50	50	50	50

E = Estimate
F = Forecast
*Including state and local taxes.

The president also thinks accounts payable should decline to no more than a payables period of 59 days. The tax rate and the dividends-to-earnings, or payout ratio, are expected to stay constant.

The resulting pro forma financial statements appear in Table 3.3. Looking first at the income statement, the implication of the preceding assumptions is that earnings after tax will decline to $234,000, down 20 percent from the prior year. The only entry on this statement requiring further comment is net interest expense. Net interest expense will clearly depend on the size of the loan the company requires. However, because we do not know this yet, net interest expense has initially been assumed to equal last year's value, with the understanding that this assumption may have to be modified later.

Estimating the External Funding Required

To most operating executives, a company's income statement is more interesting than its balance sheet because the income statement measures profitability. The reverse is true for the financial executive. When the object of the exercise is to estimate future financing requirements, the income statement is interesting only insofar as it affects the balance sheet. To the financial executive, the balance sheet is key.

The first entry on R&E's pro forma balance sheet (Table 3.3) requiring comment is prepaid expenses. Prepaid expenses, like accrued wages further down the balance sheet, is a small item that increases erratically with sales.

TABLE 3.3 Pro Forma Financial Statements for R&E Supplies, Inc., December 31, 2018 ($ thousands)

Income Statement		
	2018	**Comments**
Net sales	$25,766	25% increase
Cost of goods sold	22,159	86% of sales
Gross profit	3,607	
Expenses:		
General, selling, and administrative expenses	3,092	12% of sales
Net interest expense	90	Initially constant
Earnings before tax	425	
Tax	191	45% tax rate
Earnings after tax	$ 234	

Balance Sheet		
Assets		
Current assets:		
Cash and securities	$ 1,271	18 days sales
Accounts receivable	3,600	51-day collection period
Inventories	2,462	9 times turnover
Prepaid expenses	20	Rough estimate
Total current assets	7,353	
Net fixed assets	280	See text discussion
Total assets	$ 7,633	
Liabilities and Owners' Equity		
Current liabilities:		
Bank loan	$ 0	
Accounts payable	3,582	59-day payables period
Current portion of long-term debt	100	See text discussion
Accrued wages	22	Rough estimate
Total current liabilities	3,704	
Long-term debt	660	
Common stock	150	
Retained earnings	1,697	See text discussion
Total liabilities and owners' equity	$ 6,211	
External funding required	**$ 1,422**	

Because the amounts are small and the forecast does not require a high degree of precision, rough estimates will suffice.

When asked about new fixed assets, the president indicated that a $43,000 capital budget had already been approved for 2018. Further, depreciation for the year would be $50,000, so net fixed assets would decline $7,000 to $280,000 ($280,000 = $287,000 + $43,000 − $50,000).

Note that the bank loan is initially set to zero. We will calculate the external funding required momentarily and will then be in a position to consider a possible bank loan. Continuing down the balance sheet, "current portion of long-term debt" is simply the principal repayment due in 2019. It is a contractual commitment specified in the loan agreement. As this required payment becomes a current liability, the accountant shifts it from long-term debt to current-portion long-term debt.

The last entry needing explanation is retained earnings. Because the company does not plan to sell new equity in 2018, common stock remains constant. Retained earnings are determined as follows:

$$\begin{array}{c} \text{Retained} \\ \text{earnings '18} \end{array} = \begin{array}{c} \text{Retained} \\ \text{earnings '17} \end{array} + \begin{array}{c} \text{Earnings} \\ \text{after tax '18} \end{array} - \text{Dividends '18}$$

$$\$1,697,000 = \$1,580,000 + \$234,000 - \$117,000$$

In other words, when a business earns a profit larger than its dividend, the excess adds to retained earnings. The retained earnings account is the principal bridge between a company's income statement and its balance sheet; so as profits rise, retained earnings grow and loan needs decline.[2]

The last step in constructing R&E's pro formas is to estimate the amount of external funding required. Using the expression defined earlier,

$$\begin{array}{c} \text{External} \\ \text{funding required} \end{array} = \begin{array}{c} \text{Total} \\ \text{assets} \end{array} - \left(\text{Liabilities} + \begin{array}{c} \text{Owners'} \\ \text{equity} \end{array} \right)$$

$$= \$7,633,000 - \$6,211,000$$

$$= \$1,422,000$$

According to our first-pass forecast, R&E Supplies needs not $500,000 but more than *$1.4 million* to achieve the president's objectives.

Mindful of the cautionary tale of the grateful borrower who rises to shake the hand of his banker and exclaims, "I don't know how I'll ever repay you," the lending officer for Suburban National Bank is apt to be of two minds about this result. On the one hand, R&E has a projected 2018 accounts receivable balance equal to $3.6 million, which would probably provide excellent security for a $1.4 million loan. On the other hand, R&E's cavalier attitude toward financial planning and the president's obvious lack of knowledge about where his company is headed are definite negatives. But before getting too involved in the implications of the forecast, we need to recall that our projection does not yet include the higher interest expense on the new, larger loan.

---

[2] Sometimes companies will complicate this equation by charging certain items, such as gains or losses on foreign currency translation, directly to retained earnings. But this is not a problem here.

Interest Expense

One thing that bothers attentive novices about pro forma forecasting is the circularity involving interest expense and indebtedness. As noted earlier, interest expense cannot be estimated accurately until the amount of external funding required has been determined. Yet because the external funding depends in part on the amount of interest expense, it would appear one cannot be accurately estimated without the other.

There are two common ways around this dilemma. The more responsible approach is to use a computer spreadsheet to solve for the interest expense and external funding simultaneously. We will look at this approach in more detail in the section titled Forecasting with Spreadsheets. The other, more cavalier approach is to ignore the problem with the expectation that the first-pass estimate will be close enough. Given the likely errors in predicting sales and other variables, the additional error caused by a failure to determine interest expense accurately is usually not all that critical.

To illustrate, R&E Supplies' first-pass pro formas assumed a net interest expense of $90,000, whereas the balance sheet indicates total interest-bearing debt of almost $2.2 million. At a 10 percent interest rate, this implies an interest expense of about $220,000, or $130,000 more than our first-pass estimate. But think what happens as we trace the impact of a $130,000 addition to interest expense through the income statement. First, the $130,000 expense is before taxes. At a 45 percent tax rate, the decline in earnings after tax will be only $71,500. Second, because R&E Supplies distributes half of its earnings as dividends, a $71,500 decline in earnings after tax will result in only a $35,750 decline in the addition to retained earnings. So after all the dust settles, our initial estimate of the external funding required will be about $35,750 low. But when the need for new external financing is already over $1.4 million, what's another $35,750 among friends? Granted, increased interest expense has a noticeable percentage effect on earnings, but by the time the increase filters through taxes and dividend payments, the effect on the external funding needed is modest. Moreover, the effect would be even smaller if the borrowing rate were lower than the assumed 10 percent. The moral to the story is that quick-and-dirty financial forecasts really can be quite useful. Unless you are naturally inclined toward green eyeshades or have the luxury of charging by the hour, you will find that simple forecasts are just fine for many purposes.

Seasonality

A more serious potential problem with pro forma statements—and, indeed, with all of the forecasting techniques mentioned in this chapter—is that the results are applicable only on the forecast date. The pro formas in Table 3.3 present an estimate of R&E Supplies' external financing requirements on December 31, 2018.

They say nothing about the company's need for financing on any other date before or after December 31. If a company has seasonal financing requirements, knowledge of year-end loan needs may be of little use in financial planning, because the year end may bear no relation whatever to the date of the company's peak financing need. To avoid this problem, you should make monthly or quarterly forecasts rather than annual ones. Or, if you know the date of the peak financing need, you can simply make this date the forecast horizon.

Pro Forma Statements and Financial Planning

To this point, R&E's pro forma statements simply display the financial implications of the company's operating plans. This is the forecasting half of the exercise. It is time now for R&E to do some serious financial planning. Using the techniques described in earlier chapters, management must analyze the forecast carefully to decide if it is acceptable or whether it must be changed to avoid identified problems. In particular, R&E management must decide whether the estimated external funding requirement is too large. If the answer is yes, either because R&E does not want to borrow $1.4 million or because the bank is unwilling to grant such a large loan, management must change its plans to conform to the financial realities. This is where operating plans and financial plans merge (or, too often, collide) to create a coherent strategy. Fortunately, the pro forma forecast provides an excellent template for such iterative planning.

To illustrate the process, suppose that Suburban National Bank, concerned about R&E management's obvious lack of financial acumen, will not lend the company more than $1 million. Ignoring the possibility of trying another bank, or selling new equity, R&E's challenge is to modify its operating plans to shave $400,000 off the projected external funding requirement. There are many ways to meet this challenge, each involving subtle trade-offs among growth, profitability, and funding needs. And while we are not in a position to evaluate these trade-offs, as R&E management would be, we can illustrate the mechanics. Suppose that, after much debate, management decides to test the following revised operating plan:

- Tighten up collection of accounts receivable so that the collection period falls from 51 days to 47.

- Settle for a more modest improvement in trade payables so that the payables period rises from 59 days to 60.

Finally, because a tougher collection policy will drive away some customers and because higher trade payables will sacrifice some prompt payment discounts, let us presume that management believes the revised plan will reduce

TABLE 3.4   **Revised Pro Forma Financial Statements for R&E Supplies, Inc., December 31, 2018**
($ thousands, changes in bold)

Income Statement		
	2018	**Comments**
Net sales	**$24,736**	**20% increase**
Cost of goods sold	21,273	86% of sales
Gross profit	3,463	
Expenses:		
General, selling, and administrative expenses	**3,092**	**12.5% of sales**
Net interest expense	90	Initially constant
Earnings before tax	281	
Tax	126	45% tax rate
Earnings after tax	$ 155	

Balance Sheet		
Assets		
Current assets:		
Cash and securities	$ 1,220	18 days sales
Accounts receivable	**3,185**	**47-day collection period**
Inventories	2,364	9 times turnover
Prepaid expenses	20	Rough estimate
Total current assets	6,789	
Net fixed assets	280	See text discussion
Total assets	$ 7,069	
Liabilities and Owners' Equity		
Current liabilities:		
Bank loan	$ 0	
Accounts payable	**3,497**	**60-day payables period**
Current portion of long-term debt	100	See text discussion
Accrued wages	22	Rough estimate
Total current liabilities	3,619	
Long-term debt	660	
Common stock	150	
Retained earnings	1,657	See text discussion
Total liabilities and owners' equity	$ 6,086	
External funding required	$ 982	

sales growth from 25 percent to 20 percent and increase general, selling, and administrative expenses from 12 percent to 12.5 percent.

To test this revised operating plan, we need only make the indicated changes in assumptions and roll out a revised pro forma forecast. Table 3.4 presents the results of this exercise. The good news is that external funding required is now below the $1 million target; the bad news is that this improvement is not free. Earnings after tax in the revised forecast trail the original projection in Table 3.3 by 34 percent [($234 − $155)/$234].

Is R&E Supplies' revised operating plan optimal? Is it superior to all other possible plans? We cannot say; these are fundamental questions of business strategy that can never be answered with complete assurance. We can say, however, that pro forma forecasts contribute mightily to the planning process by providing a vehicle for evaluating alternative plans, by quantifying the anticipated costs and benefits of each, and by indicating which plans are financially feasible.

Forecasting with Spreadsheets

Readily available spreadsheets make it possible for anyone with a modicum of computer skill to spin out elegant (and occasionally useful) pro forma forecasts and sophisticated risk analysis. To demonstrate how effective it is to create forecasts with a spreadsheet, Table 3.5 presents an abbreviated one-year forecast for R&E Supplies as it might appear in a spreadsheet program.[3] The first area on the simulated screen is an *assumptions box,* containing all of the information and assumptions required to construct the forecast. Gathering all of the necessary input information in an assumptions box can be a real timesaver later if you want to change assumptions. The 2018 data in the assumptions box correspond closely to the data used earlier in our original forecast for R&E Supplies.

The forecast begins immediately below the assumptions box. The first column, labeled "Equations 2018," is included for explanatory purposes and would not appear on a conventional forecast. Entering the equations shown causes the computer to calculate the quantities appearing in the second column, labeled "Forecast 2018." The third column, labeled "Forecast 2019," is presently blank.

Two steps are required to get from the assumptions to the completed forecast. First, it is necessary to enter a series of equations tying the inputs to the forecasted outputs. These are the equations appearing in the first column. Here is how to read them. The first equation for net sales is $= B3 + B3 * C4$. This instructs the spreadsheet to get the number in cell B3 and add to it that number times the number in cell C4—in other words, $\$20{,}613 + \$20{,}613 \times 25\%$. The second equation instructs the spreadsheet to multiply forecasted net sales by the forecasted cost of goods sold percentage. The third says to calculate gross profit by subtracting cost of goods sold from net sales. And so on.

---

[3] Our examples are created using Excel, but other spreadsheet programs such as Calc or Google Sheets have similar functionality in most cases.

TABLE 3.5 **Forecasting with a Spreadsheet: Pro Forma Financial Forecast for R&E Supplies, Inc., December 31, 2018 ($ thousands)**

	A	B	C	D
1				
2	*Year*	*2017 Actual*	*2018*	*2019*
3	Net sales	$20,613		
4	Growth rate in net sales		25.0%	
5	Cost of goods sold/net sales		86.0%	
6	Gen., sell., and admin. expenses/net sales		12.0%	
7	Long-term debt	$ 760	$660	
8	Current portion long-term debt	$ 100	$100	
9	Interest rate		10.0%	
10	Tax rate		45.0%	
11	Dividend/earnings after tax		50.0%	
12	Current assets/net sales		29.0%	
13	Net fixed assets		$280	
14	Current liabilities/net sales		14.5%	
15	Owners' equity	$ 1,730		
16	**INCOME STATEMENT**			
17		*Equations*	*Forecast*	*Forecast*
18	*Year*	*2018*	*2018*	*2019*
19	Net sales	= B3 + B3*C4	$25,766	
20	Cost of goods sold	= C5*C19	22,159	
21	Gross profit	= C19 − C20	3,607	
22	Gen., sell., and admin. exp.	= C6*C19	3,092	
23	Interest expense	= C9*(C7 + C8 + C40)	231	
24	Earnings before tax	= C21 − C22 − C23	285	
25	Tax	= C10*C24	128	
26	Earnings after tax	= C24 − C25	156	
27	Dividends paid	= C11*C26	78	
28	Additions to retained earnings	= C26 − C27	78	
29				
30	**BALANCE SHEET**			
31	Current assets	= C12*C19	7,472	
32	Net fixed assets	= C13	280	
33	Total assets	= C31 + C32	7,752	
34				
35	Current liabilities	= C14*C19	3,736	
36	Long-term debt	= C7	660	
37	Owners' equity	= B15 + C28	1,808	
38	Total liabilities and owners'	= C35 + C36 + C37	6,204	
39	equity			
40	**EXTERNAL FUNDING REQUIRED**	= C33 − C38	**$ 1,548**	

Why Are Lenders So Conservative?

Some would answer, "Too much Republican in-breeding," but there is another possibility: low returns. Simply put, if expected loan returns are low, lenders cannot accept high risks.

Let us look at the income statement of a representative bank lending operation with, say, 100 $1 million loans, each paying 10 percent interest:

($ thousands)	
Interest income (10% × 100 × $1 million)	$10,000
Interest expense	7,000
Gross income	3,000
Operating expenses	1,000
Income before tax	2,000
Tax at 40% rate	800
Income after tax	$ 1,200

The $7 million interest expense represents a 7 percent return the bank must promise depositors and investors to raise the $100 million lent. (In bank jargon, these loans offer a 3 percent lending margin, or spread.) Operating expenses include costs of the downtown office towers, the art collection, wages, and so on.

These numbers imply a minuscule return on assets of 1.2 percent ($1.2 million/[100 × $1 million]). We know from the levers of performance that to generate any kind of reasonable return on equity, banks must pile on the financial leverage. Indeed, to generate a 12 percent ROE, our bank needs a 10-to-1 assets-to-equity ratio or, equivalently, $9 in liabilities for every $1 in equity.

Worse yet, our profit figures are too optimistic because they ignore the reality that not all loans are repaid. Banks typically are able to recover only about 40 percent of the principal value of defaulted loans, implying a loss of $600,000 on a $1 million default. Ignoring tax losses on defaulted loans, this means that if only two of the bank's 100 loans go bad annually, the bank's $1.2 million in expected profits will evaporate. Stated differently, a loan officer must be almost certain that each loan will be repaid just to break even. (Alternatively, the officer must be almost certain of being promoted out of lending before the loans start to go bad.) So why are lenders conservative? Because the aggressive ones have long since gone bankrupt.

There are only three tricky equations. Interest expense, row 23, is the interest rate times end-of-period long-term debt, including the current portion, plus the forecasted external funding required. As discussed earlier, the tricky part here is the interdependence between interest expense and external funding required. (I will talk more about this in step 2.) The other two equations are simple by comparison. The equity equation, row 37, is end-of-period equity plus additions to retained earnings; the external funding required equation, row 40, is total assets minus total liabilities and owners' equity.

The second required step is to incorporate the interdependence between interest expense and external funding required. Without some adjustment on your part, the spreadsheet will likely signal a "Circular Reference Warning" when you enter the equation for interest expense. To avoid this, you need to modify the way the spreadsheet calculates formulas in this file. In Excel, click the File tab, click Options, and click the Formulas category. In the "Calculation Options" section, select the "Enable iterative calculation" box and then click "OK". Your forecast should now be complete.

Now the fun begins. To modify a forecast assumption, just change the appropriate entry in the assumptions box, and the spreadsheet updates the rest of the forecast. To extend the forecast one more year, simply complete the entries in the assumptions box, highlight the 2018 forecast, and copy or fill one column to the right. Then, make some obvious changes in the equations for net sales and equity, and the spreadsheet does the rest.

Coping with Uncertainty

Sensitivity Analysis

Executives grappling with the uncertainty inherent in all realistic financial projections can turn to several techniques. The simplest is *sensitivity analysis,* known colloquially as "what if " questions: What if R&E's sales grow by 15 percent instead of 25 percent? What if cost of goods sold is 84 percent of sales instead of 86 percent? It involves systematically changing one of the assumptions in the pro forma statements and observing how the forecast responds. The exercise is useful in at least two ways. First, it provides information about the range of possible outcomes. For example, sensitivity analysis on R&E Supplies' original forecast might reveal that depending on the future sales volume attained, the company's need for external financing could vary between $1.4 million and $2 million. This would tell management that it had better have enough flexibility in its financing plans to add an extra $600,000 in external funding as the future unfolds. Second, sensitivity analysis encourages management by exception. It enables managers to determine which assumptions most strongly affect the forecast and which are secondary. This allows them to concentrate their data-gathering and forecasting efforts on the most critical assumptions. Subsequently, during implementation of the financial plan, the same information enables management to focus on those factors most critical to the plan's success.

Scenario Analysis

Sensitivity analysis has its uses, but it is important to realize that forecasts seldom err on one assumption at a time. That is, whatever events throw one assumption in a financial forecast off the mark will likely affect other assumptions as well. For example, suppose we want to estimate R&E Supplies' external financing needs, assuming sales fall 15 percent below expectations. Sensitivity analysis would have us simply cut forecasted sales growth by 15 percent and recalculate the external financing required. However, this approach implicitly assumes the shortfall in sales will not affect any of the other estimates underlying the forecast. If the proper assumptions are that inventories will initially rise when sales drop below expectations and the profit margin will decline as the company slashes prices to maintain volume, failure to include these complementary effects will cause an underestimate of the need for outside financing.

Instead of manipulating one assumption at a time, *scenario analysis* broadens the perspective to look at how a number of assumptions might change in response to a particular economic event. The first step in a scenario analysis is to identify a few carefully chosen events, or scenarios, that might plausibly befall the company. Common scenarios include loss of a key customer, successful introduction of a major new product, or entry of an important new competitor. Then, for each scenario identified, the second step is to carefully rethink the variables in the original forecast to either reaffirm the original assumption or substitute a new, more accurate one. The last step in the analysis is to generate a separate forecast for each scenario. The result is a limited number of detailed projections describing the range of contingencies the business faces.

Simulation

Simulation is a computer-assisted extension of sensitivity analysis. To perform a simulation, begin by assigning a probability distribution to each uncertain element in the forecast. The distribution describes the possible values the variable could conceivably take on and states the probability of each value occurring. Next, ask a computer to pick at random a value for each uncertain variable consistent with the assigned probability distribution and generate a set of pro forma statements based on the selected values. This creates one trial. Performing the last step many times produces a large number of trials. The output from a simulation is a table or, more often, a graph summarizing the results of many trials.

As an example, Figure 3.1 displays the results of a simulation of R&E's external funding needs using Crystal Ball, a popular simulation program. Our original forecast assumed a 25 percent sales growth in 2018, but this, of course, is only a guess. The figure shows a frequency chart of R&E's external funds required as the estimated sales growth varies in a range of about 10 to 40 percent. To generate the chart, I selected a normal distribution for the sales growth estimate from the gallery of distributions provided by Crystal Ball and shown at the bottom of the figure. For the parameters of the normal distribution I entered a mean of 25 percent and a standard deviation of 5 percent. Then, using the spreadsheet model in Table 3.5, I asked Crystal

FIGURE 3.1 **Simulating R&E Supplies' Need for External Funding: Frequency Chart and Distribution Gallery for Sales Growth**

Source: Oracle

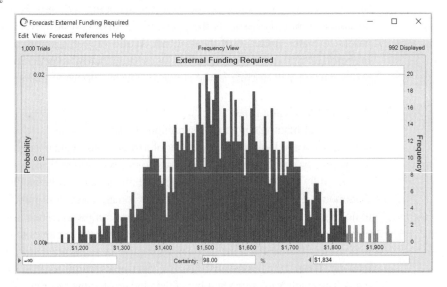

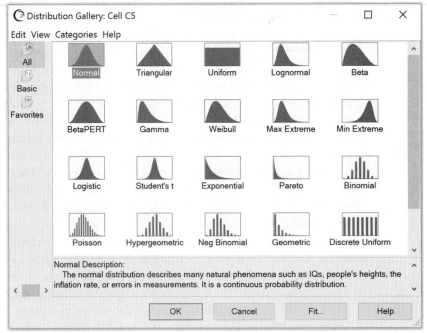

Ball to display the results of 1,000 trials as a frequency chart. I could have allowed virtually all of the assumptions in the spreadsheet to vary, and to vary in correlation with one another, but this is enough to provide a taste of how simulations work.

The principal advantage of simulation relative to sensitivity analysis and scenario analysis is that it allows all of the uncertain input variables to change at once. The principal disadvantage, in my experience, is that the results are often hard to interpret. One reason is that few executives are used to thinking about future events in terms of probabilities. The frequency chart in Figure 3.1 indicates there is a 2.00 percent chance that R&E's external funding needs will exceed $1.834 million. Is a 2 percent chance so remote that R&E can safely raise less than $1.834 million, or might the prudent course be to raise even more just in case? How big a chance should the company be willing to take that it will be unable to meet its external funding requirement: 10 percent, 2 percent, or is .02 percent the right number? The answer isn't obvious. A second difficulty with simulation in practice recalls President Eisenhower's dictum "Plans are worthless, but planning is everything." With simulation, much of the "planning" goes on inside the computer, and managers too often see only the results. Consequently, they may not gain the depth of insight into the company and its future prospects that they would if they used simpler techniques.

The complete Crystal Ball program is available on a 30-day trial basis at **oracle.com/crystalball.** For practice using the program to build a simulation model, see problem 17 at the end of this chapter. The additional resources at the end of this chapter includes some freeware alternatives to Crystal Ball.

Cash Flow Forecasts

A cash flow forecast is simply a listing of all anticipated sources of cash to, and uses of cash by, the company over the forecast period. The difference between forecasted sources and forecasted uses is the external financing required. Table 3.6 shows a 2018 cash flow forecast for R&E Supplies. The assumptions underlying the forecast are the same as those used to construct R&E's initial pro forma statements in Table 3.3.

Cash flow forecasts are straightforward, easily understood, and commonly used. Their principal weakness compared to pro forma statements is that they are less informative. R&E's pro forma statements not only indicate the size of the external funding required but also provide information that is useful for evaluating the company's ability to raise this amount of money. Thus, a loan officer can use standard analysis tools on a company's pro forma statements to assess its ability to service a requested loan. Because the cash flow forecast presents only *changes* in the quantities represented, a similar analysis using cash flow forecasts would be much more difficult.

TABLE 3.6 Cash Flow Forecast for R&E Supplies, Inc., 2018 ($ thousands)

Sources of Cash	
Net income	$ 234
Depreciation	50
Decreases in assets or increases in liabilities:	
Increase in accounts payable	370
Increase in accrued wages	4
Total sources of cash	$ 658
Uses of Cash	
Dividends	$ 117
Increases in assets or decreases in liabilities:	
Increase in cash and securities	859
Increase in accounts receivable	714
Increase in inventories	195
Increase in prepaid expenses	2
Increase in fixed assets	43
Decrease in long-term debt	100
Decrease in short-term debt	50
Total uses of cash	$2,080

Determination of external funding required:
      Total sources + External funding required = Total uses
        $658,000 + External funding required = $2,080,000
External funding required = $1,422,000

Cash Budgets

A *cash budget* is what you and I are apt to prepare when we are worried about our personal finances. We make a list of all expected cash inflows and outflows over coming months, and earnestly hope the former exceeds the latter. When the news is bad, and outflows exceed inflows, we know that reduced savings or a new loan is in our future. Similarly, a corporate cash budget is a simple listing of projected cash receipts and disbursements over a forecast period for the purpose of anticipating future cash shortages or surpluses. Many firms use a nested set of financial forecasts, relying on pro forma projections to plan operations and estimate external funding needs, and cash budgets, prepared on a weekly or even daily basis, to manage short-term cash.

The only conceptual challenge to preparing a cash budget for a company lies in the fact that company accounts are based on accrual accounting, while cash budgets use strictly cash accounting. This makes it necessary to translate company projections regarding sales and purchases into their cash equivalents. For credit sales, this means adjusting for the time lag between a sale

TABLE 3.7   Cash Budget for Jill Clair Fashions, 3rd Quarter, 2018 ($ thousands)

	Actual		Projected		
	May	June	July	Aug.	Sept.
I. Determination of Cash Collections and Payments					
Projected sales	$150	$200	$300	$400	$250
Collection of sales					
During month of sale			88	118	74
(0.3) (.98) (month's sales)					
During 1st month after sale			120	180	240
0.6 (prior month's sales)					
During 2nd month after sale			15	20	30
0.1 (sales two months ago)					
Total collections			$223	$318	$344
Purchases 0.6 (next month's projected sales)		$180	240	$150	
Payments (prior month's purchases)			$180	$240	$150
II. Cash Receipts and Disbursements					
Total collections (from above)			$223	$318	$344
Sale of used equipment				79	
Total cash receipts			$223	$397	$344
Payments (from above)			180	240	150
Wages and salaries			84	82	70
Interest payments			8	8	8
Rent			10	10	10
Taxes					12
Principal payment on loan					40
Other disbursements			1	27	14
Total cash disbursements			$283	$367	$304
Net cash receipts (disbursements)			$ (60)	$ 30	$ 40
III. Determination of Cash Surplus or Deficit					
Beginning cash			220	160	190
Net cash receipts (disbursements)			(60)	30	40
Ending cash			160	190	230
Minimum desired cash			200	200	200
Cash surplus (deficit)			**$ (40)**	**$ (10)**	**$ 30**

and receipt of cash from the sale. Analogously, for credit purchases, it means adjusting for the lag between the purchase of an item and payment of the resulting account payable.

To see the mechanics, Table 3.7 presents Jill Clair Fashions' monthly cash budget for the third quarter of 2018. Jill Clair is a modest-sized manufacturer and distributor of women's apparel. Sales are quite seasonal, reaching a peak in midsummer, and the company treasurer is concerned about maintaining adequate cash balances during this critical period. For simplicity, the table presents a monthly cash budget. In practice, a treasurer working with volatile sales and limited cash would likely want weekly and perhaps daily budgets as well.

The top part of the budget, labeled "Determination of Cash Collections and Payments," makes the necessary conversion between accrual and cash accounting. The company's stated credit terms are 2 percent/10 net 30 days, meaning customers receive a 2 percent discount when they pay within 10 days, but otherwise the bill is due in full in 30 days. Based on past experience, the treasurer anticipates that 30 percent of customers will pay in the month of purchase and claim the discount, 60 percent will pay in the following month, and 10 percent will pay two months after purchase. Looking at July's numbers, we see that projected sales are $300,000 but collections are only $223,000. Approximately $88,000 of this total comes from collections of sales made in July. This figure equals 30 percent of 98 percent of July's sales. (Ninety-eight percent reflects the two percent discount for prompt payment.) Approximately $120,000 of July collections comes from sales booked in June, reflecting the expectation that 60 percent of June buyers will pay the following month. Finally, $15,000 of July collections originates from sales made two months ago and equals 10 percent of May sales.

Jill Clair purchases raw materials equal to 60 percent of next month's projected sales. So with August projected sales of $400,000, July purchases are $240,000. However, because the company pays its accounts payable 30 days after purchase, cash payments equal June purchases, or only $180,000.

The second section in Table 3.7, labeled "Cash Receipts and Disbursements," records all anticipated cash inflows and outflows for each month. Also appearing is the monthly difference between these quantities, labeled "Net cash receipts (disbursements)." Observe that Jill Clair anticipates receiving cash from two sources: collections from credit sales, as estimated in the top part of the table, and an additional $79,000 from the sale of used equipment. Other possible sources of cash not contemplated here include such things as proceeds from a new bank loan, interest income, and cash from the exercise of employee stock options. In the lower part of this section, cash disbursements record all anticipated cash payments for each month, including payments for credit purchases as estimated earlier, wages and salaries, interest payments, rent, taxes, a loan principal payment, and other miscellaneous disbursements. In each category, the treasurer has recorded the anticipated cash cost in the month paid. Note that depreciation does not appear among the disbursements because as a non-cash charge it has no place in a cash budget.

The bottom portion of Jill Clair's cash budget shows the effect of the company's anticipated cash inflows and outflows on its need for external funding.

The logic is quite simple. One month's ending cash balance becomes the next month's beginning balance, and throughout each month cash rises or falls according to that month's net cash receipts or disbursements. For example, August's beginning cash balance of $160,000 is July's ending balance, and during August, net cash receipts of $30,000 boost cash to an ending figure of $190,000. Comparing each month's ending cash balance with the minimum desired level of cash as specified by the treasurer yields a monthly estimate of the company's cash surplus or deficit. A deficit measures the amount of money the company must raise on the forecast date to cover anticipated disbursements, and leave ending cash at the desired minimum. A forecasted surplus, on the other hand, means the company can cover anticipated disbursements and still have cash in excess of the desired minimum. Stated differently, the cash surplus or deficit figures in a cash budget are equal in all respects to the figures for external funding required that appear on a pro

A Problem with Depreciation

XYZ Corporation is forecasting its financing needs for next year. The original forecast shows an external financing need of $10 million. On reviewing the forecast, the production manager, having just returned from an accounting seminar, recommends increasing depreciation next year—for reporting purposes only, not for tax purposes—by $1 million. She explains, rather condescendingly, that this will reduce net fixed assets by $1 million and, because a reduction of an asset is a source of cash, this will reduce the external funding required by a like amount. Explain why the production manager is incorrect.

Answer: Increasing depreciation will reduce net fixed assets. However, it will also reduce provision for taxes and retained earnings by the same amount. Because both are liability accounts and reduction of a liability is a use of cash, the whole exercise is a wash with respect to determination of external financing requirements. This is consistent with cash budgeting, which ignores depreciation entirely. Here is a numerical example:

	Original Depreciation	Increase in Depreciation	Change in Liability Account
Operating income	$10,000	$10,000	
Depreciation	4,000	5,000	
Earnings before tax	6,000	5,000	
Provision for tax @ 40%	2,400	2,000	−400
Earnings after tax	3,600	3,000	
Dividends	1,000	1,000	
Additions to retained earnings	$ 2,600	$ 2,000	−$ 600
Total change in liabilities			−$1,000

forma projection or a cash flow forecast. They all measure the company's future need for external financing or its projected surplus cash.

Jill Clair's cash budget suggests that the treasurer needs to borrow $40,000 in July, but should be able to reduce the loan to $10,000 the following month, and will be able to repay the loan in full by the end of September. In fact, it appears the company will have $30,000 in excess cash by then, which can be used to pay down other debt, purchase marketable securities, or invest elsewhere in the business.

The Techniques Compared

Although the formats differ, it should be a relief to learn that all of the forecasting techniques considered in this chapter produce the same results. As long as the assumptions are the same and no arithmetic or accounting mistakes are made, all of the techniques will produce the same estimate of external funding required. Moreover, if your accounting skills are up to the task, it is possible to reconcile one format with another. Problems 10, 11, and 12 at the end of the chapter allow you to demonstrate this fact for yourself.

A second reassuring fact is that regardless of which forecasting technique is used, the resulting estimate of new financing needs is not biased by inflation. Consequently, there is no need to resort to elaborate inflation adjustments when making financial forecasts in an inflationary environment. This is not to say that the need for new financing is independent of the inflation rate. Indeed, as will become apparent in Chapter 4, the financing needs of most companies rise with inflation. Rather, it means that direct application of the previously described forecasting techniques will correctly indicate the need for external financing even in the presence of inflation.

Mechanically, then, the three forecasting techniques are equivalent, and the choice of which one to use can depend on the purpose of the forecast. For most planning purposes and for credit analysis, I recommend pro forma statements because they present the information in a form suitable for additional financial analysis. For short-term forecasting and the management of cash, the cash budget is appropriate. A cash flow forecast lies somewhere between the other two. It presents a broader picture of company operations than a cash budget does and is easier to construct and more accessible to accounting novices than pro formas are, but it is also less informative than pro formas.

Regardless of which forecasting technique you use, keep in mind that—as mentioned in the opening paragraph to this chapter—financial forecasts are only the tip of the planning iceberg. Especially in large, multidivision corporations, effective planning usually involves multiple steps. First, headquarters executives and division managers hammer out a corporate strategy. Second, division managers and department personnel translate the corporate strategy into a set of division activities that help achieve the agreed-on goals. Third, department personnel develop a set of quantitative plans and budgets based on the defined division activities. Then, finally, the integration of the detailed divisional budgets at headquarters produces the corporation's financial forecast. In proper perspective, then, financial forecasting is a family of techniques for translating creative ideas and strategies into concrete action plans, and while proper technique cannot guarantee success, the lack of same certainly heightens the odds of failure.

SUMMARY

1. Pro forma statements
   - Are the principal means by which operating managers can predict the financial implications of their decisions.
   - Are predictions of what a company's financial statements will look like at the end of the forecast period.
   - Are commonly used to estimate a company's future need for external funding and a great way to test the feasibility of current operating plans.
   - Are often based on percent-of-sales forecasts that assume many balance sheet and income statement entries vary in constant proportion to sales.
   - Involve four steps:
     1. Review of past financial statements to identify quantities that have varied in proportion to sales historically.
     2. Careful projection of future sales.
     3. Preparation of independent projections of quantities, such as fixed plant and equipment, that have not varied in proportion to sales historically.
     4. Testing the sensitivity of forecast results to variations in projected sales.
   - Generate forecasts that are strictly applicable only on the forecast date and thus require care when dealing with seasonal businesses.
   - Contain a circularity involving interest expense and total debt outstanding, which can be easily handled with a computer spreadsheet set to enable iterative calculation.
   - Are a great platform for effective financial planning where management carefully analyzes their forecast to decide if it is acceptable or whether it must be changed to avoid identified problems.
2. Cash flow forecasts
   - Project external funding required as the difference between anticipated sources and uses of cash over the forecast period.

- Yield the same need for external funding as a pro forma projection, given the same assumptions.
- Are less informative than pro forma forecasts because they do not provide information useful for evaluating how best to meet the indicated need for financing.

3. Cash budgets
   - Project the change in cash balance over the forecast period as the difference between anticipated cash receipts and disbursements.
   - Rely on cash rather than accrual accounting.
   - Yield the same need for external funding as a pro forma projection, given the same assumptions.
   - Are commonly used for short-term forecasts ranging from a day to a month.
   - Are less informative than pro forma forecasts but easier for accounting neophytes to understand.

4. Three ways to cope with uncertainty in financial forecasts are
   - Sensitivity analysis: change one uncertain input at a time and observe how the forecast responds.
   - Scenario analysis: make coordinated changes in several inputs to mirror the occurrence of a particular scenario, such as loss of a major customer, or a major recession.
   - Simulation: assign probability distributions to a number of uncertain inputs and use a computer to generate a distribution of possible outcomes.

ADDITIONAL RESOURCES

Benninga, Simon. *Financial Modeling.* 4th ed. Cambridge, MA: The MIT Press, 2014. 1,144 pages.

Covers a number of financial models, including pro forma forecasting and simulation techniques, as well as more advanced models such as portfolio analysis, options, duration, and immunization. Microsoft Excel is used throughout.

Mayes, Timothy R. *Financial Analysis with Microsoft Excel.* 7th ed. Cengage Learning, 2014. 544 pages.

An introductory-level look at the use of Microsoft Excel for financial analysis. Nowhere near as sophisticated or ambitious as the Benninga book.

office.com/training

If you are new to Excel or need to refresh your skills, go to this site for some interactive Excel training.

Excel Tutorial Apps

If you would like to learn Excel on your handheld device, many tutorials are available for both iOS and Android (search Apple's app store or Google Play for "Excel Tutorial").

youtube.com/user/MotionTraining

If you would like to learn Excel through videos, this link goes to a popular series of tutorials.

exinfm.com/free_spreadsheets.html

Links to 121 free Excel spreadsheets for analyzing a wide variety of financial issues, plus other Excel tools. Compiled by a financial consultant.

oracle.com/crystalball

Visit this site to download a full-featured, 30-day trial copy of Crystal Ball, a powerful addition to Excel for simulation analysis. Select "Oracle Crystal Ball Free Trial" and follow the instructions.

tukhi.com; yasai.rutgers.edu

If you prefer a free alternative to Crystal Ball using Excel, check out one of these websites.

PROBLEMS

Answers to odd-numbered problems appear at the end of the book. Answers to even-numbered problems and additional exercises are available in the Instructor Resources within McGraw-Hill's *Connect* (see the Preface for more information).

1. Suppose you constructed a pro forma balance sheet for a company and the estimate for external financing required was negative. How would you interpret this result?

2. Pro forma financial statements, by definition, are predictions of a company's financial statements at a future point in time. So why is it important to analyze the historical performance of the company before constructing pro forma financial statements?

3. Suppose you constructed a pro forma balance sheet and a cash budget for a company for the same time period and the external financing required from the pro forma forecast exceeded the cash deficit estimated on the cash budget. How would you interpret this result?

4. Answer true or false to each of the following. Briefly explain your reasoning for each answer.
    a. All else equal, increasing the projected amount of accounts receivable in a financial forecast will increase external funding required.

b. Estimates of external funding required based on cash flow forecasts are usually higher than estimates based on pro forma financial statements.

c. An annual financial forecast for 2018 showing no external funding required assures a company that no cash shortfalls are likely to occur during 2018.

5. Universal Products Co. has almost finished its pro forma financial statements for 2018, as shown next.

Universal Products Co.
Financial Statements, 2017 and Pro Forma 2018 ($ thousands)

INCOME STATEMENT			BALANCE SHEET		
	Actual	Forecast		Actual	Forecast
	2017	2018		2017	2018
Sales	$5,000	$5,500	Current assets	$2,500	$2,750
Cost of goods sold	4,000	4,400	Net fixed assets	2,000	
Operating expense	500	550	Total assets	$4,500	
Depreciation expense	250	260			
Interest expense	50	50	Current liabilities	$1,050	$1,155
Earnings before tax	200	240	Long-term debt	500	500
Tax	70	84	Owners' equity	2,950	
Net income	$130	$156	Total liabilities & equity	$4,500	

a. Assume that Universal plans to purchase $500,000 in fixed assets during 2018 and to dispose of no fixed assets during 2018. What would be its forecast for net fixed assets in 2018?

b. Assume that Universal plans to have a dividend payout ratio of 50 percent in 2018 and will neither sell nor repurchase equity during 2018. What would be its forecast for owners' equity in 2018?

c. Given the assumptions in questions (a) and (b), what is Universal's projected external funding required for 2018?

6. Sequoia Furniture Company's sales over the past three months, half of which are for cash, were as follows:

March	April	May
$400,000	$650,000	$520,000

a. Assume that Sequoia's collection period is 60 days. What would be its cash receipts in May? What would be its accounts receivable balance at the end of May?

b. Now assume that Sequoia's collection period is 45 days. What would be its cash receipts in May? What would be its accounts receivable balance at the end of May?

7. Table 3.3 shows the December 31, 2018 pro forma balance sheet and income statements for R&E Supplies, Inc. The pro-forma balance sheet shows that R&E Supplies will need external funding from the bank of $1.4 million. However, they show almost $1.3 million in cash and short-term securities. Why are they talking to the bank for such a large amount when they have most of this sum in their cash account?

8. Table 3.5 presents a computer spreadsheet for estimating R&E Supplies' external financing required for 2018. The text mentions that with modifications to the equations for equity and net sales, the forecast can easily be extended through 2019. Write the modified equations for equity and net sales.

9. A spreadsheet containing R&E Supplies' 2018 pro forma financial forecast, as shown in Table 3.5, is available for download from McGraw-Hill's *Connect* or your course instructor (see the Preface for more information). Using the spreadsheet information presented next, and the modified equations determined in question 8 earlier, extend the forecast for R&E Supplies contained in Table 3.5 through 2019.

R&E Supplies Assumptions for 2019 ($ thousands)			
Growth rate in net sales	30.0%	Tax rate	45.0%
Cost of goods sold/net sales	86.0%	Dividend/earnings after tax	50.0%
Gen., sell., & admin.		Current assets/net sales	29.0%
expenses/net sales	11.0%	Net fixed assets	$ 270
Long-term debt	$560	Current liabilities/net sales	14.4%
Current portion long-term debt	$100		
Interest rate	10.0%		

a. What is R&E's projected external financing required in 2019? How does this number compare to the 2018 projection?

b. Perform a sensitivity analysis on this projection. How does R&E's projected external financing required change if the ratio of cost of goods sold to net sales declines from 86.0 percent to 84.0 percent?

c. Perform a scenario analysis on this projection. How does R&E's projected external financing required change if a severe recession occurs in 2019? Assume net sales decline 5 percent, cost of goods sold rises to 88 percent of net sales due to price cutting, and current assets increase to 35 percent of net sales as management fails to cut purchases promptly in response to declining sales.

The following three problems demonstrate that pro forma forecasts, cash budgets, and cash flow forecasts all yield the same estimated need for external financing—provided you don't make any mistakes. For problems 10, 11, and 12, you may ignore the effect of added borrowing on interest expense.

10. The treasurer of Westmark Industrial, Inc., a wholesale distributor of household appliances, wants to estimate his company's cash balances for the first three months of 2018. Using the following information, construct a monthly cash budget for Westmark for January through March 2018. Westmark's sales are 20 percent for cash, with the rest on 30-day credit terms. Its purchases are all on 60-day credit terms. Does it appear from your results that the treasurer should be concerned about investing excess cash or looking for a bank loan?

Westmark Industrial, Inc. Selected Information ($ thousands)						
	2017 (Actual)			2018 (Projected)		
	October	November	December	January	February	March
Sales	360	420	1,200	600	240	240
Purchases	510	540	1,200	300	120	120
Wages payable monthly				180		
Principal payment on debt due in March				210		
Interest due in March				90		
Dividend payable in March				300		
Taxes payable in February				180		
Addition to accumulated depreciation in March				30		
Cash balance on January 1, 2018				300		
Minimum desired cash balance				150		

11. Continuing problem 10, Westmark Industrial's annual income statement and balance sheet for December 31, 2017, are shown next. Additional information about the company's accounting methods and the treasurer's expectations for the first quarter of 2018 appear in the footnotes.

Income Statement	
January 1, 2017 to December 31, 2017 ($ thousands)	
Net sales	$6,000
Cost of goods sold[1]	3,900
Gross profits	2,100
Selling and administrative expenses[2]	1,620
Interest expense	90
Depreciation[3]	90
Net profit before tax	300
Tax (33%)	99
Net profit after tax	$ 201

Balance Sheet
December 31, 2017 ($ thousands)

Assets

Cash	$ 300
Accounts receivable	960
Inventory	1,800
Total current assets	3,060
Gross fixed assets	900
Accumulated depreciation	150
Net fixed assets	750
Total assets	$3,810

Liabilities

Bank loan	$ 0
Accounts payable	1,740
Miscellaneous accruals[4]	60
Current portion long-term debt[5]	210
Taxes payable	300
Total current liabilities	2,310
Long-term debt	990
Shareholders' equity	510
Total liabilities and equity	$3,810

[1] Cost of goods sold consists entirely of items purchased in first quarter.
[2] Selling and administrative expenses consist entirely of wages.
[3] Depreciation is at the rate of $30,000 per quarter.
[4] Miscellaneous accruals are not expected to change in the first quarter.
[5] $210 due in March 2018. No payments for remainder of year.

    a. Use this information and the information in problem 10 to construct a pro forma income statement for the first quarter of 2018 and a pro forma balance sheet for March 31, 2018. What is your estimated external financing need for March 31?

    b. Does the March 31, 2018 estimated external financing equal your cash surplus (deficit) for this date from your cash budget in problem 10? Should it?

    c. Do your pro forma forecasts tell you more than your cash budget does about Westmark's financial prospects?

    d. What do your pro forma income statement and balance sheet tell you about Westmark's need for external financing on February 28, 2018?

12. Based on your answer to question 11, construct a first-quarter 2018 cash flow forecast for Westmark Industrial.

13. Toys-4-Kids manufactures plastic toys. Sales and production are highly seasonal. The following is a quarterly pro forma forecast indicating external financing needs for 2018. Assumptions are in parentheses.

Toys-4-Kids
2018 Quarterly Pro Forma Forecast
($ thousands)

	Qtr 1	Qtr 2	Qtr 3	Qtr 4
Net sales	300	375	3,200	5,000
Cost of sales (70 percent of sales)	210	263	2,240	3,500
Gross profit	90	113	960	1,500
Operating expenses	560	560	560	560
Profit before tax	(470)	(448)	400	940
Income taxes	(188)	(179)	160	376
Profit after tax	(282)	(269)	240	564
Cash (minimum balance = $200,000)	1,235	927	200	200
Accounts receivable				
(75 percent of quarterly sales)	225	281	2,400	3,750
Inventory (12/31/17 balance = $500,000)	500	500	500	500
Current assets	1,960	1,708	3,100	4,450
Net plant & equipment	1,000	1,000	1,000	1,000
Total assets	2,960	2,708	4,100	5,450
Accounts payable				
(10 percent of quarterly sales)	30	38	320	500
Accrued taxes (payments quarterly in arrears)	(188)	(179)	160	376
Current liabilities	(158)	(142)	480	876
Long-term debt	400	400	400	400
Equity (12/31/17 balance = $3,000,000)	2,718	2,450	2,690	3,254
Total liabilities and equity	2,960	2,708	3,570	4,530
External financing required	0	0	530	920

a. How do you interpret the negative numbers for income taxes in the first two quarters?

b. Why are cash balances in the first two quarters greater than the minimum required $200,000? How were these numbers determined?

c. How was "external financing required" (appearing at the bottom of the forecast) determined?

d. Do you think Toys-4-Kids will be able to borrow the external financing required as indicated by the forecast?

14. Continuing with Toys-4-Kids, introduced in the preceding problem, the company's production manager has argued for years that it is inefficient to produce on a seasonal basis. She believes the company should switch to level production throughout the year, building up finished goods

inventory in the first two quarters to meet the peak selling needs in the last two. She believes the company can reduce its cost of goods sold from 70 percent to 65 percent with level production. (Recall that production managers typically want to restrict production to left shoes only so as to reduce costs.)

   a. Prepare a revised pro forma forecast assuming level production. In your forecast, assume that quarterly accounts payable under level production equal 10 percent of *average* quarterly sales for the year. To estimate quarterly inventory, use the following two formulas:

$$\text{Inventory}_{eoq} = \text{Inventory}_{boq} + \text{Quarterly production} - \frac{\text{Quarterly}}{\text{cost of sales}}$$

$$\text{Quarterly production} = \text{Annual cost of sales}/4$$

   where eoq and boq refer to end of quarter and beginning of quarter, respectively. Please ignore the effect of increased external financing required on interest expense.

   b. What is the effect of the switch from seasonal to level production on annual profits?

   c. What effect does the switch have on the company's quarterly ending inventory? On the company's quarterly need for external financing?

   d. Do you think the company will be able to borrow the amount of money required by level production? What obsolescence risks does the company incur by building up inventory in anticipation of future sales? Might this be a concern to lenders?

15. This problem asks you to prepare one- and five-year financial forecasts and conduct some sensitivity analysis and scenario analysis for Aquatic Supplies Company. A spreadsheet containing the company's 2017 financial statements and management's projections is available for download from McGraw-Hill's *Connect* or your course instructor (see the Preface for more information). Use this information to answer the questions posed in the spreadsheet.

16. Financial statements and additional information for Noble Equipment Corp. are available for download from McGraw-Hill's *Connect* or your course instructor (see the Preface for more information). The company's fiscal year end is September 30. Noble's management wants to estimate the company's cash balances for the last three months of calendar year 2017, which are the first three months of fiscal year 2018. The questions accompanying the spreadsheet ask you to prepare a monthly cash budget, pro forma financial statements, and a cash flow forecast for the period.

17. This problem asks you to construct a simple simulation model. If you do not own simulation software, see the options for downloading simulation software under Additional Resources.

   a. Problem 9 earlier asked you to extend the forecast for R&E Supplies contained in Table 3.5 through 2019. Using the same spreadsheet, simulate R&E Supplies' external funding requirements in 2019 under the following assumptions.

      i. Represent the growth rate in net sales as a triangular distribution with a mean of 30 percent and a range of 25 to 35 percent.

      ii. Represent the interest rate as a uniform distribution varying from 9 percent to 11 percent.

      iii. Represent the tax rate as a lognormal distribution with a mean of 45 percent and a standard deviation of 2 percent.

   b. If the treasurer wants to be 95 percent certain of raising enough money in 2019, how much should he raise? (Grab the triangle below the frequency chart on the right and move it to the left until 95.00 appears in the "Certainty" window.)

Managing Growth

Alas, the road to success is always under repair.

Anonymous

Growth and its management present special problems in financial planning, in part because many executives see growth as something to be maximized. They reason simply that, as growth increases, the firm's market share and profits should rise as well. From a financial perspective, however, growth is not always a blessing. Rapid growth can put considerable strain on a company's resources, and unless management is aware of this effect and takes active steps to control it, rapid growth can lead to bankruptcy. Companies can literally grow broke. It is a sad truth that rapid growth has driven almost as many companies into bankruptcy as slow growth has. It is doubly sad to realize that those companies that grew too fast met the market test by providing a product people wanted and failed only because they lacked the financial acumen to manage their growth properly.

At the other end of the spectrum, companies growing too slowly have a different but no less pressing set of financial concerns. As will become apparent, if these companies fail to appreciate the financial implications of slow growth, they will come under increasing pressure from restive shareholders, irate board members, and potential raiders. In either case, the financial management of growth is a topic worthy of close inspection.

We begin our look at the financial dimensions of growth by defining a company's *sustainable growth rate*. This is the maximum rate at which company sales can increase without depleting financial resources. Then, we look at the options open to management when a company's target growth rate exceeds its sustainable growth rate and, conversely, when growth falls below sustainable levels. An important conclusion will be that growth is not necessarily something to be maximized. In many companies, it may be necessary to limit growth to conserve financial strength. In others, the money used to finance unprofitable growth might better be returned to owners. The need to limit growth is a hard lesson for operating managers used to thinking that more is better. It is a critical one, however, because operating executives bear major responsibility for managing growth.

Sustainable Growth

We can think of successful companies as passing through a predictable life cycle. The cycle begins with a startup phase in which the company loses money while developing products or services and establishing a foothold in the market. This is followed by a rapid growth phase in which the company is profitable but is growing so rapidly that it needs regular infusions of outside financing. The third phase is maturity, characterized by a decline in growth and a switch from absorbing outside financing to generating more cash than the firm can profitably reinvest. The last phase is decline, during which the company is perhaps marginally profitable, generates more cash than it can reinvest internally, and suffers declining sales. Mature and declining companies frequently devote considerable time and money to seeking investment opportunities in new products or firms that are still in their growth phase.

We begin our discussion by looking at the growth phase, when financing needs are most pressing. Later, we will consider the growth problems of mature and declining firms. Central to our discussion is the notion of sustainable growth. Intuitively, sustainable growth is merely a formalization of the old adage "It takes money to make money." Increased sales require more assets of all types, which must be paid for. Retained profits and the accompanying new borrowing generate some cash, but only limited amounts. Unless the company is prepared to sell common stock or borrow excessive amounts, this limit puts a ceiling on the growth it can achieve without straining its resources. This is the firm's sustainable growth rate.

The Sustainable Growth Equation

Let's begin by writing a simple equation to express the dependence of growth on financial resources. For this purpose, assume

- The company has a target financing, or capital, structure and a target dividend policy it wishes to maintain.

- Management is unable or unwilling to sell new equity.

We will say more about these assumptions soon. For now, it is enough to realize that although they may not be appropriate for all firms, the assumptions describe a great many.

Figure 4.1 shows the rapidly growing company's plight. It represents the firm's balance sheet as two rectangles, one for assets and the other for liabilities and owners' equity. The two long, unshaded rectangles represent the balance sheet at the beginning of the year. The rectangles are, of course, the same height because assets must equal liabilities plus owners' equity. Now, if the company wants to increase sales during the coming year, it must also increase assets such as inventory, accounts receivable, and productive capacity. The shaded area

FIGURE 4.1 **New Sales Require New Assets, Which Must Be Financed**

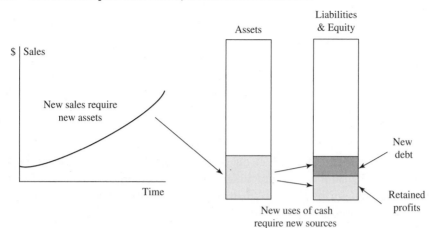

on the assets side of the figure represents the value of new assets necessary to support the increased sales. Because the company will not be selling equity by assumption, the cash required to pay for this increase in assets must come from retained profits and new debt.

We want to know what limits the rate at which the company in Figure 4.1 can increase sales. Assuming, in effect, that all parts of a business expand in strict proportion like a balloon, what limits the rate of this expansion? To find out, start in the lower-right corner of the figure with owners' equity. As equity grows, the firm can borrow more money without altering the capital structure—together, the growth of liabilities and the growth of equity determine the rate at which assets expand. This, in turn, limits the growth rate in sales. So after all the dust settles, what limits the growth rate in sales is the rate at which owners' equity expands. A company's sustainable growth rate therefore is nothing more than its growth rate in equity.

Letting g^* represent the sustainable growth rate,

$$g^* = \frac{\text{Change in equity}}{\text{Equity}_{bop}}$$

where bop denotes beginning-of-period equity. Because the firm will not be selling any new shares by assumption, the only source of new equity will be from retained profits, so we can rewrite this expression as

$$g^* = \frac{R \times \text{Earnings}}{\text{Equity}_{bop}}$$

where R is the firm's "retention rate." R is the fraction of earnings retained in the business, or 1 minus the dividend payout ratio. If a company's target dividend policy is to distribute 10 percent of earnings as dividends, its retention ratio is 90 percent.

The ratio "Earnings/Equity" in this expression should look familiar; it is the firm's return on equity, or ROE. Thus,

$$g^* = R \times \text{ROE}_{\text{bop}}$$

Finally, recalling the levers of performance discussed in Chapter 2, we can rewrite this expression yet again as

$$g^* = PRA\hat{T}$$

where P, A, and $\hat{T}$ are our old friends from Chapter 2, the levers of performance, where P is the profit margin, A is the asset turnover ratio, and $\hat{T}$ is the assets-to-equity ratio. The assets-to-equity ratio wears a hat here as a reminder that it is assets divided by *beginning-of-period* equity instead of end-of-period equity as defined in Chapter 2.

This is the sustainable growth equation.[1] Let's see what it tells us. Given the assumptions just noted, the equation says that a company's sustainable growth rate in sales, g^*, equals the product of four ratios, P, R, A, and $\hat{T}$. Two of these ratios, P and A, summarize the operating performance of the business, while the other two describe the firm's principal financial policies. Thus, the retention rate, R, captures management's attitudes toward the distribution of dividends, and the assets-to-equity ratio, $\hat{T}$, reflects its policies regarding financial leverage.

An important implication of the sustainable growth equation is that *g^* is the only growth rate in sales that is consistent with stable values of the four ratios.* If a company increases sales at any rate other than g^*, one or more of the ratios *must* change. This means that when a company grows at a rate in excess of its sustainable growth rate, it had better improve operations (represented by an increase in the profit margin or the asset turnover ratio) or prepare to alter its financial policies (represented by increasing its retention rate or its financial leverage).

Too Much Growth

This is the crux of the sustainable growth problem for rapidly expanding firms: Because increasing operating efficiency is not always possible and altering financial policies is not always wise, we see that it is entirely possible for a company to grow too fast for its own good. This is particularly true for smaller companies, which may do inadequate financial planning. Such companies see sales growth as something to be maximized and think too little of

---

[1] I shall refrain from admonishing you to avoid "prat̂" falls.

the financial consequences. They do not realize that rapid growth has them on a treadmill; the faster they grow, the more cash they need, even when they are profitable. They can meet this need for a time by increasing leverage, but eventually they will reach their debt capacity, lenders will refuse additional credit requests, and the companies will find themselves without the cash to pay their bills. All of this can be prevented if managers understand that growth above the company's sustainable rate creates financial challenges that must be anticipated and managed.

Please understand; I am not suggesting that a company's actual growth rate should always equal its sustainable growth rate, or even closely approximate it. Rather, I am saying that management must anticipate any disparity between actual and sustainable growth and have a plan in place for managing that disparity. The challenge is, first, to recognize the disparity and, second, to create a viable strategy to manage it.

Balanced Growth

Here is another way to think about sustainable growth. Recalling that a company's return on assets, ROA, can be expressed as the product of its profit margin times its asset turnover, we can rewrite the sustainable growth equation as[2]

$$g^* = R\hat{T} \times \text{ROA}$$

Here, R and $\hat{T}$ reflect the company's financial policies, while ROA summarizes its operating performance. So if a company's retention ratio is 25 percent and its assets-to-equity ratio is 1.6, its sustainable growth equation becomes simply

$$g^* = 0.4 \times \text{ROA}$$

This equation says that given stable financial policies, sustainable growth varies linearly with return on assets. Figure 4.2 graphs this relationship with sales growth on the vertical axis, ROA on the horizontal axis, and the sustainable growth equation as the upward-sloping, solid, diagonal line.

The line bears the label "Balanced growth" because the company can self-finance only the sales growth–ROA combinations lying on this line. All growth-return combinations lying off this line generate either cash deficits or cash surpluses. Thus, rapidly growing, marginally profitable companies will plot in the upper-left portion of the graph, implying cash deficits, while slowly expanding, highly profitable companies will plot in the lower-right portion, implying cash surpluses. I should emphasize that the phrase "self-finance"

---

[2] Strictly speaking, this equation should be expressed in terms of return on invested capital, not return on assets, but the gain in precision is too modest to justify the added mathematical complexity. See Gordon Donaldson, *Managing Corporate Wealth* (New York: Praeger, 1984), Chapter 4, for a more rigorous exposition.

FIGURE 4.2   **A Graphical Representation of Sustainable Growth**

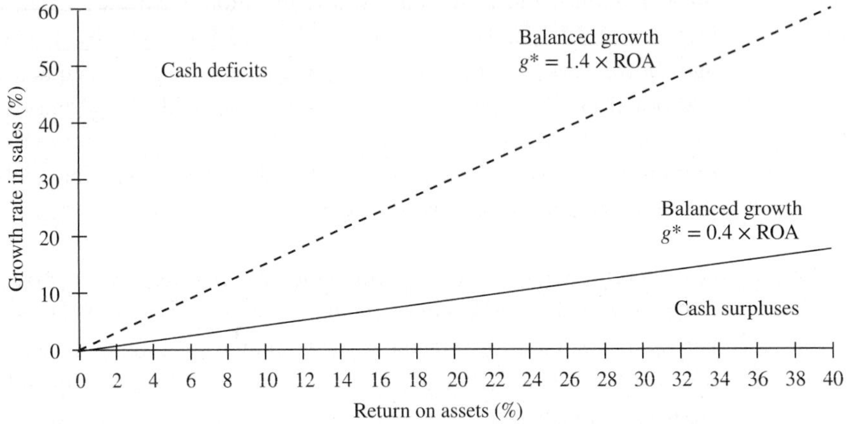

does not imply constant debt but rather a constant debt-to-equity ratio. Debt can increase but only in proportion to equity.

When a company experiences unbalanced growth of either the surplus or the deficit variety, it can move toward the balanced growth line in any of three ways: It can change its growth rate, alter its return on assets, or modify its financial policies. To illustrate the last option, suppose the company with the balanced growth line depicted in Figure 4.2 is in the deficit region of the graph and wants to reduce the deficit. One strategy would be to increase its retention ratio to, say, 50 percent and its assets-to-equity ratio to, say, 2.8 to 1, thereby changing its sustainable growth equation to

$$g^* = 1.4 \times \text{ROA}$$

In Figure 4.2, this is equivalent to rotating the balanced growth line upward to the left, as shown by the dotted line. Now any level of profitability will support a higher growth rate than before.

In this perspective, the sustainable growth rate is the nexus of all growth-return combinations yielding balanced growth, and the sustainable growth challenge is that of managing the surpluses or deficits caused by unbalanced growth. We will return to strategies for managing growth after looking at a numerical example.

Nobility Homes' Sustainable Growth Rate

To illustrate the growth management challenges a rapidly growing business faces, let's look at Nobility Homes, Inc., a small maker of manufactured homes sold throughout the state of Florida. Table 4.1 presents the company's actual and sustainable growth rates from 2012 through 2016. For each year, I calculated Nobility's sustainable growth rate by plugging the four required

TABLE 4.1 A Sustainable Growth Analysis of Nobility Homes Inc., 2012–2016*

Source: Data from Nobility Homes 2012–2016 annual reports

	2012	2013	2014	2015	2016
Required ratios:					
Profit margin, P (%)	0.3	4.0	5.9	10.5	17.5
Retention ratio, R (%)	100.0	100.0	100.0	100.0	100.0
Asset turnover, A (times)	0.44	0.50	0.54	0.66	0.67
Financial leverage, T (times)	1.04	1.08	1.11	1.16	1.30
Nobility Homes' sustainable growth rate, g^* (%)	0.1	2.2	3.6	8.0	15.3
Nobility Homes' actual growth rate in sales, g (%)	17.9	17.0	14.2	31.6	22.3

	What If?		
	Profit Margin 20.0%	Financial Leverage 1.5 Times	Both Occur
Nobility Homes' sustainable growth rate in 2016 (%)	17.4	17.6	20.1

*Totals may not add due to rounding.

ratios into the sustainable growth equation. I calculated the ratios from the company's financial statements, which are not shown. Observe that Nobility's sales grew more than 20 percent a year, on average, over the period, almost four times its sustainable growth rate.

How did Nobility Homes cope with actual growth above sustainable levels? A look at the four required ratios reveals that the company's response was to increase every ratio except the retention rate, which was already at a maximum of 1.00. On the operating side, return on assets jumped from almost nothing to a hearty 11.7 percent, while on the financial side, financial leverage rose 25 percent. Management is undoubtedly pleased by the improving returns, but also aware that increasing indebtedness is not a long-run answer to the problems of rapid growth.

Figure 4.3 says the same thing graphically. It shows Nobility Homes' balanced growth lines in 2012 and 2016, as well as the growth-return combinations the company achieved each year. Despite a beneficial increase in the slope of the company's balanced growth line produced by the previously mentioned increase in leverage, Nobility remained well into the cash deficit portion of the graph every year. The persistent gap between the yearly growth-return combinations and the balanced growth lines throughout the period confirms that Nobility's growth management challenges persist. Such is the life of a cyclical home builder during an upturn.

FIGURE 4.3 **Nobility Homes' Sustainable Growth Challenges, 2012–2016**

Source: Data from Nobility Homes 2012–2016 annual reports

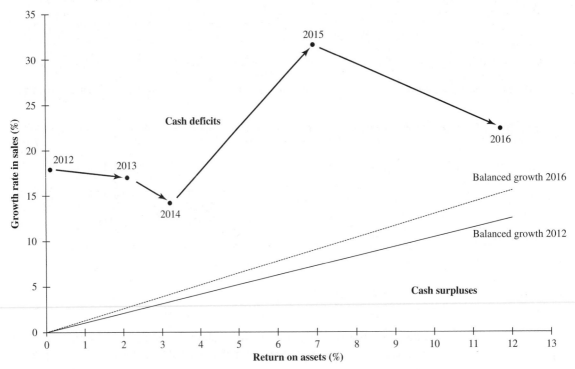

"What If" Questions

When management faces growth problems, the sustainable growth equation can be useful in searching for solutions. This is done by asking a series of "what if" questions, as shown in the bottom portion of Table 4.1. We see, for example, that in coming years Nobility can raise its sustainable growth rate to 17.4 percent by increasing its profit margin to 20.0 percent. Alternatively, it can boost its sustainable growth rate to 17.6 percent by raising financial leverage to 1.5 times. Doing both simultaneously will raise sustainable growth to 20.1 percent, still well below its recent actual growth rates in sales.

What to Do When Actual Growth Exceeds Sustainable Growth

We have now developed the sustainable growth equation and illustrated its use for rapidly growing companies. The next question is: What should management do when actual growth exceeds sustainable growth? The first step is to determine how long the situation will continue. If the company's growth rate is likely to decline in the near future as the firm reaches maturity, the problem is only a transitory one that can probably be solved by further borrowing. In the future, when the actual growth rate falls below the sustainable rate, the company will switch from being an absorber of cash to being a generator of cash and can repay the loans. For longer-term sustainable growth problems, some combination of the following strategies will be necessary.

- Sell new equity

- Increase financial leverage

- Reduce the dividend payout

- Prune away marginal activities

- Outsource some or all of production

- Increase prices

- Merge with a "cash cow"

Let's consider each of these strategies in more detail.

Sell New Equity

If a company is willing and able to raise new equity by selling shares, its sustainable growth problems vanish. The increased equity, plus whatever added borrowing it makes possible, become sources of cash with which to finance further growth.

The problem with this strategy is that it is unavailable to many companies and unattractive to others. In many countries throughout the world, equity markets are poorly developed or nonexistent. To sell equity in these countries, companies must go through the laborious and expensive task of seeking out investors one by one to buy the new shares. This is a difficult undertaking because without active stock market trading of the shares, new investors will be minority owners of illiquid securities. In effect, they will be along for the ride, unable to steer the corporate ship and without a graceful way to bail out. Consequently, those investors interested in buying the new shares will be limited largely to family and friends of existing owners.

Even in countries with well-developed stock markets, such as the United States and Britain, many companies find it very difficult to raise new equity. This is particularly true of smaller concerns that, unless they have a glamorous product, find it difficult to attract venture capital money or to secure the services of an investment banker to help them sell the shares to other investors. Without such help, the firms might just as well be in a country without developed markets, for a lack of trading in the stock will again restrict potential buyers largely to family and friends.

Dell Grows Up

Even well-known, successful companies such as tech giant Dell Technologies, Inc. have experienced life-threatening growing pains. The company's founder, Michael Dell, now admits that in 1993 Dell's growth spurt had come at the expense of a sound financial position. He says the company's cash reserves were down to $20 million at one point. "We could have used that up in a day or two. For a company our size, that was ridiculous. I realized we had to change the priorities."

Had Dell's priorities remained "growth, growth, growth," it might not be around today. Michael Dell founded Dell Computer before he was 20 years old. After several years of prodigious growth and with his company at the financial precipice, he lacked the expertise to manage the growth. Fortunately, he had the sense to hire more seasoned managers who could calm security analysts and steer Dell in a more conservative direction. Those managers urged Dell to focus on earnings and liquidity rather than sales growth. Slowing growth in 1994 cost the company market share, but it also helped convert a loss a year earlier into a $106.6 million profit. The company also instituted formal planning and budgeting processes. Today, Dell is one of the world's largest computer manufacturers. As of 2017, Dell maintains a healthy balance sheet with cash balances of over $17 billion, about 15 percent of total assets.

Finally, even many companies that are able to raise new equity prefer not to do so. This is evidenced in Table 4.2, which shows the sources of capital to U.S. nonfinancial corporations over the past decade. Observe that internal sources, depreciation and retained profits, were by far the most important sources of corporate capital, accounting for two-thirds of the total. At the other extreme, *new equity has been not a source of capital at all but a use,* meaning American corporations, on average, retired more stock than they issued over this period.

TABLE 4.2   Sources of Capital to U.S. Nonfinancial Corporations, 2007–2016

Source: Federal Reserve System, *Financial Accounts of the United States.* From data at **federalreserve.gov/releases/z1/current/data.htm.**

Internal		
Retained profits	23.4%	
Depreciation	45.5%	
Subtotal	68.9%	
External		
Increased liabilities	47.5%	
New equity issues	−16.3%	
Subtotal	31.1%	
Total		100.0%

We will return to the puzzling question of why companies do not issue more new equity at the end of the chapter. For now, let us provisionally accept that many companies cannot or will not sell new stock, and consider other strategies for managing unsustainably rapid growth.

Increase Leverage

If selling new equity is not a solution to a company's sustainable growth problems, two other financial remedies are possible. One is to cut the dividend payout ratio, and the other is to increase financial leverage. A cut in the payout ratio raises sustainable growth by increasing the proportion of earnings retained in the business, while increasing the leverage ratio raises the amount of debt the company can add for each dollar of retained profits.

I like to think of increasing leverage as the "default" option, in two senses of the word. From a computer programming perspective, an increase in leverage will be what occurs by default when management does not plan ahead. Over time, the company will find there is too little cash to pay creditors in a timely fashion, and accounts payable will rise by default. Increasing leverage is also the default option in the financial sense that creditors will eventually balk at rising debt levels and force the company into default—step one on the path to bankruptcy.

We will have considerably more to say about financial leverage in the next two chapters. It should be apparent already, however, that there is an upper limit to a company's use of debt financing. And part of the growth management challenge is to identify an appropriate degree of financial leverage for a company and to ensure this ceiling is not broached.

Reduce the Payout Ratio

Just as there is an upper limit to leverage, there is a lower limit of zero to a company's dividend payments, and most companies are already at this limit. Over half of the over six thousand public companies for which data are available on Standard & Poor's Compustat data service paid no dividends at all in 2016.[3] In general, owners' interest in dividend payments varies inversely

---

[3] This does not imply that dividends are in any way insignificant or unimportant in the U.S. economy. For in the same year that less than half of companies were paying dividends, over 80 percent of the nation's largest firms, represented by members of the S&P 500 Index, were distributing over $435 billion in cash to shareholders, a sum equal to almost one-half of earnings. Add in another $531 billion spent on share repurchases, and the total distributed to shareholders exceeds net income in the year. The proper inference is that small, young firms tend not to pay dividends, while large, mature ones do, and that there are many more small, young firms in our economy than large, mature ones.

with their perceptions of the company's investment opportunities. If owners believe the retained profits can be put to productive use earning attractive rates of return, they will happily forgo current dividends in favor of higher future ones. (There have been few complaints among Facebook's shareholders about the lack of dividends.) On the other hand, if company investment opportunities do not promise attractive returns, a dividend cut will anger shareholders, prompting a decline in stock price. An additional concern for closely held companies is the effect of dividend changes on owners' income and on their tax obligations.

Profitable Pruning

Beyond modifications in financial policy, a company can make several operating adjustments to manage rapid growth. One is called "profitable pruning." In past times, some financial experts emphasized the merits of product diversification. The idea was that companies could reduce risk by combining the income streams of businesses in different product markets. The thought was that as long as these income streams were not affected in exactly the same way by economic events, the variability inherent in each stream would "average out" when combined with others. We now recognize two problems with this conglomerate diversification strategy. First, although it may reduce the risks seen by management, it does nothing for the shareholders. If shareholders want diversification, they can get it on their own by just purchasing shares of different independent companies. Second, because most companies have limited resources, and a limited ability to manage disparate activities, they cannot be important competitors in a large number of product markets at the same time. Instead, they are apt to be followers in many markets, unable to compete effectively with the dominant firms. An apparent exception to this rule presently is Amazon, which appears to conquer one disparate market after another—from online retailing, to cloud computing, to smart speakers—with apparent ease.

Profitable pruning is the opposite of conglomerate merger. This strategy recognizes that when a typical company spreads its resources across too many products, it may be unable to compete effectively in any. Better to sell off marginal operations and plow the money back into remaining businesses.

Profitable pruning reduces sustainable growth problems in two ways: It generates cash directly through the sale of marginal businesses, and it reduces actual sales growth by eliminating some of the sources of the growth.

The tactic is also possible for a single-product company. Here the idea is to prune out slow-paying customers or slow-turning inventory. This lessens sustainable growth problems in three ways: It frees up cash, which can be used to support new growth; it increases asset turnover; and it reduces sales. Sales decline because tightening credit terms and reducing inventory selection drive away some customers.

Outsourcing

Outsourcing involves the choice of whether to perform an activity in-house or purchase it from an outside vendor. A company can increase its sustainable growth rate by outsourcing more and doing less in-house. When a company outsources, it releases assets that would otherwise be tied up in performing the activity, and it increases its asset turnover. Both results diminish growth problems. An extreme example of this strategy is a franchisor that sources out virtually all of the company's capital-intensive activities to franchisees and, as a result, has very little investment. More recent examples include ride-sharing services, like Lyft and Uber, that outsource driving and vehicle ownership to independent contractors. Indeed, outsourcing is central to much of the new sharing economy.

The key to effective outsourcing is to determine where the company's unique abilities—or, as consultants would put it, "core competencies"—lie. If certain activities can be performed by others without jeopardizing the firm's core competencies, these activities are candidates for outsourcing.

Pricing

An obvious inverse relationship exists between price and volume. When sales growth is too high relative to a company's financing capabilities, it may be necessary to raise prices to reduce growth. If higher prices increase the profit margin, the price increase will also raise the sustainable growth rate.

In effect, the recommendation here is to make growth itself a decision variable. If rapid growth is a problem, attack the problem directly by cutting growth. And while closing early on alternate Wednesdays or turning away every 10th customer might get the job done, the most effective way to cut growth is usually to raise prices.

Is Merger the Answer?

When all else fails, it may be necessary to look for a partner with deep pockets. Two types of companies are capable of supplying the needed cash. One is a mature company, known in the trade as a "cash cow," looking for profitable investments for its excess cash flow. The other is a conservatively financed company that would bring liquidity and borrowing capacity to the marriage. Acquiring another company or being acquired is a drastic solution to growth problems, but it is better to make the move when a company is still financially strong than to wait until excessive growth forces the issue.

Too Little Growth

Slow-growth companies—those whose sustainable growth rate exceeds actual growth—have growth management problems too, but of a different kind. Rather than struggling continually for fresh cash to stoke the fires of growth, slow-growth companies face the dilemma of what to do with profits in excess of company needs. This might appear to be a trivial or even enviable problem, but to many enterprises it is a very real and occasionally frightening one.

To get a closer look at the difficulties insufficient growth creates, let's look again at Hasbro Inc., the company featured in earlier chapters. Table 4.3 presents a five-year sustainable growth analysis of Hasbro. (Hasbro's financial statements for 2015 and 2016 appear in Tables 1.2 and 1.3 in Chapter 1; other relevant ratios are in Table 2.2 in Chapter 2.) It shows that Hasbro's sustainable growth rate in sales has exceeded its actual growth rate every year for the last five years and by more than a three-to-one ratio on average. Moreover, a rising profit margin and retention ratio have heightened the challenge by increasing the firm's sustainable growth rate over the period. What did management do with all the excess cash generated? They returned it to owners in the form of cash dividends and share repurchases. In total, Hasbro distributed $1,073 million in dividends and $898 million in share repurchases over the period, totaling 97 percent of earnings. Fortunately, by 2016, rising sales growth has brought the gap between sustainable and actual sales down to the lowest level in five years, although excess cash remains a nagging problem going forward.

Figure 4.4 says the same thing graphically. Hasbro has raised its balanced growth line over the period, due primarily to a rising retention ratio, and it

TABLE 4.3 A Sustainable Growth Analysis of Hasbro Inc., 2012–2016*

Source: Data from Hasbro 2012–2016 annual reports.

	2012	2013	2014	2015	2016
Required ratios:					
Profit margin, P (%)	8.2	7.0	9.7	10.2	11.0
Retention ratio, R (%)	32.9	45.4	47.9	50.0	54.9
Asset turnover, A (times)	0.95	0.93	0.94	0.94	0.99
Financial leverage, T (times)	3.05	2.92	2.69	3.22	3.06
Hasbro's sustainable growth rate, g^* (%)	7.8	8.6	11.8	15.4	18.2
Hasbro's actual growth rate in sales, g (%)	(4.6)	(0.2)	4.8	4.0	12.9

*Totals may not add due to rounding.

FIGURE 4.4   Hasbro's Sustainable Growth Challenges, 2012–2016

Source: Data from Hasbro 2012–2016 annual reports

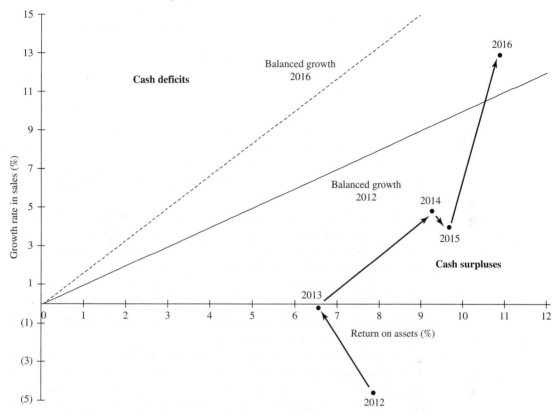

has consistently operated in the cash surplus portion of the graph. Improving sales growth throughout the period has improved the situation markedly, but a gap remains.

What to Do When Sustainable Growth Exceeds Actual Growth

The first step in addressing problems of inadequate growth is to decide whether the situation is temporary or longer term. If temporary, management can simply continue accumulating resources in anticipation of future growth.

When the difficulty is longer term, the issue becomes whether the lack of growth is industrywide—the natural result of a maturing market—or unique to the company. If the latter, the reasons for inadequate growth and possible sources of new growth are to be found within the firm. In this event, management must look carefully at its own performance to identify and remove the internal constraints on company growth, a potentially painful process involving organizational changes as well as increased developmental expenses. The nerve-wracking aspect of such soul searching is that the strategies initiated to enhance growth must bear fruit within a few years or management will be forced to seek other, often more drastic solutions.

When a company is unable to generate sufficient growth from within, it has three options: ignore the problem, return the money to shareholders, or buy growth. Let us briefly consider each alternative.

Ignore the Problem

This response takes one of two forms: Management can continue investing in its core businesses despite the lack of attractive returns, or it can simply sit on an ever-larger pile of idle resources. The difficulty with either response is that, like dogs to a fire hydrant, underutilized resources attract unwelcome attention. Poorly utilized resources depress a company's stock price and make the firm a feasible and attractive target for a raider. If a raider has done her sums correctly, she can redeploy the target firm's resources more productively and earn a substantial profit in the process. And among the first resources to be redeployed in such a raid are usually incumbent managers, who find themselves suddenly reading help-wanted ads. Even if a hostile raid does not occur, boards of directors and activist shareholders are increasingly likely to give the boot to underperforming managements.

Another way to characterize the relationship between investment and growth is to distinguish between good growth and its evil twin, bad growth. Good growth occurs when the company invests in activities offering returns in excess of cost, including the cost of capital employed. Good growth benefits owners and is rewarded by a higher stock price and reduced threat of takeover. Bad growth involves investing in activities with returns at or below cost. Because ill-advised activities are always readily available, a bad growth strategy is easy to execute. If all else fails, the company can always overpay to purchase the sales and assets of another business. Such a strategy disposes of excess cash and makes the firm larger, but these cosmetic results only mask the fact that a bad growth strategy wastes valuable resources—and stock markets are increasingly adept at distinguishing between good and bad growth, and punishing the latter. The moral to the story, then, is that it is not enough for slow-growth companies to grow more rapidly; they must do so in a way that benefits shareholders. All other forms of growth are a snare and a delusion. (We will say more about value-creating investment activities in Chapters 7 and 8.)

Return the Money to Shareholders

The most direct solution to the problem of idle resources is to simply return the money to owners by increasing dividends or repurchasing shares. However, while this solution is increasingly common, it is still not the strategy of choice among some executives. The chief reason is that these executives appear to have a bias in favor of growth, even when the growth creates little or no value for shareholders. At the personal level, these executives resist paying large dividends or repurchasing shares because the practices hint of failure. Shareholders entrust managers with the task of profitably investing their capital, and for the company to return the money suggests an inability to perform a basic managerial function. A cruder way to say the same thing is that dividends and share repurchases reduce the size of management's empire, an act counter to basic human nature.

Gordon Donaldson and others also document a bias toward growth at the organizational level.[4] In a carefully researched review and synthesis of the decision-making behavior of senior executives in a dozen large companies, Donaldson noted that executives commonly opt for growth, even uneconomic growth, out of concern for the long-run viability of their organizations. As senior managers see it, size offers some protection against the vagaries of the marketplace. Moreover, growth contributes significantly to company morale by creating stimulating career opportunities for employees throughout the organization, and when growth slackens, the enterprise risks losing its best people.

Buy Growth

The third way to eliminate slow-growth problems is to buy growth. Motivated by pride in their ability as managers, concern for retaining key employees, and fear of raiders, managers often respond to excess cash flow by attempting to diversify into other businesses. Management systematically searches for worthwhile growth opportunities in other, more vibrant industries. And because time is a factor, this usually involves acquiring existing businesses rather than starting new ones from scratch.

The proper design and implementation of a corporate acquisition program is a challenging task that need not detain us here. Two points, however, are worth noting. First, in many important respects, the growth management problems of mature or declining companies are just the mirror image of those faced by rapidly growing firms. Slow-growth businesses are generally seeking productive uses for their excess cash, while rapidly growing ones are in search of additional cash to finance their unsustainably rapid growth. It is natural, therefore, that high- and low-growth companies frequently solve their respective growth management problems by merging so that the excess cash generated by one organization can finance the rapid growth of the other. Second, accumulating evidence increasingly suggests that, from the shareholders' perspective, buying

---

[4] Donaldson, *Managing Corporate Wealth.*

growth is distinctly inferior to returning the money to owners. More often than not, the superior growth prospects of potential acquisitions are fully reflected in the target's stock price, so that after paying a substantial premium to acquire another firm, the buyer is left with a mediocre investment or worse. The conflict between managers and owners in this regard is a topic of Chapter 9.

Sustainable Growth and Pro Forma Forecasts

It is important to keep the material presented here in perspective. I find that comparison of a company's actual and sustainable growth rates reveals a great deal about the principal financial concerns confronting senior management. When actual growth exceeds sustainable growth, management's focus will be on getting the cash to fund expansion; conversely, when actual growth falls below sustainable growth, the financial agenda will swing 180 degrees to one of productively spending the excess cash flow. The sustainable growth equation also describes the way many top executives view their jobs: Avoid external equity financing and work to balance operating strategies, growth targets, and financial policies so that the disparity between actual and sustainable growth is manageable. Finally, for nonfinancial types, the sustainable growth equation is a useful way to highlight the tie between a company's growth rate and its financial resources.

The sustainable growth equation, however, is essentially just a simplification of pro forma statements. If you really want to study a company's growth management challenges in detail, therefore, I recommend you take the time to construct pro forma financial statements. The sustainable growth equation may be great for looking at the forest but is considerably less helpful when studying individual trees.

New Equity Financing

Earlier in the chapter I noted that a fundamental assumption of sustainable growth analysis is that the company cannot or will not issue new equity. Consistent with this assumption, I also noted in Table 4.2 that over the past decade new equity has been a use of cash to American companies, not a source, meaning that businesses have retired more stock than they have issued. It is time now to explore this phenomenon in more detail with particular emphasis on explaining why companies are so reticent to sell new stock.

Figure 4.5 shows the annual value of new equity issues, net of repurchases, by nonfinancial corporations in the United States from 1980 through 2016. Net new equity issues grew erratically to about $28 billion in 1983, then plunged sharply, and have essentially been negative ever since. The figure reached an all-time low of minus $706 billion in 2007 when companies took

FIGURE 4.5   Net New Equity Issues 1980–2016

Source: Federal Reserve System, *Financial Accounts of the United States,* Table F.223 nonfinancial corporate business, **federalreserve.gov/releases/z1/current/data.htm.**

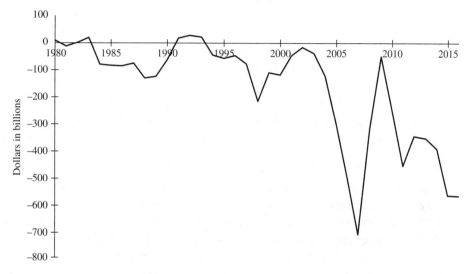

advantage of healthy internal cash flows and low borrowing rates to repurchase shares aggressively. The repurchase binge ended abruptly the following year when the sharp recession cut internal cash flows, but has increased since.

Reductions in common stock outstanding occur in two ways: when a company repurchases its own stock or when a company acquires the stock of another firm for cash or debt. The best available evidence suggests that the sharp reduction in equity outstanding in recent decades was initially triggered by a change in regulations accommodating repurchases and the hostile takeover battles that swept the economy in the last half of the 1980s.

In more recent years, the reduction in U.S. equity is attributable to the growing popularity of share repurchase as a way to distribute cash to shareholders and to manage reported earnings per share. If security analysts are projecting a 15 percent growth in EPS, but management can only deliver 10, one way to bridge the gap is to repurchase 5 percent of the shares outstanding. The same logic applies when the goal is to reach EPS-based performance targets or to offset the dilution in shares created by the exercise of employee stock options. In each instance, it can be easier just to tell a broker to buy a few thousand shares than to create the organic growth necessary to produce desired results.

A second explanation for the popularity of share repurchase points to a problem with dividends as a means of distributing cash. Many investors view dividends as an important signal of managements' beliefs about the future, buying when dividends increase and selling when they fall. In response, companies typically follow a conservative policy of setting dividends at a modest sustainable level and increasing them only when the addition can be maintained over time. Dividend cuts are to be avoided if at all possible. Surveys suggest that many executives are even prepared to cut growth when it threatens the firm's ability to pay dividends or to meet analyst's earnings expectations.[5]

Because share repurchase carries no such informational baggage, companies view it as the more flexible, less disruptive means of distributing cash. Better to repurchase shares than to get locked into higher dividend payments for an extended period. Such flexibility also explains why share repurchase does not appear in the sustainable growth expression. As a discretionary expenditure, share repurchase need never constrain a company's sustainable growth rate, quite unlike cash dividends.

These data suggesting that new equity capital is not a source of financing to American business are consistent with evidence showing that, in an average year, only about 5 percent of publicly traded companies in the United States sell additional common stock. This means that a typical publicly traded company raises new equity capital in public markets only once every 20 years.[6]

Recalling the cautionary tale of the statistician who calculated that, on average, humans have only one testicle, we need to bear in mind that the equity figures presented are the net result of new issues and retirements. Figure 4.6 shows the *gross* proceeds from new common stock sales in the United States from 1980 to 2016. The average over the period was $71.2 billion, and the high in 2000 was $295.4 billion. To put these numbers in perspective, gross proceeds from new stock sales by non-financial corporations over the past decade equaled 3.0 percent of total sources and 10.0 percent of external sources.

Figure 4.6 also shows the money raised from initial public offerings of common stock (IPOs) from 1980 through 2016. Observe that the aggregate amount of money raised is comparatively modest, amounting to about one-third of gross new equity proceeds over the period. In 2000, the peak year for IPOs, total money raised equaled only 5 percent of total corporate external sources of capital.

I see these graphs as a testament to the dynamism of the American economy in which many firms are retiring equity at the same time others are

---

[5] Alon Brav, John R. Graham, Campbell R. Harvey, and Ron Michaely, "Payout Policy in the 21st Century," *Journal of Financial Economics,* September 2005, pp. 483–527.

[6] Aydoğan Altı and Johan Sulaeman, "When Do High Stock Returns Trigger Equity Issues?" *Journal of Financial Economics,* January 2012, pp. 61–87. Although public issues of equity are infrequent, firms also add new equity to their balance sheet in other ways, such as through private placements or the exercise of employee stock options. Typically, the amounts so raised are modest. See Eugene Fama and Kenneth French, "Financing Decisions: Who Issues Stock?" *Journal of Financial Economics,* June 2005, pp. 549–582.

FIGURE 4.6   **Gross New Stock Issues by Nonfinancial Corporations and Initial Public Offerings, 1980–2016**

Sources: U.S. Federal Reserve, Data Sources Webpage, Table 1.46 "New Security Issues U.S. Corporations," **Federalreserve.gov/publications/bulletin/htm;** Jay Ritter, "Initial Public Offerings Updated Statistics," Tables 8. **bear.warrington.ufl.edu/ritter.**

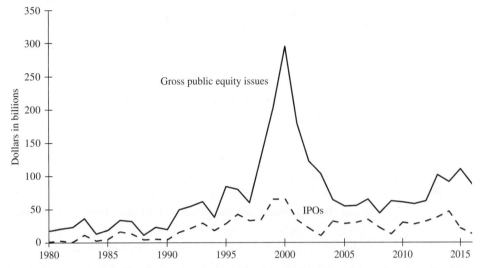

Note: Prior to 1995, issues are total corporate issues less those by real estate and financial corporations; afterward, they are issues by nonfinancial corporations. New equity includes preferred stock. IPOs exclude overallotment options but include the international tranche, if any.

selling new shares. On balance, the appropriate conclusion is that while the stock market is not an important source of capital to corporate America in the aggregate, it is critical to some companies. Companies making extensive use of the new equity market tend to be what brokers call "story paper," potentially high-growth enterprises with a particular product or concept that brokers can hype to receptive investors (the words high-tech and biotech come most readily to mind).

Why Don't U.S. Corporations Issue More Equity?

Here are several reasons. We will consider others in Chapter 6 when we review financing decisions in more detail.

- Companies in the aggregate simply have not needed new equity. Retained profits and new borrowing have been sufficient.

- Equity is expensive to issue. Issue costs commonly run in the neighborhood of 5 to 10 percent of the amount raised, and the percentage on small issues is even higher. These figures are at least twice as high as the issue costs for a comparable-size debt issue. (On the other hand, the equity can be outstanding forever, so its effective annualized cost is less onerous.)

- Many managers, especially U.S. managers, have a fixation with earnings per share (EPS). They translate a complicated world into the simple notion that whatever increases EPS must be good and whatever reduces EPS must be bad. In this view, a new equity issue is bad because, at least initially, the number of shares outstanding rises but earnings do not. EPS is said to be *diluted.* Later, as the company makes productive use of the money raised, earnings should increase, but in the meantime EPS suffers. Moreover, as we will see in Chapter 6, EPS is almost always higher when debt financing is used in favor of equity.

- There is also the "market doesn't appreciate us" syndrome. When a company's stock is selling for $10 a share, management tends to think the price will be a little higher in the future as soon as the current strategy begins to bear fruit. When the price rises to $15, management begins to believe this is just the beginning and the price will be even higher in the near future. Managers' inherent enthusiasm for their company's prospects produces a feeling that the firm's shares are undervalued at whatever price they currently command, and this view creates a bias toward forever postponing new equity issues. A 2001 survey of 371 chief financial officers of U.S. corporations by researchers at Duke University illustrates this syndrome. Despite the fact that the Dow Jones Industrial Average was approaching a new record high at the time of the survey, fewer than one-third of respondents thought the stock market correctly valued their stock; only 3 percent believed their stock was overvalued, and fully 69 percent felt it was undervalued.[7]

- Finally, many managers perceive the stock market to be an unreliable funding source. In addition to uncertainty about the price a company can get for new shares, managers also face the possibility that during some future periods the stock market will not be receptive to new equity issues on any reasonable terms. In finance jargon, the "window" is said to be shut at these times. Naturally, executives are reluctant to develop a growth strategy that depends on such an unreliable source of capital. Rather, the philosophy is to formulate growth plans that can be financed from retained profits and accompanying borrowing and relegate new equity finance to a minor backup role. More on this topic in later chapters.

---

[7] John R. Graham and Campbell R. Harvey, "The Theory and Practice of Corporate Finance: Evidence from the Field," *Journal of Financial Economics,* May–June 2001, pp. 187–243.

SUMMARY

1. A firm's sustainable growth rate
   - Reminds managers that more growth is not always a blessing and that companies can literally "grow broke."
   - Is the maximum rate at which a firm can increase sales without raising new equity or increasing its financial leverage.
   - Assumes company debt increases in proportion to equity.
   - Equals the product of four ratios:
     - Profit margin.
     - Retention ratio.
     - Asset turnover.
     - Financial leverage, defined as assets divided by beginning of period equity.
   - Also equals the firm's retention ratio times return on beginning of period equity.

2. Actual sales growth above a firm's sustainable growth rate
   - Causes one or more of the defining ratios to change.
   - Must be anticipated and planned for.
   - Can be managed by
     - Increasing financial leverage.
     - Reducing the dividend payout ratio.
     - Pruning away marginal activities, products, or customers.
     - Outsourcing some or all of production.
     - Increasing prices.
     - Merging with a "cash cow."
     - Selling new equity.

3. Actual sales growth below a firm's sustainable growth rate
   - Produces excess cash that can enhance a firm's appeal as a takeover target.
   - Forces management to find productive uses for the excess cash, such as
     - Reducing financial leverage.
     - Returning the money to shareholders.
     - Cutting prices.
     - "Buying growth" by acquiring rapidly growing firms in need of cash.

4. New equity financing
   - Has been a *use* of cash to American companies for most of the past 35 years, meaning firms have retired more equity than they have issued.

- Is an important source of cash to a number of smaller, rapidly growing companies with exciting prospects.
- Among other reasons, is seldom used because
  - Companies in the aggregate have not needed the additional cash.
  - Issue costs of equity are high relative to those of debt.
  - New equity tends to reduce earnings per share, something most managers abhor.
  - Managers commonly believe their current share price is unreasonably low and they can get a better price by waiting.
  - Equity is perceived as an unreliable source of financing, not something a prudent manager should count on.

ADDITIONAL RESOURCES

Higgins, Robert C. "Sustainable Growth under Inflation." *Financial Management,* August 1981, pp. 36–40.

A look at the dependence of a company's sustainable growth rate on the inflation rate. The paper concludes that inflation will reduce sustainable growth only if an "inflation illusion" exists, and that such an illusion likely exists.

dividend.com

A website devoted to everything related to dividends: news, data, education, and more.

fred.stlouisfed.org

Lots of good data on interest rates, employment, and so on. A treasure trove of current and historical economic data. Also available as a free app for iOS and Android (search Apple's app store or Google Play for "FRED Economic Data").

pages.stern.nyu.edu/~adamodar

NYU professor Aswath Damodaran's home page. This site contains an exhaustive but no-nonsense selection of financial data sets and spreadsheets, as well as quite a bit of academic and instructional material. Data sets include spreads and interest coverage ratios by firms; historical returns on stocks, bonds, and bills; and return on equity and levers of performance by industry.

PROBLEMS

Answers to odd-numbered problems appear at the end of the book. Answers to even-numbered problems and additional exercises are available in the

Instructor Resources within McGraw-Hill's *Connect* (see the Preface for more information).

1. To what extent do you agree or disagree with the following statement? "An important top-management job is to make certain that the company's actual growth rate and sustainable growth rate are as close together as possible."

2. This chapter distinguishes between good and bad growth. How do they differ, and why does the distinction matter?

3. Are the following statements true or false? Please explain why.
   a. The only way a company can grow at a rate above its current sustainable growth rate is by issuing new stock.
   b. The stock market is a ready source of new capital when a company is incurring heavy losses.
   c. Share repurchases usually increase earnings per share.
   d. Companies often buy back their stock because managers believe the shares are undervalued.
   e. Only rapidly growing firms have growth management problems.
   f. Increasing growth increases stock price.

4. Table 3.1 in the last chapter presents R&E Supplies' financial statements for the period 2014 through 2017, and Table 3.5 presents a pro forma financial forecast for 2018. Use the information in these tables to answer the following questions.
   a. Calculate R&E's sustainable growth rate in each year from 2015 through 2018.
   b. Comparing the company's sustainable growth rate with its actual and projected growth rates in sales over these years, what growth management problems does R&E appear to face in this period?
   c. How did the company cope with these problems? Do you see any difficulties with the way it addressed its growth problems over this period? If so, what are they?
   d. What advice would you offer management regarding managing future growth?

5. Looking at Figure 4.5, describe the trend in net equity financing in the United States during the last 35 years. What does this say about the use of equity financing in U.S. corporations?

6. Looking at Figure 4.6, describe the trend in gross public equity issues and IPOs in the United States during the last 35 years. How do you explain this trend given what we observe in Figure 4.5? Explain.

7. Medifast, Inc. is a producer and marketer of weight-loss meals and other health and weight-loss products. The following are selected financial data for the company for the period 2006–2010.

	2006	2007	2008	2009	2010
Profit margin (%)	6.0	7.0	4.6	5.2	7.2
Retention ratio (%)	99.5	100.0	100.0	100.0	100.0
Asset turnover (X)	1.3	2.0	1.9	2.1	2.6
Financial leverage (X)	1.6	1.7	1.6	1.6	1.6
Growth rate in sales (%)	46.8	84.6	13.1	25.9	57.1

Source: Data from Medifast 2006–2010 annual reports

a. Calculate Medifast's annual sustainable growth rate for the years 2006 through 2010.
b. Comparing the company's sustainable growth rate with its actual growth rate in sales, what growth management challenge did Medifast face over this period?
c. How did the company cope with this challenge?

8. Under Armour, Inc. is an American supplier of sportswear and casual apparel. Following are selected financial data for the company for the period 2009–2013.

	2009	2010	2011	2012	2013
Profit margin (%)	5.5	6.4	6.6	7.0	7.0
Retention ratio (%)	100.0	100.0	100.0	100.0	100.0
Asset turnover (X)	1.6	1.6	1.6	1.6	1.5
Financial leverage (X)	1.7	1.7	1.9	1.8	1.9
Growth rate in sales (%)	18.1	24.2	38.4	24.6	27.1

Source: Data from Under Armour 2009–2013 annual reports

a. Calculate Under Armour's annual sustainable growth rate for the years 2009 through 2013.
b. Did Under Armour face a growth management challenge during this period? Please explain briefly.
c. How did Under Armour cope with this challenge?
d. Calculate Under Armour's sustainable growth rate in 2013 assuming a profit margin of 8.0%. Calculate the sustainable growth rate in 2013 assuming a financial leverage of 2.40 times. Calculate the sustainable growth rate in 2013 assuming both of these changes occur.

9. Jos. A. Bank Clothiers, Inc. is a direct marketer of men's clothing, with over 800 retail stores in 42 states, that was acquired by Men's Wearhouse in 2014. The following are selected financial data for the company for the period 2006–2010.

	2006	2007	2008	2009	2010
Profit margin (%)	7.9	8.3	8.4	9.2	10.0
Retention ratio (%)	100.0	100.0	100.0	100.0	100.0
Asset turnover (X)	1.5	1.4	1.4	1.4	1.3
Financial leverage (X)	2.4	2.1	1.9	1.7	1.7
Growth rate in sales (%)	17.6	10.5	15.2	10.7	11.4

Source: Data from Jos. A. Banks Clothiers 2006–2010 annual reports

  a. Calculate Jos. A. Bank's annual sustainable growth rate from 2006 through 2010.
  b. What growth management challenge did Jos. A. Bank face during these years?
  c. How did Jos. A. Bank deal with this challenge?

10. Stryker Corporation is a leading medical technology company headquartered in Kalamazoo, Michigan, that trades on the New York Stock Exchange. Following are selected financial data for Stryker for the period 2009–2013.

	2009	2010	2011	2012	2013
Profit margin (%)	16.5	17.4	16.2	15.0	11.2
Retention ratio (%)	82.1	81.3	79.3	75.0	60.1
Asset turnover (X)	0.7	0.7	0.7	0.7	0.6
Financial leverage (X)	1.7	1.7	1.7	1.7	1.8
Growth rate in sales (%)	0.1	8.9	13.5	4.2	4.2

Source: Data from Stryker 2009–2013 annual reports.

  a. Calculate Stryker's annual sustainable growth rate from 2009 through 2013.
  b. What growth management challenge did Stryker face during these years?
  c. How did Stryker deal with its growth management challenge?

11. A spreadsheet containing selected financial information for Tournament Sporting Goods is available for download from McGraw-Hill's *Connect* or your course instructor (see the Preface for more information). Using this information, answer the questions appearing in the spreadsheet regarding Tournament's growth management challenges.

12. Chapter 3, Problem 15, part f asks you to construct a five-year financial projection for Aquatic Supplies beginning in 2018. Based on your forecast, or the suggested answer available for download from McGraw-Hill's *Connect* or your course instructor, calculate Aquatic Supplies' sustainable and actual growth rates in these years. What do these numbers suggest to you?

13. A spreadsheet containing completed pro forma financial statements for Ottawa Corporation is available for download from McGraw-Hill's *Connect* or your course instructor (see the Preface for more information). Your task is to use the pro forma financial statements to analyze and propose a solution for Ottawa's growth challenges. Answer the questions shown in the spreadsheet.

PART THREE

Financing Operations

Financial Instruments
and Markets

"Don't tell Mom I'm an investment banker. She still thinks I play piano in a brothel."

Anonymous

A major part of a financial executive's job is to raise money to finance current operations and future growth. In this capacity, the financial manager acts much as a marketing executive. He or she has a product—claims on the company's future cash flow—that must be packaged and sold to yield the highest price to the company. The financial manager's customers are creditors and investors who put money into the business in anticipation of future cash flows. In return, these customers receive a piece of paper such as a stock certificate, a bond, or a loan agreement, that describes the nature of their claim on the firm's future cash flow. When the paper can be bought and sold in financial markets, it is customarily called a *financial security.*

In packaging the product, the financial executive must select or design a financial security that meets the needs of the company and is attractive to potential creditors and investors. To do this effectively requires knowledge of financial instruments, the markets in which they trade, and the merits of each instrument to the issuing company. In this chapter, we consider the first two topics, financial instruments and markets. In the next chapter, we look at a company's choice of the proper financing instrument.

Although corporate financing decisions are usually the responsibility of top executives and their finance staffs, there are several reasons managers at all levels need to understand the logic on which these decisions rest. First, we all make similar financing decisions in our personal lives whenever we borrow money to buy a home, a car, or return to school. Second, as investors, we are often consumers of the financial securities that companies issue, and it is always wise to be an informed consumer. Third, and most important for present purposes, sound financing decisions are central to effective financial management. This is witnessed by the fact that financial leverage is one of the levers of performance by which managers seek to generate competitive returns, and it is a principal determinant of a company's sustainable growth rate. So failure to appreciate the logic driving an enterprise's financing decisions robs managers of a complete understanding of their company and its challenges.

Before beginning, a few words about what this chapter is not. "Financial markets" is the name given to a dynamic, heterogeneous distribution system through which cash-surplus entities provide money to cash-deficit entities. Businesses are by no means the only, or even the most prominent players in these markets. Other active participants include national, state, and local governments and agencies, pension funds, endowments, individuals, commercial banks, insurance companies, and the list goes on and on. This chapter is not a balanced overview of financial markets; rather it is a targeted look at the financing instruments most used by nonfinancial corporations and the means by which they are sold. A further restriction is that we will not consider short-term instruments. When speaking of financial markets, it is common to distinguish between *money markets,* in which securities having a maturity of less than one year trade, and *capital markets,* in which longer-term instruments are bought and sold. Because nonfinancial businesses rely much more on capital markets for financing, we will say little about money markets, even though they are the larger and more liquid of the two. (For a more comprehensive look at financial markets and instruments, see one of the books recommended at the end of this chapter.)

Financial Instruments

Fortunately, lawyers and regulators have not yet taken all of the fun and creativity out of raising money. When selecting a financial instrument for sale in securities markets, a company is *not* significantly constrained by law or regulation. The company is largely free to select or design any instrument, provided only that the instrument appeals to investors and meets the needs of the company. Securities markets in the United States are regulated by the Securities and Exchange Commission (SEC) and, to a lesser extent, by state authorities. SEC regulation can create red tape and delay, but the SEC does not pass judgment on the investment merits of a security. It requires only that investors have access to all information relevant to valuing the security and have adequate opportunity to evaluate it before purchase. This freedom has given rise to such unusual securities as Foote Minerals' $2.20 cumulative, if earned, convertible preferred stock and Sunshine Mining's silver-indexed bonds. In 2016, Credit Suisse issued bonds that pay interest but fall in value if Credit Suisse suffers losses due to rogue trading or cybercrime. My all-time favorite is a 6 percent bond issued by Hungary in 1983 that, in addition to paying interest, included a firm promise of telephone service within three years. The usual wait for a phone at the time was said to run up to 20 years. A close second is a bond proposed by a group of Russian vodka distillers. Known as *Lial,* or "Liter" bonds, they were to pay annual interest of 20 percent in hard currency or 25 percent in vodka. According to one of the promoters, "Vodka has been currency for 1,000 years. We have just made the relationship formal."

But, do not let the variety of securities obscure the underlying logic. When designing a financial instrument, the financial executive works with three variables: investors' claims on future cash flow, their right to participate in company decisions, and their claims on company assets in liquidation. We will now describe the more popular security types in terms of these three variables. In reading the descriptions, bear in mind that the characteristics of a specific financial instrument are determined by the terms of the contract between issuer and buyer, not by law or regulation. So the descriptions that follow should be thought of as indicating general security types rather than exact definitions of specific instruments.

Bonds

Economists like to distinguish between physical assets and financial assets. A physical asset, such as a home, a business, or a painting, is one whose value depends on its physical properties. A financial asset is a piece of paper or, more formally, a security representing a legal claim to future cash payouts. The entity agreeing to make the payouts is the issuer, and the recipient is the investor. It is often useful to draw a further distinction among financial assets depending on whether the claim to future payments is fixed as to dollar amount and timing or residual, meaning the investor receives any cash remaining after all prior fixed claims have been paid. Debt instruments offer fixed claims, while equity, or common stock, offers residual claims. Human ingenuity being what it is, you should not be surprised to learn that some securities, such as convertible preferred stock, are neither fish nor fowl, offering neither purely fixed nor purely residual claims.

Derivatives constitute a third fundamental security type. A derivative security is distinguished by the fact that its claim to future payments depends upon the value of some other underlying asset. For example, an option to purchase IBM stock is a derivative because its value depends on the price of IBM shares. The popularity and importance of derivatives have grown enormously since Fisher Black and Myron Scholes first proposed a rigorous way to value options in 1973. The appendix to this chapter considers derivatives briefly as part of a discussion of financial risk management, and Chapter 8 revisits the topic in the context of evaluating investment opportunities.

A bond, like any other form of indebtedness, is a *fixed-income* security. The holder receives a specified annual interest income and a specified amount at maturity—no more and no less (unless the company goes bankrupt).

The difference between a bond and other forms of indebtedness such as trade credit, bank loans, and private placements is that bonds are sold to the public in small increments, usually $1,000 per bond. After issue, the bonds can be traded by investors on organized security exchanges.

I noted in the last chapter that internal financing, in the form of retained profits and depreciation, has provided about 69 percent of the money used by American business over the past decade. Looking at external financing, aggregate data indicate that over the past two decades corporate bonds have been the largest source, accounting for about 44 percent of the total. Loans and advances of various kinds from banks and others have contributed another 10 percent. Before dismissing bank loans as of only secondary importance, it is important to bear in mind that although they are not a major source of financing in the aggregate, they are important to smaller firms. For example, in 2016, the ratio of bank loans to total liabilities among billion dollar–plus manufacturing firms was only 8 percent, while the comparable number for small manufacturers having assets of $25 million or less was 36 percent.[1]

Three variables characterize a bond: its *par value,* its *coupon rate,* and its *maturity date.* For example, a bond might have a $1,000 par value, a 5 percent coupon rate, and a maturity date of December 31, 2027. The par value is the amount of money the holder will receive on the bond's maturity date. By custom, the par value of bonds issued in the United States is usually $1,000. The coupon rate is the percentage of par value the issuer promises to pay the investor annually as interest income. Our bond will pay $50 per year in interest (5% × $1,000), usually in two semiannual payments of $25 each. On the maturity date, the company will pay the bondholder $1,000 per bond and will cease further interest payments.

On the issue date, companies usually try to set the coupon rate on the new bond equal to the prevailing interest rate on other bonds of similar maturity and quality. This ensures that the bond's initial market price will about equal its par value. After issue, the market price of a bond can differ substantially from its par value as market interest rates and credit risk perceptions change. As we will see in Chapter 7, when interest rates rise, bond prices fall, and vice versa.

Many forms of long-term indebtedness require periodic repayment of principal. This principal repayment is known as a *sinking fund.* Readers who have studied too much accounting will know that technically a sinking fund is a sum of money the company sets aside to meet a future obligation, and this is the way bonds used to work, but no more. Today, a bond sinking fund is a direct payment to creditors that reduces principal. Depending on the indenture agreement,

---

[1] U.S. Federal Reserve, "Financial Accounts of the United States," **federalreserve.gov/ releases/z1.** U.S. Census Bureau, "Quarterly Financial Report for Manufacturing, Mining, Trade, and Selected Service Industries: 2016 Quarter 4," Tables 1.1 and 80.1, **census.gov/econ/qfr.**

When Investing Internationally, What You See Isn't Always What You Get

A 6 percent interest rate on a dollar-denominated bond is not directly comparable to a 3 percent rate on a yen bond or an 8 percent rate on a British sterling bond. To see why, let's calculate the rate of return on $1,000 invested today in a one-year, British sterling bond yielding 8 percent interest. Suppose today's exchange rate is £1 = $1.25 and the exchange rate in one year is £1 = $1.20.

$1,000 will buy £800 today ($1,000/1.25 = £800), and in one year the interest and principal on the sterling bond will total £864 (£800 [1 + 0.08] = £864). Converting this amount back into dollars yields $1,036.80 in one year (£864 × 1.2 = $1,036.80). So the investment's rate of return, measured in dollars, is only 3.68 percent ([$1,036.80 − $1,000]/$1,000 = 3.68%).

Why is the dollar return so low? Because investing in a foreign asset is really two investments: purchase of a foreign-currency asset and speculation on future changes in the dollar value of the foreign currency. Here, the foreign asset yields a healthy 8 percent, but sterling depreciates 4 percent against the dollar ([$1.25 − $1.20]/$1.25), so the combined return is roughly the difference between the two. The exact relationship is

$$(1 + \text{Return}) = (1 + \text{Interest rate})(1 + \text{Change in exchange rate})$$
$$(1 + \text{Return}) = (1 + 8\%)(1 - 4\%)$$
$$\text{Return} = 3.68\%$$

Incidentally, we know that sterling depreciated relative to the dollar over the year because a pound costs less at the end of the year than at the start.

---

there are several ways a firm can meet its sinking-fund obligation. It can repurchase a certain number of bonds in securities markets, or it can retire a certain number of bonds by paying the holders par value. When a company has a choice, it will naturally repurchase bonds if the market price of the bonds is below par value.

I have just described a fixed-interest-rate bond. An alternative more common to loans than bonds is floating-rate debt in which the interest rate is tied to a short-term interest rate such as the 90-day U.S. Treasury bill rate. If a floating-rate instrument promises to pay, say, one percentage point over the 90-day bill rate, the interest to be paid on each payment date will be calculated anew by adding one percentage point to the then prevailing 90-day bill rate. Because the interest paid on a floating-rate instrument varies in harmony with changing interest rates over time, the instrument's market value always approximates its principal value.

Call Provisions

Some corporate bonds contain a clause giving the issuing company the option to retire the bonds prior to maturity. Frequently, the call price for early retirement will be at a modest premium above par; or the bond may have a *delayed call,* meaning the issuer may not call the bond until it has been outstanding for a specified period, usually 5 or 10 years.

Companies want call options on bonds for two obvious reasons. One is that if interest rates fall, the company can pay off its existing bonds and issue new ones at a lower interest cost. The other is that the call option gives a company flexibility. If changing market conditions or changing company strategy requires it, the call option enables management to rearrange its capital structure.

At first glance, it may appear that a call option works entirely to the company's advantage. If interest rates fall, the company calls the bonds and refinances at a lower rate. But if rates rise, investors have no similar option. They must either accept the low interest income or sell their bonds at a loss. From the company's perspective, it looks like "heads I win, tails you lose," but investors are not so naive. As a general rule, the more attractive the call provisions to the issuer, the higher the coupon rate on the bond.

Covenants

Under normal circumstances, no creditors, including bondholders, have a direct voice in company decisions. Bondholders and other long-term creditors exercise control through *protective covenants* specified in the indenture agreement. Typical covenants include a lower limit on the company's current ratio, an upper limit on its debt-to-equity ratio, and perhaps a requirement that the company not acquire or sell major assets without prior creditor approval. Creditors have no say in company operations as long as the firm is current in its interest and sinking-fund payments and no covenants have been violated. If the company falls behind in its payments or violates a covenant, it is in *default,* and creditors gain considerable power. At the extreme, creditors can force the company into bankruptcy and possible liquidation. In liquidation, the courts supervise the sale of company assets and distribution of the proceeds to the various claimants.

Rights in Liquidation

The distribution of liquidation proceeds in bankruptcy is determined by what is known as the *rights of absolute priority.* First in line are, naturally, the government for past-due taxes. Among investors, the first to be repaid are *senior* creditors, then *general* creditors, and finally *subordinated* creditors. Preferred stockholders and common shareholders bring up the rear. Because each class of claimant is paid off in full before the next class receives anything, equity shareholders frequently get nothing in liquidation.

Secured Creditors

A *secured credit* is a form of senior credit in which the loan is collateralized by a specific company asset or group of assets. In liquidation, proceeds from the sale of this asset go only to the secured creditor. If the cash generated from the sale exceeds the debt to the secured creditor, the excess cash goes into the pot for distribution to general creditors. If the cash is insufficient, the lender becomes a general creditor for the remaining liability. Mortgages are a common example of a secured credit in which the asset securing the loan is land or buildings.

Bonds as an Investment

For many years, investors thought bonds to be very safe investments. After all, interest income is specified and the chances of bankruptcy are remote. However, this reasoning ignored the pernicious effects of inflation on fixed-income securities. For although the *nominal* return on fixed-interest-rate bonds is specified, the value of the resulting interest and principal payments to the investor is much less when inflation is high. This implies that investors need to concern themselves with the *real,* or inflation-adjusted, return on an asset, not the nominal return. And according to this yardstick, even default-free bonds can be quite risky in periods of high and volatile inflation.

Table 5.1 presents the nominal rate of return U.S. investors earned on selected securities over the period 1928 to 2016. Looking at long-term corporate bonds, you can see that had an investor purchased a representative portfolio of corporate bonds at the beginning of 1928 and held them through 2016 (while reinvesting all interest income and principal payments in similar bonds), the annual return would have been 5.7 percent over the entire 89-year period. By comparison, the annual return on an investment in long-term U.S. government bonds would have been 5.2 percent over the same period. We can attribute the 0.5 percent difference to a "risk premium." This is the added return investors in corporate bonds earn over government bonds as compensation for the risk that the corporations will default on their liabilities or call their bonds prior to maturity.

TABLE 5.1   **Rate of Return on Selected Securities, 1928–2016**

Sources: Professor Aswath Damodaran's website: **pages.stern.nyu.edu/~adamodar;** Bureau of Labor Statistics, "CPI Detailed Report," Table 24. Return on long-term corporate bonds estimated by authors.

Security	Return*
Common stocks	11.4%
Long-term corporate bonds	5.7%
Long-term government bonds	5.2%
Short-term government bills	3.5%
Consumer price index	3.1%

*Arithmetic mean annual returns ignoring taxes and assuming reinvestment of all interest and dividend income.

The bottom entry in Table 5.1 contains the annual percentage change in the consumer price index over the period. Subtracting the annual inflation rate from 1928 through 2016 of 3.1 percent from these nominal returns yields real, or inflation-adjusted, returns of 2.6 percent for corporates and 2.1 percent for governments.[2] Long-term bonds did little more than keep pace with inflation over this period.

Bond Ratings

Several companies analyze the investment qualities of many publicly traded bonds and publish their findings in the form of bond ratings. A bond rating is a letter grade, such as AA, assigned to an issue that reflects the analyst's appraisal of the bond's default risk. Analysts determine these ratings using many of the techniques discussed in earlier chapters, including analysis of the company's balance sheet debt ratios and its coverage ratios relative to competitors. Table 5.2 summarizes the debt-rating definitions of Standard & Poor's (S&P), a major rating firm. Table 6.5 in the next chapter shows the differences in key performance ratios by rating category.

TABLE 5.2 S&P Debt-Rating Definitions

Source: S&P Global Long-Term Issue Credit Ratings, **standardandpoors.com.**

The credit ratings issued by S&P are based on their analysis of three considerations: the capacity and willingness of the debtor to repay the debt, the specific provisions of the debt obligation, and the seniority position of creditors in the event of bankruptcy. (The ratings issued by the other major credit rating agencies, Moody's and Fitch, follow a similar pattern.)

Rating	Summarized Definition
AAA	Extremely strong capacity to meet obligations
AA	Very strong capacity to meet obligations
A	Strong capacity to meet obligations
BBB	Adequate capacity; susceptible to adverse conditions
BB	Adequate capacity; major exposure to adverse conditions
B	Adequate capacity; nonpayment likely in adverse conditions
CCC	Currently vulnerable to nonpayment
CC	Currently highly vulnerable to nonpayment
C	Currently highly vulnerable to nonpayment; lower seniority
D	In default

Plus (+) or minus (−): The ratings from "AA" to "CCC" may be modified by the addition of a plus (+) or minus (−) sign to show relative standing within the major rating categories.

[2] These numbers are approximate. The exact equation is $i_r = (1 + i_n)(1 + p) - 1$, where i_r = real return, i_n = nominal return, and p = inflation rate. Applying this equation, the real returns on corporate and government bonds are 2.5 percent and 2.0 percent, respectively.

Junk Bonds

A company's bond rating is important because it affects the interest rate the company must offer. Moreover, many institutional investors are prohibited from investing in bonds that are rated less than "investment" grade, where investment grade is usually defined as BBB– and above. As a result, there have been periods in the past when companies with lower-rated bonds had great difficulty raising debt in public markets. Below-investment-grade bonds are known variously as *speculative, high-yield,* or simply *junk* bonds.

Until the emergence of a vibrant market for speculative-grade bonds in the 1980s, public debt markets were largely the preserve of huge, blue-chip corporations. Excluded from public bond markets, smaller, less prominent companies in need of debt financing were forced to rely on bank and insurance company loans. Although bond markets are still closed to most smaller businesses, the junk bond market has been a boon to many mid-size and emerging companies, which now find public debt an attractive alternative to traditional bank financing. The market has also been an important financing source to corporate raiders and private equity investors for use in highly levered transactions.

Rating agencies have justly been criticized for their role in fostering the financial crisis of 2008 when their ratings of complex mortgage-based securities proved to be wildly optimistic. They appear to have made two egregious errors. First, based on the review of limited historical evidence in a rapidly changing market, the agencies discounted the possibility that housing prices could fall nationwide. Their models convinced them that any decline in housing prices would be only regional, not national. As Mark Adelson, former senior director at Moody's rating agency, put it later, their method was "like observing 100 years of weather in Antarctica to forecast the weather in Hawaii."[3] Second, the agencies all but ignored the possibility that loan origination standards might deteriorate, assuming instead that the credit quality of the mortgages underpinning the securities to be rated was constant over time. In their minds, it was not appropriate to study individual loan files because their job was to rate the quality of the securities, not the underlying mortgages. In the words of Claire Robinson, a 20-year veteran at Moody's, "We aren't loan officers. Our expertise is as statisticians on an aggregate basis."[4]

Common Stock

Common stock is a *residual income* security. The stockholder has a claim on any income remaining after the payment of all obligations, including interest on debt. If the company prospers, stockholders are the chief beneficiaries; if it falters, they are the chief losers. The amount of money a stockholder receives

[3] Source: Roger Lowenstein, "Triple-A-Failure," *New York Times Magazine,* April 27, 2008.
[4] Ibid.

What Do Bond Ratings Tell Investors About the Chance of Default?

Take a look at the following figures showing bond default rates by rating category and investment horizon. The numbers span the years 1981–2016 and are from Standard & Poor's. Note, for instance, that, on average, only 0.72 percent of AAA-rated bonds defaulted over a 10-year holding period, while the same figure for C-rated bonds of all types was 51.03 percent. Default is clearly a distinct possibility among lower-rated bonds; no wonder they carry higher interest rates.

The fact that default rates consistently rise as bond ratings fall offers convincing evidence that ratings are indeed useful predictors of default. Notice too the sharp break between investment grade and speculative grade bonds. At, say, a five-year investment horizon, the default rate on BBB bonds—the lowest investment-grade rating—is less than 2 percent, while the same figure for BB bonds—the highest speculative rating—is over 7 percent.

Historical Global Average Cumulative Bond Default Rates 1981–2016

Bond Rating	Time Horizon (Years)		
	1	5	10
AAA	0.00%	0.35%	0.72%
AA	0.02%	0.33%	0.77%
A	0.06%	0.53%	1.41%
BBB	0.18%	1.78%	3.76%
BB	0.72%	7.45%	13.33%
B	3.76%	18.32%	25.43%
CCC/C	26.78%	46.42%	51.03%

Source: S&P Global, "2016 Annual Global Corporate Default Study and Rating Transitions".

annually depends on the dividends the company chooses to pay, and the board of directors, which makes this decision quarterly, is under no obligation to pay any dividend at all.

Shareholder Control

At least in theory, stockholders exercise control over company affairs through their ability to elect the board of directors. In the United States, the wide distribution of share ownership and the laws governing election of the board have sometimes combined to reduce this authority. In some companies, ownership of as little as 10 percent of the stock has been sufficient to control the entire board. In many others, there is no dominant shareholder group, and management has been able to control the board even if it owns little or none of the company's shares.

This does not imply that managers in such companies are free to ignore shareholder interests entirely, for they face at least two potential constraints on their actions. One is created by their need to compete in product markets.

If management does not make a product or provide a service efficiently and sell it at a competitive price, the company will lose market share to more aggressive rivals and will eventually be driven from the industry. The actions managers take to compete effectively in product markets are most often consistent with shareholder interests.

Securities markets provide a second check on management discretion. If a company wants to raise debt or equity capital in future years, it must maintain its profitability to attract money from investors. Moreover, if managers ignore shareholder interests, stock price will suffer, and the firm may become the target of a hostile takeover. Even when not facing a takeover, company boards, often prodded by large institutional shareholders, are sometimes quite diligent in monitoring management performance and replacing poor performers. Between 2000 and 2008, an average of 37 percent of chief executive departures each year were forced by their boards, although this number was only 18 percent between 2009 and 2016.[5] We will have more to say about corporate takeovers and the role of the board of directors in Chapter 9.

In some countries, owners have traditionally exercised more direct control over company managements than have their U.S. or UK counterparts. In Germany, for example, banks have often been the controlling shareholders of many businesses, with representation on the board of directors and effective control over the business's access to debt and equity capital. In Japan and South Korea, firms have often been controlled by groups of companies—called *keiretsu* in Japan and *chaebol* in South Korea—that purchase sizable ownership interests in one another as a means of cementing important business relations. However, evidence suggests that these more direct approaches to corporate control are being employed less frequently.

Common Stock as an Investment

Common stockholders receive two types of investment return: dividends and possible share price appreciation. If d_1 is the dividends per share during the year and p_0 and p_1 are the beginning-of-the-year and end-of-the-year stock price, respectively, the *annual income* a stockholder earns is

$$d_1 + p_1 - p_0$$

Dividing by the beginning-of-the-year stock price, the *annual return* is

$$\frac{\text{Annual}}{\text{return}} = \frac{\text{Dividend}}{\text{yield}} + \frac{\text{Percentage change in}}{\text{share price}}$$

$$= \frac{d_1}{p_0} + \frac{p_1 - p_0}{p_0}$$

---

[5] Strategy&, *2016 CEO Success Study.*

Over the 1928–2016 period, equity investors in large-company common stocks received an average dividend yield of 3.7 percent and average capital appreciation of 7.5 percent. Over the past decade, these figures have been 2.1 percent and 6.4 percent, respectively.

Common stocks are an ownership claim against primarily real, or productive, assets. If companies can maintain profit margins during inflation, real, inflation-adjusted profits should be relatively unaffected by inflation. For years, this reasoning led to the belief that common stocks are a hedge against inflation, but this did not prove to be the case during the bout of high inflation during the 1970s. Looking at Table 5.1 again, we see that had an investor purchased a representative portfolio of common stocks at the beginning of 1928 and reinvested all dividends received in the same portfolio, his average annual return in 2016, over the entire 89 years, would have been 11.4 percent. However, from 1973 through 1981, a period when prices rose an average of 9.2 percent a year, the average annual nominal return on common stocks was only 5.2 percent. This implies a negative *real* return of about 4 percent. The comparable figures for corporate bonds over this period were a nominal return of 2.5 percent and a negative real return of about 6.7 percent.

The common stock return of 11.4 percent from 1928 through 2016 compares with a return of 5.2 percent on government bonds over the same period. The difference between the two numbers of 6.2 percent can be thought of as a *risk premium,* the extra return common stockholders earned as compensation for the added risks they bore. Comparing the return on common stocks to the annual percentage change in consumer prices, we see that the *real* return to common stock investors over the period was about 8.3 percent (11.4% − 3.1%).

Figure 5.1 presents much of the same information more dramatically. It shows an investor's wealth at year-end 2016 had she invested $1 in various assets at the beginning of 1928. Common stocks are the clear winners here. By 2016, the original $1 investment in common stock would have grown to

---

Do Dividends Increase Annual Return?

It may appear from the preceding equation that annual return rises when dividends rise. But the world is not so simple. An increase in current dividends means one of two things: The company will have less money to invest, or it will have to raise more money from external sources to make the same investments. Either way, an increase in current dividends reduces the stockholders' claim on future cash flow, which reduces share price appreciation. Depending on which effect dominates, annual returns may or may not increase as dividends rise.

FIGURE 5.1 **If Your Great-Grandmother Had Invested a Dollar in 1928; Nominal Returns on U.S. Assets, 1928–2016**

(Assumed initial investment of $1 at year-end 1927; includes reinvestment income.)

Sources: Professor Aswath Damodaran's website: **pages.stern.nyu.edu/~adamodar;** Bureau of Labor Statistics, CPI Detailed Report, Table 24.

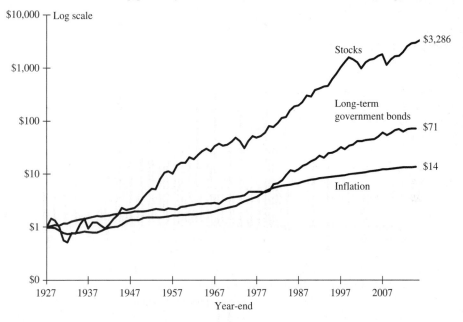

a whopping $3,286. In contrast, $1 invested in long-term government bonds would have been worth only $71 in 2016. Reflecting the pernicious effect of inflation, the corresponding real numbers are $238 for common stock and $5 for government bonds. Common stocks, however, have proven to be a much more volatile investment than bonds, as Figure 5.2 attests.

Preferred Stock

Preferred stock is a hybrid security: like debt in some ways, like equity in others. Like debt, preferred stock is a fixed-income security. It promises the investor an annual fixed dividend equal to the security's coupon rate times its par value. Like equity, the board of directors need not distribute this dividend unless it chooses. Also like equity, preferred dividend payments are *not* a deductible expense for corporate tax purposes. For the same coupon rate, this makes the *after-tax* cost of bonds much less than that of preferred shares. Another similarity with equity is that although preferred stock may have a call option, it frequently has no maturity. The preferred shares are outstanding indefinitely unless the company chooses to call them.

FIGURE 5.2 **Distribution of Annual Return on Stocks and Bonds, 1928–2016**

Source: Professor Aswath Damodaran's website: **pages.stern.nyu.edu/~adamodar.**

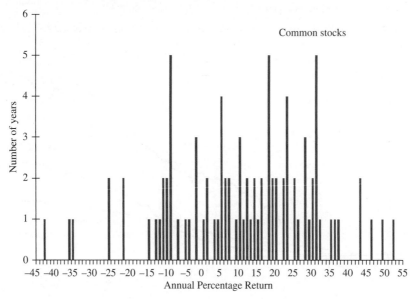

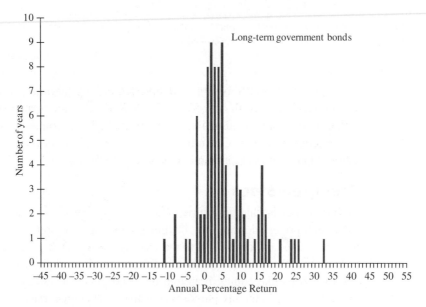

Cumulative Preferred

Company boards of directors have two strong incentives to pay preferred dividends. One is that preferred shareholders have priority over common shareholders with respect to dividend payments. Common shareholders receive no dividends unless preferred holders are paid in full. Second, virtually all pre-ferred stocks are *cumulative.* If a firm passes a preferred dividend, the arrear-age accumulates and must be paid in full before the company can resume common dividend payments.

The control that preferred shareholders have over management deci-sions varies. In some instances, preferred shareholders' approval is routinely required for major decisions; in others, preferred shareholders have no voice in management unless dividend payments are in arrears.

Preferred stock is not a widely used form of financing; at present, only about 16 percent of S&P 500 companies have any preferred stock on their balance sheet. Some managers see preferred stock as *cheap equity.* They observe that preferred stock gives management much of the flexibility regard-ing dividend payments and maturity dates that common equity provides. Yet because preferred shareholders have no right to participate in future growth, they see preferred stock as less expensive than equity. The majority, however, see preferred stock as *debt with a tax disadvantage.* Because few compa-nies would ever omit a preferred dividend payment unless absolutely forced to, most managers place little value on the flexibility of preferred stock. To them, the important fact is that interest payments on bonds are tax deductible, whereas dividend payments on preferred stock are not.

Financial Markets

Having reviewed the basic security types, let us now turn to the markets in which these securities are issued and traded. Of particular interest will be the provocative notion of market efficiency.

Broadly speaking, financial markets are the channels through which inves-tors provide money to companies. Because these channels differ greatly depending on the nature of the company and securities involved, they can best be described by considering the financing needs of three representative firms: a startup, a candidate for an initial public offering, and a multinational. Although these brief vignettes certainly do not exhaust the topic, I hope they offer a use-ful overview of financial markets and their more important participants.

Venture Capital Financing

Janet Holmes has developed a promising new medical device and now wants to start a company to capitalize on her research. Her problem is finding the financing. After a brief inquiry, she learns that conventional financing sources such as bank loans and public stock or bond offerings are out of the question. Her venture is far too risky to qualify for a bank loan and too small to attract public funding. A banker has expressed interest in a small loan collateralized by accounts receivable, machinery, and any personal assets she owns, but this

Internet-Driven Finance

Startup companies hungry for capital are increasingly turning to Internet sites that allow them to reach new groups of potential investors. *Crowdfunding,* a process of pooling together small investments from many investors, is what Goldman Sachs has called "potentially the most disruptive of all of the new models in finance."[a] Prior to 2016, U.S. regulations prohibited the sale of stocks or bonds to small investors, so most crowdfunding to date has instead offered investors rewards such as discounted products. In recent years, rewards-based crowdfunding websites like Kickstarter and Indiegogo together have raised a few billion dollars per year for startup ventures worldwide. That's not much compared to the amounts raised in traditional equity and debt markets, but rewards-based crowdfunding appears to be a viable financing option for certain types of companies—those that have modest funding needs and products with social media buzz. In 2015, for example, Baubax raised over $10 million for a travel jacket with a built-in inflatable neck pillow.

Still, rewards-based crowdfunding can seem unfair at times, such as when Oculus raised $2.4 million for its virtual reality headset in 2012 and then sold out to Facebook two years later for almost 1,000-times that amount, without passing a single penny on to the original donors. So crowdfunding's new frontier is the expansion of online fund-raising to include the sale of stock to small investors, often referred to as *equity crowdfunding* or *regulation crowdfunding.* The 2012 JOBS Act authorized regulation crowdfunding in the U.S., but it was not legal for small investors until the SEC's final rules became effective in 2016. The SEC regulations, concisely stated in a 685-page document, seek to protect investors by limiting their annual investment to a small percentage of their net worth or income, and by restricting companies from raising more than $1 million per year. In addition, all regulation crowdfunding investments are required to flow through online intermediaries called *funding portals* that are registered with the SEC. Within the first year of legalized regulation crowdfunding, over two dozen funding portals registered with the SEC, and a few startups reached the $1 million funding maximum, including Beta Bionics, the maker of a wearable device that automatically manages blood sugar levels in people with diabetes.

A close cousin to crowdfunding, *peer-to-peer (P2P) lending,* consists of online marketplaces that match borrowers and lenders without using a bank as an intermediary, a process which can potentially reduce transaction costs and result in cheaper funding. As with crowdfunding, P2P lending is more useful for smaller companies that lack traditional financing options. P2P marketplaces such as Lending Club and Funding Circle raised a total of $25 billion in loans in 2015, and market observers expect the total to be hundreds of billions of dollars per year by the early 2020s.[b] Although crowdfunding and P2P lending markets are relatively new and still face challenges—including how to protect unwary investors from fraud—online finance could soon reach the point where it accounts for more funding worldwide than traditional venture capital.[c]

[a] Source: Heath Terry, Debra Schwartz, and Tina Sun, "The Future of Finance," *Goldman Sachs Equity Research,* March 13, 2015.

[b] Prableen Bajpai, "The Rise of Peer-to-Peer (P2P) Lending," Nasdaq, September 27, 2016. The totals include other types of loans in addition to business loans.

[c] Chance Barnett, "Trends Show Crowdfunding to Surpass VC in 2016," *Forbes,* June 9, 2015.

will not be nearly enough. Instead, it looks as if Ms. Holmes will have to rely primarily on the traditional four-Fs of new venture financing: founders, family, friends, and fools. Other possible financing sources are strategic investors and venture capitalists, from whom Ms. Holmes might legitimately aspire to raise as much as $15 million in return for a large fraction, possibly controlling interest, of her new company.

Strategic investors are operating companies—frequently potential competitors—that make significant equity investments in startups as a way to gain access to promising new products and technology. Some strategic investors, including Microsoft, Intel, and Cisco Systems, have come to view new venture investing as a means of outsourcing research and development. Rather than develop all new products in-house, they sprinkle money across a number of promising startups, expecting to acquire any that prove successful.

Venture capitalists come in two flavors: wealthy individuals, often referred to as "angel investors," and professional venture capital companies. Venture capital companies are financial investors who make high-risk equity investments in entrepreneurial businesses deemed capable of rapid growth and high investment returns. They purchase a significant fraction of a company and take an active policy role in management. Their goal is to liquidate the investment in five or six years when the company goes public or sells out to another firm. Venture capital firms routinely consider dozens of candidates for every investment made and expect to suffer a number of failures for each investment success. In return, they expect winners to return 5 to 10 times their initial investment. According to the National Venture Capital Association, venture capital firms in the United States invested about $69 billion across some 8,000 deals in 2016. The dollar volume is well below the Internet-fueled record of $105 billion in 2000, but it is higher than most years in the past decade, which has seen average volume of $48 billion per year. Most venture capital investments are in technology firms of one kind or another.

Private Equity

Venture capital companies are prominent examples of a broader class of companies known as "private equity" firms. Although private equity firms invest in a wide variety of opportunities, including new ventures, leveraged buyouts, and distressed businesses, they all share an important trait: They employ a unique organizational form known as a private equity partnership. Instead of the conventional public-company form, private equity investments are structured as limited partnerships with a specified duration, usually of 10 years. Acting as the general partner, the private equity firm raises a pool of money from limited partners, consisting primarily of institutional investors, such as pension funds, college endowments, and insurance companies. As limited partners, these investors enjoy the same limited liability protections afforded conventional shareholders. The private equity sponsor then invests the money raised, actively manages the investments for a period of years, liquidates the portfolio, and returns the proceeds to the limited partners. In return, the private equity firm charges the limited partners handsome fees consisting of an annual management charge equaling about 2 percent of the original investment, plus what is known as *carried interest,* often 20 percent or more of any capital appreciation earned on the portfolio. For example, the carried interest on a $1 billion portfolio subsequently liquidated for $3 billion would be $400 million ($400 million = 20% × [$3 billion − $1 billion]). At any one time, private equity firms may be managing a number of limited partnerships of differing size and years to maturity.

Private equity markets have become increasingly popular over the years for a number of reasons. Management of some companies see private equity financing as an attractive alternative to public equity markets because being privately funded allows them to avoid some of the hassle and expense of being a public company, such as meetings with analysts, increased disclosure requirements, and an intense focus on quarterly earnings. In addition, private equity partnerships appear to address several incentive problems inherent in more conventional investment forms.

- The partnership form minimizes any differences between owners and managers. As knowledgeable, active owners, private equity investors make it clear that management works for them and that their goal is not to meet artificial short-run earnings targets, but to create value for owners.

- The fixed life of the partnership imposes an aggressive, buy-fix-sell attitude on managers, prompting them to take decisive actions.

- As humorist Dave Barry might put it, the limited time horizon also assures investors that they will eventually get their money back, rather than having to stand by idly watching management feed it to chipmunks.

How big is the private equity business? Big. Malcolm Gladwell, in his *New Yorker* story on the rescue of General Motors, notes "In the past twenty-five years, private equity has risen from obscurity to become one of the most powerful forces in the American economy."[6] *The Economist* reports that private equity controls about a quarter of midsized companies and a tenth of large companies in the U.S. The portfolios of companies held by Carlyle and KKR, two of the largest private equity firms, each account for the employment of over 700,000 people. If considered as single employers, the Carlyle and KKR portfolios would be the second- and third-largest employers among U.S. listed companies, behind only Walmart.[7]

[6] Source: Malcolm Gladwell, "Overdrive: Who Really Rescued General Motors?" *The New Yorker,* November 1, 2010.
[7] "The Barbarian Establishment," *The Economist,* October 22, 2016.

Initial Public Offerings

Genomic Devices got its start six years ago when it raised $15 million from three venture capital firms. After two more rounds of venture financing totaling $40 million, Genomic is now a national company with sales of $125 million and an annual growth rate of more than 40 percent. To finance this rapid growth, management estimates the company needs another $25 million equity infusion. At the same time, company founders and venture capital investors are anxious to see some cash from their years of toil. This has led to active consideration of an initial public offering (IPO) of common stock. By creating a public market for the company's shares, an IPO will provide desired liquidity to existing owners, as well as supply necessary funding.

Investment Banking

Genomic Devices' first step toward an IPO will be to conduct what is known in the trade as a "bake-off." This involves reviewing proposals from several investment bankers detailing the mechanics of how they would sell the new shares and what a great job each could do for the company. Investment bankers can be thought of as the grease that keeps financial markets running smoothly. They are finance specialists who assist companies in raising money. Other activities include stock and bond brokerage, investment counseling, merger and acquisition analysis, and corporate consulting. Some banking companies, such as Bank of America, employ thousands of brokers and have offices all over the world. Others, such as Lazard Ltd., specialize in working with companies or trading securities, and consequently are less in the public eye. As to the range of services provided, H. F. Saint said it best in his Wall Street thriller *Memoirs of an Invisible Man:* "[Investment bankers] perform all sorts of interesting services and acts—in fact, any service or act that can be performed in a suit, this being the limitation imposed by their professional ethics."[8]

When a company is about to raise new capital on public markets, an investment banker's responsibilities are not unlike his fees: many and varied. (Capital raising techniques differ from one country to another depending on custom and law. In the interest of space, and with apologies to non-American readers, I will confine my comments here to the American scene.) The winner of the bake-off receives the mantle "managing underwriter" and immediately begins advising the company on detailed design of the security to be issued. Then, the banker helps the company register the issue with the SEC. This usually takes 30 to 90 days and includes detailed public disclosure of information about the company's finances, its officer compensation, plans, and so on—information some managements would prefer to keep confidential. Under the JOBS Act passed in

---

[8] Source: H. F. Saint, *Memoirs of an Invisible Man,* New York: Dell, 1987, 290.

2012, firms with less than $1 billion in annual revenues may now keep some of this information confidential during the IPO process.

While the registration wends its way toward approval, the managing underwriter orchestrates the "road show," during which top company executives market the issue to institutional investors in New York and other financial centers. The managing underwriter also puts together a *selling* and an *underwriting syndicate*. A syndicate is a team of as many as 100 or more investment banking firms that join forces for a brief time to sell new securities. Each member of the selling syndicate accepts responsibility for selling a specified portion of the new securities to investors. Members of the underwriting syndicate in effect act as wholesalers, purchasing all of the securities from the company at a guaranteed price and attempting to sell them to the public at a higher price. The "Rules of Fair Practice" of the National Association of Securities Dealers prohibit underwriters from selling new securities to the public at a price above the original offer price quoted to the company. If necessary, however, the syndicate may sell them at a lower price.

Given the volatility of stock markets and the length of time required to go through registration, it may appear that underwriters bear significant risks when they guarantee the issuer a fixed price for the shares. This is not the way the world works, however. Underwriters do not commit themselves to a firm price on a new security until just hours before the sale, and if all goes as planned, the entire issue will be sold to the public on the first day of offer. It is the company, not the underwriters, that bears the risk that the terms on which the securities can be sold will change during registration.

The life of a syndicate is brief. Syndicates form several months prior to an issue for the purpose of "building the book," or pre-selling the issue, and disband as soon as the securities are sold. Even on unsuccessful issues, the syndicate breaks up several weeks after the issue date, leaving the underwriters to dispose of their unsold shares on their own. I will have more to say about the issue costs and pricing of IPOs in a few paragraphs.

Seasoned Issues

Our third representative firm in need of financing is Trilateral Enterprises, a multinational consumer products company with annual sales of almost $90 billion. Trilateral wants to raise $200 million in new debt and has narrowed the choices down to a "shelf registration," a "private placement," or an international issue executed through the company's Netherlands Antilles subsidiary.

Shelf Registration

A shelf registration allows frequent security issuers to avoid the cumbersome traditional registration process by filing a general-purpose registration, good for two to three years, indicating in broad terms the securities the company may decide to issue. Once the registration is approved by the SEC, and provided it is updated periodically, the company can put the registration on the "shelf," ready for use as desired. Trilateral may be interested in a shelf-registered debt issue, but shelf-registered equity issues are also very popular. Recent figures indicate they account for something like half of all money raised in seasoned equity issues. (A seasoned equity issue, or SEO, refers to an equity issue by a company that is already publicly traded. It contrasts with an initial public offering, undertaken by a private firm.) Moreover, the advent of "universal" shelf registrations, covering both debt and equity issues, allows the issuer to defer the choice of whether to issue debt or equity to a later date.

A shelf registration cuts the time lag between the decision to issue a security and receipt of the proceeds from as long as a few months to as little as 48 hours. Because 48 hours is far too little time for investment bankers to throw a syndicate together, shelf registrations are often "bought deals" in which a single investment house buys the entire issue in the hope of reselling it piecemeal at a profit. Also, because it is just as easy for the issuer to get price quotes from two banks as from one, shelf registrations increase the likelihood of competitive bidding among banks. Research shows that issue costs for shelf-registered equity issues are as much as 15 percent to 20 percent lower than for traditionally registered issues.[10]

Private Placement

If it wishes, Trilateral Enterprises can avoid SEC registration entirely by placing its debt privately with one or more large institutional investors. The SEC does not regulate such private placements on the expectation that large investors, such as insurance companies and pension funds, can fend for themselves without government protection. Prior to the financial crisis of 2008, private placements of debt were relatively popular, making up about half the size of U.S. public corporate debt markets in terms of total funds provided. However, in recent years private placements of debt have provided only about one-tenth the amount of funds generated by public markets. Private placements of equity are also possible, but account for an even smaller fraction of total capital raised.[11]

Private placements are especially attractive to smaller, less well-known firms and to the so-called "information-problematic" companies whose complex organization structures or financing needs make them difficult for individual investors to evaluate. Private placements can also be custom-tailored to specific company needs, arranged quickly, and renegotiated as needed with comparative ease.

[10] Don Autore, Raman Kumar, and Dilip Shome, "The Revival of Shelf-Registered Corporate Equity Offerings," *Journal of Corporate Finance,* February 2008, pp. 32–50.
[11] SIFMA Research Department, *2016 Fact Book.*

A major disadvantage of private placements has traditionally been that as unregistered securities the SEC prohibits their purchase or sale on public financial markets. As a result, issuers have historically found it necessary to offer more favorable terms on private placements than on public issues to compensate for their lack of liquidity. This began to change, at least for less information-problematic issuers, in 1990 when the SEC released Rule 144A permitting the trading of private placements among large institutional investors. Rule 144A is part of a determined effort by the SEC to encourage what are essentially two parallel markets for corporate securities: a closely regulated public market for individual investors and a more loosely monitored private market for institutional investors.

International Markets

Large corporations can raise money on any of three types of markets: *domestic, foreign,* or *international.* A domestic financial market is the market in the company's home country, while foreign markets are the domestic markets of other countries. U.S. financial markets are thus domestic to IBM and General Motors but foreign to Sony Corporation and British Petroleum; Japanese markets are domestic to Sony but foreign to IBM, General Motors, and British Petroleum.

Companies find it attractive to raise money in foreign markets for a variety of reasons. When the domestic market is small or poorly developed, a company may find that only foreign markets are large enough to absorb the contemplated issue. Companies may also want liabilities denominated in the foreign currency instead of their own. For example, when Walt Disney expanded into Japan, it sought yen-denominated liabilities to reduce the foreign exchange risk created by its yen-denominated revenues. Finally, issuers may believe foreign-denominated liabilities will prove cheaper than domestic ones in view of anticipated exchange rate changes.

The third type of market on which companies can raise money, international financial markets, is best viewed as a free market response to the regulatory constraints endemic in domestic and foreign markets. A transaction is said to occur in the international financial market whenever the currency employed is outside the control of the issuing monetary authority. A dollar-denominated loan to an American company in London, a euro-denominated loan to a Japanese company in Singapore, and a British pound bond issue by a Dutch company underwritten in Frankfurt are all examples of international financial market transactions. In each instance, the transaction occurs in a locale that is beyond the direct regulatory reach of the issuing monetary authority. Thus, the U.S. Federal Reserve has trouble regulating banking activities in London even when the activities involve American companies and are denominated in dollars. Similarly, the European Central Bank has difficulty regulating euro activities in Singapore.

International financial markets got their start in London shortly after World War II and were originally limited to dollar transactions in Europe. From this beginning, the markets have grown enormously to encompass most major currencies and trading centers around the globe. Today, international financial markets give companies access to large pools of capital, at very competitive prices, with minimal regulatory or reporting requirements.

Two important reasons international markets have often been able to offer lower-cost financing than domestic markets are the absence of reserve requirements on international bank deposits and the ability to issue bonds in what is known as *bearer form.* In the United States and many other domestic markets, banks must abide by reserve requirements stipulating that they place a portion of each deposit in a special account at the central bank. Because these reserves tie up resources while yielding only modest returns, domestic loans must carry a higher interest rate than international loans to yield the same profit.

The chief appeal of bearer bonds is that they make it easier for investors to avoid paying taxes on interest income. The company issuing a bearer bond never knows the bond's owners and simply makes interest and principal payments to anyone who presents the proper coupon at the appropriate time. In contrast, the issuer of a registered security maintains records of the owner and the payments made. Because bearer securities facilitate tax avoidance, they are illegal in the United States. This is why Trilateral Enterprises anticipates issuing their bonds to non-U.S. residents through its Netherlands Antilles subsidiary. The use of bearer bonds in international markets means international bonds can carry lower coupon rates than comparable domestic bonds and still yield the same after-tax returns.

The ability of international financial markets to draw business away from domestic markets acts as a check on efforts to impose regulations in domestic markets. As long as companies and investors can avoid onerous domestic regulations by simply migrating to international markets, regulators are forced to take into account the degree to which new regulations will hurt domestic markets by driving business overseas. Some wonder if recent legislation intended to strengthen U.S. public markets could drive business overseas. The concern is that the long-term effect of regulatory initiatives, including the Sarbanes–Oxley Act of 2002 and the Dodd–Frank Wall Street Reform and Consumer Protection Act of 2010, will be simply to drive business offshore and on to private markets. Although largely circumstantial, evidence consistent with this concern is accumulating. It includes a shift in IPO activity to non-U.S. markets,[12] apparent increased popularity of going-private transactions among smaller public companies,[13] growth of unregulated private markets, called "shadow markets," on

---

[12] Craig Doidge, George Karolyi, and René Stulz, "The U.S. Left Behind: The Rise of IPO Activity Around the World," *Journal of Financial Economics,* December 2013, pp. 546–573.
[13] Ellen Engel, Rachel Hayes, and Xue Wang, "The Sarbanes-Oxley Act and Firms' Going-Private Decisions," *Journal of Accounting and Economics,* September 2007.

which investors can buy and trade shares of private companies, and a reduction in the number of smaller foreign companies willing to list on U.S. stock exchanges.

Not all regulations are bad, of course. Regulatory oversight of financial markets and the willingness of governments to combat financial panics have greatly stabilized markets and economies for over 70 years. The ongoing question is whether these types of regulations improve public markets or drive business to less-fettered locales. Stay tuned.

Issue Costs

Financial securities impose two kinds of costs on the issuer: annual costs, such as interest expense, and issue costs. We will consider the more important annual costs later. Issue costs are the costs the issuer and its shareholders incur on initial sale. For privately negotiated transactions, the only substantive cost is the fee charged by the investment banker in his or her capacity as agent. On a public issue, there are legal, accounting, and printing fees, plus those paid to the managing underwriter. The managing underwriter states his fee in the form of a *spread.* To illustrate, suppose ABC Corporation is a publicly traded company that wants to sell 10 million new shares of common stock using traditional registration procedures, and its shares presently trade at $20 on the New York Stock Exchange (NYSE). A few hours prior to public sale, the managing underwriter might inform ABC management, "Given the present tone of the markets, we can sell the new shares at an issue price of $19.00 and a spread of $1.50, for a net to the company of $17.50 per share." This means the investment banker intends to *underprice* the issue $1.00 per share ($20 market price less $19 issue price) and is charging a fee of $1.50 per share, or $15 million, for his services. This fee will be split among the managing underwriter and the syndicate members by prior arrangement according to each bank's importance in the syndicates.

To underprice an issue means to offer the new shares at a price below that of existing shares, or in the case of an IPO, below the market price of the shares shortly after the issue is completed. One obvious motivation investment bankers have for underpricing is to make their own job easier. Selling something worth $20 for $19 is a lot easier than selling for $20. But there appears to be more to the practice than this. In any public sale of securities, well-informed insiders are selling paper of uncertain value to less informed outsiders. One way to quell outsiders' natural concern with being victimized by insiders is to consistently underprice new issues. This gives uninformed buyers the expectation the shares will more likely rise than fall after issue. Underpricing is not an out-of-pocket cost to the company, but it is a cost to shareholders. The greater the underpricing, the more securities a company must issue to raise a given amount of money. If the securities are bonds, this translates into higher interest expense, and if they are shares, it translates into a reduced percentage ownership for existing owners.

Empirical studies of issue costs confirm two prominent patterns. First, equity is much more costly than debt. Representative costs of raising capital in public markets, ignoring underpricing, average about 2.2 percent of proceeds for debt, 3.8 percent for convertible bonds, and 7.1 percent for offerings of equity by publicly traded companies. This figure rises to 11.0 percent for IPOs. Second, issue costs for all security types rise rapidly as issue size declines. Issue costs as a percentage of gross proceeds for equity are as low as 3 percent for issues larger than $100 million but rise to more than 20 percent for issues under $500,000. Comparable figures for debt financing are from below 0.9 percent for large issues to more than 10 percent for very small ones.[14]

Efficient Markets

A recurring issue in raising new capital is *timing.* Companies are naturally anxious to sell new securities when prices are high. Toward this end, managers routinely devote considerable time and money to predicting future price trends in financial markets.

Concern for proper timing of security issues is natural, but there is a perception among many academicians and market professionals that attempting to forecast future prices in financial markets is a loser's game. Such pessimism follows from the notion of *efficient markets,* a much-debated and controversial topic in recent years. A detailed discussion of efficient markets would take us too far afield, but because the topic has far-reaching implications, it merits some attention.

Market efficiency is controversial in large part because many proponents have overstated the evidence supporting efficiency and have misrepresented its implications. To avoid this, let us agree on two things right now. First, market efficiency is a question not of black or white but of shades of gray. A market is not efficient or inefficient but *more* or less efficient. Moreover, the degree of efficiency is an empirical question that can be answered only by studying the particular market under consideration. Second, market efficiency is a matter of perspective. The NYSE can be efficient to a dentist in Des Moines who doesn't know an underwriter from an undertaker; at the same time, it can be highly *in*efficient to a specialist at the exchange who has detailed information about buyers and sellers of each stock and up-to-the-second prices.

---

[14] Wayne H. Mikkelson and M. Megan Partch, "Valuation Effects of Security Offerings and the Issuing Process," *Journal of Financial Economics,* January–February 1986; Inmoo Lee, Scott Lockhead, Jay Ritter, and Quanshui Zhao, "The Cost of Raising Capital," *Journal of Financial Research,* Spring 1996; Securities and Exchange Commission, "Report of the Advisory Committee on the Capital Formation and Regulatory Process" (Washington, DC: U.S. Government Printing Office, July 24, 1996).

What Is an Efficient Market?

Market efficiency describes how prices in competitive markets respond to new information. The arrival of new information at a competitive market can be likened to the arrival of a lamb chop at a school of flesh-eating piranha, where investors are, plausibly enough, the piranha. The instant the lamb chop hits the water, turmoil erupts as the fish devour the meat. Very soon the meat is gone, leaving only the worthless bone behind, and the waters soon return to normal. Similarly, when new information reaches a competitive market, much turmoil erupts as investors buy and sell securities in response to the news, causing prices to change. Once prices adjust, all that is left of the information is the worthless bone. No amount of gnawing on the bone will yield any more meat, and no further study of old information will yield any more valuable intelligence.

An efficient market, then, is one in which prices adjust rapidly to new information, and current prices fully reflect available information about the assets traded. "Fully reflect" means investors rapidly pounce on new information, analyze it, revise their expectations, and buy or sell securities accordingly. They continue to buy or sell securities until price changes eliminate the incentive for further trades. In such an environment, current prices reflect the cumulative judgment of investors. They *fully reflect* available information.

The degree of efficiency a particular market displays depends on the speed with which prices adjust to news and the type of news to which they respond. It is common to speak of three levels of informational efficiency:

1. A market is *weak-form* efficient if current prices fully reflect all information about past prices.

2. A market is *semistrong-form* efficient if current prices fully reflect all publicly available information.

3. A market is *strong-form* efficient if current prices fully reflect all information public or private.

Extensive tests of many financial markets suggest that with limited exceptions, most financial markets are semistrong-form efficient but not strong-form efficient. In other words, you generally cannot make money trading on public information; insider trading, however, based on private information, can be lucrative. This statement needs to be qualified in two respects. First, there is the issue of perspective. The preceding statement applies to the typical investor, who is subject to brokerage fees and lacks special information-gathering equipment. It does *not* apply to market makers. Second, it is impossible to test every conceivable type and combination of public information for efficiency. All we can say is that the most plausible types of information tested with the most sophisticated techniques available indicate efficiency. This does not

How Rapidly Do Stock Prices Adjust to New Information?

Figure 5.3 gives an indication of the speed with which common stock prices adjust to new information. It is a result of what is known as an *event study*. In this instance, the researchers are studying the effect of acquisition offers on the stock prices of target firms. The graph plots the cumulative percentage change in a target firm's stock price from a period beginning 40 days before the announcement of the acquisition offer and ending 10 days after. The price changes shown are averaged over 6,150 acquisition announcements in the U.S. between 1980 and 2008. The date for each announcement is defined as day 0, so that all announcements can be shown on the same timeline.

An acquisition offer is invariably good news to the target firm's shareholders, because the offer is at a price well above the prevailing market price of the firm's shares, so we expect to see the target company's stock price rise after the announcement. The question is: How rapidly? The answer evident from the graph is: Very rapidly. We see that the stock price drifts upward prior to the announcement (perhaps due to rumors of a pending announcement), shoots up dramatically on the announcement day, and then drifts with little direction after the announcement. Clearly, if you read about the announcement in your Twitter feed one day and buy the stock from an online broker the next, you will miss out on the major price move. The market will already have responded to the new information. Over the years, academics have performed a great number of event studies involving different markets and events, and the preponderance of these studies indicates that financial markets respond to new, publicly available information very rapidly.

However, an event study using daily stock price data, such as the one summarized in Figure 5.3, does not tell the whole story. In today's financial markets, the reaction of stock prices to news is better measured in seconds, or even fractions of seconds. For example, when the Federal Reserve announced in September 2013 that it would continue its bond-buying program—unexpectedly good news for stock markets—stock prices started responding within *microseconds* of the news release.[a] If that doesn't seem humanly possible, that's because it isn't, at least not without the help of automated trading, a system in which high-speed computers automatically submit buy or sell orders in response to information. In one type of automated trading, news analytics providers process news releases using textual analysis and then deliver estimates of the impact on specific companies to high-speed traders, all within about a third of a second.[b] The high-speed traders' automated programs then immediately execute trades to attempt to profit from the news.

So if you want to make money in financial markets trading on news, you'd better be quick about it. You don't necessarily have to be the fastest trader to profit from news, but the faster you are, the higher your potential profits. In their quest for speed, high-frequency traders have invested heavily in cutting-edge hardware and software, and have gone so far as to pay stock exchanges for the right to "co-locate" their computers in the same building as the exchange's computer servers, thus saving precious microseconds of transmission time. Just try competing with that on your home computer.

[a] Maureen Farrell, "High Speed Traders Reacted Instantly to Fed," CNN Money, September 19, 2013.

[b] Bastian von Beschwitz, Donald Keim, and Massimo Massa, "First to 'Read' the News: News Analytics and High Frequency Trading," CEPR Discussion Paper, October 2015.

FIGURE 5.3 Average Stock Price Reaction to Takeover Announcements for 6,150 Target Firms

Source: Sandra Betton, Espen Eckbo, Rex Thompson, and Karin Thorburn, "Merger Negotiations with Stock Market Feedback", *Journal of Finance,* vol. 69, no. 4, 2014.

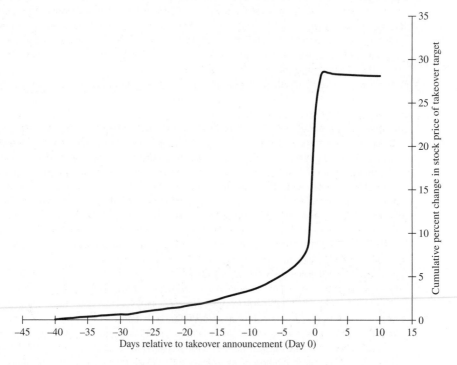

preclude the possibility that a market will be inefficient with respect to some as yet untested information source. Nor does it preclude researchers who find evidence of profitable market inefficiencies and choose to exploit them rather than publish their findings.

Implications of Efficiency

If financial markets are semistrong-form efficient, the following statements are true:

- Publicly available information is not helpful in forecasting future prices.

- In the absence of private information, the best forecast of future price is current price, perhaps adjusted for a long-term trend.

- Without private information, a company cannot improve the terms on which it sells securities by trying to select the optimal time to sell.

- Without private information or the willingness to accept above-average risk, investors should not expect to consistently earn above the market-average rate of return.

Individuals without private information have two choices: They can admit that markets are efficient and quit trying to forecast security prices, or they can attempt to make the market inefficient from their perspective. This involves acquiring the best available information-gathering system in the hope of learning about events before others do. A variation on this strategy, usually illegal,

---

Did Belief in Market Efficiency Contribute to the Financial Crisis?

Market efficiency did not fare well in the financial crisis of 2008. Among other epitaphs, commentators labeled the concept "incredibly inaccurate," and "an academic nostrum" that caused "a lethally dangerous combination of asset bubbles, lax controls, pernicious incentives and wickedly complicated instruments [that] led to our current plight."[a]

Is such vitriol warranted? Did the conviction that markets are efficient contribute to the crisis? The answer in my mind is "yes and no." As noted by Meir Statman of the University of Santa Clara, there are at least two definitions of market efficiency in common use.[b] The modest definition used here says efficient markets are unbeatable markets in the sense that it is very difficult for investors to consistently outperform market averages on a risk-adjusted basis. Prices in unbeatable markets respond very quickly to new information, and their response is neither consistently too great nor too small. For if either of these conditions did not hold, markets would no longer be unbeatable. Importantly, the modest definition of efficiency says nothing about whether the response of prices to new information is necessarily correct or not. Rather, it says only that the response will reflect prevailing investor sentiment, which might well be misguided. This means that prices might well deviate from their intrinsic values in efficient markets, and price bubbles are eminently possible.

In contrast, the ambitious definition is that efficient markets are not only unbeatable but also rational in the sense that prices always equal intrinsic values. As a result, prices in efficient markets are always "right," and bubbles cannot occur. Despite ample evidence to the contrary, the ambitious definition has proven intoxicating to some proponents of financial market deregulation, who appear to believe that unregulated markets are also necessarily rational markets.

How much blame does the notion of market efficiency bear for the financial crisis? In truth, early academic proponents of market efficiency did lean toward the rational markets definition, so they must bear some responsibility for initially over-interpreting the significance of their findings. But that was decades ago. Finance scholars today overwhelmingly agree on the modest, unbeatable markets definition of efficiency. In fact, the increasingly popular academic discipline known as "behavioral finance" is essentially the study of how market sentiment might cause prices to deviate systematically from their intrinsic values.

Much more blame lies with those who continue to believe that efficient markets are equivalent to rational markets. Whether out of intellectual laziness or an overriding philosophical commitment to deregulation, a widespread conviction that unregulated markets are necessarily rational might well have contributed to the lethally dangerous combination of factors that led to the financial panic of 2008.

[a] Jeremy Grantham quoted by Joe Nocera, "Poking Holes in a Theory of the Markets," *The New York Times*, June 5, 2009, and Roger Lowenstein, "On Wall Street, the Price Isn't Right," *The Washington Post*, June 7, 2009.

[b] Meir Statman, "Efficient Markets in Crisis," *Journal of Investment Management*, 2nd Quarter 2011, pp. 4–13.

is to seek inside information. Or as Chinese fortune cookies have said for years, "A friend in the market is better than money in the purse." A third gambit used by some investors is to purchase the forecasts of prestigious consulting firms. The chief virtue of this approach appears to be that there will be someone to blame if things go wrong. After all, if the forecasts were really any good, the consulting firms could make money by trading, thereby eliminating the need to be nice to potential customers.

As the preceding comments attest, market efficiency is a subtle and provocative notion with a number of important implications for investors as well as companies. Our treatment of the topic here has been necessarily brief, but it should be sufficient to suggest that unless executives have inside information or superior information gathering and analysis systems, they may have little to gain from trying to forecast prices in financial markets. This conclusion applies to many markets in which companies participate, including those for government and corporate securities, foreign currencies, and commodities.

There is, however, one important caveat to this conclusion: Because managers clearly possess private information about their own companies, they should have some ability to predict future prices of their own securities. This means managers' efforts to time new security issues based on inside knowledge of their company and its prospects may in fact be appropriate. But notice the distinction. The decision to postpone an equity issue because the president believes the company will significantly outperform analysts' expectations in the coming year is fully defensible in a world of semistrong-form-efficient markets, but the decision to postpone an issue because the treasurer believes stocks in general will soon rise is not. The former decision is based on inside information; the latter is not.

APPENDIX

Using Derivatives to Manage Risks

A discussion of financial instruments would not be complete without at least an introduction to financial derivatives. As mentioned earlier in the chapter, the term *derivative* refers to a broad class of financial instruments whose value depends upon, or is "derived" from, the value of some other asset. Derivatives have received some bad press over the years, perhaps rightfully so. Warren Buffett famously stated in Berkshire Hathaway's 2002 annual report that "derivatives are financial weapons of mass destruction, carrying dangers that, while now latent, are potentially lethal." And, in fact, derivatives were very much entwined with many of the regrettable events of the financial crisis of 2008.

However, blaming derivatives for financial disasters is a bit like blaming a baseball bat for a vandalized storefront. Misuse of derivatives can be damaging, but in the right hands, derivatives help financial managers to mitigate risk and thereby create substantial value for companies. Indeed, the view of some executives is that a major element of modern business is getting paid to undertake intelligent risks, while deftly avoiding others. According to this view, a steel maker is well positioned to manage the vagaries of changing steel demand, but ill-equipped to cope with volatile interest rates or exchange rates. A logical response then is for the company to use financial instruments systematically to sidestep unwanted risks, enabling it to better focus on the activities at which it excels.

Despite the occasional complexity of derivatives, operating executives need to understand the basics of using derivatives for financial risk management for at least three reasons:

- The market for derivatives is huge. Statistics put the total value of derivative contracts of all types outstanding in 2016 at over $600 *trillion*.[1] While the amount of money actually at risk in derivatives contracts is closer to "only" $30 trillion, the markets are huge by any measure, and size alone warrants a basic familiarity. By comparison, the total value of all stocks trading on all exchanges worldwide in 2016 was $70 trillion.[2]

- Most large companies use derivatives. A survey of the world's 500 largest companies found that 94 percent use derivatives for risk management.[3] It is very likely that anyone embarking on a career as a financial manager will encounter derivatives of some type sooner or later.

- Misuse of derivatives can be dangerous. A number of otherwise sophisticated companies have reported multimillion-dollar losses on what were originally intended as risk-reducing activities. Moreover, although financial risk management is an indisputably valuable activity, it is not a panacea. Executives throughout the firm need a clear understanding of what the techniques can and cannot do if they are to use them effectively.

In this appendix, we focus on the use of derivatives to implement a simple risk management technique known as *hedging*. Hedging means to reduce or eliminate a risk by taking a position in an instrument that will offset, or counterbalance, the existing risk. As a simple example of hedging, suppose that an irresistible impulse has prompted you to remortgage your home and bet $100,000 on Manchester United to defeat Real Madrid in an upcoming Champions League

---

[1] Bank for International Settlements, available at **bis.org/statistics.**
[2] Data available at **world-exchanges.org.**
[3] International Swaps and Derivatives Association, Derivatives Usage Survey 2009.

soccer match. Your spouse, however, is not amused to learn of your wager and threatens serious consequences unless you immediately cancel the bet. But, of course, bets are seldom canceled without a broken kneecap or two.

So what do you do? You hedge your bet. Acknowledging that your mother was wrong all those years ago—that two wrongs may indeed make one right— you place a second wager, but this time on Real Madrid to beat Manchester United. Now, no matter who wins, the proceeds from your winning wager will cover the cost of your losing one, and except for the bookie's take, it's just as though you had never made the first bet. You have covered your bet. Companies use financial market "wagers" analogously to hedge unavoidable commercial risks, and derivatives provide the tools to make the hedges possible. We will consider three important types of derivatives in the executive's risk management toolbox: forwards (or futures), swaps, and options.

Forward Markets

Most markets are *spot* markets, in which a price is set today for immediate exchange. In a *forward* market, the price is set today but exchange and payment occurs at some stipulated future date. Buying milk at the grocery store is a spot market transaction, while reserving a hotel room to be paid for later is a forward market transaction. Most assets trading in forward markets also trade spot. To illustrate these markets, suppose the spot price of a bushel of wheat today is $4.40, meaning payment of this amount will buy one bushel of wheat for immediate delivery. In contrast, assume the six-month forward rate is $4.60, meaning payment of this higher amount in six months will buy one bushel of wheat for delivery at that time. A *forward contract* is an irrevocable transaction in which the parties set the price today at which they will trade wheat for dollars at a specific future date.

Hedging with Forward Contracts

How do forward contracts help companies manage risk? Suppose that Amber Waves Inc. (AWI), a wheat farming company, is cultivating wheat to be harvested and sold six months in the future. AWI knows that today the spot price for wheat is $4.40 per bushel, but they are exposed to the risk that the spot price in six months—when they are ready to sell their wheat—will be lower. They know, in fact, that if the price is below $4.00 when they sell their wheat that they will not have enough revenue to cover their expenses and may take an operating loss for the year.

Meanwhile, Midwest Bread Inc. (MBI), a baking company, knows that they will need to purchase wheat in six months, but they are exposed to the risk that spot prices in six months will be higher. MBI estimates that if they have to pay more than $5.00 per bushel for wheat, they will not make a profit on their bread products. In this situation, AWI and MBI can both manage their risk by using forward markets. They can agree to a forward contract in which MBI agrees to buy, say, 100,000 bushels of wheat from AWI in six months at a price of, say, $4.60 per bushel or $460,000 in total. In this way, both companies ensure that they can transact at a price that allows them to be profitable, and their financial forecast becomes much more certain. We would then say that both companies have hedged the risk of wheat price fluctuations.

Hedging with Futures Contracts

One potential difficulty with the scenario described above is that AWI and MBI could have trouble finding each other or, for that matter, any partner willing to take the opposite side of a forward contract in the same quantity and time to maturity that they require. So an alternative for companies looking to hedge risk is to deal with a *futures exchange* that facilitates the matching of parties to forward transactions, which in this case are called *futures contracts.* A futures contract is the same as a forward contract in spirit, but its terms (i.e, the amount, the time to maturity, and so on) are standardized to make it easier for them to be bought and sold between different parties.

Suppose that in March, MBI knows that it needs to buy 100,000 bushels of wheat in September and decides to hedge the risk of wheat price fluctuations using the Chicago Board Options Exchange (CBOE), the largest futures exchange in the U.S. The CBOE buys and sells wheat futures contracts in increments of 5,000 bushels per contract and they offer contracts that mature in various months of the year, including September. To hedge its risk, MBI would buy (or *long,* as a purchase is often called) 20 September wheat futures contracts in March. If the price of the September futures in March was $4.60 per bushel, this would mean that MBI was effectively locking in a price of $460,000 (20 × 5,000 × $4.60) for 100,000 bushels of wheat in September. This *long position* ensures that MBI can obtain wheat in September at a cost that will allow them to be profitable.

At the same time, AWI can go to the CBOE in March and sell (or *short*) 20 September wheat futures contracts at a price of $4.60 per bushel. This *short position* allows AWI to lock in a selling price of $460,000 for the wheat they need to sell in September. The CBOE acts as an intermediary to match up the buyer and the seller, eliminating the need for AWI and MBI to deal with each other. AWI does not even need to know that a company called MBI exists, and vice versa.

It is important to recognize that companies can hedge price risk using futures contracts without holding the contract to maturity and without making or taking delivery of the underlying asset through the exchange. Unlike with forward contracts, companies can (and almost always do) close out their futures contracts at some point prior to delivery and take profits or losses that have accrued on the contract to that point. Then, they simply buy or sell the underlying asset as they normally would in the spot market. When the hedge is set up properly, the company profits from its futures contract when spot market prices move against it, and suffers losses on its futures contract when spot market prices move in its favor. The company ends up paying or receiving roughly the same net amount regardless of which direction prices move.

To illustrate how this works, consider MBI's long position in 20 September wheat futures contracts, which it bought in March at a price of $4.60 per bushel. Suppose that come September, when MBI needs to purchase wheat, poor weather conditions have caused the futures price for September wheat to rise to $5.10 per bushel. The price increase is profitable for MBI's futures contracts, because the contracts they purchased at $4.60 per bushel are now worth $5.10 per bushel. Their profit from the futures can be calculated as the change in the futures price per bushel times the number of bushels contracted.

$$\text{Gain on futures} = (\$5.10 - \$4.60) \times 100,000 \ bushels = \$50,000$$

MBI then purchases wheat from their preferred supplier at the spot price of $5.10 per bushel, or $510,000 total. (Important sidenote: If the futures price is $5.10 in September, then the spot price in September must also be approximately $5.10. That's because, in September, a futures contract to purchase wheat in September can be executed immediately, which is essentially the same as purchasing in the spot market.) When offset by its profit from the futures market, MBI's net cost for wheat is $510,000 – $50,000 = $460,000 for 100,000 bushels of wheat, which is the price MBI locked in back in March.

If, instead, September wheat futures prices declined to, say, $4.35 per bushel by September, MBI would lose money on its futures contracts.

$$\text{Gain on futures} = (\$4.35 - \$4.60) \times 100,000 \ bushels = -\$25,000$$

However, that bad news is offset by the good news that MBI can purchase wheat in the spot market at the cheaper price of $4.35 per bushel. MBI's net cost for wheat would be $435,000 + $25,000 = $460,000, just the same as when futures prices went up. In this way, MBI's futures contracts ensure that it pays a net cost of $460,000 for its wheat in the spot market without having to take delivery of wheat through the CBOE. Taking delivery through the CBOE is always a possibility, of course, but firms avoid doing this so as not to risk having to deal with an unfamiliar supplier at an inconvenient location.

Types of Forwards and Futures

The above example focused on hedging wheat price fluctuations, but it might just as well have focused on hedging risks inherent in many other types of assets. The following are the most common types of futures and forward contracts that companies use for hedging purposes:

In *commodity futures* (of which wheat futures are one example), a company can lock in a future price for buying or selling any number of commodities. Organized exchanges facilitate trading in many types of commodity futures, including foods like milk and sugar, metals like gold and copper, livestock like hogs and cattle, and energy products like oil and natural gas. Of course, if a company wants to hedge the price risk of a commodity not found on an organized exchange, it still has the possibility of finding a counterparty for a forward contract on any commodity.

In *currency futures* or *foreign exchange futures,* a company can contract to exchange one currency for another at a predetermined exchange rate on a future date. For example, suppose Boeing contracts to sell a 787 jet to All Nippon Airways in one year at the yen-denominated price of ¥30 billion. At the spot exchange rate of 100 ¥/$, this would bring Boeing revenue of $300 million. But Boeing is exposed to the risk that the ¥/$ rate will rise before the payment is made, thereby reducing Boeing's profit in dollar terms. To hedge this risk, Boeing can use yen futures to lock in a set exchange rate one year hence. If the one-year forward rate is also 100 ¥/$ (in reality it could be higher or lower than the spot rate), Boeing can sell ¥30 billion one year forward and ensure the receipt of $300 million in one year.

In *interest rate futures,* a company can contract to buy or sell an interest-bearing financial instrument, such as a Treasury bond, at a predetermined price on a future date, which effectively locks in a future lending or borrowing interest rate. For example, if Intel needs to borrow $100 million in six months to build a new plant, it is exposed to the risk that interest rates will rise in the intervening six months, resulting in higher borrowing costs. To hedge this risk, Intel can take an appropriate position in Treasury bond futures that will increase in value when interest rates rise. (As with bonds, the prices of bond futures are sensitive to changes in interest rates.) Intel's higher borrowing costs will be offset by the gain on its Treasury bond futures.

Hedging with Swaps

Another derivative security, known as a swap, has altered the way many financial executives think about issuing and managing company debt. A swap is an agreement between two parties in which each commits to give a series of one type of payments to the other party and receive a series of another type of payments from the other party. The two most common types of swaps are *interest rate swaps* and *currency swaps.* An interest rate swap entails the trade of fixed-rate payments for floating-rate payments, while a currency swap involves the trade of liabilities denominated in different currencies. Swaps are so commonplace that an active market exists in which standard swaps are bought and sold much like stocks and bonds.

Interest Rate Swaps

In terms of market value, the interest rate swap is the king of all derivatives. Over half of the $600 trillion in total value of derivatives outstanding is attributable to interest rate swaps. In the most popular type of interest rate swap, often called a *plain vanilla* swap, one party pays the other a fixed interest rate in return for a floating interest rate, often LIBOR (the London Interbank Offered Rate). These payments are made on specified regular dates on a specified amount of *notional* principal. The notional principal itself is never exchanged between the parties; they only exchange the interest on the principal.

As an example, suppose that BP contacts a swap dealer (perhaps a large bank such as HSBC) wanting to make fixed-rate payments and receive floating-rate payments on $100 million notional principal. HSBC quotes BP a fixed rate of 2.1 percent in exchange for LIBOR payments to be made annually for the next five years. If the swap is initiated on May 15, 2017, then on May 15 of each year BP will pay 2.1 percent of $100 million and receive the LIBOR rate prevailing at the *beginning* of the year on $100 million. Depending on where LIBOR rates end up in the future, the swap payments will look something like this:

BP's Interest Rate Swap Payments			
Date	LIBOR rate	BP pays	BP receives
May 15, 2017	1.75%		
May 15, 2018	1.95%	$ 2,100,000	$1,750,000
May 15, 2019	1.89%	$ 2,100,000	$1,950,000
May 15, 2020	2.18%	$ 2,100,000	$1,890,000
May 15, 2021	2.31%	$ 2,100,000	$2,180,000
May 15, 2022		$ 2,100,000	$2,310,000

How can this swap help BP with risk management? Suppose BP is paying LIBOR on $100 million of debt issued several years ago when BP wanted floating-rate debt. But now, with five years remaining on the debt, BP no longer wants floating-rate debt, perhaps because management believes rates are poised to increase and they do not want to risk being saddled with higher interest payments. The interest rate swap solves this problem. Combining the original debt with the above swap, BP is effectively paying a net fixed rate on $100 million in debt. The LIBOR payment it receives from HSBC "cancels out" the LIBOR payment it makes on the original debt, leaving BP with the fixed payment to HSBC. The interest rate swap allows BP to easily shed its interest rate risk without retiring the current debt and issuing new debt, an alternative which may be impractical or too costly.

In addition to risk management, interest rate swaps can also help companies with cost reduction. Prior to the advent of swaps, a company's decision about what type of debt to issue often involved a compromise between what the company really wanted and what investors were willing to buy. For example, suppose that BP wants to issue $100 million of fixed-rate debt but settles for floating-rate debt because investors are willing to offer better terms on floating-rate debt. The swap allows BP to have its cake and eat it too. It can issue floating-rate debt and immediately swap into a fixed rate. In effect, swaps enable the issuer to separate concerns about what type of debt the company needs from those regarding what type investors want to buy, thereby greatly simplifying the issuance decision and reducing borrowing costs.

Currency Swaps

Though not as ubiquitous as interest-rate swaps, currency swaps are very popular for companies seeking to manage foreign exchange risk. Suppose, for example, that McDonald's, encouraged by the surprising popularity of its McCurrywurst sausage entree, decides on a major expansion in Germany. McDonald's knows that the increased business in Germany will generate additional euro revenues, but it faces exchange rate risk when translating the euros into dollars in future periods. So McDonald's contacts Deutsche Bank for a five-year currency swap on $100 million, which at the prevailing exchange rate is equal to €90 million. Deutsche Bank's quote for the currency swap allows McDonald's to receive a fixed rate of 2.5 percent on $100 million in exchange for paying a 3.0 percent rate on €90 million. In contrast to interest rate swaps, in currency swaps the principal amounts are exchanged at the beginning and end of the swap. If the swap is initiated on May 15, 2017, then payments on the swap will look like this (negative signs indicate payments made by McDonald's, positive signs indicate receipts):

McDonald's Currency Swap Payments		
Date	Dollar cash flows	Euro cash flows
May 15, 2017	−$100,000,000	+€90,000,000
May 15, 2018	+2,500,000	−2,700,000
May 15, 2019	+2,500,000	−2,700,000
May 15, 2020	+2,500,000	−2,700,000
May 15, 2021	+2,500,000	−2,700,000
May 15, 2022	+102,500,000	−92,700,000

Note how effective this swap is for McDonald's. At the initiation of the swap, it gives $100 million to Deutsche Bank and receives €90 million that it can use to expand in Germany. Then, each year thereafter, it gives euro cash flows generated in Germany to Deutsche Bank and receives a set amount of dollars in return. For that five-year period, McDonald's exchange rate risk on €2.7 million per year is hedged. At the termination of the swap, McDonald's makes the last exchange of interest payments and gives back the €90 million in return for $100 million.

You might notice that each individual annual exchange of payments looks very much like a currency futures contract in which McDonald's and Deutsche Bank have agreed to exchange a set amount dollars for euros at a future point in time at a predetermined exchange rate. Indeed, one useful way to think about a swap is as a series of futures contracts, appropriate for companies that need to hedge the risk of many regular future cash flows instead of a single cash flow.

Currency swaps offer companies advantages comparable to those mentioned above for interest rate swaps: risk management and cost reduction. Does your company have existing Swiss franc debt, but you are worried that the franc/dollar exchange rate will fall, thereby increasing the dollar burden of the debt? No problem: Swap out of francs into dollars. Do you want yen-denominated debt, but find that your company can issue dollar-denominated debt at better terms? Piece of cake: Issue dollar debt and then use a swap to transform the dollars into yen.

Hedging with Options

Whereas a forward contract is an agreement to buy or sell an asset at a specified price at a specified future time, an *option* is a security giving the holder the right, *but not the obligation,* to buy or sell an asset at a specified price for a specified time. Options come in two flavors: A *call* option conveys the right to buy the underlying asset, while a *put* is the right to sell it. Options are available to hedge the risk of fluctuations in stock prices, commodity prices, interest rates, and exchange rates.

To demonstrate the basics of how call and put options work, let's consider options on a share of stock. Assume that today the price of Snap stock is $25 per share, and that for $5 you can buy (or long) a call option that gives you the right to buy a share of Snap stock for $30 any time in the next 60 days. As a matter of semantics, $30 is known as the option's *exercise,* or *strike,* price, 60 days is its *maturity,* and the $5 purchase price, payable today, is referred to as the *premium.*

Figure 5A.1(a) shows a diagram of the payoff for this call option at maturity for different prices of Snap stock. The lower, dotted line includes the $5 premium, while the solid line omits it. Concentrating first on the solid line, we see that the call is worthless at maturity when the stock price is below the call option's strike price. The right to buy Snap stock for $30 obviously isn't very enticing when it can be purchased for less than that on the open market. In this event, the option will expire worthless, and you will have spent the $5 premium for nothing. The outcome is very different, however, when the stock price is above the strike price at maturity. If the stock price rises to $40, for instance, the option to buy Snap stock for $30 is worth $10, because your

FIGURE 5A.1 **Option Payoffs**

(a) Call option on Snap stock

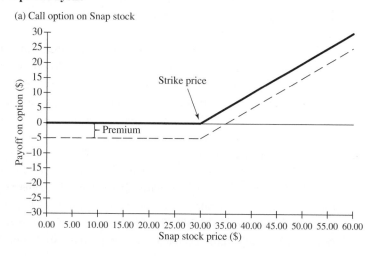

(b) Put option on Snap stock

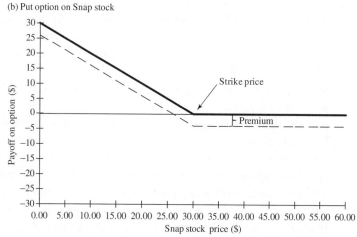

option allows you to buy the stock for $30 and immediately sell it on the open market for $40. Subtracting the original $5 cost of the option, your net profit would be $5.

The payoff diagram for put options is just the reverse of that for calls. Assume that based on today's prices, 60-day put options on Snap stock with a strike price of $30 are available for a premium of $4. As shown in Figure 5A.1(b), this put will expire worthless unless the stock price falls below the strike price; the right to sell something for less than its current market price has no value. But once below the strike price, the value of the put rises dollar for dollar as the stock price falls. If the stock price falls to $25, for instance, you can buy the stock for $25 and exercise your put to sell the stock for $30. This payoff of $5, less the initial cost of $4, yields a $1 net profit. In the best-case scenario (provided you are not a Snap employee), Snap stock becomes worthless and you receive a $26 net profit—not bad for a $4 investment.

To compare options with forwards as hedging instruments, let's return to the previous example of Boeing's pending receipt of ¥30 billion from All Nippon Airways in one year. Using forwards as a hedge, assuming a one-year forward rate of 100 ¥/$, we saw that Boeing could lock in a receipt of $300 million in one year's time. Now let's suppose that for a premium of $2 million today, Boeing can, as an alternative, purchase put options to sell ¥30 billion in one year at an exchange rate of 100 ¥/$.

Consider first the case where the spot exchange rate falls to 95 ¥/$ in one year. In the forward contract scenario, Boeing would exchange the ¥30 billion for $300 million as planned, but would feel a twinge of regret knowing that it could have received $315,789,474 ($300,000,000/95) if it had skipped the forward contract and simply exchanged currency in the spot market. In the options scenario, Boeing would let its put options expire, and sell the yen in the spot market for $315,789,474, netting $313,789,474 after the cost of the premium.

Next, consider the case where the spot exchange rate rises to 105 ¥/$ in one year. In the forward contract scenario, Boeing would exchange the ¥30 billion for $300 million as planned, and would feel relieved to have the forward contract in place, as it otherwise would have received only $285,714,286 ($300,000,000/105). In the options scenario, Boeing would exercise its put options to sell ¥30 billion for $300 million, netting $298 million after the cost of the premium.

So which works better as a hedging device for Boeing, forwards or options? As is often the case, the answer is "it depends." Forwards do not require a premium payment, but they also do not allow for any potential upside gains. Options require a premium payment up front, but in return the holder can choose whether or not to exercise the options, maintaining a possibility of upside gains. Boeing's choice of forwards or options may depend upon its expectations for exchange rate movements, its risk preferences, or its current availability of cash.

Limitations of Financial Market Hedging

Because new initiates to the world of hedging frequently overestimate the technique's power, a few cautionary reflections on the limitations of financial market hedges are in order.

First, it is more difficult to hedge risks if the asset creating the risk does not actively trade in financial markets. In commodity markets, for example, hedging wheat price risk is straightforward because the CBOE offers wheat futures contracts. Hedging asparagus price risk is more difficult—it requires either finding a willing counterparty for a forward contract or identifying a closely correlated futures contract that can serve as a "substitute" hedging instrument. In currency markets, hedging exchange rate risk for common

The Ups and Downs of Hedging: Southwest Airlines

It costs a lot to fuel an aircraft. In the airline industry, operating costs are dominated by fuel and labor. Fuel costs can be very volatile, so the price at which airlines purchase fuel can often make or break their profitability. In such an environment, airlines naturally consider using forwards, futures, swaps, or options to hedge the risk of fuel price increases.

In the early 2000s, Southwest Airlines had a strategy of hedging the majority of its fuel costs, and it worked brilliantly. As fuel prices rose, Southwest was able to offset the higher costs with hedging gains of hundreds of millions of dollars per year. Because other major airlines did not hedge as aggressively, Southwest enjoyed continued profitability while other airlines suffered losses.[a]

Then came the second half of 2008, when fuel prices dropped like a rock. Southwest *lost* hundreds of millions of dollars on its hedges, and for the first time in 17 years, it reported a quarterly loss.[b] Investors who once praised Southwest for their prescient hedging were now disappointed that Southwest's strategy had seemingly backfired. More recently, the strategy appeared to backfire again, as Southwest reported more massive losses on fuel hedges in 2016.[c]

The important lesson from Southwest's experience is that hedges look very different in the rear-view mirror. Ahead of time, a hedge may be viewed as a prudent measure to eliminate an impending risk. But after the fact, there can be some second guessing, both by executives and investors. After all, roughly half the time a hedge will end up protecting the company from unfavorable price changes, but the other half of the time the company will realize it would have been better off without the hedge. In the latter cases, investors may complain that the company "guessed wrong" or "bet wrong," even though the company was hedging, not speculating. Managers need to be highly confident in their hedging strategies so that they can withstand criticism when others view the strategy as ill-advised in hindsight.

[a] Jeff Bailey, "Southwest Airlines Gains Advantage by Hedging on Long-Term Oil Contracts," *The New York Times,* November 28, 2007.
[b] Jim Jelter, "Southwest's Treacherous Fuel Hedges," *MarketWatch,* October 16, 2008.
[c] Adam Levine-Weinberg, "Southwest Gets Burned by Fuel Hedges—Again," *The Motley Fool,* July 25, 2016.

currencies like the euro will be easier than for lesser-used currencies like the Zambian kwacha.

Second, hedging becomes more complicated and imprecise if the amount and timing of the risk to be hedged is not known with reasonable certainty. For example, in the case of foreign exchange risk, hedging is fairly straightforward when the cash flow is a foreign receivable or payable. But when it is an operating cash flow, such as expected sales, cost of sales, or earnings, the company must somehow hedge an uncertain amount of cash flow that will occur at an uncertain time. Moreover, if the cash flows being hedged are expected to continue into the foreseeable future, then the company must deal with exposure that extends far beyond next year's sales or earnings.

Our final caveat about financial market hedging is more philosophical. Empirical studies suggest that foreign exchange, commodity, and debt markets are all "fair games," meaning the chance of benefiting from unexpected price changes in these markets about equals the chance of losing. If this is so, companies facing repeated risk exposures, or those with a number of exposures in different markets, might justifiably dispense with hedging altogether on the grounds that over the long run, losses will about equal gains anyway. (Shareholders in the company are probably even less concerned about hedging than managers, given that their risk in the company is likely balanced out with the risks of their shareholdings in other companies.) According to this philosophy, hedging is warranted only when the company seldom faces a particular risk, when the potential loss is too big for the company to absorb gracefully, or when the elimination of a risk yields administrative benefits such as more accurate planning, better performance evaluation, or improved employee morale.

Valuing Options

Because options have applications in corporate finance ranging from incentive compensation to analysis of investment opportunities, a brief primer on option valuation is appropriate.

Suppose you hold a five-year option to purchase 100 shares of eBay stock for $27 a share when the stock is selling for $25, and you want to know what the option is worth today. It is apparent that your option would be worthless if you had to exercise it immediately, because the privilege of buying something for $27 when it is freely available elsewhere for $25 is not highly prized. Your option is said to be *out of the money*. Fortunately, however, you do not have to exercise the option immediately. You can wait for up to five years before acting. Looking to the future, chances are good that sometime before the option matures, eBay stock will sell for more than $27. The option will then be *in the money*, in which case you can exercise it and sell the stock for a profit. We conclude that the value of the option today depends fundamentally on two things: the chance that eBay's stock will rise above the option's strike price prior to maturity and the potential amount by which it might exceed the strike price. The challenge in valuing an option is to decide what these two things are worth.

Options have been around for many years, but it was not until 1973 that Fisher Black and Myron Scholes offered the first practical solution to this valuation challenge. Their solution is remarkable both for what it contains and for what it omits.[4] Black and Scholes demonstrated that the value of an option depends on five variables, four of which are quite easy to observe. They are

- The current price of the underlying asset (in our example, eBay stock)

- The option's time to maturity

---

[4] Robert Merton was also instrumental in solving the option valuation problem. Their solution was revolutionary enough that in 1997 Scholes and Merton were awarded the Nobel Prize in Economics (Fisher Black had since passed away).

- The option's strike price

- The interest rate

The value of a call option rises with the price of the underlying asset. The eBay call option is more valuable when eBay is selling at $50 than at $25. The value of a call option is lower when the strike price is higher. An eBay call is worth less if its strike price is $40 as opposed to $27. The opposite is true for put options— low underlying-asset prices and high strike prices are better for put values. A longer time to maturity generally results in higher option values for calls and puts, because the holder of the option has a longer period of time in which to exercise the option.

The one unobservable determinant of an option's value is the expected volatility of return on the underlying asset. In other words, the value of the eBay option depends on how uncertain investors are about the return on eBay stock over the life of the option. The standard approach to estimating expected volatility is to look at the stock's past volatility, as measured by the standard deviation of past returns. (Standard deviation is a widely used statistical measure of dispersion, which we will consider in more detail in Chapter 8.) If the standard deviation of return on eBay stock in the recent past has been 25 percent, this is a plausible estimate of its future volatility.

The intriguing thing about volatility is that option value rises with volatility. This is true of both calls and puts. In other words, a call option on a speculative stock is actually worth more than an identical option on a blue chip. That's right. Options run contrary to intuition and to most of finance, where volatility means risk, and risk is bad. With options, volatility is good. To see why, recall that an option allows its owner to walk away unscathed when things go poorly. In our example, if eBay stock never rises above $27, the worst that can happen is you will have some new wallpaper. This means that an option owner is only concerned with upside potential, and the greater the volatility, the greater this potential. If you received a dollar every time a batter hit a home run, wouldn't you rather back an erratic slugger than a steady singles hitter? The same is true of options. Uncertainty is good for options.

Remarkably, an input variable that is not required for the Black–Scholes formula is the predicted future value of the underlying asset. In our example, there is no need to forecast the value of eBay stock over the next five years to value the option because the market's forecast is already embedded in the current stock price.

With the Black–Scholes option-pricing formula in hand, valuing an option is now a straightforward, three-step process. First, find the current values of the four observable variables. Second, estimate the future volatility of the underlying asset's return, usually by extrapolating its past volatility. Third, throw these numbers into the Black–Scholes option pricing formula and calculate the answer. As an example, let's value the eBay call option under the following conditions:

Option strike price	$27
Option maturity	5 years
Current eBay stock price	$25
5-year government interest rate	2.0%
Volatility of eBay stock price	30.0%

Rather than manipulating the Black–Scholes formula myself—a tedious task—I will use an online option price calculator. You can easily find one by googling "Black–Scholes calculator". I like a simple one found at **erieri. com/blackscholes.** Plugging the requisite five numbers into the option pricer, we learn that the estimated value of the option on 100 eBay shares is $678. At a volatility of 45 percent, the value jumps to $981.[5]

Growth of the options industry since introduction of the Black–Scholes pricing model recalls the popular adage, "If your only tool is a hammer, pretty soon all the world appears to be a nail." The ability to price options with reasonable accuracy has led to a remarkable growth in the volume and variety of options traded, including those on interest rates, stocks, stock indices, foreign exchange, weather, and a wide variety of physical commodities. In addition to traded options, we have discovered the presence of embedded options lurking in many conventional financial instruments such as home mortgages and commercial bank loans. In the past, these options were either ignored or only crudely reflected in the pricing of the instrument. Now it is possible to value each option separately and price it accordingly. From the discovery of embedded options in conventional instruments, it has been a small step to the creation of innovative new instruments that include heretofore unavailable options. Finally, we have realized that many corporate investment decisions, such as whether or not to introduce a new product, contain embedded options that, at least in theory, can be priced using the techniques described. Examples of what are known as *real options* include the choice to expand production, to terminate production, or to change the product mix. The ability to price these options can greatly improve corporate investment decisions. (We will discuss this topic in further detail in Chapter 8.) Once you know how to price them, all the world indeed appears to be an option.

---

[5] It is time for a little disclaimer here. Technically, the Black–Scholes formula is accurate only for *European* options, defined as those that can be exercised only on the maturity date. Most stock options are, in fact, *American* options, defined as those that can be exercised at any time up to maturity. Often, the difference in price between European and American options is not large, and for our present purposes, we will ignore it.

SUMMARY

1. Financial instruments
   - Are claims to a company's cash flows and assets designed to meet the financing needs of the business and to appeal to investors.
   - Are not greatly constrained by law or regulation but are subject to full disclosure requirements.
   - Are often grouped into four categories:
     - Fixed-income securities known as bonds.
     - Residual-income securities known as common stock.
     - Hybrid securities having characteristics of both bonds and of stocks.
     - Derivative securities whose value depends on that of some underlying asset.

2. Realized returns on U.S. common stocks over the years since 1928 have
   - Averaged 11.4 percent a year.
   - Outpaced inflation by an average of 8.3 percent a year.
   - Been more volatile, and thus riskier, than returns on bonds.
   - Exceeded the return on government bonds by an average of 6.2 percent a year.

3. Financial markets
   - Are the channels through which companies sell financial instruments to investors.
   - Include such diverse segments as
     - Private equity financing: where buyout and venture capital firms, organized as limited partnerships, make often high-risk, intermediate-term investments.
     - Initial public offerings: where private companies, with the help of investment bankers, sell ownership interests to public investors.
     - Seasoned issues: where larger public companies use often-specialized techniques such as private placements, shelf registrations, and Rule 144A offerings to raise money.
     - Cross-border financing: where large companies raise money in other countries' financial markets, or in international markets, which are best thought of as a free market response to regulatory constraints imposed in domestic markets.

4. Efficient markets

- Are markets in which prices respond rapidly to new information such that current prices fully reflect available information about the assets traded.

- Typically impound new information into prices in a matter of seconds.

- Are often divided into three categories:

  - Weak-form efficient: when current prices fully reflect all information about past prices.

  - Semistrong-form efficient: when current prices fully reflect all publicly available information.

  - Strong-form efficient: when current prices fully reflect all information public or private.

- Is a relative term in that the same market can be simultaneously efficient to retail investors and inefficient to market specialists.

5. In semistrong-form efficient markets, in the absence of private information

- Publicly available information is not helpful in forecasting future prices.

- The best forecast of future price is current price, perhaps adjusted for a long-run trend.

- A company cannot improve the terms on which it sells securities by attempting to time the issue.

- Investors should not expect to consistently earn above-average returns without accepting above-average risks.

ADDITIONAL RESOURCES

Allen, Steven. *Financial Risk Management: A Practitioner's Guide to Managing Market and Credit Risk,* 2nd ed. New York: John Wiley & Sons, 2012. 579 pages.

Our discussion of financial risk management in the appendix is necessarily brief, so here is a suggestion for a more in-depth look.

Dimson, Elroy, Paul Marsh, and Mike Staunton. *Global Investment Returns Yearbook.* Credit Suisse Research Institute, 2017.

An authoritative source for returns earned on financial instruments in 23 countries from 1900 to the present. The summary edition is available for free online and is updated annually.

Fox, Justin. *The Myth of the Rational Market: A History of Risk, Reward, and Delusion on Wall Street.* New York: Harper Paperbacks, 2011. 416 pages.

Tells the story of the rise and fall of the efficient markets hypothesis. An excellent intellectual history of modern finance. A *New York Times* Notable Book of 2009.

Lewis, Michael. *Flash Boys: A Wall Street Revolt.* New York: W. W. Norton & Company, 2015. 320 pages.

>   Not everyone agrees with the author's opinions, but this #1 New York Times bestseller provides insight into market efficiency in today's world of high-frequency trading.

Malkiel, Burton G. *A Random Walk Down Wall Street: The Time-Tested Strategy for Successful Investing.* 11th ed. New York: W. W. Norton & Company, 2016. 496 pages.

>   The classic best-selling introduction to market efficiency and personal investing by someone who knows both the academic and professional sides of the story.

Mishkin, Frederic, and Stanley Eakins. *Financial Markets and Institutions.* 8th ed. London: Pearson Education, 2015. 704 pages.

cboe.com

Home of the Chicago Board Options Exchange. The site includes option quotes, market news, and options education. The CBOE also has a free app for iOS or Android (search Apple's app store or Google Play for "CBOE Mobile").

erieri.com/blackscholes

An online calculator for option prices. Input the five necessary bits of information and the calculator gives you theoretical option prices based on the Black–Scholes formulas.

IPO

A free app for iOS that provides up-to-date pricing information and news for upcoming IPOs. Provided by money management firm Renaissance Capital (search Apple's app store for "IPO Renaissance Capital").

PROBLEMS

Answers to odd-numbered problems appear at the end of the book. Answers to even-numbered problems and additional exercises are available in the Instructor Resources within McGraw-Hill's *Connect* (see the Preface for more information).

1. Table 5.1 indicates that the average annual rate of return on common stocks over many years has exceeded the return on government bonds in the United States. Why do we observe this pattern?

2. Suppose the realized rate of return on government bonds exceeded the return on common stocks one year. How would you interpret this result?

3. What is most important to investors: the number of a company's shares they own, the price of the company's stock, or the value of their shareholdings in the company? Why?

4. Two 20-year bonds are identical in all respects except that one allows the issuer to call the bond in return for $1,000 cash at any time after five years, while the other contains no call provisions. Will the yield to maturity on the two bonds differ? If so, which will be higher? Why?

5. The return an investor earns on a bond over a period of time is known as the *holding period return,* defined as interest income plus or minus the change in the bond's price, all divided by the beginning bond price.

   a. What is the holding period return on a bond with a par value of $1,000 and a coupon rate of 6 percent if its price at the beginning of the year was $1,050 and its price at the end was $940? Assume interest is paid annually.

   b. Can you give two reasons the price of the bond might have fallen over the year?

6. Information about three securities appears next.

	Beginning-of-Year Price	End-of-Year Price	Interest/Dividend Paid
Stock 1	$42.50	$46.75	$ 1.50
Stock 2	$ 1.25	$ 1.36	$ 0.00
Bond 1	$1,020	$1,048	$41.00

   a. Assuming interest and dividends are paid annually, calculate the annual holding period return on each security.

   b. During the year, management of Stock 2 spent $10 million, or $0.50 a share, repurchasing 7.7 million of the company's shares. How, if at all, does this information affect calculation of the holding period return on Stock 2?

7. A company wants to raise $500 million in a new stock issue. Its investment banker indicates that the sale of new stock will require 8 percent underpricing and a 7 percent spread. (Hint: the underpricing is 8 percent of the current stock price, and the spread is 7 percent of the issue price.)

   a. Assuming the company's stock price does not change from its current price of $75 per share, how many shares must the company sell and at what price to the public?

   b. How much money will the investment banking syndicates earn on the sale?

   c. Is the 8 percent underpricing a cash flow? Is it a cost? If so, to whom?

8. Magenta Corporation wants to raise $50 million in a seasoned equity offering, net of all fees. Magenta stock currently sells for $10 per share. The underwriters will require a spread of $0.50 per share, and indicate that the issue must be underpriced by 5 percent. In addition to the underwriter's fee, the firm will incur $1,000,000 in legal, accounting, and other costs. How many shares must Magenta sell?

9. You see an article in the newspaper that details the performance of mutual funds over the last five years. You see that, out of 5,600 actively managed mutual funds in the study, 104 outperformed the market in each of the last five years. The author of the article argues that these mutual funds are examples of market inefficiency. "If markets are efficient, you would expect to see mutual funds outperforming the market for short periods of time. But when more than 100 mutual funds are able to outperform the market in each of the last five years, you can no longer suppose that markets are truly efficient. Obviously, these 100 fund managers have figured out a way to beat the market every year." Do you think this is evidence that markets are not efficient?

10. Suppose in Figure 5.3 that the stock prices of target firms in acquisitions responded to acquisition announcements over a three-day period rather than almost instantly.

    a. Would you describe such an acquisition market as efficient? Why or why not?

    b. Can you think of any trading strategy to take advantage of the delayed price response?

    c. If you and many others pursued this trading strategy, what would happen to the price response to acquisition announcements?

    d. Some argue that market inefficiencies contain the seeds of their own destruction. In what ways does your answer to this problem illustrate the logic of this statement, if at all?

    e. Immediately after some merger announcements, the stock price of the target firm jumps to a level higher than the bid price. Is this proof of market inefficiency? What might explain this price pattern?

11. a. Suppose that Liquid Force, Inc.'s stock price consistently falls by an amount equal to one-half the dividend it pays on the payment date. Ignoring taxes, can you think of an investment strategy to take advantage of this information?

    b. If you and many others pursued this strategy, predict what would happen to Liquid Force's stock price on the dividend payment date.

    c. Suppose that Liquid Force's stock price consistently falls by an amount equal to twice the dividend payment on the payment date. Ignoring taxes, can you think of an investment strategy to take advantage of this information?

    d. If you and many others pursued this strategy, predict what would happen to Liquid Force's stock price on the dividend payment date.

    e. In an efficient market, ignoring taxes and transaction costs, how do you think stock prices will change on dividend payment dates?

    f. Given that investors receive returns from common stock in the form of dividends and capital appreciation, do you think that increasing dividends will benefit investors in the absence of taxes and transactions costs?

12. If the U.S. stock market is efficient, how do you explain the fact that some people make very high returns? Would it be more difficult to reconcile very high returns with efficient markets if the same people made extraordinary returns year after year?

13. Why do you suppose that smaller firms tend to rely on bank financing, while larger companies are more apt to sell bonds in financial markets?

The following four problems test your understanding of the chapter appendix.

14. Kansas Corp., an American company, has a payment of €5 million due to Tuscany Corp. one year from today. At the prevailing spot rate of 0.90 €/$, this would cost Kansas $5,555,556, but Kansas faces the risk that the €/$ rate will fall in the coming year, so that it will end up paying a higher amount in dollar terms. To hedge this risk, Kansas has two possible strategies. Strategy 1 is to buy €5 million forward today at a one-year forward rate of 0.89 €/$. Strategy 2 is to pay a premium of $100,000 for a one-year call option on €5 million at an exchange rate of 0.88 €/$.

    a. Suppose that in one year the spot exchange rate is 0.85 €/$. What would be Kansas's net dollar cost for the payable under each strategy?
    b. Suppose that in one year the spot exchange rate is 0.95 €/$. What would be Kansas's net dollar cost for the payable under each strategy?
    c. Which hedging strategy would you recommend to Kansas Corp.? Why?

15. Yosemite Corp. has an outstanding debt of $10 million on which it pays a 5 percent fixed interest rate annually. Yosemite just made its annual interest payment and has three years remaining until maturity. Yosemite believes that interest rates will fall over the next three years and that floating-rate debt will allow it to reduce its overall borrowing costs. A bank offers Yosemite a three-year interest rate swap with annual payments in which Yosemite will pay LIBOR, currently at 5.1 percent, and receive a 4.8 percent fixed rate on $10 million notional principal. Suppose that LIBOR turns out to be 4.7 percent in one year and 4.4 percent in two years. Including interest payments on Yosemite's outstanding debt and payments on the swap, what will be Yosemite's net interest payments for the next three years?

16. The common shares of Twitter, Inc. (TWTR) recently traded on the NYSE for $18.50 per share. You have employee stock options to purchase 1,000 TWTR shares for $16 per share. The options expire in three years. Assume that the annualized volatility of TWTR stock is 85.4 percent and that the interest rate is 2.5 percent. (Assume the options are European options that may only be exercised at the maturity date.)

a. Is this option a call or a put?

b. Using an option pricing calculator such as the one at **erieri.com/ blackscholes,** estimate the value of your TWTR options.

c. What is the estimated value of the options if their maturity is six months instead of three years? Why does the value of the options decline as the maturity declines?

d. What is the estimated value of the options if their maturity is three years, but TWTR's volatility is 60 percent? Why does the value of the options decrease as volatility decreases?

17. Some refer to common stock in a company with debt outstanding as an option on a company's assets. Do you see any logic to this statement? What is the logic, if any?

The Financing Decision

Equity Capital: The least amount of money owners can invest in a business and still obtain credit.

Michael Sperry

In the last chapter, we began our inquiry into financing a business by looking at financial instruments and the markets in which they trade. In this chapter, we examine the company's choice of the proper financing instruments.

Selecting the proper financing instruments is a two-step process. The first step is to decide how much external capital is required. Frequently, this is the straightforward outcome of the forecasting and budgeting process described in Chapter 3. Management estimates sales growth, the need for new assets, and the money available internally. Any remaining monetary needs must be met from outside sources. Often, however, this is only the start of the exercise. Next comes a careful consideration of financial markets and the terms on which the company can raise capital. If management does not believe it can raise the required sums on agreeable terms, a modification of operating plans to bring them within budgetary constraints is initiated.

Once the amount of external capital to be raised has been determined, the second step is to select—or, more accurately, design—the instrument to be sold. This is the heart of the financing decision. As indicated in the last chapter, an issuer can choose from a tremendous variety of financial securities. The proper choice will provide the company with needed cash on attractive terms. An improper choice will result in excessive costs, undue risk, or an inability to sell the securities. In this context, it is important to keep in mind that most operating companies make money by creatively acquiring and deploying assets, not by dreaming up clever ways to finance these assets. This means that the focus of the financing decision should generally be on supporting the company's business strategy, and that care should be taken to avoid financing choices that carry even a modest chance of derailing this strategy. Better to make company financing the passive handmaiden of operating strategy than to jeopardize that strategy in pursuit of marginally lower financing costs. This is especially true for rapidly growing companies where aggressive financing choices can be especially costly.

For simplicity, we will concentrate on a single financing choice: ABC Company needs to raise $200 million this year, so should it sell bonds or stock? Do not let this narrow focus obscure the complexity of the topic, however. First, bonds and stocks are just extreme examples of a whole spectrum of possible security types. Fortunately, the conclusions drawn regarding these extremes will apply to a modified degree to other instruments along the spectrum. Second, many businesses, especially smaller ones, are often unable or unwilling to sell stock. For these firms, the relevant financing question is not whether to sell debt or equity but how much debt to sell. As will become apparent later in the chapter, the inability to raise equity forces companies to approach financing decisions as part of the broader challenge of managing growth. Third and most important, financing decisions are seldom one-time events. Instead, the raising of money at any point in time is just one event in an evolving financial strategy. Yes, ABC Company needs $200 million today, but it will likely need $150 million in two years and an undetermined amount in future years. Consequently, a major element of ABC's present financing decision is the effect today's choice will have on the company's future ability to raise capital. Ultimately, then, a company's financing strategy is closely intertwined with its long-run competitive goals and the way it intends to manage growth.

A word of warning before we begin: Questions of how best to finance a business recall the professor's admonition to students in a case discussion class: "You will find that there are no right answers to these cases, but many wrong ones." In the course of this chapter, you will learn there is no single right answer to the question of how best to finance a business, but you will also discover some important guidelines to help you avoid the many wrong answers.

This chapter addresses a central topic in finance known as OPM: other people's money. We look first at how OPM fundamentally affects the risk and return faced by the owners of any risky asset. We then examine several practical tools for measuring these risk-return effects in a corporate setting, and we conclude by reviewing current thinking on the determinants of the optimal use of debt by a business. In the course of our review, we will consider the tax implications of various financing instruments, the distress costs a company faces when it relies too heavily on OPM, the incentive effects of high leverage, the challenges faced by companies unable to sell new equity, and what are known as signaling effects. These refer to the way a company's stock price reacts to news that the company intends to sell a particular financing instrument. This chapter's Appendix takes up a major conceptual building block in finance known variously as the irrelevance proposition or the M&M theorem.

Financial Leverage

In physics, a lever is a device to increase force at the cost of greater movement. In business, OPM, or what is commonly called *financial leverage,* is a device to increase owners' expected return at the cost of greater risk. Mechanically, financial leverage involves the substitution of fixed-cost debt financing for owners' equity, and because this substitution increases fixed interest expenses, it follows that financial leverage increases the variability of returns to owners— a common surrogate for risk. Financial leverage is, thus, the proverbial two-edged sword, increasing owners' expected return, but also their risk.

Table 6.1 illustrates this fundamental point in the form of a very simple risky investment. Ignoring taxes, the investment requires a $1,000 outlay today in return for a 50-50 chance at either $900 or $1,400 in one year. We are interested in how the owners' expected return and risk vary as we alter the type of financing. Panel A at the top of the table assumes all-equity financing. Observe that the investment promises an equal chance at a return of minus 10 percent or plus 40 percent (a $400 profit on a $1,000 investment implies a 40 percent return). Looking at the bold figures in Panel A, we see that these numbers imply an expected return on the investment of 15 percent, with a range of possible outcomes between −10 percent and +40 percent.

TABLE 6.1   **Debt Financing Increases Expected Return and Risk to Owners**

The Investment: Pay $1,000 today for a 50-50 chance at $900 or $1,400 in one year.				
Panel A: 100% Equity Financing. Owners Invest $1,000.				
Investment Outcome	Probability	To Owners	Return to Owners	Probability Weighted Return
$ 900	0.50	$ 900	−10%	−5%
1,400	0.50	1,400	**40**	20
				Expected return = **15%**

Panel B: 80% Debt Financing; 1-Year Loan at 10% Interest. Owners Invest $200.					
Investment Outcome	Probability	Due Lender	Residual to Owners	Return to Owners	Probability Weighted Return
$ 900	0.50	$880	$ 20	−90%	−45%
1,400	0.50	880	520	**160**	80
					Expected return = **35%**

Now let's pile on the debt and see what happens. Assume we finance 80 percent of the cost of the same investment with an $800, one-year loan at an interest rate of 10 percent. This reduces the owners' investment to $200. Panel B of Table 6.1 shows that while the investment cash flows are unchanged, the residual cash flows to owners change dramatically. Because owners must pay $880 in principal and interest to creditors before receiving anything, they now stand an equal chance of getting back $20 or $520 on their $200 investment. Looking again at the bold numbers in Panel B, this translates into an attractive expected return of 35 percent and a daunting range of possible outcomes between −90 percent and +160 percent.

This example clearly demonstrates that debt financing does two things to owners: It increases their expected return and it increases their risk. The example also illustrates that a single risky investment can be converted into a wide variety of risk-return combinations by simply varying the means of financing. Want to minimize risk and return on an investment? Finance with equity. Willing to take a gamble? Make the same investment, but finance it with some debt. Want to really roll the dice? Crank up the leverage. These same observations apply to companies as well as individual investments: Financial leverage increases expected return and risk to shareholders, and companies are able to generate a wide array of shareholder, risk-return combinations by varying the way they finance the business. (Incidentally, if you are worried about what happens to the $800 owners have left over in Panel B, don't. The same conclusions follow if we assume owners combine their $1,000 of equity with $4,000 of borrowed money to invest $5,000 in the risky asset. All of the dollar figures in Panel B go up, but the returns remain the same.)

A second way to look at financial leverage is to note that it is a close cousin to *operating leverage,* defined as the substitution of fixed-cost methods of production for variable-cost methods. Replacing hourly workers with a robot increases operating leverage because the robot's initial cost pushes up fixed costs, while the robot's willingness to work longer hours without additional pay reduces variable costs. This produces two effects: Sales required to cover fixed costs rise, but once breakeven is reached, profits grow more quickly with additional sales. Analogously, the substitution of debt for equity financing increases fixed costs in the form of higher interest and principal payments, but because creditors do not share in company profits, it also reduces variable costs. Increased financial leverage thus has two effects as well: More operating income is required to cover fixed financial costs, but once breakeven is achieved, profits grow more quickly with additional operating income.

To see these effects more clearly, let's look at the influence of financial leverage on return on equity. Recall from Chapter 2 that despite some problems, ROE is a widely used measure of financial performance defined as profit after tax divided by owners' equity. As shown in the following foot-note, ROE can be written for our purposes as

$$ROE = ROIC + (ROIC - i')\,D/E$$

where ROIC is the company's return on invested capital (defined in Chapter 2 as EBIT after tax divided by all sources of cash on which a return must be earned); i' is the after-tax interest rate, $(1-t)i;$ D is interest-bearing debt; and E is the book value of equity.[1] You can think of ROIC as the return a company earns before the effects of financial leverage are considered. Looking at i', recall that because interest is a tax-deductible expense, a company's tax bill declines whenever its interest expense rises; i' captures this effect.

To illustrate this equation, we can write ROE for Hasbro in 2016 as

$$ROE = 17.5\% + (17.5\% - 4.4\%)\,\$1{,}721/\$1{,}863$$
$$29.6\% = 17.5\% + 12.1\%$$

where 4.4 percent is Hasbro's after-tax borrowing rate, \$1,721 million is its interest-bearing debt, and \$1,863 million is its book value of equity. Hasbro earned a basic return of 17.5 percent on its assets, which it levered into a 29.6 percent return on equity by substituting \$1,721 million of debt for equity in its capital structure.

This revised expression for ROE is revealing. It shows clearly that the impact of financial leverage on ROE depends on the size of ROIC relative to i'. If ROIC exceeds i', financial leverage, as measured by $D/E,$ increases ROE. The reverse is also true: If ROIC is less than i', leverage reduces ROE. In English, the equation states that when a company earns more on borrowed money than it pays in interest, return on equity will rise, and vice versa. Leverage thus improves financial performance when things are going well, but worsens performance when things are going poorly. It is the classic fair-weather friend.

And lest you think that earning a return above borrowing cost is an easy target, be aware that in 2016 only 63 percent of the publicly traded, nonfinan-cial firms accomplished this feat. Even among larger firms with sales above \$200 million, the comparable figure was just 71 percent. In business, as in other walks of life, expectations are often unfulfilled.

Figure 6.1 is a graphical representation of the earlier ROE equation. The steeply pitched, solid curve represents a typical distribution of possible ROEs

---

[1] Write profit after tax as $(EBIT - iD)(1 - t)$, where EBIT is earnings before interest and tax, iD is interest expense—written as the interest rate, $i,$ times interest-bearing debt outstanding, D—and t is the firm's tax rate. This equation reflects the steps an accountant goes through to calculate profit after tax from EBIT. The rest is algebra, as shown in the following equation:

$$ROE = \frac{(EBIT - iD)(1 - t)}{E} = \frac{EBIT(1 - t)}{E} - \frac{iD(1 - t)}{E} = ROIC \times \frac{D + E}{E} - i'\frac{D}{E}$$

FIGURE 6.1 **Leverage Increases Risk and Expected Return**

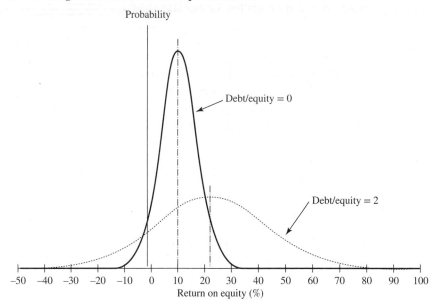

for an all-equity company. Note that the expected ROE is 10 percent and the range of possible outcomes is from a loss of about 12 percent to a gain of 35 percent. The flatter, dotted curve shows the possible ROEs for the same distribution of all-equity returns when the company's debt-to-equity ratio is 2.0 and the after-tax borrowing rate is 4 percent. Debt financing not only levers the expected ROE from 10 percent up to 22 percent but also greatly broadens the range of possible outcomes. Now a loss of as much as 40 percent or a gain of 80 percent can occur.

For at least two reasons, it is appropriate to think of the range of possible ROEs as a measure of risk. First, a larger range of possible outcomes means greater uncertainty about what ROE the company will earn. Second, a larger range of possible outcomes means a greater chance of bankruptcy. Look at the left-side tails of the two distributions; it is apparent that with zero leverage, the worst the company will do is lose about 12 percent on equity, but with a debt-to-equity ratio of 2 to 1, the same level of operating income generates a loss of about 40 percent, more than a threefold increase. In this situation, operating income is not sufficient to cover interest expense, and debt magnifies the loss. If the loss is large enough or persistent enough, bankruptcy can occur. We see again that financial leverage increases both expected return to owners and risk.

Measuring the Effects of Leverage on a Business

For a practical look at measuring the risks and rewards of debt financing in a corporate setting, let us return to the challenge faced by Hasbro in 2017. Recall from Chapter 2 that Hasbro is a stable company with strong profitability relative to its industry peers. Hasbro's high asset turnover suggests that it utilizes its assets efficiently. Although its book value leverage ratios are above the industry average, its market value leverage ratios affirm that Hasbro is conservatively financed. Its chief financial challenge is what to do with the excess cash it is generating.

Here is my fictionalized account of an important financing decision faced by the company. Suppose that in early 2017 Hasbro reaches a tentative agreement to purchase an independent toy manufacturer in China that Hasbro hopes will increase its market share in Asia. The agreed-upon price is $1.8 billion, and Deborah Thomas, Hasbro's CFO, must decide how best to finance it. The firm's investment bankers indicate the company can raise money in either of two ways:

- Sell 20 million new shares of common stock at a net price of $90 a share.

- Sell $1.8 billion of bonds with an interest rate of 5 percent and 10 years to maturity. The bonds would carry an annual sinking fund of $100 million, with the remaining principal of $800 million due in a single balloon payment at maturity.

Hasbro's debt-to-assets ratio has remained fairly constant over the past five years. In book value terms, Hasbro's debt ratio is 63 percent (the industry average is 51 percent), and in market value terms it is 25 percent (the industry average is 35 percent). Higher debt ratios are favored by several younger members of senior management, and they prefer to issue debt for the acquisition. In their words, "We are leaving money on the table and shortchanging our shareholders by not levering up this business." One source of their enthusiasm for debt financing appears to be the perception that higher leverage increases return on equity and earnings per share, key determinants of the company's executive bonuses.

Ms. Thomas is concerned, however, that debt financing for an acquisition of this size, more than doubling total debt outstanding, would put too much strain on the company's financial resources. However, the board of directors deems this new opportunity too important to pass up and has directed Ms. Thomas to prepare a financing recommendation for consideration at their next board meeting. These executives see the current situation as an ideal opportunity to find the right balance between debt and equity financing.

Looking to the future, Ms. Thomas believes that the acquisition would increase Hasbro's earnings before interest and taxes to about $1 billion in 2017. As shown in the following figures, the company's EBIT has been growing quite steadily in recent years. Ms. Thomas further anticipates that Hasbro's need for outside financing in coming years will be modest, unless another acquisition opportunity arises. The company expects to pay annual dividends of $2.35 a share in 2017, and Ms. Thomas believes the board would be quite reluctant to reduce this amount in future years.

	2009	2010	2011	2012	2013	2014	2015	2016	2017F
EBIT ($ millions)	591	590	575	545	445	636	706	807	1,000

F – forecast.

Source: Data from Hasbro annual reports and Compustat.

Hasbro's investment bankers have advised Ms. Thomas that due to substantial fixed issue costs, it makes sense to raise the entire amount through a single issuance of debt or equity. It is possible Hasbro could ultimately choose to use some of its existing cash to help pay for the acquisition, but Ms. Thomas intends initially to analyze the deal assuming the full purchase price is financed externally.

Table 6.2 presents selected information about the two financing options. The table sets up a "what if" analysis, assuming the deal is completed in early 2017. The information in the left-most column in the table represents current assumptions for Hasbro as of early 2017. The table shows that in the absence of any new financing, Hasbro will have $1,721 million in debt outstanding, interest expense of $97 million, and $50 million in principal repayments due. All of these numbers escalate sharply with $1.8 billion in new debt financing. A new stock issue, on the other hand, will leave these quantities unchanged but will increase common shares outstanding from 124.5 million to 144.5 million and total dividend payments from $293 to $340 million ($340 million = 144.5 million shares × $2.35 per share).

TABLE 6.2   Selected Information about Hasbro's Financing Options in 2017 (in millions)

Source: Data from Hasbro annual reports and Compustat.

	2017 Projected		
	Before New Financing	Stock Financing	Bond Financing
Interest-bearing debt outstanding	$1,721	$1,721	$3,521
Interest expense	$ 97	$ 97	$ 187
Principal payments	$ 50	$ 50	$ 150
Shareholders' equity (book value)	$1,863	$3,663	$1,863
Common shares outstanding	124.5	144.5	124.5
Dividends paid at $2.35 per share	$ 293	$ 340	$ 293

Leverage and Risk

Ms. Thomas's first task in analyzing the financing options should be to decide if Hasbro can safely carry the financial burden imposed by the new debt. The best way to do this is to compare the company's forecasted operating cash flows to the annual financial burden imposed by the debt. There are two ways to do this: construct pro forma financial forecasts of the type discussed in Chapter 3, perhaps augmented by sensitivity analysis and simulations, or more simply, calculate several coverage ratios. To provide a flavor of the analysis without repeating much of Chapter 3, I will confine discussion here to coverage ratios on the understanding that if real money were involved, detailed financial forecasting would be the order of the day. Because coverage ratios were treated in Chapter 2, our discussion can be brief.

The before- and after-tax burdens of Hasbro's financial obligations under the two financing options appear in the top portion of Table 6.3. Recall that because we want to compare these financial obligations to the company's EBIT, a before-tax number, we must gross up the after-tax amounts to their before-tax equivalents. This involves dividing the after-tax numbers by $(1 - t)$ where t is the company's tax rate. For this analysis, $t = 30\%$.

Three coverage ratios, corresponding to the progressive addition of each financial obligation listed in Table 6.3, appear in the bottom portion of the table for a projected EBIT of $1,000 million. To illustrate the calculation of these ratios, "times common covered" equals $1,000 million EBIT divided by the sum of all three financial burdens stated in before-tax dollars. For example, in

TABLE 6.3 Hasbro's Projected Financial Obligations and Coverage Ratios in 2017 ($ millions)

Expected EBIT = $1,000	Tax rate = 0.30			
Financial Obligations				
	Stock		**Bonds**	
	After Tax	Before Tax	After Tax	Before Tax
Interest expense		$ 97		$187
Principal payment	$ 50	$ 71	$150	$214
Common dividends	$340	$486	$293	$419
Coverage Ratios				
	Stock		**Bonds**	
	Coverage	Percentage EBIT Can Fall	Coverage	Percentage EBIT Can Fall
Times interest earned	10.3	90%	5.3	81%
Times burden covered	6.0	83%	2.5	60%
Times common covered	1.5	35%	1.2	18%

the bond financing option, $1.2 = 1,000/(187 + 214 + 419)$. Note that our analysis here is not an incremental one. We are interested in the total burden imposed by new *and* existing debt, not just that of the new borrowings.

The column headed "Percentage EBIT Can Fall" offers a second way to interpret coverage ratios. It is the percentage amount that EBIT can decline from its expected level before coverage drops to 1.0. For example, interest expense with bond financing is $187 million; thus, EBIT can fall from $1,000 million to $187 million, or 81 percent, before times interest earned equals 1.0. A coverage of 1.0 is critical, because any lower coverage indicates that operating income will be insufficient to cover the financial burden under consideration, and another source of cash must be available.

As expected, these figures confirm the greater risk inherent in debt financing. In every instance, Hasbro's coverage of its financial obligations will be worse with debt financing than without. In fact, with debt financing, a decline in EBIT of only 18 percent from the projected level will put the company's dividend in jeopardy, although in the short term Hasbro could make up this deficit with excess cash on hand. Missing a dividend payment is admittedly less catastrophic than missing an interest or principal payment, but it is still an eventuality most companies would just as soon avoid. At the same time, the risk of missing a dividend payment may be a manageable one for Hasbro in light of its previously noted operating stability. Hasbro did experience a drop in EBIT of 18 percent in 2013, but in succeeding years its EBIT has increased steadily.

To put these numbers in further perspective, Ms. Thomas will next want to compare them with various industry figures. As an example, the top part of Table 6.4 shows times-interest-earned and debt-to-asset ratios over the past decade for nonfinancial companies in the Standard & Poor's 500 stock index, while the bottom part shows the same information by selected industry in 2016. Note that both ratios show increasing indebtedness, particularly in the more recent years. Ms. Thomas will be especially interested in the numbers for the "consumer discretionary" industry, of which Hasbro is a member. Hasbro's projected 5.3 times interest earned with debt financing is below the industry median of 8.1, while the corresponding number for stock financing of 10.3 would be above it.

Table 6.5 offers a second comparison. It shows the variation in key performance ratios across Standard & Poor's bond-rating categories in 2016. Note that the median times-interest-earned ratio falls from a high of 21 times for AAA companies down to just over one time for B firms (the median CCC firm had negative EBIT). By this yardstick, Hasbro's prospective coverage ratio of 5.3 times with bonds would put it in the BBB range.

TABLE 6.4 Median Corporate Debt Ratios 2007–2016 and Industry Debt Ratios 2016

Source: Data compiled from Compustat database.

Nonfinancial companies in the Standard and Poor's 500 index and industry components. (Numbers in parentheses are the number of companies in sample.)										
	2007	2008	2009	2010	2011	2012	2013	2014	2015	2016
Times interest earned	8.4	7.1	6.5	8.5	9.2	8.7	9.2	9.4	8.0	7.2
Debt to total assets (%)	22.7	24.9	23.4	23.0	23.2	24.8	25.1	26.3	30.2	30.3

Industry Debt Ratios 2016		
	Times interest earned	Debt to total assets (%)
Energy (35)	NM	29.7
Materials (25)	5.3	30.8
Industrials (67)	8.4	30.1
Consumer discretionary (81)	8.1	32.8
Consumer staples (32)	11.1	30.7
Health care (55)	8.9	29.0
Information technology (58)	14.4	23.5
Telecommunicaton services (5)	2.5	43.7
Utilities (28)	3.3	35.9

Debt to total assets is in book values and includes all interest-bearing debt. NM = Not meaningful (median industry EBIT was negative).

TABLE 6.5 Key Ratios by Standard & Poor's Rating Category

Source: Data compiled from Compustat database.

(Median values for nonfinancial firms in 2016)	AAA	AA	A	BBB	BB	B	CCC
Times interest earned	20.9	15.7	6.7	4.7	3.3	1.1	NM
Debt to total assets (%)	23.4	24.2	28.9	31.7	39.3	48.4	67.9
Return on invested capital (%)	14.9	10.4	6.9	5.2	4.2	−2.1	−8.3
Number of companies	2	28	190	418	357	245	46
Percent of sample companies (%)	0.2	2.2	14.8	32.5	27.8	19.1	3.6

Debt to total assets is in book values and includes all interest-bearing debt. NM = Not meaningful (median EBIT for category was negative in 2016).

Leverage and Earnings

Our brief look at Hasbro's coverage ratios under the two financing options suggests that a $1.8 billion bond offering is at least feasible. Next, let's see how the two financing schemes are likely to affect reported income and return on equity. Ms. Thomas can do this by looking at the company's projected income statement under the two options. Ignoring for the moment the possibility that the company's financing choice might affect its sales or operating income, Ms. Thomas can begin her analysis with projected EBIT. Table 6.6 shows the bottom portion of a 2017 pro forma income statement for Hasbro under boom and bust conditions. Bust corresponds to a recessionary EBIT of $200 million, while boom represents a healthy EBIT of $1,200 million.

Several noteworthy observations emerge from these figures. One involves the tax advantage of debt financing. Observe that Hasbro's tax bill is always $27 million lower under bond financing than under the alternative, leaving more operating income to be divided among owners and creditors. It is as if the government pays companies a subsidy, in the form of reduced taxes, to encourage the use of debt financing. Letting t be the company's tax rate and I its interest expense, the subsidy equals tI annually. In Hasbro's case, this subsidy would be $29 million ($tI = $97 million $\times$ 30%) with stock financing, or $56 million ($tI = $187 million $\times$ 30%) with debt financing. The difference between these two numbers is the $27 million mentioned earlier. Many believe this subsidy, frequently referred to as the *interest tax shield* from debt financing, is a chief attraction of debt financing. It is available to any company using debt financing, provided only that it has sufficient taxable income to shield.

A second observation is that debt financing reduces earnings after tax, an apparent disadvantage to debt. However, it is important to realize that this is only half the story, for although debt financing does reduce earnings after tax, it also reduces shareholders' investment in the firm. And, personally, I would rather earn $90 on a $500 investment than $100 on a $1,000 investment. To capture both effects, it is useful to look at earnings per share and return on

TABLE 6.6 Hasbro Inc.'s Partial Pro Forma Income Statements in 2017 under Bust and Boom Conditions (numbers in millions except EPS)

	Bust		Boom	
	Stock	**Bonds**	**Stock**	**Bonds**
EBIT	$ 200	$ 200	$1,200	$1,200
Interest expense	97	187	97	187
Earnings before tax	103	13	1,103	1,013
Tax at 30%	31	4	331	304
Earnings after tax	$ 72	$ 9	$ 772	$ 709
Number of shares	145	125	145	125
Earnings per share	$ 0.50	$ 0.07	$ 5.34	$ 5.70
Book value of equity	3,663	1,863	3,663	1,863
Return on equity	2.0%	0.5%	21.1%	38.1%

equity, two widely tracked indicators of equity performance. First, examining the boom conditions in Table 6.6, we see the expected effect of leverage on shareholder performance: EPS with debt financing is 7 percent higher than with equity, while ROE is a robust 81 percent higher. Under bust conditions, however, the reverse is true: Stock financing in difficult times produces a higher EPS and ROE than debt. This corresponds to our earlier example when the return on invested capital (ROIC) was less than the after-tax interest rate.

To display this information more informatively, Ms. Thomas can construct a range of earnings chart relating either ROE or EPS to EBIT. To do so using ROE, she need only plot the EBIT–ROE pairs calculated in Table 6.6 on a graph and connect the appropriate points with straight lines. Figure 6.2 shows the resulting range of earnings chart for Hasbro. It presents the return on equity Hasbro will report for any level of EBIT under the two financing options. Consistent with our boom-bust pro formas, note that the debt financing line passes through a ROE of 0.5 percent at $200 million EBIT and 38.1 percent at $1,200 million EBIT, while the corresponding figures for stock financing are 2.0 percent and 21.1 percent, respectively.

Ms. Thomas will be particularly interested in two aspects of the range of earnings chart. One is the increase in ROE Hasbro will report at the expected EBIT level if the company selects bonds over stock financing. As the graph shows, ROE will be an attractive 76 percent higher at the expected EBIT of $1 billion. Ms. Thomas will also observe that in addition to generating an immediate increase in ROE, bond financing puts Hasbro on a faster growth

FIGURE 6.2 Range of Earnings Chart for Hasbro

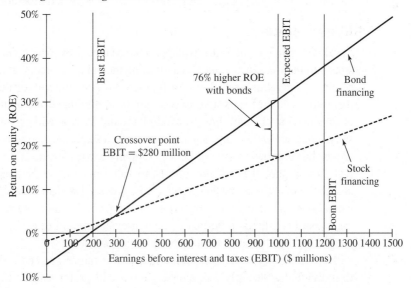

trajectory. This is represented by the steeper slope of the bond financing line. For each dollar Hasbro adds to EBIT, ROE will rise more with bond financing than with equity. Unfortunately, the reverse is also true: For each dollar EBIT declines, ROE will fall more with bond financing than with equity financing.

The second aspect of the range of earnings chart that will catch Ms. Thomas's eye is that debt financing does not always yield a higher ROE. If Hasbro's EBIT falls below a critical crossover value of $280 million, ROE will actually be higher with stock financing than with bonds. Hasbro's expected EBIT is comfortably above the crossover value today, and past EBIT has been quite stable, but there are no guarantees going forward. Higher ROE with bond financing is clearly not a certainty.

How Much to Borrow

Coverage ratios, pro forma forecasts, and range of earnings charts yield important information about Hasbro's ability to support various amounts of debt and about the effect of different debt levels on shareholder returns and earnings. With this foundation, it is now time to confront the chapter's central question: How do we determine what level of debt financing is best for a firm? How does Deborah Thomas decide whether Hasbro should issue debt or equity? There is general agreement that the purpose of a firm's financing decision should be to increase firm value. But what does this imply for specific financing decisions? As noted earlier, the current state of the art will not enable us to answer this question definitively. We can, however, identify the key decision variables and suggest practical guides to Ms. Thomas's deliberations.

Irrelevance

Speaking broadly, there are two possible channels by which financing decisions might affect firm value: by increasing the value investors attach to a given stream of operating cash flows, or by increasing the amount of the cash flows themselves. Some years ago, two economists eliminated the apparently more promising first channel. Franco Modigliani and Merton Miller, known universally today as M&M, demonstrated that when expected operating cash flows are unchanged, the amount of debt a company carries has no effect on its value and, hence, should be of no concern to value-maximizing managers or their shareholders. In their provocative words, when cash flows are constant, "the capital structure decision is irrelevant." In terms of risk and return, M&M demonstrated that what's important is the aggregate amount of each, not how they are divided up among shareholders and creditors.

Note the irony here. Questions of risk and return are centrally important to individuals. Strongly risk-averse people will prefer safe equity financing, while risk-indifferent folks will prefer debt. And, if financing choices are so important at the individual level, it seems only natural to conclude they must also be important to firms. However, this conclusion does not necessarily follow. Indeed, the genius of M&M's irrelevance proposition is to demonstrate that under certain conditions, firm financing choices need not affect value—despite the importance of financing decisions in our personal lives.

Intuitively, M&M's irrelevance argument comes down to this: Companies own physical assets, like trucks and buildings, and owe paper liabilities, like stocks and bonds. A company's physical assets are the true creators of value, and as long as the cash flows from these assets stay constant, it is hard to imagine how simply renaming paper claims to the cash flows could create value. The company is worth no more with one set of paper claims than another.

Just for good measure, here is a second intuitive argument supporting the M&M irrelevance proposition, based on what is known as "homemade" leverage. It rests on the observation that investors have two ways to lever an investment: They can rely on the company to borrow money, or they can borrow money themselves and buy the stock on margin. It is like a boat with two tillers, and whatever leverage tack the company takes with its corporate financing decision, the investor can override with her homemade decision. But if investors can readily substitute homemade leverage for corporate leverage, why would they care how much debt the company employs? How could firm leverage affect its value? (See the Appendix of this chapter for more on the irrelevance proposition and homemade leverage, including a numerical example.)

No rational executive believes M&M's irrelevance proposition is literally true, but most acknowledge it to be the starting point for practical consideration of how financing decisions affect firm value. By demonstrating that renaming paper claims to a firm's cash flows alone does not affect value, M&M direct our attention to the second channel by which financing decisions might affect firm value. They thus confirm that firm financing decisions are important to the extent that they affect the *amount* of the cash flows themselves, and that the best capital structure is the one that maximizes these flows. To decide whether Hasbro should issue debt or equity, Deborah Thomas needs to consider how the change in debt will affect company cash flows.

In the following sections, we examine five ways in which a company's financing decision can affect its cash flows. With a nod to strategy guru Michael Porter, creator of the five forces model, Figure 6.3 outlines the financing decision in what I will modestly call the Higgins 5-Factor Model. The figure also shows each factor's direction of influence when considered in isolation. Thus, tax benefits considered alone suggest more debt financing, while distress costs caution more equity. Ms. Thomas's job is to consider each of these five factors in light of Hasbro's specific circumstances, and come to a reasoned judgment about their collective effect on company cash flows.

FIGURE 6.3 The Higgins 5-Factor Model for Financing Decisions

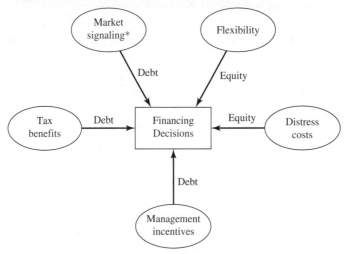

*Technically, market signaling affects investor perceptions of company cash flows, not the cash flows themselves. However, this distinction is not important for present purposes.

Tax Benefits

The tax advantages of debt financing are readily apparent. As noted in Table 6.6, Hasbro's tax bill falls $27 million annually when it increases debt by $1.8 billion—a clear benefit to the firm and its owners. As Warren Buffett so deftly put it, back in the days of a 48 percent corporate tax rate, "If you can eliminate the federal government as a 48 percent partner in your business, it's got to be worth more." As the tax bill goes down, the cash flow available for distribution to owners and creditors rises dollar for dollar. General Electric is an example of one of the biggest beneficiaries of interest tax shields among nonfinancial companies in the U.S. In 2016, G.E. had interest expense of about $5 billion. At a tax rate of 25 percent (G.E.'s average from 2014 to 2016), its interest tax shield was around $1.25 billion, or about 15 percent of G.E.'s net income for the year.

Distress Costs

One popular perspective on selecting an appropriate debt level views the decision as a trade-off between the just-noted tax advantages of debt financing and various costs a company incurs when it uses too much debt. Collectively, these costs are known as the costs of *financial distress.* According to this view, the tax benefits of debt financing predominate at low debt levels, but as debt increases, the costs of financial distress grow to the point where they outweigh the tax advantages. The appropriate debt level, then, involves a judicious balancing of these offsetting costs and benefits.

The costs of financial distress are more difficult to quantify than the benefits of increased interest tax shields, but they are no less important to financing decisions. These costs come in at least three flavors, which we will review briefly under the headings of bankruptcy costs, indirect costs, and conflicts of interest.

Bankruptcy Costs

The expected cost of bankruptcy equals the probability bankruptcy will occur times the costs incurred when it does. As a glance at Hasbro's coverage ratios attests, an obvious problem with aggressive debt financing is that rising debt levels increase the probability the business will be unable to meet its financial obligations. With high debt, what might otherwise be a modest downturn in profits can turn into a contentious bankruptcy as the company finds itself unable to make interest and principal payments in a timely manner.

While this is not the place for a complete review of bankruptcy laws and procedures, two points are worth making. First, bankruptcy does not necessarily imply liquidation. Many bankrupt companies are able to continue operations

---

Different Views of Bankruptcy

Historically, bankruptcy was seen as a black hole in which companies were clumsily dismembered for the benefit of creditors and where shareholders lost everything. Today, executives often view bankruptcy as a quiet refuge where the courts keep creditors at bay while management works on its problems. To be sure, many bankruptcies still signal the immediate death of the company. In a liquidation bankruptcy, often referred to as Chapter 7 bankruptcy in the U.S., the company typically shuts down operations and its assets are sold off to pay creditors. The retail industry has made frequent use of Chapter 7 bankruptcy in recent years, with once-popular stores such as Borders, Circuit City, and Mervyn's bowing out due to competition from online retailing, among other factors.

However, in a reorganization bankruptcy (Chapter 11), the company typically continues operations and hopes to emerge from the bankruptcy healthier and more valuable than when it entered. The airline industry is famous for its use of Chapter 11 over the years. Three of the four largest airlines in the U.S. (Delta, American, and United) and the largest airline in Canada (Air Canada) all successfully emerged from bankruptcy at some point between 2004 and 2013. One potential advantage to airlines in bankruptcy is the ability to reduce labor costs. Continental Airlines first employed this strategy in 1983, using bankruptcy protection to abrogate what it considered ruinous labor contracts. Research shows that from 1992 to 2006, airlines in bankruptcy reduced wage expenses by about 10 percent per year, on average.[a] There are other potential advantages to bankruptcy; some companies have found Chapter 11 an inviting haven while wrestling with product liability suits or massive legal judgments. Nevertheless, be forewarned: Although successful reorganizations of large companies make the news, the majority of Chapter 11 bankruptcies end in failure. Here's hoping your company never has to go down that road.

[a] Efraim Benmelech, Nittai Bergman, and Ricardo Enriquez, "Negotiating with Labor under Financial Distress," *Review of Corporate Finance Studies*, September 2012, 28–67.

while they reorganize their business and are eventually able to leave bankruptcy and return to normal life. Second, bankruptcy in the United States is a highly uncertain process. For once in bankruptcy, a company's fate rests in the hands of a bankruptcy judge and a multitude of attorneys, each representing an aggrieved party and each determined to pursue the best interests of his or her client until justice is done or the money runs out. Bankruptcy today is thus akin to a high-stakes poker game in which the only certain winners are attorneys. And, depending on their luck, managers and owners can come away with a revitalized business or next to nothing.

Increased debt clearly heightens the probability of bankruptcy, but this is not the whole story. The other important consideration is the cost to the business if bankruptcy does occur. If bankruptcy involves only a few amicable meetings with creditors to reschedule debt, there is little need to limit borrowing to avoid bankruptcy. On the other hand, if bankruptcy spells immediate liquidation at fire-sale prices, aggressive borrowing is obviously foolhardy. A key factor in determining the cost of bankruptcy to an individual company is what can be called the "resale" value of its assets. Two simple examples will illustrate this notion.

First, suppose ACE Corporation's principal asset is an apartment complex and, due to local overbuilding and overly aggressive use of debt financing, ACE has been forced into bankruptcy. Because apartment complexes are readily salable, the likely outcome of the proceedings will be the sale of the complex to a new owner and distribution of the proceeds to creditors. The cost of bankruptcy in this instance will be correspondingly modest, consisting of the obvious legal, appraisal, and court costs, plus whatever price concessions are necessary to sell the apartments. In substance, because bankruptcy will have little effect on the operating income generated by the apartment complex, its costs will be relatively low, and ACE can justify aggressive debt financing.

Note that the cost of bankruptcy here does *not* include the difference between what ACE and its creditors originally thought the apartments were worth and their value just prior to bankruptcy. This loss is due to over-building, not bankruptcy, and is incurred by the firm regardless of how it is financed or whether or not it declares bankruptcy. Even all-equity financing, while it may prevent bankruptcy, will not eliminate this loss.

At the other extreme, Moletek is a genetic engineering firm whose chief assets are a brilliant research team and attractive growth opportunities. If Moletek stumbles into bankruptcy, the cost is likely to be very high. Selling the company's assets individually in a liquidation will generate little cash because most of the assets are intangible. It will also be difficult to realize value by keeping the company intact, either as an independent firm or in the hands of a new owner, for in such an unsettled environment it will be hard to retain key employees and to raise the funds needed to exploit growth opportunities. In essence, because bankruptcy will adversely affect Moletek's operating income, its costs are likely to be high and Moletek would be wise to use debt sparingly.

In sum, our brief overview of bankruptcy costs suggests that they vary with the nature of a company's assets. If the resale value of the assets is high either in liquidation or when sold intact to new owners, bankruptcy costs are correspondingly modest. Such firms should be expected to make liberal use of debt financing. Conversely, when resale value is low because the assets are largely intangible and would be difficult to sell intact, bankruptcy costs are comparatively high. Companies matching this profile should use more conservative financing.

Another way to say the same thing is to suggest that the value of a company is composed of two types of assets: physical assets in place, and growth options. Growth options are the exciting investment opportunities a firm is positioned to undertake in coming years. While physical assets tend to retain value in times of financial distress, growth options clearly do not. Consequently, companies with valuable growth options are ill advised to use aggressive debt financing.

Indirect Costs

In addition to direct bankruptcy costs, companies frequently incur a number of more subtle indirect costs as the probability of bankruptcy grows. These costs are especially troublesome because they can be mutually reinforcing, causing a chain reaction in which one cost feeds on another. Internally, these costs include lost profit opportunities as management cuts back investment, R&D, and marketing to conserve cash. Externally, they include lost sales as customers become concerned about future parts and service availability, higher financing costs as investors worry about future payments, and increased operating costs as suppliers become reluctant to make long-run commitments or to provide trade credit. Lost sales and increased costs, in turn, pressure management to become even more conservative, risking further losses. And if this weren't enough, competitors, tasting blood in the water, are inclined to initiate price wars and to compete more aggressively for the company's customers.

Trade creditors in certain industries show an especially strong propensity to cut and run. With a portfolio of perhaps thousands of small-ticket receivables to manage, these suppliers are unwilling to work with ailing customers and instead rush for the exits at the first sign of trouble. With a conservative management, restless customers, aggressive competitors, and flighty suppliers, the slope between financial health and bankruptcy can be a slippery one.

Conflicts of Interest

Managers, owners, and creditors in healthy companies usually share the same fundamental objective: to see the business prosper. When a company falls into financial distress, however, this harmony can evaporate as the various parties begin to worry more about themselves than the firm. The resulting conflicts of interest are a third potential cost of aggressive debt financing. One such conflict is known as the overinvestment problem. However, it might more aptly be called the "go-for-broke" problem.

Suppose that a certain company is in serious financial difficulty due to over-borrowing, and shareholders' equity is almost worthless. Realizing that shareholders are about to be wiped out, an opportunistic banker proposes a wildly risky investment scheme. Under normal conditions, the company would never consider the investment, but it presently offers one compelling attraction: a small chance at a very large payoff. Shareholders look at the scheme and reason, "This is a truly bad investment, but if we do nothing, our shares will likely end up worthless, while if we make this investment, there is at least a small chance of hitting the jackpot. Then, we can settle our debts, and walk away with a little something for ourselves. So what have we got to lose? Let's go for broke." This reasoning accurately describes the U.S. savings and loan industry in the late 1980s when many owners, faced with the near certainty their equity would soon be wiped out, took wild risks with depositors' money in the hope of a big score.[2] In one extraordinary case, FedEx founder Fred Smith quite literally gambled with the company's money in FedEx's troubled early days. Realizing that the company lacked sufficient cash to pay its fuel bill, Smith took the company's last $5,000 to Las Vegas and won $27,000 playing blackjack—enough to pay the fuel bill and keep the company running for another week.[3]

So what do these musings about the relative importance of taxes and financial distress costs imply about how to finance a business? Our analysis suggests that managers should consider the following three firm-specific factors when making financing choices:

1. The ability of the company to utilize additional interest tax shields over the life of the debt.

2. The increased probability of incurring financial distress costs created by any new leverage.

3. The magnitude of the distress costs should they occur.

Applying this checklist to Hasbro, we can say that the first consideration should be no barrier to increased debt inasmuch as the company appears to have plenty of income to take advantage of the increased interest tax shields. Similarly, the company's past income stability suggests the increased chance

---

[2] Underinvestment problems can also arise in near-bankrupt companies when managers knowingly forgo attractive, safe investment opportunities because too much of the benefits accrue to creditors instead of shareholders.

[3] Roger Frock, *Changing How the World Does Business: FedEx's Incredible Journey to Success — The Inside Story* (San Francisco: Berrett Kohler, 2006), p. 101.

of incurring financial distress due to the new, higher debt level is probably not excessive. Finally, the distress costs incurred by Hasbro, if it were to have difficulty servicing the new debt, appear moderate. The company is not seasonal and does not appear dependent on potentially nervous supplier credit. A price war seems unlikely because Hasbro's products are differentiated from their competitors' products. Furthermore, as a mature company with mostly low-tech products, it's likely that a relatively small part of Hasbro's value comes from growth options. Finally, customers probably won't worry about Hasbro's level of financial distress when purchasing products, because toys and games carry fewer concerns about long-term servicing or warranties.

Flexibility

The tax benefits–distress costs perspective treats financing decisions as if they were one-time events. Should Hasbro raise cash today by selling debt or equity? A broader perspective views such individual decisions within the context of a longer-run financing strategy that is shaped in large part by the firm's growth potential and its access to capital markets over time.

At one extreme, if a firm has the rare luxury of always being able to raise debt or equity capital on acceptable terms, its decision is straightforward. The company can simply select a target capital structure premised on consideration of long-run tax benefits and distress costs and then base specific debt-equity choices on the proximity of its existing capital structure to the target. If the existing debt level is below target, debt financing is the obvious choice. If the current debt level is above target, time to issue equity.

In the more realistic case where continuous access to capital markets is not guaranteed, the decision becomes more complex. For now, management must worry not only about long-run targets but also about how today's decision might affect future access to capital markets. This is the notion of financial flexibility: the concern that today's decision not jeopardize future financing options.

To illustrate the importance of financial flexibility to certain firms, consider the challenges faced by XYZ Enterprises, a rapidly growing business in continuing need of external financing. Even when an immediate debt issue appears attractive, XYZ management must understand that extensive reliance of debt financing will eventually "close off the top," meaning added debt financing would no longer be available without a proportional increase in equity. (Top as used here refers to the top portion of the liabilities side of an American balance sheet. British balance sheets show equity on top of liabilities, but then they drive on the wrong side too.) Having thus reached its debt capacity, XYZ would find itself dependent on the equity market for any additional external financing over the next few years. This is a precarious position because equity can be a fickle source of financing. Depending on market conditions and recent company performance, equity may not be available at a reasonable price—or indeed any price. And XYZ would then be forced to forgo attractive investment opportunities for lack of cash. This could prove very expensive, because the inability to make competitively mandated investments can result in a permanent loss of market position. On a more personal note, the CFO's admission that XYZ must pass up lucrative investment opportunities because he cannot raise the money to finance them will not be greeted warmly by his colleagues. Consequently, a concern for financing future growth suggests that XYZ avoid over-reliance on debt financing, thereby maintaining financial flexibility to meet future contingencies.

Some companies, especially in industries with rapidly changing technology, appear to value financial flexibility above all other considerations. Facebook is one company that holds almost zero debt, despite having plenty of earnings (over $10 billion in 2016) and plenty of cash on hand (around $30 billion in 2016). Surely, Facebook could issue at least some debt, benefit from the interest tax shield, and still not incur even the slightest hint of any costs of financial distress. But Facebook's immense financial flexibility gives it the ability to make any desired acquisitions (it has made over 60, including WhatsApp for $19 billion) and to make the necessary investments to react to any competitive threats.

The situation is more extreme for most small companies and many larger ones that are unable or unwilling to sell new equity. For these firms, the financing decision is not whether to issue debt or equity, but whether to issue debt or restrict growth. Of necessity, these companies need to place their financing decision in the larger context of managing growth. Recall from Chapter 4 that when a company is unable or unwilling to sell new equity, its sustainable growth rate is

$$g^* = PRA\hat{T}$$

where P, R, A, and $\hat{T}$ are profit margin, retention ratio, asset turnover ratio, and financial leverage, respectively. In this equation, P and A are determined on the operating side of the business. The financial challenge for these companies is to develop dividend, financing, and growth strategies that enable the firm to expand at an appropriate rate without using too much debt or resorting to common stock financing.

An executive student of mine once told me I would never do anything entrepreneurial because "you know too much about what could go wrong." In the case of debt financing, I am inclined to agree. Too many entrepreneurs, convinced of the eventual success of their endeavors, appear to view debt as an unmitigated blessing. In their eyes, debt's only attribute is that it enables them to expand the size of their empire beyond their own net worth; thus, their growth management strategy becomes to borrow as much money as creditors will lend. In other words, they maximize $\hat{T}$ in the preceding equation. Delegating the financing decision to creditors certainly simplifies life, but it also unwisely puts a critical management decision in the hands of self-interested

Reverse Engineering the Capital Structure Decision

Most companies select or stumble into a particular capital structure and then pray the rating agencies will treat them kindly when rating the debt. Other businesses, however, reverse engineer the process by first selecting the bond rating they want and then working backward to estimate the maximum amount of debt consistent with the chosen rating. Several consulting companies facilitate this effort by selling proprietary models—based on the observed pattern of past rating agency decisions—for predicting what bond rating a company will receive at differing debt levels.

The appeal of reverse engineering the capital structure decision is twofold. First, it reveals how much more debt a company can take on before suffering a rating downgrade. This is important information to businesses concerned about overuse of debt and to those interested in increasing the interest tax shields associated with debt financing. Second, it eliminates all speculation about how creditors will respond to a particular financing decision, enabling executives to focus instead on the more concrete question of what credit rating is appropriate for their company given its current prospects and strategy.

outsiders. The smarter approach is to select a prudent capital structure and manage the firm's growth rate to lie within this constraint.

Market Signaling

Concern for future financial flexibility customarily favors equity financing today. A persuasive counterargument against equity financing, however, is the stock market's likely response. In Chapter 4, we mentioned that, on balance, U.S. corporations do not make extensive use of new equity financing and suggested several possible explanations for this apparent bias. It is time now to discuss another.

Academic researchers have explored the stock market's reaction to various company announcements regarding future financing, and the results make fascinating reading. Performing event studies similar to the one described in Chapter 5 on thousands of common stock offerings, researchers have consistently found that a large majority of companies experience a decline in stock price averaging two to three percent, and that the declines cannot reasonably be attributed to chance.[4]

On the surface, a loss of two to three percent of market value may not sound like much. But when measured relative to the amount of money to be raised, the loss is quite startling. In their pioneering study of 531 common stock offerings, Paul Asquith and David Mullins showed that announcement

---

[4] See, for example, Michael Lemmon and Jaime Zender, "Debt Capacity and Tests of Capital Structure Theories," *Journal of Financial and Quantitative Analysis,* October 2010, pp. 1161–1187.

losses average *more than 30 percent* of the size of the new issue.[5] To put this number in perspective, a 30 percent loss means that a company planning a $100 million equity issue can expect to suffer a $30 million decline in market value when it announces the sale. For the worst 6 percent of the issues in the Asquith and Mullins study, the unhappy companies actually lost more in market value from the announcement effect than they hoped to raise from the issue itself. The cloud communications firm Twilio fell in this unfortunate category in October 2016 when it announced a stock offering of $400 million. Within a day, the company's stock had fallen by over 14 percent, for a loss of market value of about $720 million, 180 percent of the size of the issue.

To complete the picture, similar studies of debt announcements have not observed the adverse price reactions found for equity financing. Further, it appears that equity announcements work both ways; that is, a company's announcement of its intention to repurchase some of its shares is greeted by a significant increase in stock price.

Why do these price reactions occur? Several explanations are possible. One suggested most often by executives and market practitioners attributes the observed price reactions to dilution. According to this reasoning, a new equity issue slices the corporate pie into more pieces and reduces the portion of the pie owned by existing shareholders. It is therefore natural that the shares existing shareholders own will be worth less. Conversely, when a company repurchases its shares, each remaining share represents ownership of a larger portion of the company and hence is worth more.

Other observers, including yours truly, remain unconvinced by this reasoning, pointing out that while an equity issue may be analogous to slicing a pie into more pieces, the pie also grows by virtue of the equity issue. When a company raises $100 million in new equity, it is clearly worth $100 million more than before the issue. And there is no reason to expect that a smaller slice of a larger pie is necessarily worth less; nor is there any reason to expect remaining shareholders to necessarily gain from a share repurchase. True, each post-repurchase share represents a larger percentage ownership claim, but the repurchase also reduces the size of the company.

A more intriguing explanation involves what is known as *market signaling*. Suppose, plausibly enough, that Hasbro's top managers know much more about their company than do outside investors, and consider again Hasbro's range of earnings chart in Figure 6.2. Begin by reflecting on which option you would recommend if, as Hasbro's chief financial officer, you were highly optimistic about the company's performance in coming years. After a thorough analysis

---

[5] Paul Asquith and David Mullins, Jr., "Equity Issues and Offering Dilution," *Journal of Financial Economics,* January–February 1986, pp. 61–89.

of the market for Hasbro's products and its competitors, you are confident that EBIT can only grow over the next decade. If you have been awake the last few sections, you will know that the most attractive option in this circumstance is debt financing. The higher debt level produces a higher ROE today and puts the company on a steeper growth trajectory. Moreover, growing operating income will make it easier to support the higher financial burden of the debt.

Now reverse the exercise and consider which option you would recommend if you were concerned about Hasbro's prospects, fearing that future EBIT might well decline. In this scenario, equity financing is the clear winner because of its superior coverage and higher ROE at low operating levels.

But if those who know the most about a company prefer debt when the future looks bright and equity when it looks grim, what does an equity announcement tell investors? Right: It signals the market that management is concerned about the future and has opted for the safe financing choice. Is it any wonder, then, that stock price falls on the announcement and that many companies are reluctant to even mention the "E" word, much less sell it?

The market signal conveyed by a share repurchase announcement is just the reverse. Top management is optimistic about the company's future prospects and perceives that current stock price is inexplicably low, so low that share repurchase constitutes an irresistible bargain. A repurchase announcement therefore signals good news to investors, and stock price rises.

A more Machiavellian view, which nonetheless comes to the same conclusion, sees management as exploiting new investors by opportunistically selling shares when they are overpriced and repurchasing them when they are underpriced. But regardless of whether management elects to sell new equity because it is concerned about the company's future or because it wants to gouge new investors, the signal is the same: New equity announcements are bad news and repurchase announcements are good news.

The need to sell equity at a discount is an example of what economists call the "lemons problem." Whenever the seller of an asset knows more about it than a buyer, the buyer, fearing she is being offered a lemon, will only purchase the asset at a bargain price. And the greater the information disparity between seller and buyer, the greater the discount will have to be. Your neighbor, who is trying to sell his month-old Mercedes, might be telling the truth when he says he only wants to sell it because he changed his mind about the color. But then again, maybe he is not. Maybe the car has serious problems he is not revealing. Maybe it's a lemon. To guard against this possibility, a wise but uninformed buyer will only buy the car at a steep discount from the original price. Moreover, wise sellers, knowing they can only sell almost-new cars at a steep discount, will get used to the color, which, in turn, only increases the odds that the remaining almost-new cars for sale really are lemons.

Stewart Myers of MIT reasons that this lemons problem encourages companies to adopt what he calls a "pecking order" approach to financing.[6] At the top of the pecking order as the most preferred means of financing are internal sources, retained profits, depreciation, and excess cash accumulated from past profit retentions. Companies prefer internal financing sources because they avoid the lemons problem entirely. External sources are second in order of preference, with debt financing dominating equity because it is less likely to generate a negative signal. Or said differently, debt is preferred to equity because the information disparity between seller and buyer is less with debt, resulting in a smaller lemons problem. The financing decision, then, essentially amounts to working progressively down this pecking order in search of the first feasible source. Myers also notes that the observed debt-to-equity ratios of such pecking-order companies are less a product of a rational balancing of advantages and disadvantages of debt relative to equity and more the aggregate result over time of the company's profitability relative to its investment needs. Thus, high-profit-margin, modestly growing companies can get away with little or no debt, while lower-margin, more rapidly expanding businesses may be forced to live with higher leverage ratios.

Management Incentives

Incentive effects are not relevant in most financing decisions, but when relevant, their influence can be dominating.

Managers in many companies enjoy a degree of autonomy from owners. And human nature being what it is, they are inclined to use this autonomy to pursue their own interests rather than those of owners. This separation of ownership and control enables managers to indulge their personal preferences for such things as retaining profits in the business rather than returning them to owners, pursuing growth at the expense of profitability, and settling for satisfactory performance rather than excellence.

A virtue of aggressive debt financing in some instances is that it can reduce the gap between owners' interests and those of managers. The mechanics are simple. When a company's interest and principal repayment burden is high, even the most recalcitrant manager understands that he must generate healthy cash flows or risk losing the business and his job. With creditors breathing down their necks, managers quickly find there is no room for ill-advised investments or less than maximum effort. Financier Joseph Perella explained the relationship between debt and efficiency rather bluntly, "Every company has got people sitting around who do nothing for what they get paid. If they take on a lot of debt, it forces them to cut fat."[7] As discussed in more detail in

---

[6] Stewart C. Myers, "The Capital Structure Puzzle," *Journal of Finance,* July 1984, pp. 575–592.
[7] Michael Lewis, *Liar's Poker,* New York: W.W. Norton, 2014, p. 275.

International Differences in Leverage

Recent research reveals substantial geographical differences in corporate financing practices.[a] Looking at public companies in 39 countries around the globe, the study reports that median debt ratios (measured as interest-bearing debt/firm market value) range from over 50 percent for firms in South Korea to below 10 percent for those in Australia. Although there are exceptions, the general trend is that companies headquartered in developed countries, such as Canada and the United Kingdom, carry lower debt ratios, while those in developing countries, such as Indonesia and Pakistan, have higher debt ratios.

The study also shows that the maturity of debt used by companies varies a great deal across countries. Firms in stable, developed economies strongly favor long-term debt, while those in developing economies rely much more on short-term financing. At the extremes, the median ratio of long-term debt to total debt for firms in New Zealand is almost 90 percent, while the same figure for businesses in China is less than 10 percent.

Why such large differences in leverage in different countries? Of course there are many reasons, but the research shows that much of the variation comes down to the reaction of investors and firms to the country's legal and judicial systems. Or said differently, the relative importance of the Higgins 5-Factor variables discussed here varies with the host country's legal and regulatory practices. So, when a country's tax code favors debt financing, firms in that country will use more debt. No surprise there. Similarly, if a country is lax in its enforcement of debt contracts, lenders there will insist on short-term loans to retain more control over their investment. In sum, even if two firms in different countries operate in the exact same business, don't assume that they will necessarily have similar financial structures.

[a] Joseph P. H. Fan, Sheridan Titman, and Garry Twite, "An International Comparison of Capital Structure and Debt Maturity Choices," *Journal of Financial and Quantitative Analysis,* April 2012, pp. 23–56.

Chapter 9, leveraged buyout firms have found that aggressive debt financing, especially when combined with significant management ownership, can create powerful incentives to improve performance. Ownership in such highly levered companies serves as a carrot to encourage superior performance, while the high debt level is a stick to punish inferior performance.

The Financing Decision and Growth

We have examined five ways in which a company's financing choices can affect its cash flows and hence its value. The art of the financing decision is to weigh the relative importance of these five forces for the specific firm. To illustrate the process, let's consider what these forces suggest about how debt levels should vary with firm growth.

Rapid Growth and the Virtues of Conservatism

Review of the likely effect of the five forces on rapidly growing businesses strongly suggests that high growth and high debt are a dangerous combination. First, the most powerful engine of value creation in a rapidly growing business is new investment, not interest tax shields or incentive effects that might accompany debt financing. Better, therefore, to make financing a passive servant to growth by striving to maintain unrestricted access to financial markets. This implies modest debt financing. Second, to the extent that high-growth firms generate volatile income streams, chances of financial distress rise rapidly as interest coverage falls. Third, because much of a high-growth firm's value is represented by intangible growth opportunities, expected distress costs of such firms are large.

These considerations suggest the following financing polices for rapidly growing businesses:

- Maintain a conservative leverage ratio with ample unused borrowing capacity to ensure continuous access to financial markets.

- Adopt a modest dividend payout policy that enables the company to finance most of its growth internally.

- Use cash, marketable securities, and unused borrowing capacity as temporary liquidity buffers to provide financing in years when investment needs exceed internal sources.

- If external financing is necessary, use debt only to the point where the leverage ratio begins to affect financial flexibility.

- Sell equity rather than limit growth, thereby constraining growth only as a last resort after all other alternatives have been exhausted.

Low Growth and the Appeal of Aggressive Financing

Compared to their rapidly growing brethren, slow-growth companies have a much easier time with financing decisions. Because their chief financial problem is disposing of excess operating cash flow, concerns about financial flexibility and adverse market signaling are largely foreign to them. However, beyond merely eliminating a problem, this situation creates an opportunity that a number of companies have successfully exploited. The logic goes like this. Face the reality that the business has few attractive investment opportunities, and seek to create value for owners through aggressive use of debt financing. Use the company's healthy operating cash flow as the magnet for borrowing as much money as is feasible, and use the proceeds to repurchase shares.

Such a strategy promises at least three possible payoffs to owners. First, increased interest tax shields reduce income taxes, leaving more money for investors. Second, the share repurchase announcement should generate a positive market signal. Third, the high financial leverage may significantly improve management incentives. Thus, the burden high financial leverage imposes on management to make large, recurring interest and principal payments or face bankruptcy may be just the elixir needed to encourage them to squeeze more cash flow out of the business.

In summary, an old saw among bank borrowers is that the only companies banks are willing to lend money to are those that don't need it. We see now that much the same dynamic may be at work on the borrowers' side. Slow-growth businesses that don't need external financing may find it attractive to finance aggressively, while rapidly growing businesses in need of external cash find it appealing to maintain conservative capital structures.

Empirical work supports the wisdom of this perspective. In their study of the ties between company value and the use of debt financing, John McConnell and Henri Servaes have found that, for high-growth businesses, increasing leverage reduces firm value, while precisely the reverse is true for slow-growth businesses.[8]

What does all this imply for Hasbro's decision? Based on the information available, my advice on balance is to issue debt. Unless management anticipates

Aggressive Financing Tactics

Over the years, companies have used varying degrees of aggressiveness in their attempts to increase firm value through higher leverage. Back in 1986, Colt Industries, facing slow growth, decided it was time to "go big or go home." Colt recapitalized its business by offering shareholders $85 in cash plus one share of stock in the newly recapitalized company in exchange for each old share held. To finance the $85 cash payment, Colt borrowed $1.4 billion, raising total long-term debt to $1.6 billion and reducing the book value of shareholders' equity to *minus* $157 million, meaning Colt's liabilities exceeded the book value of its assets by $157 million. We are talking serious leverage here. But how did Colt shareholders make out? Quite well, thank you. Just prior to the announcement of the exchange offer, Colt's shares were trading at $67, and immediately after the exchange, shares in the recapitalized company were trading for $10. So the offer came down to this: $85 cash plus one new share of stock worth $10 in exchange for each old share worth $67. This works out to a windfall gain to owners of $28 a share, or 42 percent ($28 = $85 + $10 − $67).

Recent examples are not as dramatic, but companies still use aggressive financing tactics to good effect. In April 2017, Costco announced a dividend of $7 per share, or $3.1 billion total. The payment to shareholders was funded primarily by an accompanying debt issue of $3.8 billion, which increased Costco's outstanding long-term debt by over 50 percent. However, despite the increase in leverage, Costco CFO Richard Galanti emphasized that the transaction would not endanger Costco's financial flexibility. Shareholders seemed to like the strategy, as Costco shares rose about 3 percent when the dividend was announced. Many other companies have employed debt-funded dividends or repurchases in recent years, including Sirius XM satellite radio, Nathan's Famous hot dogs, and McGraw-Hill Education, publisher of distinguished books such as the one you are reading right now.*

* Maxwell Murphy and Mike Cherney, "Bond-Funded Dividends, Buybacks Draw Skeptics," *Wall Street Journal*, June 26, 2015.

[8] John J. McConnell and Henri Servaes, "Equity Ownership and the Two Faces of Debt," *Journal of Financial Economics,* September 1995, pp. 131–157.

an imminent return to rapid growth or more large acquisitions, flexibility would not appear to be a major concern, and equity's $540 million signaling cost would certainly be painful ($540 million = 30% × $1.8 billion). Meanwhile, debt's $27 million first-year interest tax shield would be nice, and the increased interest and principal requirements on the new debt might encourage management to work harder and smarter. As to risks, Hasbro's historically stable cash flows suggest that expected distress costs will remain modest, even at the lower interest coverage ratios created by the debt financing. Finally, debt financing will help solve Hasbro's continuing problem of what to do with the excess cash being generated. In the future, they can use some of it to service the new debt. All in all, a nice package.

Selecting a Maturity Structure

When a company decides to raise debt, the next question is: What maturity should the debt have? Should the company take out a one-year loan, sell seven-year notes, or market 30-year bonds? Looking at the firm's entire capital structure, the minimum-risk maturity structure occurs when the maturity of liabilities equals that of assets, for in this configuration, cash generated from operations over coming years should be sufficient to repay existing liabilities as they mature. In other words, the liabilities will be self-liquidating. If the maturity of liabilities is less than that of assets, the company incurs a refinancing risk because some maturing liabilities will have to be paid off from the proceeds of newly raised capital. Also, the rollover of maturing debt is not an automatic feature of capital markets. When the maturity of liabilities is greater than that of assets, cash provided by operations should be more than sufficient to repay existing liabilities as they mature. This provides an extra margin of safety, but it also means the firm may have excess cash in some periods.

If maturity matching is minimum risk, why do anything else? Why allow the maturity of liabilities to be less than that of assets? Companies mismatch either because long-term debt is unavailable on acceptable terms or because management anticipates that mismatching will reduce total borrowing costs. For example, if the treasurer believes interest rates will decline in the future, an obvious strategy is to use short-term debt now and hope to roll it over into longer-term debt at lower rates in the future. Of course, efficient-markets advocates criticize this strategy on the grounds that the treasurer has no basis for believing she can forecast future interest rates.

Inflation and Financing Strategy

An old adage in finance is that it's good to be a debtor during inflation because the debtor repays the loan with depreciated dollars. It is important to understand, however, that this saying is correct only when the inflation is unexpected.

When creditors expect inflation, the interest rate they charge rises to compensate for the expected decline in the purchasing power of the loan principal. This means it is not necessarily advantageous to borrow during inflation. In fact, if inflation unexpectedly declines during the life of a loan, it can work to the disadvantage of the borrower. The proper statement of the old adage, therefore, is that it's good to be a borrower during *unexpected* inflation.

APPENDIX

The Irrelevance Proposition

This appendix demonstrates the irrelevance of capital structure proposition mentioned in the chapter and illustrates in greater detail why the tax deductibility of interest favors debt financing. The irrelevance proposition says that holding expected cash flows constant, the way a company finances its operations has no effect on firm or shareholder value. As far as owners are concerned, a company might just as well use 90 percent debt financing as 10 percent.

The irrelevance proposition is significant not because it describes reality, but because it directs attention to what's important about financing decisions: understanding how financing choices affect firm cash flows. The proposition is also an interesting intellectual puzzle in its own right.

No Taxes

Legend has it that a waitress once asked Yogi Berra how many pieces he'd like his pizza cut into, and he replied, "You'd better make it six; I don't think I'm hungry enough to eat eight." Absent taxes, a company's financing decision can be likened to slicing Yogi's pizza: No matter how you slice up claims to the firm's cash flow, it is still the same firm with the same earning power and hence the same market value. The benefits of increased return to shareholders from higher leverage are precisely offset by the increased risks so that market value is unaffected by leverage.

Here is an example demonstrating this assertion. Your stockbroker has come up with two possible investments: Timid Inc. and Bold Company. The two firms happen to be identical in every respect except that Timid uses no debt financing while Bold relies on 80 percent debt at an annual interest cost of 10 percent. Each has $1,000 of assets and generates expected annual earnings before interest and tax of $400 in perpetuity. For simplicity, we will suppose that both companies distribute all their earnings every year as dividends.

The first two columns of Table 6A.1 show the bottom portion of pro forma income statements for the two companies in the absence of taxes. Note that

TABLE 6A.1   In the Absence of Taxes, Debt Financing Affects Neither Income nor Firm Value; In the Presence of Taxes, Prudent Debt Financing Increases Income and Firm Value

	No Taxes		Corporate Taxes at 40%	
	Timid Inc.	Bold Co.	Timid Inc.	Bold Co.
Corporate Income				
EBIT	$ 400	$400	$ 400	$400
Interest expense	0	80	0	80
Earnings before tax	400	320	400	320
Corporate tax	0	0	160	128
Earnings after tax	$ 400	$320	$ 240	$192
Investment	$1,000	$200	$1,000	$200
Rate of return	**40%**	**160%**	**24%**	**96%**
Personal Income				
Dividends received	400	320	240	192
Interest expense	80	0	80	0
Total income	$ 320	$320	$ 160	$192
Equity invested	$ 200	$200	$ 200	$200
Rate of return	**160%**	**160%**	**80%**	**96%**
Personal Taxes at 33%				
Income before tax			160	192
Personal taxes			53	63
Income after tax			$ 107	$129
Equity invested			$ 200	$200
Rate of return			**54%**	**64%**

Timid Inc. shows higher earnings because it has no interest expense. Comparing Timid's $400 annual earnings to your prospective investment of $1,000 suggests a 40 percent annual return. Not bad! However, your broker recommends Bold Company, pointing out that because of the company's aggressive use of debt financing, you can purchase its entire equity for only $200. Comparing Bold Company's annual income of $320 to a $200 investment produces an expected annual return of 160 percent ($320/$200 = 160%). Wow!

But you have studied enough finance to know that the expected return to equity almost always rises with debt financing, so this result is not especially surprising. Moreover, a moment's reflection should convince you that it is incorrect to compare returns on two investments with different risk. If the return on investment A is greater than the return on investment B and they have the same risk, A is the better choice. But if A has a higher return and higher risk, as in the present case, all bets are off. Poker players and fighter pilots might prefer investment A despite its higher risk, while we more timid souls might reach the opposite conclusion.

More to the point, it is important to note that you are not dependent on Bold Company for financial leverage. You can borrow on your own account to help pay for your purchase of Timid's shares and in so doing precisely replicate Bold's numbers. The bottom portion of the left two columns in Table 6A.1, labeled Personal Income, show the results of your borrowing $800 at 10 percent interest to finance purchase of Timid's shares. Subtracting $80 interest and comparing your total income to your $200 equity investment, we find that your levered return on Timid stock is now also 160 percent. You can generate precisely the same return on either investment, provided you are willing to substitute personal debt for corporate debt.

So what have we proven? We have shown that when investors can substitute homemade leverage for corporate leverage in the absence of taxes, the way a business is financed does not affect the total return to owners. And if total return is not affected, neither is the value of the business. Firm value is independent of financing. If investors can replicate the leverage effects of corporate borrowing on their own account, there is no reason for them to pay more for a levered firm than an unlevered one. (If the logic here seems a bit counterintuitive, you will be heartened to learn that Franco Modigliani and Merton Miller won Nobel Prizes largely for explaining it.)

Taxes

Let us now repeat our saga in a more interesting world that includes taxes. The figures in the upper-right corner of Table 6A.1 show Timid's and Bold's earnings after taxes in the presence of a 40 percent corporate tax rate. As before, absent any borrowing on your part, Bold continues to offer the more attractive return of 96 percent versus 24 percent for Timid. But contrary to the no-taxes case, the substitution of personal borrowing for corporate borrowing does not eliminate the differential. Even after borrowing $800 to help finance purchase of Timid, your return is only 80 percent versus 96 percent on Bold's stock. The levered business now offers a higher return and thus is more valuable than its unlevered cousin.

Why does debt financing increase the value of a business in the presence of taxes? Look at the tax bills of the two companies. Timid's taxes are $160, while Bold's are only $128, a saving of $32. Three parties share in the fruits of a company's success: creditors, owners, and the tax collector. Our example shows that debt financing, with its tax-deductible interest expense, reduces the tax collector's take in favor of the owners'. In other words, the financing decision increases expected cash flow to owners.

The bottom portion of Table 6A.1 is for suspicious readers who think these results might hinge on the omission of personal taxes. There you will note that imposition of a 33 percent personal tax on income reduces the annual after-tax advantage of debt financing from $32 to $22, but does not eliminate it. Note too that this conclusion holds at any personal tax rate, as long as it is the same for both firms. Because many investors, such as mutual funds and pension funds, do not pay taxes, the convention is to dodge the problem of defining an appropriate personal tax rate by concentrating on earnings after corporate taxes but before personal taxes. We will gratefully follow that convention here.

I should note that our finding of a tax law bias in favor of debt financing is largely an American result. In most other industrialized countries, corporate and personal taxes are at least partially integrated, meaning dividend recipients receive at least partial credit on their personal tax bills for corporate taxes paid on distributed profits. As in our no-tax example, there are no tax benefits to debt financing when corporate and personal taxes are fully integrated.

In the presence of American-style corporate taxes, then, the reshuffling of paper claims to include more debt does create value—at least from the shareholders' perspective, if not from that of the U.S. Treasury—because it increases the cash flow available to private investors. The amount of the increase in annual income to shareholders created by debt financing equals the corporate tax rate times the interest expense, or what we referred to earlier as the interest tax shield. In our example, annual company earnings after tax plus interest expense increases $32 a year ($192 + $80 − $240 = $32), which also equals the tax rate of 40 percent times the interest expense of $80.

Saying the same thing in symbols, if V_L is the value of the company when levered, and V_U is its value unlevered, our example says that

$$V_L = V_U + \text{Value } (tI)$$

where t is the corporate tax rate, I is annual interest expense in dollars, and Value (tI) represents the value today of all future interest tax shields. In the next chapter, we will refer to this last term as the present value of future tax shields. In words, then, our equation says the value of a levered company equals the value of the same company unlevered plus the present value of the interest tax shields.

Taken at face value, this appendix suggests a disquieting conclusion: The value of a business is maximized when it is financed entirely with debt. But you know after reading the chapter that this is just the beginning of our story. For just as the tax deductibility of interest causes firm value to rise with leverage, the costs of financial distress cause it to fall. Add concerns about financial flexibility, market signaling, and incentive effects; season with a pinch of sustainable growth; and you have the recipe for the modern view on corporate financing decisions. Not a feast, perhaps, but certainly a hearty first course.

SUMMARY

1. Financial leverage
   - Is a fundamental financial variable affecting return on equity and sustainable growth.
   - Involves the substitution of fixed cost debt financing for variable cost equity.
   - Like operating leverage, increases breakeven sales but increases the rate of earnings per share growth once breakeven is achieved.
   - Increases expected return and risk to owners.
   - Increases expected ROE and EPS, as well as their variability.
   - Creates a wide array of risk-return combinations out of a single risky investment, depending on the amount of financial leverage used.

2. To measure the effect of leverage on company risk,
   - Stress test pro forma forecasts.
   - Estimate coverage ratios at differing debt levels.
   - Interpret coverage ratios in light of the variability of operating income, the coverage ratios of peers, and across different bond ratings.

3. To measure the effect of leverage on company returns,
   - Assess projected income statements under different economic conditions.
   - Prepare a range of earnings chart noting the increase in ROE and EPS at the projected EBIT level and the proximity of expected EBIT to the "crossover" value.

4. The irrelevance proposition
   - Argues that under idealized conditions and assuming leverage does not affect operating income, financing decisions do not affect firm or shareholder value.
   - Implies that financing decisions are important to the degree that they affect operating income.

5. The Higgins 5-Factor Model
   - Identifies five ways in which company financing can affect operating income:
     - Tax benefits: due to the tax deductibility of interest
     - Distress costs: imposed by various parties when concerns arise about a company's ability to honor its financial obligations
     - Financial flexibility: the possibility that high debt levels will limit future financing options
     - Market signaling: the information managers convey when they opt for one form of financing over another
     - Management incentives: the increased pressure to generate cash flows to meet high debt service obligations

- Emphasizes that the financing decision involves a careful assessment of each factor in light of the company's specific circumstances.
- Suggests that rapidly growing businesses are wise to maintain conservative capital structures, while slow-growth firms may want to consider the opposite strategy.

ADDITIONAL RESOURCES

Andrade, Gregor, and Steven N. Kaplan. "How Costly Is Financial (Not Economic) Distress? Evidence from Highly Leveraged Transactions That Became Distressed." *Journal of Finance,* October 1998, pp. 1443–1493.

   The authors look at 31 highly levered transactions that became distressed due to too much debt and estimate that financial distress costs are in the range of 10 to 20 percent of firm value.

Asquith, Paul, and David W. Mullins, Jr. "Signaling with Dividends, Stock Repurchases, and Equity Issues." *Financial Management,* Autumn 1986, pp. 27–44.

   A well-written summary of empirical work on measuring the capital market's reaction to major equity-related announcements. An excellent introduction to and overview of market signaling.

Hovakimian, Armen, Tim Opler, and Sheridan Titman. "The Debt-Equity Choice." *Journal of Financial and Quantitative Analysis,* March 2001, pp. 1–24.

   Presents evidence that capital structure choices are consistent with the pecking-order theory in the short run but that the tax benefits–distress costs trade-off theory is more important in the long run.

Parsons, Christopher A., and Sheridan Titman. "Empirical Capital Structure: A Review." *Foundations and Trends in Finance,* 2008. 92 pages.

   An accessible, academically oriented survey of empirical work on capital structure decisions divided into three parts: the characteristics of firms associated with different capital structure structures, factors causing firms to move away from their capital structure targets, and the consequences of leverage choices for firm behavior.

Stern, Joel M., and Donald H. Chew, Jr. (Eds.) *The Revolution in Corporate Finance,* 4th ed. Malden, MA: Blackwell Publishing, 2003. 631 pages.

   A collection of practitioner-oriented articles, many by leading academics, originally appearing in the *Journal of Applied Corporate Finance.* See especially "The Modigliani-Miller Proposition after 30 Years," by Merton Miller; "Raising Capital: Theory and Evidence," by Clifford W. Smith, Jr.; and "Still Searching for Optimal Capital Structure," by Stewart C. Myers.

abiworld.org

The American Bankruptcy Institute's website with news and statistics about many aspects of corporate and personal bankruptcy.

khanacademy.org

For brief, easy-to-follow tutorials on capital structure, bankruptcy, and related topics, select Economics and finance > Finance and capital markets > Stocks and bonds. Also available as a free app for iOS or Android.

careers-in-finance.com

This site allows you to explore different career options in finance, including information on required skills, working environments, and salaries.

ifa.com/articles/An_Interview_with_Merton_Miller

A candid interview with Merton Miller on the M&M theory and his philosophy of personal investing. See also interviews with other Nobel Prize winners Gene Fama and Bill Sharpe.

PROBLEMS

Answers to odd-numbered problems appear at the end of the book. Answers to even-numbered problems and additional exercises are available in the Instructor Resources within McGraw-Hill's *Connect* (see the Preface for more information).

1. Looking at Table 6.4, why do public utilities have such a low times-interest-earned ratio? Why is the ratio for information technology companies so high?

2. What is operating leverage? How, if at all, is it similar to financial leverage? If a firm has high operating leverage would you expect it to have high or low financial leverage? Explain your reasoning.

3. Explain why increasing financial leverage increases the risk borne by shareholders.

4. Explain how a company can incur costs of financial distress without ever going bankrupt. What is the nature of these costs?

5. One recommendation in the chapter is that companies with promising investment opportunities should strive to maintain a conservative capital structure. Yet many promising small businesses are heavily indebted.

   a. Why should most companies with promising investment opportunities strive to maintain conservative capital structures?

   b. Why do you suppose many promising small businesses fail to follow this recommendation?

6. Why might it make sense for a mature, slow-growth company to have a high debt ratio?

7. As the chief financial officer of Adirondack Designs, you have the following information:

Next year's expected net income after tax but before new financing	$42 million
Sinking-fund payments due next year on the existing debt	$15 million
Interest due next year on the existing debt	$10 million
Common stock price, per share	$28.00
Common shares outstanding	20 million
Company tax rate	30%

   a. Calculate Adirondack's times-interest-earned ratio for next year assuming the firm raises $50 million of new debt at an interest rate of 4 percent.

   b. Calculate Adirondack's times-burden-covered ratio for next year assuming annual sinking-fund payments on the new debt will equal $5 million.

   c. Calculate next year's earnings per share assuming Adirondack raises the $50 million of new debt.

   d. Calculate next year's times-interest-earned ratio, times-burden-covered ratio, and earnings per share if Adirondack sells 2 million new shares at $25 a share instead of raising new debt.

8. A broker wants to sell a customer an investment costing $100 with an expected payoff in one year of $106. The customer indicates that a 6 percent return is not very attractive. The broker responds by suggesting the customer borrow $90 for one year at 4 percent interest to help pay for the investment.

   a. What is the customer's expected return if she borrows the money?

   b. Does borrowing the money make the investment more attractive?

   c. What does the Irrelevance Proposition say about whether borrowing the money makes the investment more attractive?

9. Explain how each of the following changes will affect a company's range of earnings chart such as that shown in Figure 6.2. How would each of the changes affect the attractiveness of increased debt financing relative to increased equity financing?

   a. An increase in the interest rate on the new debt to be raised.

   b. An increase in the company's stock price.

   c. Increased uncertainty about the issuing company's future earnings.

   d. Increased cash dividends paid on common stock.

   e. An increase in the amount of debt the company already has outstanding.

10. FARO Technologies, whose products include portable 3D measurement equipment, recently had 17 million shares outstanding trading at $35 a share. Suppose the company announces its intention to raise $200 million by selling new shares.

    a. What do market signaling studies suggest will happen to FARO's stock price on the announcement date? Why?

    b. How large a gain or loss in aggregate dollar terms do market signaling studies suggest existing FARO shareholders will experience on the announcement date?

    c. What percentage of the value of FARO's existing equity prior to the announcement is this expected gain or loss?

    d. At what price should FARO expect its existing shares to sell immediately after the announcement?

11. This is a more difficult but informative problem. James Brodrick & Sons, Inc. is growing rapidly and, if at all possible, would like to finance its growth without selling new equity. Selected information from the company's five-year financial forecast follows.

Year	1	2	3	4	5
Earnings after tax ($ millions)	100	130	170	230	300
Capital Investment ($ millions)	175	300	300	350	440
Target book value debt-to-equity ratio (%)	120	120	120	120	120
Dividend payout ratio (%)	?	?	?	?	?
Marketable securities ($ millions)	200	200	200	200	200
(Year 0 marketable securities = $200 million.)					

    a. According to this forecast, what dividends will the company be able to distribute annually without raising new equity and while maintaining a balance of $200 million in marketable securities? What will the annual dividend payout ratio be? (Hint: Remember sources of cash must equal uses at all times.)

    b. Assume the company wants a stable payout ratio over time and plans to use its marketable securities portfolio as a buffer to absorb year-to-year variations in earnings and investments. Set the annual payout ratio equal to the five-year sum of total dividends paid determined in question (a) divided by total earnings. Then, solve for the size of the company's marketable securities portfolio each year.

    c. Suppose earnings fall below forecast every year. What options does the company have for continuing to fund its investments?

d. What does the pecking-order theory say about how management will rank these options?

e. Why might management be inclined to follow this pecking order?

12. An all-equity business has 100 million shares outstanding selling for $20 a share. Management believes that interest rates are unreasonably low and decides to execute a leveraged recapitalization (a recap). It will raise $1 billion in debt and repurchase 50 million shares.

a. What is the market value of the firm prior to the recap? What is the market value of equity?

b. Assuming the Irrelevance Proposition holds, what is the market value of the firm after the recap? What is the market value of equity?

c. Do equity shareholders appear to have gained or lost as a result of the recap? Please explain.

d. Assume now that the recap increases total firm cash flows, which adds $100 million to the value of the firm. Now what is the market value of the firm? What is the market value of equity?

e. Do equity shareholders appear to have gained or lost as a result of the recap in this revised scenario?

13. In recent years, Haverhill Corporation has averaged net income of $10 million per year on net sales of $100 million per year. It currently has no long-term debt, but is considering a debt issue of $5 million. The interest rate on the debt would be 6 percent. Haverhill currently faces an effective tax rate of 35 percent. What would be Haverhill's annual interest tax shield if it goes through with the debt issuance?

14. This problem asks you to analyze the capital structure of HCA, Inc., the largest private operator of health care facilities in the world. In 2006, a syndicate of private equity firms acquired the firm for $31.6 billion and took it private. In November 2010, as interest rates hit record lows, the company announced a dividend recapitalization in which it would distribute an extraordinary $2 billion dividend financed in large part by a $1.53 billion bond offering. A spreadsheet with HCA's financial statements for 2005–2009 and specific questions is available for download through McGraw-Hill's *Connect* or your course instructor (see the Preface for more information).

15. This problem asks you to evaluate a major increase in financial leverage on the part of Nova Products, Inc. The company's financial statements for 2015–2017 and specific questions are available for download through McGraw-Hill's *Connect* or your course instructor (see the Preface for more information).

16. Problem 15, part f in Chapter 3 asks you to construct a five-year financial projection for Aquatic Supplies beginning in 2018. Based on your

forecast or the suggested answer available through McGraw-Hill's *Connect*, answer the following questions.

a. Calculate the company's times-interest-earned ratio for each year from 2017 to 2022.

b. Calculate the percentage EBIT can fall before interest coverage dips below 1.0 for each year from 2017 to 2022.

c. Consulting Table 6.5 in the text, what bond rating would Aquatic Supplies have in 2017 if the rating was based solely on the firm's interest coverage ratio?

d. Based on this rating, would a significant increase in financial leverage be a prudent strategy for Aquatic Supplies?

PART FOUR

Evaluating Investment Opportunities

Discounted Cash Flow Techniques

A nearby penny is worth a distant dollar.

Anonymous

The chief determinant of what a company will become is the investments it makes today. Each investment follows the same recurring pattern of near-term outlays followed by the promise of attractive future returns. The challenge in each instance is to decide whether the uncertain future returns justify the current outlays.

To a novice, such investment choices can seem straightforward: just add up all the costs and all the benefits, and make sure the total benefits exceed total costs. Easy enough, except, of course, that money has a time value. A nearby dollar really is worth more than a distant dollar, so that comparing costs and benefits occurring at various times is anything but straightforward.

The discounted cash flow (DCF) techniques discussed here and in following chapters address this challenge. For several reasons, DCF techniques are central to finance and to business, and thus warrant your careful attention. First, a great many company decisions fall into the investment mold of costs and benefits extending over time, including such disparate activities as valuing stocks and bonds, analyzing equipment acquisitions or sales, choosing among competing production technologies, deciding whether to launch a new product, valuing divisions or whole companies for purchase or sale, assessing marketing campaigns and research and development programs, and even designing a corporate strategy.

Second, the adjustments to investment cash flows dictated by DCF techniques are far from trivial, not something that can be safely ignored as academic window-dressing or of only second-order importance. Here are a couple of benchmarks to keep in mind. At an interest rate of 7 percent, money loses half its value every decade. The promise of a dollar in 10 years is worth but 50 cents today. At a more representative corporate rate of 15 percent, money loses half its value in just 5 years. The time value of money is not trivial or second order.

Third, it is said that "if you don't know where you are going, any road will get you there," or in the words of Yogi Berra, ". . . you might wind up someplace else." Either way, the DCF techniques introduced here provide the necessary direction to finance, and indeed, to business. As the following sections reveal, DCF techniques yield a practical definition of economic value, justify "creation of shareholder value" as the appropriate firm objective in a competitive economy, and point to what is known as the *net present value,* or *NPV,* as the correct yardstick for identifying which activities promise to create value and which do not.

This chapter will rely on a common expositional technique known formally as "truncated finite induction," or more colloquially as "proof by example," to explore a selection of numerical examples, allowing the broader conceptual insights regarding value creation and destruction to emerge from the examples as appropriate.

Figures of Merit

The financial evaluation of any investment opportunity involves the following three discrete steps:

1. Estimate the relevant cash flows.

2. Calculate a figure of merit for the investment.

3. Compare the figure of merit to an acceptance criterion.

A *figure of merit* is a number summarizing an investment's economic worth. A common figure of merit is the rate of return. Like the other figures of merit to be discussed, the rate of return translates the complicated cash inflows and outflows associated with an investment into a single number summarizing its economic worth. An *acceptance criterion,* on the other hand, is a standard of comparison that helps the analyst determine whether an investment's figure of merit is attractive enough to warrant acceptance. It's like a fisher who can keep only fish longer than 10 inches. To the fisher, the length of the fish is the relevant figure of merit, and 10 inches is the acceptance criterion.

Although determining figures of merit and acceptance criteria appear to be difficult on first exposure, the first step, estimating the relevant cash flows, is the most challenging in practice. Unlike the basically mechanical problems encountered in calculating figures of merit and acceptance criteria, estimating relevant cash flows is more of an art form, often requiring a thorough understanding of a company's markets, competitive position, and long-run intentions. Difficulties range from commonplace concerns with depreciation, financing costs, and working capital investments to more arcane questions of shared resources, excess capacity, and contingent opportunities. And pervading the whole topic is the fact that many important costs and benefits cannot be measured in monetary terms and so must be evaluated qualitatively.

In this chapter, we will initially set aside questions of relevant cash flows and acceptance criteria to concentrate on figures of merit. Later, we will return to the estimation of relevant cash flows. Acceptance criteria will be addressed in the following chapter under the general heading "Risk Analysis in Investment Decisions."

To begin our discussion of figures of merit, let's consider a simple numerical example. Pacific Rim Resources, Inc. is contemplating construction of a container-loading pier in Seattle. The company's best estimate of the cash flows associated with constructing and operating the pier for a 10-year period appears in Table 7.1.

Figure 7.1 presents the same information in the form of a *cash flow diagram,* which is simply a graphical display of the pier's costs and benefits distributed along a time line. Despite its simplicity, I find that many common mistakes can be avoided by preparing such a diagram for even the most elementary investment opportunities. We see that the pier will cost $40 million to construct and is expected to generate cash inflows of $7.5 million annually for 10 years. In addition, the company expects to salvage the pier for $9.5 million at the end of its useful life, bringing the 10th-year cash flow to $17 million.

The Payback Period and the Accounting Rate of Return

Pacific's management wants to know whether the anticipated benefits from the pier justify the $40 million cost. As we will see shortly, a proper answer to

TABLE 7.1   Cash Flows for Container-Loading Pier ($ millions)

Year	0	1	2	3	4	5	6	7	8	9	10
Cash flow	($40)	7.5	7.5	7.5	7.5	7.5	7.5	7.5	7.5	7.5	17

FIGURE 7.1   Cash Flow Diagram for Container-Loading Pier

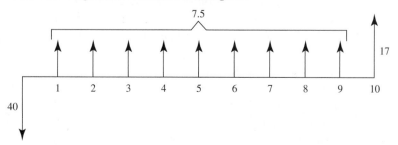

this question must reflect the *time value of money.* But before addressing this topic, let's consider two commonly used, back-of-the-envelope-type figures of merit that, despite their popularity, suffer from some glaring weaknesses. One, known as the *payback period,* is defined as the time the company must wait before recouping its original investment. The pier's payback period is $5\frac{1}{3}$ years, meaning the company will have to wait this long to recoup its original investment ($5\frac{1}{3} = 40/7.5$).

The second widely used, but nonetheless deficient, figure of merit is the *accounting rate of return,* defined as

$$\text{Accounting rate of return} = \frac{\text{Annual average cash inflow}}{\text{Total cash outflow}}$$

The pier's accounting rate of return is 21.1 percent ($[(7.5 \times 9 + 17)/10]/40$).

The problem with the accounting rate of return is its insensitivity to the timing of cash flows. For example, a postponement of all of the cash inflows from Pacific's container-loading pier to year 10 obviously reduces the value of the investment but does not affect the accounting rate of return. In addition to ignoring the timing of cash flows within the payback date, the payback period is insensitive to all cash flows occurring beyond this date. Thus, an increase in the salvage value of the pier from $9.5 million to $90.5 million clearly makes the investment more attractive. Yet it has no effect on the payback period, nor does any other change in cash flows in years 7 through 10.

In fairness to the payback period, I should add that although it is clearly an inadequate figure of investment merit, it has proven to be useful as a rough measure of investment risk. In most settings, the longer it takes to recoup an original investment, the greater the risk. This is especially true in high-technology environments where management can forecast only a few years into the future. Under these circumstances, an investment that does not promise to pay back within the forecasting horizon is equivalent to a night in Las Vegas without the floorshow.

The Time Value of Money

An accurate figure of merit must reflect the fact that a dollar today is worth more than a dollar in the future. This is the notion of the time value of money, and it exists for at least three reasons. One is that inflation reduces the purchasing power of future dollars relative to current ones; another is that in most instances, the uncertainty surrounding the receipt of a dollar increases as the date of receipt recedes into the future. Thus, the promise of $1 in 30 days is usually worth more than the promise of $1 in 30 months, simply because it is customarily more certain.

A third reason money has a time value involves the important notion of opportunity costs. By definition, the *opportunity cost* of any investment is the return one could earn on the next best alternative. A dollar today is worth more than a dollar in one year because the dollar today can be productively invested and will grow into more than a dollar in one year. Waiting to receive the dollar until next year carries an opportunity cost equal to the return on the forgone investment. Because there are always productive opportunities for investment dollars, all investments involve opportunity costs.

Compounding and Discounting

Because money has a time value, we cannot simply combine cash flows occurring at different dates as we do in calculating the payback period and the accounting rate of return. To adjust investment cash flows for their differing time value, we need to use the ideas of compounding and discounting. Anyone who has ever had a bank account knows intuitively what compounding is. Suppose you have a bank account paying 10 percent annual interest, and you deposit $1 at the start of the year. What will it be worth at the end of the year? Obviously, $1.10. Now suppose you leave the dollar in the account for two years. What will it be worth then? This is a little harder, but most of us realize that because you earn interest on your interest, the answer is $1.21. *Compounding* is the process of determining the future value of a present sum. The following simple cash flow diagrams summarize the exercise. And note the pattern: As the number of years increases, so too does the power by which we raise the interest rate term $(1 + .10)$. By extension, the future value of $1.00 in, say, 19 years at 10 percent interest is thus, $F_{19} = \$1(1 + .10)^{19} = \$6.12$.

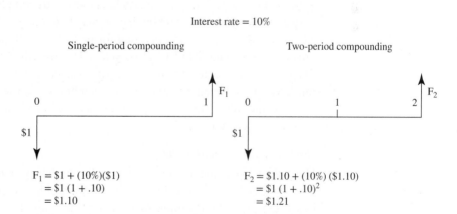

Interest rate = 10%

Single-period compounding   Two-period compounding

$$F_1 = \$1 + (10\%)(\$1)$$
$$= \$1 (1 + .10)$$
$$= \$1.10$$

$$F_2 = \$1.10 + (10\%) (\$1.10)$$
$$= \$1 (1 + .10)^2$$
$$= \$1.21$$

Discounting is simply compounding turned on its head: It is the process of finding the present value of a future sum. Yet despite the obvious similarities, many people find discounting somehow mysterious. And as luck would have it, the convention has become to use discounting rather than compounding to analyze investment opportunities.

Here is how discounting works. Suppose you can invest money to earn a 10 percent annual return and you are promised $1 in one year. What is the value of this promise today? Clearly, it is worth less than $1, but the exact figure is probably not something that pops immediately to mind. In fact, the answer is $0.909. This is the *present value* of $1 to be received in one year, because if you had $0.909 today, you could invest it at 10 percent interest, and it would grow into $1 in one year [$1.00 = 0.909(1 + 0.10)].

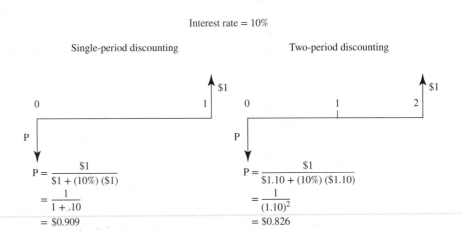

Now, if we complicate matters further and ask what is the value of one dollar to be received in two years, intuition fails most of us completely. We know the answer must be less than $0.909, but beyond that, things are a fog. In fact, the answer is $0.826. This sum, invested for two years at 10 percent interest, will grow, or compound, into $1 in two years. The preceding cash flow diagrams illustrate these discounting problems. Note the formal similarity to compounding. The only difference is that in compounding we know the present amount and seek the future sum, whereas in discounting we know the future sum and seek the present amount.

Present Value Calculations

How did I know the answers to these discounting problems? I could have done the arithmetic in at least three ways: Solve the formulas appearing below the cash flow diagrams by hand, or with a simple calculator; punch the numbers into a financial calculator; or use a computer spreadsheet, such as Excel. Financial calculators and spreadsheets can be thought of as basically a family of present value formulas where you provide the information and the device does the arithmetic. All three methods, of course, yield the same answer, but as discounting problems become more complex, the appeal of a computer spreadsheet grows accordingly.

Financial calculators use five basic variables to perform present value calculations, four to describe the cash flows and one for the interest rate. Each variable corresponds to a separate key on the calculator. The four cash flow variables are: **n,** the number of periods; **PV,** a present cash flow; **PMT,** a uniform cash flow occurring each period—also known as an *annuity;* and **FV,** a future cash flow. The diagram below shows how the variables relate to one another.

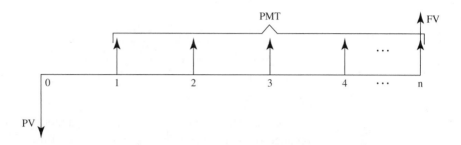

The fifth variable, **i,** the interest rate, plays a pivotal role and deserves brief additional comment. In present value calculations, the interest rate is frequently called the *discount rate.* It can be interpreted either of two ways. When a company already has cash in hand, the discount rate is the rate of return available on alternative, similar-risk investments. In other words, it is the company's *opportunity cost of capital.* When a firm must raise the cash by selling securities, the discount rate is the rate of return expected by buyers of the securities. In other words, it is the investors' *opportunity cost of capital.* As we will see in Chapter 8, the discount rate is frequently used to adjust an investment's cash flows for risk and hence is also known as a *risk-adjusted discount rate.*

To solve a discounting problem using a financial calculator, begin by deciding which variable you want to calculate, enter the other four variables you know (in any order), and ask the calculator to find the unknown quantity. So, for example, to solve the single-period discounting problem above, input the number of periods (1), the interest rate (10), and the future value (1). Enter zero for the periodic payment (PMT) because there are none. Then, ask the calculator to calculate the PV, and it will return the answer of −0.909. The answer has a minus sign to indicate that $0.909 must be paid today to receive $1 in one period.

The following schematic illustrates the solution to this problem using a financial calculator.

Input: 1   10   ?   0   1

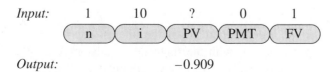

Output: −0.909

Solving the two-period discounting problem above is a simple matter of replacing the 1 stored in the *n* key with a 2, and recalculating the PV.

As a more challenging example, let us calculate the future value of a $100 investment in 22 years when the interest rate is 7 percent. Entering these values into a financial calculator and solving for FV this time, the answer is $443.04. The investment's value rises over fourfold in 22 years at only 7 percent interest. Perhaps patience really is a virtue.

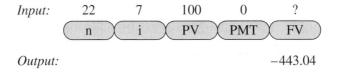

Input: 22   7   100   0   ?
             n   i   PV   PMT   FV

Output: −443.04

To replicate these calculations using a computer spreadsheet, we first need to change a couple of symbols describing the cash flows. Specifically, replace **n** with **NPER** to describe the number of periods, and **i** with **RATE** to capture the interest rate. With these modest changes, the egg-shaped icon below shows how to solve the one-period discounting problem with a spreadsheet. Begin by opening Excel, or an equivalent spreadsheet program, and placing the cursor in a blank cell where you want the answer to appear. Then, as with a financial calculator, decide which variable you want to calculate; here we want the Present Value, PV. As you begin to type the first few symbols of the desired variable,

$$=PV(\ldots$$

the spreadsheet instantly recognizes your intent and produces the prompt appearing in the icon's second line. Following the prompted instructions, complete the top line of the icon by entering the indicated variables in the specified order, and, voila, the spreadsheet produces the desired answer, ($0.909). Yes, it's that simple. Try it. To solve the two-period discounting problem, just change the nper variable from 1 to 2, and the answer changes to ($0.826).

=PV(.1,1,0,1) = ($0.909)
PV(**rate**, nper, pmt, [fv], [type])

As a detail, notice that the interest rate is now a decimal rather than a percentage as with the financial calculator. Also, note that the variables in square brackets in the prompt are optional. If left blank, the spreadsheet will treat them as zero. The optional variable "[type]" allows the user to specify whether payments are due at the beginning or the end of the period, and can usually be left blank.[1]

For ease of exposition, I will use this egg-shaped icon often to describe subsequent discounted cash flow calculations, without meaning to suggest that a spreadsheet is the only way to perform them.

Equivalence

As further practice, and to begin discussion of an important topic known as *equivalence,* suppose the Cincinnati Reds baseball team offers a talented young catcher a contract promising $2 million a year for four years. The athlete's agent wants to know the value of the contract today when the ballplayer has similar-risk investment opportunities promising 15 percent a year.

The cash flow diagram for the contract is

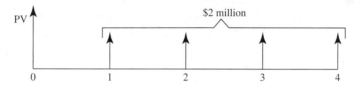

The icon for determining the value of the contract today is

$$=PV(.15,4,2) = (\$5.71)$$
PV(**rate**, nper, pmt, [fv], [type])

Although the baseball player expects to receive a total of $8 million over the next four years, the present value of these payments is barely over $5.7 million. Such is the power of compound interest.

The important fact about the $5.71 million present value here is that it is *equivalent* in value to the future flows promised by the contract. It is equivalent because if the athlete had the present value today, he could transform it into the future cash flows simply by investing it at the discount rate.

To confirm this important fact, the following table shows the cash flows involved in transforming $5.71 million today into the baseball player's contract offer of $2 million a year for four years. We begin by investing the present value at 15 percent interest. At the end of the first year, the investment grows to over $6.5 million, but the first $2 million salary payment reduces the principal to just over $4.5 million. In the second year, the investment grows to over $5.2 million, but the second salary installment brings the principal down to just over $3.2 million. And so it goes until at the end of four years, the $2 million salary payment just exhausts the account. Hence, from the baseball player's perspective, $5.71 million today is equivalent in value to $2 million a year for four years because he can readily convert the former into the latter by investing it at 15 percent.

Year	Beginning-of-Period Principal	Interest at 15%	End-of-Period Principal	Withdrawal
1	$5,710,000	$856,500	$6,566,500	$2,000,000
2	4,566,500	684,975	5,251,475	2,000,000
3	3,251,475	487,721	3,739,196	2,000,000
4	1,739,196	260,879	2,000,075	2,000,000

Note: The $75 remaining in the account after the last withdrawal is due to round-off error.

The Net Present Value

Now that you have mastered compounding, discounting, and equivalence, let's use these concepts to analyze the container pier investment. More specifically, let us replace the future cash flows appearing in Figure 7.1 with a single cash flow of equivalent worth occurring today. Because all cash flows will then be in current dollars, we will have eliminated the time dimension from the decision and can proceed to a direct comparison of present value cash inflows against present value outflows.

Here is the arithmetic. Assuming other similar-risk investment opportunities are available yielding 10 percent annual interest, the present value of the cash inflows from the pier investment is $49.75 million.

$$=PV(.10,10,7.5,9.5) = (\$49.75)$$
$$PV(\textbf{rate}, \text{nper, pmt, [fv], [type]})$$

Note that the cash flow in year 10 is composed of the last year of a $7.5 million annuity plus a $9.5 million salvage value, for a total of $17 million.

The cash flow diagrams that follow provide a schematic representation of this calculation. The present value calculation transforms the messy original cash flows on the left into two cash flows of equivalent worth on the right, each occurring at time zero. And our decision becomes elementary. Should Pacific invest $40 million today for a stream of future cash flows with a value today of $49.75 million? Yes, obviously. Paying $40 million for something worth $49.75 million makes eminent sense.

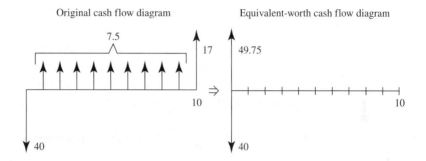

What we have just done is calculate the pier's *net present value,* or *NPV,* an important figure of investment merit:

$$\text{NPV} = \frac{\text{Present value of}}{\text{cash inflows}} - \frac{\text{Present value of}}{\text{cash outflows}}$$

The NPV for the container pier is $9.75 million.

NPV and Value Creation

The declaration that an investment's NPV is $9.75 million may not generate a lot of enthusiasm around the water cooler, so it is important to provide a more compelling definition of the concept. An investment's NPV is nothing less than a measure of how much richer you will become by undertaking the investment. Thus, Pacific's wealth, or value, rises $9.75 million when it builds the pier because it pays $40 million for an asset worth $49.75 million.

This is an important insight. For years, a common mantra among academics, management gurus, and senior executives has been that managers' purpose in life should be to create value for owners. A crowning achievement of finance has been to transform value creation from a catchy management slogan into a practical decision-making tool that not only indicates which activities create value but also estimates the amount of value created. Want to create value for owners? Here's how: Embrace positive-NPV activities—the higher the NPV, the better—and eschew negative-NPV activities. Treat zero-NPV activities as marginal because they neither create nor destroy wealth.

In symbols, when

NPV > 0, accept the investment.

NPV < 0, reject the investment.

NPV = 0, the investment is marginal.

The Benefit-Cost Ratio

The net present value is a perfectly respectable figure of investment merit, and if all you want is one way to analyze investment opportunities, feel free to skip ahead to the section "Determining Relevant Cash Flows." On the other hand, if you want to be able to communicate with people who use different but equally acceptable figures of merit, and if you want to reduce the work involved in analyzing certain types of investments, you will need to slog through a few more pages.

A second time-adjusted figure of investment merit popular in government circles is the *benefit-cost ratio (BCR)*, also known as the *profitability index,* defined as

$$BCR = \frac{Present\ value\ of\ cash\ inflows}{Present\ value\ of\ cash\ outflows}$$

The container pier's BCR is 1.24 ($49.75/$40). Obviously, an investment is attractive when its BCR exceeds 1.0 and is unattractive when its BCR is less than 1.0.

The Internal Rate of Return

Without doubt, the most popular figure of merit among executives is a close cousin to the NPV known as the investment's *internal rate of return,* or *IRR.* To illustrate the IRR and show its relation to the NPV, let's follow the fanciful exploits of the Seattle area manager of Pacific Rim Resources as he tries to win approval for the container pier investment. After determining that the pier's NPV is positive at a 10 percent discount rate, the manager forwards his analysis to the company treasurer with a request for approval. The treasurer responds that she is favorably impressed with the manager's methodology but believes that in today's interest rate environment, a discount rate of 12 percent is more appropriate. So the Seattle manager calculates a second NPV at a 12 percent discount rate and finds it to be $5.44 million—still positive but considerably lower than the original $9.75 million ($5.44 million = $45.44 million, as shown next, −$40 million).

=PV(.12,10,7.5,9.5) = ($45.44)
PV(**rate**, nper, pmt, [fv], [type])

Confronted with this evidence, the treasurer reluctantly agrees that the project is acceptable and forwards the proposal to the chief financial officer. (That the NPV falls as the discount rate rises here should come as no surprise, for all of the pier's cash inflows occur in the future, and a higher discount rate reduces the present value of future flows.)

The chief financial officer, who is even more conservative than the treasurer, also praises the methodology but argues that with all the risks involved and the difficulty in raising money, an 18 percent discount rate is called for. After doing his calculations a third time, the dejected Seattle manager now finds that at an 18 percent discount rate, the NPV is −$4.48 million (−$4.48 million = $35.52 million, as shown next, −$40 million).

$$=PV(.18,10,7.5,9.5) = (\$35.52)$$
$$PV(\textbf{rate}, \text{nper}, \text{pmt}, [\text{fv}], [\text{type}])$$

Because the NPV is now negative, the chief financial officer, betraying his former career as a bank loan officer, gleefully rejects the proposal. The manager's efforts prove unsuccessful, but in the process he has helped us understand the IRR.

Table 7.2 summarizes the manager's calculations. From these figures, it is apparent that something critical happens to the investment merit of the container pier as the discount rate increases from 12 to 18 percent. Somewhere within this range, the NPV changes from positive to negative and the investment changes from acceptable to unacceptable. The critical discount rate at which this change occurs is the investment's IRR.

Formally, an investment's IRR is defined as

IRR = Discount rate at which the investment's NPV equals zero

The IRR is yet another figure of merit. The corresponding acceptance criterion against which to compare the IRR is the opportunity cost of capital for the

TABLE 7.2   **NPV of Container Pier at Different Discount Rates**

Discount Rate	NPV
10%	$9.75 million
12	5.44
	⟵———— IRR = 15%
18	−4.48

investment. If the investment's IRR exceeds the opportunity cost of capital, the investment is attractive, and vice versa. If the IRR equals the cost of capital, the investment is marginal.

In symbols, if K is the percentage cost of capital, then if

IRR $> K$, accept the investment.

IRR $< K$, reject the investment.

IRR $= K$, the investment is marginal.

You will be relieved to learn that in most, but regrettably not all, instances, the IRR and the NPV yield the same investment recommendations. That is, in most instances, if an investment is attractive based on its IRR, it will also have a positive NPV, and vice versa. Figure 7.2 illustrates the relation between the container pier's NPV and its IRR by plotting the information in Table 7.2. Note that the pier's NPV = 0 at a discount rate of about 15 percent, so this by definition is the project's IRR. At capital costs below 15 percent, the NPV is positive and the IRR also exceeds the cost of capital, so the investment is acceptable on both counts. When the cost of capital exceeds 15 percent, the reverse is true, and the investment is unacceptable according to both criteria.

Figure 7.2 suggests several informative ways to interpret an investment's IRR. One is that the IRR is a breakeven return in the sense that at capital costs below the IRR the investment is attractive, but at capital costs greater than the IRR it is unattractive. A second, more important interpretation is that the IRR is the rate at which money remaining in an investment grows, or compounds. As such, an IRR is comparable in all respects to the interest rate on a bank loan or a savings deposit. This means you can compare the IRR of an investment

FIGURE 7.2   **NPV of Container Pier at Different Discount Rates**

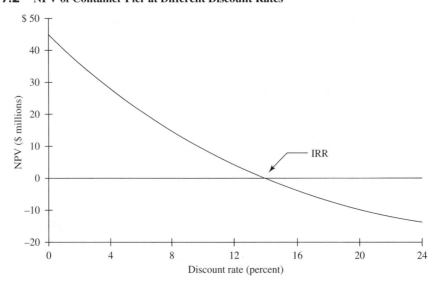

The Container Pier Investment Is Economically Equivalent to a Bank Account Paying 15 Percent Annual Interest

To confirm that an investment's IRR is equivalent to the interest rate on a bank account, suppose that instead of building the pier, Pacific Rim Resources puts the $40 million cost of the pier in a clearly hypothetical bank account earning 15 percent annual interest. The following table demonstrates that Pacific can then use this bank account to replicate precisely the cash flows from the pier and that, just like the investment, the account will run dry in 10 years. In other words, ignoring any differences in risk, the fact that the pier's IRR is 15 percent means the investment is economically equivalent to a bank savings account yielding this rate.

	($ millions)			
Year	Beginning-of-Period Principal	Interest Earned at 15%	End-of-Period Principal	Withdrawals = Investment Cash Flows
1	$40.0	$6.0	$46.0	$7.5
2	38.5	5.8	44.3	7.5
3	36.8	5.5	42.3	7.5
4	34.8	5.2	40.0	7.5
5	32.5	4.9	37.4	7.5
6	29.9	4.5	34.4	7.5
7	26.9	4.0	30.9	7.5
8	23.4	3.5	26.9	7.5
9	19.4	2.9	22.3	7.5
10	14.8	2.2	17.0	17.0

directly to the annual percentage cost of the capital to be invested. We cannot say the same thing about other, simpler measures of return, such as the accounting rate of return, because they do not properly incorporate the time value of money.

The following icon confirms that the container pier's IRR is indeed 15 percent. Feel free to ignore the optional [guess] variable here. IRR calculations commonly involve a bit of trial-and-error searching on the part of the computer for the right number, and the guess variable can simplify the computer's task by defining a plausible starting point. But in all but rare instances, using it is not worth the effort.

$$=RATE(10,7.5,-40,9.5) = 15\%$$
RATE(**nper,** pmt, pv, [fv], [type], [guess])

Uneven Cash Flows

Perceptive readers may have noticed a problem with what we have covered to this point: All of the cash flows in all of the examples can be described using the four variables defined earlier. What happens when the cash flows are not so well behaved? What happens when they are more erratic? To illustrate the problem, let's modify our container pier example a bit and assume that Pacific Container now estimates it will take time to ramp up to full capacity and that first-year cash flows will be only $3.5 million, not $7.5 million as originally projected. The revised cash flow diagram is

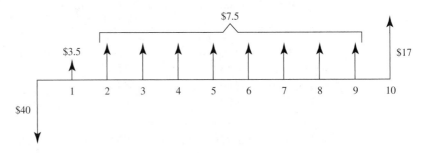

And we are now stuck because it is no longer possible to describe the investment's cash flows purely in terms of the original four variables: nper, pv, pmt, and fv.

Fortunately, spreadsheets offer a simple, elegant solution to this problem involving two new functions known as **=IRR** and **=NPV.** Table 7.3 shows an Excel spreadsheet illustrating their use. The numbers on the left are the revised container pier cash flows. The icons for the two new functions appear to the right. Looking first at the IRR icon, note that the prompt replaces the usual PV, PMT, and FV variables with a new variable called **values.** The values point the speadsheet to a range of cells containing the investment's cash flows. Here, the cash flows are in cells B3 through B13, and the values appear in the formula as B3:B13. All you need to do to calculate the IRR of an arbitrary list of numbers, then, is to enter the relevant range containing the numbers into the =IRR function.

The =NPV function is similar. It calls for an interest rate and a range of cash flows containing at least one nonzero value and returns the cash flows' net present value. Here I have entered the cash flows in the range B4 through B13. "But wait," you exclaim, "why did you omit the cash flow in B3 from this range?" The answer is that, by definition, the =NPV function calculates the net present value of the specified range as of *one period before the first cash flow.* Had I entered "=NPV (C15,B3:B13)" the computer would have calculated the NPV of the investment as of time *minus* 1. To avoid this error, I calculated the NPV of the cash flows from years 1 through 10, which by definition the computer will calculate as of time 0, and then I added the time 0 cash flow separately. Remember this annoying convention, and the =NPV function can be very handy.

TABLE 7.3 Working with Uneven Cash Flows

	A	B	C	D	E	F	G	H	I	J	K
1		Revised Container Pier Cash Flows									
2	Year	($ in millions)									
3	0	$ (40.0)									
4	1	3.5									
5	2	7.5									
6	3	7.5									
7	4	7.5									
8	5	7.5									
9	6	7.5									
10	7	7.5									
11	8	7.5									
12	9	7.5									
13	10	17.0									
14											
15	Discount rate:		10%								
16											

=IRR(B3:B13) = 13%
IRR(**values**, [guess])

IRR Icon

=NPV(C15,B4:B13) + B3 = $6.11
NPV(**rate**, value1, [value2]...)

NPV Icon

A Few Applications and Extensions

Discounted cash flow concepts are the foundation for much of finance. To demonstrate their versatility, to sharpen your mastery of the concepts, and to introduce some topics we will refer to later in the book, I want to consider several useful applications and extensions.

Bond Valuation

Investors regularly use discounted cash flow techniques to value bonds. To illustrate, suppose ABC Corporation bonds have an 8 percent coupon rate paid annually, a par value of $1,000, and nine years to maturity. An investor wants to determine the most she can pay for the bonds if she wants to earn at least 7 percent on her investment. The relevant cash flow diagram is:

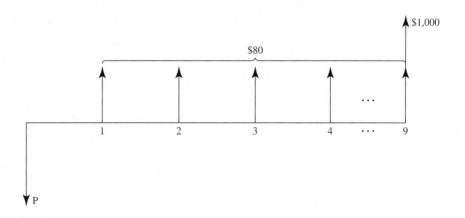

In essence, the investor wants to find P such that it is equivalent in value to the future cash receipts discounted at 7 percent. Calculating the present value, we find it equals $1,065.15, meaning her return over nine years will be precisely 7 percent when she pays this amount for the bond.

$$=\text{PV}(.07,9,80,1000) = (\$1,065.15)$$
$$\text{PV}(\textbf{rate}, \text{nper, pmt, [fv], [type]})$$

Moreover, we know her return will fall below 7 percent when she pays above this price, and rise above 7 percent when she pays less.

More commonly, an investor knows the price of a bond and wants to know what return it implies. If ABC Corporation bonds are selling for $1,030, the investor wants to know the return she will earn if she buys the bonds and holds them to maturity. In the jargon of the trade, she wants to know the bond's *yield to maturity*. Performing the necessary calculation, we learn the bond's yield to maturity, or IRR, is 7.53 percent.

$$=\text{RATE}(9,80,-1030,1000) = 7.53\%$$
$$\text{RATE}(\textbf{nper}, \text{pmt, pv, [fv],[type],[guess]})$$

The IRR of a Perpetuity

Some financial instruments, including certain British and French government bonds, have no maturity date and simply promise to pay the stated interest every year forever. Annuities that last forever are called *perpetuities*. Many preferred stocks are perpetuities. Later in Chapter 9 when valuing companies, we will occasionally find it convenient to think of company cash flows as perpetuities.

How can we calculate the present value of a perpetuity? It turns out to be embarrassingly easy. Begin by noting that the present value of an annuity paying $1 a year for 100 years discounted at, say, 12 percent is only $8.33!

$$=\text{PV}(.12,100,1) = (\$8.33)$$
$$\text{PV}(\textbf{rate}, \text{nper, pmt, [fv], [type]})$$

Think of it: Although the holder will receive a total of $100, the present value is less than $9. Why? Because if the investor put $8.33 in a bank account today yielding 12 percent a year, he could withdraw approximately $1 in interest every year *forever* without touching the principal (12% × $8.33 = $0.9996). Consequently, $8.33 today has approximately the same value as $1 a year forever.

This suggests the following simple formula for the present value of a perpetuity. Letting A equal the annual receipt, r the discount rate, and P the present value,

$$P = \frac{A}{r}$$

and

$$r = \frac{A}{P}$$

To illustrate, suppose a share of preferred stock sells for $480 and promises an annual dividend of $52 forever. Then, its IRR is 10.8 percent (52/480). Because the equations are so simple, perpetuities are often used to value long-lived assets and in many textbook examples.

Equivalent Annual Cost

In most discounted cash flow calculations, we seek a present value or an internal rate of return, but this is not always the case. Suppose, for example, that Pacific Rim Resources is considering leasing its $40 million container pier to a large Korean shipping company for a period of 12 years. Pacific Rim believes the pier will have a $4 million continuing value at the end of the lease period. To consummate the deal, the company needs to know the annual fee it must charge to recover its investment, including the opportunity cost of the funds used. In essence, Pacific Rim needs a number that converts the initial expenditure and the salvage value into an equal value annual payment. At a 10 percent interest rate and ignoring taxes, the required annual lease payment is $5.68 million.

=PMT(.10,12,-40,4) = ($5.68)
PMT(**rate**, nper, pv, [fv], [type])

This quantity, known as the investment's *equivalent annual cost,* is the effective, time-adjusted annual cost of the pier. The calculation tells us that if Pacific Rim sets the lease payment equal to the pier's equivalent annual cost, it will earn an IRR of precisely 10 percent on the investment. We will discuss more about equivalent annual costs in this chapter's Appendix.

A Note on Differing Compounding Periods

For simplicity, I have assumed that the compounding period for all discounted cash flow calculations is one year. Of course, this is not always the case. In the United States and Britain, bond interest is calculated and paid semi-annually, many credit card issuers use monthly compounding, and some savings instruments advertise daily compounding.

The existence of different compounding intervals forces us to distinguish between two interest rates: a quoted interest rate, often called the *annual percentage rate* or *APR,* and a true rate, known as the *effective annual rate* or *EAR.*

To appreciate the distinction, you know that $1 put to work at 10 percent interest, compounded annually, will be worth $1.10 in one year. But what will it be worth when the compounding period is semi-annual? To find out, we need to divide the stated interest rate by 2 and double the number of compounding periods. Thus, at the end of six months, the investment will be worth $1.05, and at the end of the year it will be worth $1.1025 ($1.05 + .05 × $1.05). With semi-annual compounding, the interest earned in the first compounding period earns interest in the second, leading to a slightly higher ending value. So although the stated interest rate is 10 percent, semi-annual compounding boosts the effective return to 10.25 percent. The account's APR is 10 percent, but its EAR is 10.25 percent.

Letting *m* equal the number of compounding periods in a year, we can generalize this example to the following expression.

$$EAR = \left(1 + \frac{APR}{m}\right)^m - 1$$

Thus, the effective annual interest rate on a 6 percent savings account with daily compounding is $(1 + .06/365)^{365} - 1 = 6.18\%$, while the effective annual rate on a credit card loan charging 18 percent, compounded monthly, is $(1 + .18/12)^{12} - 1 = 19.56\%$.

There are two morals to this story. First, when an instrument's compounding period is less than one year, its true interest rate is its EAR, not its APR. And second, when comparing instruments with different compounding periods, you must look at their EARs, not their APRs. This might all be of only minor interest were it not for the fact that common practice, strongly supplemented by Federal Truth in Lending laws, emphasizes APRs to the virtual exclusion of EARs.

Mutually Exclusive Alternatives and Capital Rationing

We now consider briefly two common occurrences that often complicate investment selection. The first is known as *mutually exclusive alternatives.* Frequently, there is more than one way to accomplish an objective, and the investment problem is to select the best alternative. In this case, the investments are said to be mutually exclusive. Examples of mutually exclusive alternatives abound, including the choice of whether to build a concrete or a wooden structure, whether to drive to work or take the bus, and whether to build a 40-story or a 30-story building. Even though each option gets the job done and may be attractive individually, it does not make economic sense to do more than one. If you decide to take the bus to work, driving to work as well could prove a difficult feat. When confronted with mutually exclusive alternatives, then, it is not enough to decide if each option is attractive individually; you must determine which is best. Mutually exclusive investments are in contrast to independent investments, where the capital budgeting problem is simply to accept or reject a single investment.

When investments are independent, all three figures of merit introduced earlier—the NPV, BCR, and IRR—will generate the same investment decision, but this is no longer true when the investments are mutually exclusive. In all of the preceding examples, we implicitly assumed independence.

A second complicating factor in many investment appraisals is known as *capital rationing.* So far, we have implicitly assumed that sufficient money is available to enable the company to undertake all attractive opportunities. In contrast, under capital rationing, the decision maker has a fixed investment budget that may not be exceeded. Such a limit on investment capital may be imposed externally by investors' unwillingness to supply more money, or it may be imposed internally by senior management as a way to control the amount of investment dollars each operating unit spends. In either case, the investment decision under capital rationing requires the analyst to *rank* the opportunities according to their investment merit and accept only the best.

Both mutually exclusive alternatives and capital rationing require a ranking of investments, but here the similarity ends. With mutually exclusive investments, money is available, but for technological reasons only certain investments can be accepted; under capital rationing, a lack of money is the complicating factor. Moreover, even the criteria used to rank the investments differ in the two cases, so the best investment among mutually exclusive alternatives may not be the best under conditions of capital rationing. The Appendix to this chapter discusses these technicalities and indicates which figures of merit are appropriate under which conditions.

The IRR in Perspective

Before turning to the determination of relevant cash flows in investment analysis, I want to offer a few concluding thoughts about the IRR. The IRR has two clear advantages over the NPV and the BCR. First, it has considerably more intuitive appeal. The statement that an investment's IRR is 45 percent is more likely to get the juices flowing than the exclamation that its NPV is $12 million or its BCR is 1.41. Second, the IRR sometimes makes it possible to sidestep the challenging task of determining the appropriate discount rate for an investment. Thus, when a normal-risk opportunity's IRR is 80 percent, we can be confident that it is a winner at any reasonable discount rate. And when the IRR is 2 percent, we can be equally certain it is a loser regardless of the rate. The only instances in which we have to worry about coming up with an accurate discount rate are when the IRR is in a marginal range of, say, 5 to 25 percent. This differs from the NPV and the BCR, where we have to know the discount rate before we can even begin the analysis.

Unfortunately, the IRR also suffers from several technical problems that compromise its use, and while this is not the place to describe these problems in detail, you should know they exist. (See one of the books recommended at the end of this chapter for further information.) One difficulty is that on rare occasions an investment can display multiple IRRs; that is, its NPV can equal zero at two or more different discount rates. Other investments can have no IRR; their NPVs are either positive at all discount rates or negative at all rates. A second, more serious problem to be discussed in this chapter's Appendix is that the IRR is an invalid yardstick for analyzing mutually exclusive alternatives and under capital rationing.

On balance then, the IRR is, like many things in life, appealing but flawed. And although a diligent technician can circumvent each of the problems mentioned, I have to ask if it is worth the effort when the NPV offers a simple, straightforward alternative. In my view, the appropriate watchword for the IRR is to appreciate its intuitive appeal but read the warning label before applying.

Determining the Relevant Cash Flows

It's time now to set aside the computer and confront the really difficult part of evaluating investment opportunities. Calculating a figure of merit requires an understanding of the time value of money and equivalence, and it necessitates a modicum of algebra. But these difficulties pale to insignificance compared to those arising in estimating an investment's relevant cash flows. Calculating figures of merit requires only technical competence; determining relevant cash flows demands business judgment and perspective.

Two principles govern the determination of relevant cash flows. Both are obvious when stated in the abstract but can be devilishly difficult to apply in practice:

1. *The cash flow principle:* Because money has a time value, record investment cash flows when the money actually moves, not when the accountant using accrual concepts says they occur. And if the money doesn't move, don't count it.

2. *The with-without principle:* Imagine two worlds, one in which the investment is made and one in which it is rejected. All cash flows that are different in these two worlds are relevant to the decision, and all those that are the same are irrelevant.

The following extended example illustrates the practical application of these principles to a number of commonly recurring cash flow estimation problems.

Nina Sanders, newly appointed general manager of the Handheld Devices Division of Plasteel Communications, has a problem. Prior to her appointment, division executives had put together a proposal to introduce an exciting new line of smartphones with flexible screens. The numbers spun out by division analysts looked excellent, but when the proposal was presented to the company's Capital Expenditure Review Committee, it was attacked from all sides. One committee member called the presentation "plain amateurish"; another accused Ms. Sanders's division of "trying to steal" his assets. Surprised by the strong emotions expressed and anxious to avoid further confrontation, the committee chair quickly tabled the proposal pending further review and likely revision by Ms. Sanders. Her task now was to either substantiate or correct the work of her subordinates.

Table 7.4 shows the projected costs and benefits of the new product as presented to the committee, with the most contentious issues highlighted.

TABLE 7.4 Division Financial Analysis of New Line of Smartphones ($ millions)

				Year		
	0	**1**	**2**	**3**	**4**	**5**
Plant and equipment	$(30)					$ 15
Increased working capital	**(14)**					
Preliminary engineering	**(2)**					
Excess capacity	**0**					
Total investment	$(46)					
Total salvage value						$ 15
Sales		$60	$82	$140	$157	$120
Cost of sales		26	35	60	68	52
Gross profit		34	47	80	89	68
Interest expense		**5**	**4**	**4**	**3**	**3**
Allocated expenses		**0**	**0**	**0**	**0**	**0**
Selling and administrative expenses		10	13	22	25	19
Total operating expenses		14	17	26	28	22
Operating income		20	29	54	61	46
Depreciation		**3**	**3**	**3**	**3**	**3**
Income before tax		17	26	51	58	43
Tax at 40 percent		7	11	20	23	17
Income after tax		$10	$16	$ 30	$ 35	$ 26
Free cash flow	$(46)	$10	$16	$ 30	$ 35	$ 41
Net present value @ 15%	$ 35					
Benefit-cost ratio	1.76					
Internal rate of return	37%					

Totals may not add due to rounding.

The top part of the table shows the initial investment and anticipated salvage value in five years. The smartphone business was changing so rapidly that executives believed improved new devices would make the contemplated product obsolete within about five years. The center portion of the table is essentially a projected income statement for the new product, while the bottom portion, beginning with "Free Cash Flow," contains the financial analysis. According to these figures, the new line costs $46 million and promises a 37 percent internal rate of return.

Free cash flow (FCF) is the "bottom line" of investment projections. It is the estimated total cash consumed or generated each year by the investment, and as such is the cash flow stream we discount to calculate the investment's NPV or IRR. A generic definition is

$$FCF = \text{Earnings after tax} + \text{Noncash charges} - \text{Investment}$$

where we think of a project's salvage value as a negative investment. We will say more about FCF in later chapters.

Depreciation

The first point of contention at the meeting was the division's treatment of depreciation. As shown in Table 7.4, division analysts had followed conventional accounting practice by subtracting depreciation from gross profit to calculate profit after tax. Upon seeing this, one committee member asserted that depreciation was a noncash charge and therefore irrelevant to the decision, while other participants agreed that depreciation was relevant but maintained the division's approach was incorrect. Ms. Sanders needed to determine the correct approach.

Accountants' treatment of depreciation is reminiscent of the Swiss method of counting cows: Count the legs and divide by four. It gets the job done, but not always in the most direct manner. Division analysts are correct in noting that the physical deterioration of assets is an economic fact of life that must be included in investment evaluation. However, they did this when they forecasted that the salvage value of new plant and equipment would be less than its original cost. Thus, new plant and equipment constructed today for $30 million and salvaged five years later for $15 million is clearly forecasted to depreciate over its life. Having included depreciation by using a salvage value below initial cost, it would clearly be double-counting to also subtract an annual amount from operating income as accountants would have us do.

And here our story would end were it not for the tax collector. Although annual depreciation is a noncash charge and hence irrelevant for investment analysis, annual depreciation does affect a company's tax bill, and taxes *are* relevant. So we need to use the following two-step procedure: (1) Use standard accrual accounting techniques, including the treatment of depreciation as a cost, to calculate taxes due; then (2) add depreciation back to income after tax to calculate the investment's after-tax cash flow (ATCF). ATCF is the correct measure of an investment's operating cash flow. Note that ATCF equals the first two terms in the free cash flow expression just defined, where depreciation is the most common noncash charge.

Table 7.4 reveals that division analysts did step 1 but not step 2. They neglected to add depreciation back to income after tax to calculate ATCF. Given their estimates, the appropriate number for year 1 is

$$\text{After-tax cash flow} = \text{Earnings after tax} + \text{Depreciation}$$
$$\$13 \qquad = \qquad \$10 \qquad + \qquad \$3$$

I should hasten to add that in the course of the next few sections, we will make further corrections to the table, resulting in additional changes in ATCF. But focusing now solely on depreciation, $13 million is the correct number.

Depreciation as a Tax Shield

Here is yet another way to view the relation between depreciation and ATCF.

The recommended way to calculate an investment's ATCF is to add depreciation to profit after tax. In symbols,

$$ATCF = (R - C - D)(1 - t) + D$$

where R is revenue, C is cash costs of operations, D is depreciation, and t is the firm's tax rate. Combining the depreciation terms, this expression can be written as

$$ATCF = (R - C)(1 - t) + tD$$

where the last term is known as the *tax shield from depreciation*.

This expression is interesting in several respects. First, it shows unambiguously that, were it not for taxes, annual depreciation would be irrelevant for estimating an investment's ATCF. Thus, if t is zero in the expression, depreciation disappears entirely.

Second, the expression demonstrates that ATCF rises with depreciation. The more depreciation a profitable company can claim, the higher its ATCF. On the other hand, if a company is not paying taxes, added depreciation has no value.

Third, the expression is useful for evaluating a class of investments known as *replacement decisions*, in which a new piece of equipment is being considered as a replacement for an old one. In these instances, cash operating costs and depreciation may vary among equipment options, but not revenues. Because revenues do not change among equipment options, the with-without principle tells us they are not relevant to the decision. Setting R equal to zero in the preceding equation,

$$ATCF = (-C)(1 - t) + tD$$

In words, the relevant cash flows for replacement decisions are operating costs after tax plus depreciation tax shields.

The following table shows the full two-step process for calculating year 1 ATCF:

Operating income	$20
Less: Depreciation	3
Profit before tax	17
Less: Tax at 40%	7
Income after tax	10
Plus: Depreciation	3
After-tax cash flow	$13

Note the subtraction of depreciation to calculate taxable income and the subsequent addition of depreciation to calculate ATCF.

The table also suggests a second way to calculate ATCF:

$$\text{After-tax cash flow} = \text{Operating income} - \text{Taxes}$$
$$\$13 \quad = \quad \$20 \quad - \quad \$7$$

This formulation shows clearly that depreciation is irrelevant for calculating ATCF except as it affects taxes.

Working Capital and Spontaneous Sources

In addition to increases in fixed assets, many investments, especially those for new products, require increases in working-capital items such as inventory and receivables. According to the with-without principle, changes in working capital that are the result of an investment decision are relevant to the decision. Indeed, in some instances, they are the largest cash flows involved.

Division analysts thus are correct to include a line item in their spreadsheet for changes in working capital. However, working capital investments have several unique features not captured in the division's numbers. First, working-capital investments usually rise and fall with the new product's sales volume. Second, they are reversible in the sense that at the end of the investment's life, the liquidation of working-capital items usually generates cash inflows approximately as large as the original outflows. Or, said differently, working-capital investments typically have large salvage values. The third unique feature is that many investments requiring working-capital increases also generate *spontaneous sources* of cash that arise in the natural course of business and have no explicit cost. Examples include increases in virtually all non-interest-bearing short-term liabilities such as accounts payable, accrued wages, and accrued taxes. The proper treatment of these spontaneous sources is to subtract them from the increases in current assets when calculating the project's working-capital investment.

To illustrate, the following table shows a revised estimate of the working-capital investment required to support the division's new product assuming (1) new current assets, net of spontaneous sources, equal 20 percent of sales and (2) full recovery of working capital at the end of the product's life. Note that the annual investment equals the year-to-year change in working capital so that it rises and falls with sales.

Year	0	1	2	3	4	5
New-phone sales	$ 0	$ 60	$82	$140	$157	$120
Working capital @ 20% of sales	0	12	16	28	31	24
Change in working capital	0	12	4	12	3	(7)
Recovery of working capital						24
Total working capital investment	$ 0	$(12)	$(4)	$(12)	$ (3)	$ 31

Sunk Costs

A *sunk cost* is one that has already been incurred and that, according to the with-without principle, is not relevant to present decisions. By this criterion, the division's inclusion of $2 million in already incurred preliminary engineering expenses is clearly incorrect and should be eliminated. The division's response that "we need to record these costs somewhere or the engineers will spend preproduction money like water" has merit. But the proper place to recognize them is in a separate expense budget, not in the new-product proposal. When making investment decisions, it is important to remember that we are seekers of truth, not auditors controlling costs or managers measuring performance. We are thus not captives of the particular reporting or performance appraisal systems used by the company.

This seems easy enough, but here are two examples where ignoring sunk costs is psychologically harder to do. Suppose you purchased some common stock a year ago at $100 a share and it is presently trading at $70. Even though you believe $70 is an excellent price for the stock given its current prospects, would you be prepared to admit your mistake and sell it now, or would you be tempted to hold it in the hope of recouping your original investment? The with-without principle says the $100 price is sunk and hence irrelevant, except for possible tax effects, so sell the stock. Natural human reluctance to admit a mistake and the daunting prospect of having to justify the mistake to a skeptical boss or spouse frequently muddy our thinking.

As another example, suppose the R&D department of a company has devoted 10 years and $10 million to perfecting a new, long-lasting light bulb. Its original estimate was a development time of two years at a cost of $1 million, but every year since then R&D has progressively extended the development time and increased the cost. Now it is estimating only one more year and an added expenditure of only $1 million. Because the present value of the benefits from such a light bulb is only $4 million, there is strong feeling in the company that the project should be killed and whoever had been approving the budget increases throughout the years should be fired.

In retrospect, it is clear the company should never have begun work on the light bulb. Even if successful, the cost will be well in excess of the benefits. Yet at any point along the development process, including the current decision, it may have been perfectly rational to continue work. Past expenditures are sunk, so the only question at issue is whether the anticipated benefits exceed the *remaining* costs required to complete development. Past expenditures are relevant only to the extent that they influence one's assessment of whether the remaining costs are properly estimated. So if you believe the current estimates, the light bulb project should continue for yet another year.

Allocated Costs

The proper treatment of depreciation, working capital, and sunk costs in investment evaluation is comparatively straightforward. Now things get a bit murkier. According to Plasteel Communications's *Capital Budgeting Manual,*

> New investments that increase sales must bear their fair share of corporate overhead expenses. Therefore, all new-product proposals must include an annual overhead charge equal to 14 percent of sales, without exception.

Yet, as Table 7.4 reveals, division analysts ignored this directive in their analysis of the new smartphone. They did so on the grounds that the manual is simply wrong, that allocating overhead expenses to new products violates the with-without principle and stifles creativity. In their words, "If exciting projects like this one have to bear the deadweight costs of corporate overhead, we'll never be competitive in this business."

The point at issue here is whether expenses not directly associated with a new investment, such as the president's salary, legal department expenses, and accounting department expenses, are relevant to the decision. A straightforward reading of the with-without principle says that if the president's salary will not change as a result of the new investment, it is not relevant, nor are legal and accounting department expenses, if they will not change. This is clear enough. If they won't change, they aren't relevant.

But who is to say these expenses will not change with the new investment? Indeed, it appears to be an inexorable fact of life that over time, as companies grow, presidents' salaries become larger while legal and accounting departments expand. The issue therefore is not whether expenses are allocated but whether they vary with the size of the business. Although we may be unable to see a direct cause-effect tie between such expenses and increasing sales, a longer-run relation likely exists between the two. Consequently, it does make sense to require all sales-increasing investments to bear a portion of those allocated costs that grow with sales. Remember, allocated costs are not necessarily fixed costs.

A related problem arises with cost-reducing investments. To illustrate, as a part of their performance appraisal system, many companies allocate overhead costs to departments or divisions in proportion to the amount of direct labor expense the unit incurs. Suppose a department manager in such an environment has the opportunity to invest in a labor-saving asset. From the department's narrow perspective, such an asset offers two benefits: (1) a reduction in direct labor expense and (2) a reduction in the overhead costs allocated to the department. Yet from the total-company perspective and from the correct economic perspective, only the reduction in direct labor is a benefit because the total-company overhead costs are unaffected by the decision. They are simply reallocated from one cost center to another, and thus are not relevant to the investment decision.

Cannibalization

During the meeting, a product manager in another division argued that the new smartphone proposal was "incomplete and overly optimistic." He stressed two points. First, the decision should be made from a corporate perspective, not from a narrow divisional one. Second, from this perspective the projected cash flows must reflect the reality that the new device will cannibalize sales of existing offerings. That is, the new device will attract a number of customers who would otherwise purchase one of the company's existing products. By his estimate, the new device would attract about 10 percent of his division's customer base, resulting in lost cash flows of approximately $7 million a year. He argued that, at a minimum, this figure must appear as an annual cost in the new device's projected cash flows.

The product manager is correct that the decision should be made from a corporate perspective. Moreover, the with-without principle appears to support his contention that the new product should bear any cannibalization costs. But does it really? Plasteel Communications is certainly not the only innovator among smartphone manufacturers. Suppose, for example, that Samsung or LG Electronics will likely introduce a similar flexible-screen smartphone whether Plasteel does or not. In this circumstance, the sales in question will be lost whatever Plasteel decides to do, and are thus not relevant to the decision. Ultimately, then, whether losses due to cannibalization are relevant hinges on the degree of competition, and the proper mantra in competitive markets is "better we eat our lunch than our competitors do." I believe Nina Sanders is correct to ignore cannibalization costs in Table 7.4. To do otherwise would be to erect a dangerous barrier to innovation.

The treatment of cannibalization in resource allocation decisions can have important strategic implications. Frequently, dominant firms in an industry are reluctant to adopt new, disruptive technologies due to concern about cannibalizing existing lucrative activities. This reluctance to innovate can open the door for smaller new entrants, who have no such worries, to compete effectively against entrenched giants. A case in point is the cell phone industry itself, in which pipsqueak McCaw Cellular Communications competed effectively against giant AT&T for many years, in large part because AT&T was concerned that cell phone revenues would just cannibalize land line revenues to no net gain. It was not until 1994, when the cell phone industry truly threatened to eat AT&T's lunch, that the behemoth finally acted by purchasing McCaw for over $10 billion.

Excess Capacity

The most acrimonious debate over the proposed new product involved the Handheld Division's plan to use another division's excess production capacity. Three years earlier, the Switching Division had added a new production line that was presently operating at only 50 percent capacity. Handheld analysts reasoned that they could put this idle capacity to good use by manufacturing several subcomponents of their new smartphone there. As they saw it, using idle capacity avoided a major capital expenditure and saved the corporation money. They therefore had assigned zero cost to use of the excess capacity. The general manager of the Switching Division saw things rather differently. He argued vehemently that those assets were his, he had paid for them, and he damned sure wasn't going to give them away. He demanded that the Handheld Division either purchase his idle capacity for a fair price or build their own production line. He estimated that the excess capacity was worth at least $20 million. Handheld analysts responded that this was nonsense. The excess capacity had already been paid for and was thus a sunk cost for the current decision.

For technological reasons, it is frequently necessary to acquire more capacity than needed to accomplish a task, and the question arises of how to handle the excess. In this instance, as is often the case, the answer depends on the company's future plans. If the Switching Division has no alternative use for the excess capacity now or in the future, no cash flows are triggered when the Handheld Division uses it. The idle capacity thus is a free good with zero cost. On the other hand, if the Switching Division has alternative uses for the capacity now, or if it is likely to need the capacity in the future, there are costs associated with its use by the Handheld Division, and they should appear in the new-product proposal.

As a concrete example, suppose the Switching Division estimates that it will need the excess capacity in two years to accommodate its own growth. In this event, it is appropriate to assign zero cost to the capacity for the first two years but to require the Handheld Division's new product to bear the cost of new capacity at the end of year 2. Even though the Handheld Division may not ultimately occupy the new capacity, its acquisition is contingent on today's decision and therefore relevant to that decision. After the dust settles, the Handheld Division benefits from the temporarily idle capacity by deferring expenditures on new capacity for two years.

Sharing resources among divisions in this way raises a host of practical accounting questions such as whether the first division should compensate the second for resources used, how the transaction will affect divisional performance measures, and how the cost of new capacity in two years will be recorded. However, because these questions do not involve the movement of cash to or from the firm, they are not germane to the investment decision. The watchword thus should be to make the correct investment choice today and worry about accounting issues such as these later.

The reverse excess capacity problem also arises: A company is contemplating acquisition of an asset that is too large for its present needs and must decide how to treat the excess capacity created. For example, suppose a company is considering the acquisition of a hydrofoil boat to provide passenger service across a lake, but effective use of the hydrofoil will require construction of two very expensive special-purpose piers. Each pier will be capable of handling 10 hydrofoils, and for technical reasons it is impractical to construct smaller piers. If the full cost of the two piers must be borne by the one boat presently under consideration, the boat's NPV will be large and negative, suggesting rejection of the proposal; yet if only one-tenth of the pier costs are assigned to the boat, its NPV will be positive. How should the pier costs be treated?

The proper treatment of the pier costs again depends on the company's future plans. If the company does not anticipate acquiring any additional hydrofoils in the future, the full cost of the piers is relevant to the present decision. On the other hand, if this boat is but the first of a contemplated fleet of hydrofoils, it is appropriate to consider only a fraction of the pier's costs today. More generally, the problem the company faces is that of defining the investment. The relevant question is not whether the company should acquire a boat but whether it should enter the hydrofoil transportation business. The broader question forces the company to look at the investment over a longer time span and consider explicitly the number of boats to be acquired.

Financing Costs

Financing costs refer to any dividend, interest, or principal payments associated with the particular means by which a company intends to finance an investment. As shown in Table 7.4, Handheld Division analysts anticipate financing a significant fraction of the new product's cost with debt and have included a line item in their projections for the interest cost on the debt. Nina Sanders realized that according to the with-without principle, financing costs of some sort are relevant to the decision; money is seldom free. But she was not sure her analysts had treated them properly.

Ms. Sanders's intuition is correct. Her analysts have indeed erred by including interest expense among the cash flows. Financing costs are certainly relevant to investment decisions, but care must be taken not to double-count them. As Chapter 8 will clarify, the most common discount rate used in calculating any of the recommended figures of merit equals the annual percentage cost of capital to the company. It would obviously be double-counting to subtract financing costs from an investment's annual cash inflows and expect the investment to also generate a return greater than the cost of the capital employed. The standard procedure, therefore, is to reflect the cost of money in the discount rate and ignore all financing costs when estimating an investment's cash flows. We will revisit this problem in the next chapter.

Table 7.5 presents Ms. Sanders's revised figures for her division's new-product proposal reflecting all of the suggested corrections. The new line of smartphones

TABLE 7.5 Revised Financial Analysis of New Line of Smartphones ($ millions)

Assumptions:						
Increased working capital	20% of sales, full recovery at end of year 5					
Preliminary engineering	Already spent—sunk cost					
Excess capacity	$20 million cost of new capacity in year 2,					
	$2 million annual depreciation, continuing value in year 5 of $14 million					
Interest expense	Subsumed in discount rate					
Allocated expenses	Variable allocated costs equal to 14% of sales					

		Year				
	0	**1**	**2**	**3**	**4**	**5**
Plant and equipment	$(30)					15
Increased working capital	0	(12)	(4)	(12)	(3)	31
Preliminary engineering	0					
Excess capacity			(20)			14
Total costs	$(30)	$(12)	$(24)	$ (12)	$ (3)	
Total salvage value						$ 60
Sales		$ 60	$82	$140	$157	$120
Cost of sales		26	35	60	68	52
Gross profit		34	47	80	89	68
Interest expense		0	0	0	0	0
Allocated expenses		8	11	20	22	17
Selling and administrative expenses		10	13	22	25	19
Total operating expenses		18	25	42	47	36
Operating income		16	22	38	42	32
Depreciation		3	3	5	5	5
Income before tax		13	19	33	37	27
Tax at 40%		5	8	13	15	11
Income after tax		$ 8	$11	$ 20	$ 22	$ 16
Add back depreciation		3	3	5	5	5
After-tax cash flow		$11	$14	$ 25	$ 27	$ 21
Free cash flow	$(30)	$ (1)	$(10)	$ 13	$ 24	$ 82
Net present value @ 15%	$25					
Benefit-cost ratio*	1.64					
Internal rate of return	30%					

Totals may not add due to rounding.
*BCR = PV$_{inflows}$/PV$_{outflows}$ = $63.0/$38.4 = 1.64

still looks attractive, with an IRR of 30 percent, and Ms. Sanders now has reason to be more confident of her division's recommendations and to expect a more cordial welcome from her colleagues on the Capital Budget Review Committee.

From these examples, I hope you have gained an appreciation for the challenges executives face in identifying relevant costs and benefits in new investment opportunities and why this is a job for operating managers, not finance specialists.

APPENDIX

Mutually Exclusive Alternatives and Capital Rationing

I noted briefly in the chapter that the presence of mutually exclusive alternatives or capital rationing complicates investment analysis. This appendix explains how investments should be analyzed in these cases.

Two investments are mutually exclusive if accepting one precludes further consideration of the other. The choices between building a steel or a concrete bridge, laying a 12-inch pipeline instead of an 8-inch one, or driving to Boston instead of flying are all mutually exclusive alternatives. In each case, there is more than one way to accomplish a task, and the objective is to choose the best way. Mutually exclusive investments stand in contrast to independent investments, where each opportunity can be analyzed on its own without regard to other investments.

When investments are independent and the decision is simply to accept or reject, the NPV, the BCR, and the IRR are equally satisfactory figures of merit. You will reach the same investment decision regardless of the figure of merit used. When investments are mutually exclusive, the world is not so simple. Let's consider an example. Suppose Petro Oil and Gas Company is considering two alternative designs for new service stations and wants to evaluate them using a 10 percent discount rate. As the cash flow diagrams in Figure 7A.1 show, the inexpensive option involves a present investment of $522,000 in return for an anticipated $100,000 per year for 10 years; the expensive option costs $1.1 million but, because of its greater customer appeal, is expected to return $195,000 per year for 10 years.

Table 7A.1 presents the three figures of merit for each investment. All the figures of merit signal that both options are attractive, the NPVs are positive, the BCRs are greater than 1.0, and the IRRs exceed Petro's opportunity cost of capital. If it were possible, Petro should make both investments, but because they are mutually exclusive, this does not make technical sense. So

FIGURE 7A.1   **Cash Flow Diagrams for Alternative Service Station Designs**

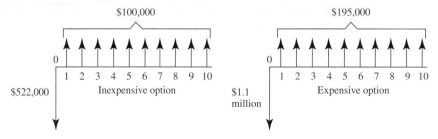

TABLE 7A.1   **Figures of Merit for Service Station Designs**

	NPV at 10%	BCR at 10%	IRR
Inexpensive option	$92,500	1.18	14%
Expensive option	98,200	1.09	12

rather than just accepting or rejecting the investments, Petro must rank them and select the better one. When it comes to ranking the alternatives, however, the three figures of merit no longer give the same signal, for although the inexpensive option has a higher BCR and a higher IRR, it has a lower NPV than the expensive one.

To decide which figure of merit is appropriate for mutually exclusive alternatives, we need only remember that the NPV is a direct measure of the anticipated increase in wealth created by the investment. Because the expensive option will increase wealth by $98,200, as opposed to only $92,500 for the inexpensive option, the expensive option is clearly superior.

The problem with the BCR and the IRR for mutually exclusive alternatives is that they are insensitive to the scale of the investment. As an extreme example, would you rather have an 80 percent return on a $1 investment or a 50 percent return on a $1 million investment? Clearly, when investments are mutually exclusive, scale is relevant, and this leads to the use of the NPV as the appropriate figure of merit.

What Happened to the Other $578,000?

Some readers may think the preceding reasoning is incomplete because I have said nothing about what Petro can do with the $578,000 it would save by choosing the inexpensive option. It would seem that if this saving could be invested at a sufficiently attractive return, the inexpensive option might prove to be superior after all. We will address this concern in the section titled "Capital Rationing." For now, it is sufficient to say that the problem arises only when there is a fixed limit on the amount of money Petro has available to invest. When the company can raise enough money to make all investments promising positive NPVs, the best use of any money saved by selecting the inexpensive option must be to invest in zero-NPV opportunities. And because zero-NPV investments do not increase wealth, any money saved by selecting the low-cost option does not alter our decision.

Unequal Lives

The Petro Oil and Gas example conveniently assumed that both service station options had the same 10-year life. This, of course, is not always the case. When the alternatives have different lives, a simple comparison of NPVs is usually inappropriate. Consider the problem faced by a company trying to decide whether to build a wooden bridge or a steel one:

- The wooden bridge has an initial cost of $125,000, requires annual maintenance expenditures of $15,000, and will last 10 years.

- The steel bridge costs $200,000, requires $5,000 annual maintenance, and will last 40 years.

Which is the better buy? At a discount rate of, say, 15 percent, the present value cost of the wooden bridge over its expected life of 10 years is $200,282 ($125,000 initial cost + $75,282 present value of maintenance expenditures as shown next).

$$=PV(.15,10,15) = (\$75.282)$$
$$PV(\textbf{rate}, nper, pmt, [fv], [type])$$

This compares with a figure for the steel bridge over its 40-year life of $233,209 ($200,000 initial cost + $33,209 present value of maintenance expenditures as shown next).

$$=PV(.15,40,5) = (\$33.209)$$
$$PV(\textbf{rate}, nper, pmt, [fv], [type])$$

So if the object is to minimize the cost of the bridge, a simple comparison of present values would suggest that the wooden structure is a clear winner. However, this obviously overlooks the differing life expectancy of the two bridges, implicitly assuming that if the company builds the wooden bridge, it will not need a bridge after 10 years.

The message is clear: When comparing mutually exclusive alternatives having different service lives, it is necessary to reflect this difference in the analysis. One approach is to examine each alternative over the same common investment horizon. For example, suppose our company believes it will need a bridge for 20 years; due to inflation, the wooden bridge will cost $200,000 to reconstruct at the end of 10 years; and the salvage value of the steel bridge in 20 years will be $90,000. The cash flow diagrams for the two options are thus as follows:

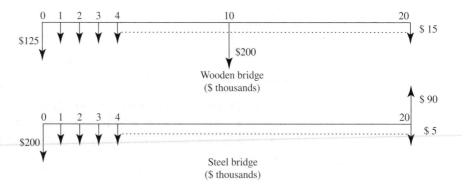

Now the present value cost of the wooden bridge is $268,327 ($125,000 initial cost + $93,890 present value of maintenance expenditures as shown below + $49,437 present value cost of a new bridge in 10 years as shown below).

=PV(.15,20,15) = ($93.890)
PV(**rate**, nper, pmt, [fv], [type])

=PV(.15,10,0,200) = ($49.437)
PV(**rate**, nper, pmt, [fv], [type])

And the cost of the steel bridge is $225,798 ($200,000 initial cost + $25,798 present value of maintenance expenditures net of salvage value).

$$=PV(.15,20,5,-90) = (\$25.798)$$
$$PV(\textbf{rate}, \text{nper, pmt, [fv], [type]})$$

Compared over a common 20-year investment horizon, the steel bridge has the lower present value cost and is thus superior.

A second way to choose among mutually exclusive alternatives with differing lives is to calculate the equivalent annual cost of each. Here's the arithmetic for the two bridges.

Wooden bridge

$$=PMT(.15,10,200.282) = (\$39.9)$$
$$PMT(\textbf{rate}, \text{nper, pv, [fv], [type]})$$

Steel bridge

$$=PMT(.15,40,233.209) = (\$35.1)$$
$$PMT(\textbf{rate}, \text{nper, pv, [fv], [type]})$$

Spreading the $200,282 present value cost of the wooden bridge over its 10-year life expectancy, we find that the bridge's equivalent annual cost is $39,900, while the analogous figure over a 40-year life for the steel bridge is only $35,100. Looking at the decision over a 40-year horizon, and assuming no change in the cost of a new wooden bridge every 10 years, our decision is now obvious. Because we can have the steel bridge at an equivalent annual cost below that of the wooden bridge, the steel bridge is the better choice.

But notice the assumption necessary to reach this conclusion. If due to technological improvements, we believe the replacement cost of the wooden bridge will fall over time, its higher equivalent annual cost in the first decade might well be offset by lower annual costs in subsequent decades, tipping the balance in favor of the wooden bridge. Similarly, if we believe inflation will cause the replacement cost of the wooden bridge to rise over time, its equivalent annual cost in the first decade is again insufficient information on which to base an informed decision. We conclude that equivalent annual costs are a slick way to analyze mutually exclusive alternatives with differing lives when prices are constant. However, the technique is more difficult to apply in the face of changing prices.

Capital Rationing

Implicit in our discussion to this point has been the assumption that money is readily available to companies at a cost equal to the discount rate. The other extreme is capital rationing. Under *capital rationing,* the company has a fixed investment budget that it may not exceed. As was true with mutually exclusive alternatives, capital rationing requires us to rank investments rather than simply accept or reject them. Despite this similarity, however, you should understand that the two conditions are fundamentally different. With mutually exclusive alternatives, the money is available but, for technical reasons, the company cannot make all investments. Under capital rationing, it may be technically possible to make all investments, but there is not enough money. This difference is more than semantic, for, as the following example illustrates, the nature of the ranking process differs fundamentally in the two cases.

Suppose Sullivan Electronics Company has a limited investment budget of $200,000 and management has identified the four independent investment opportunities appearing in Table 7A.2. According to the three figures of merit, all investments should be undertaken, but this is impossible because the total cost of the four investments exceeds Sullivan's budget. Looking at the investment rankings, the NPV criterion ranks A as the best investment, followed by B, C, and D in that order, while the BCR and IRR rank C best, followed by D, B, and A. So we know that A is either the best investment or the worst.

To make sense of these rankings, we need to remember that the underlying objective in evaluating investment opportunities is to increase wealth, or

TABLE 7A.2   **Four Independent Investment Opportunities under Capital Rationing (capital budget = $200,000)**

Investment	Initial Cost	NPV at 12%	BCR at 12%	IRR
A	$200,000	$10,000	1.05	14.4%
B	120,000	8,000	1.07	15.1
C	50,000	6,000	1.12	17.6
D	80,000	6,000	1.08	15.5

value. Under capital rationing, this means the company should undertake that *bundle* of investments generating the highest *total* NPV. How is this to be done? One way is to look at every possible bundle of investments having a total cost less than the budget constraint and select the bundle with the highest *total* NPV. A shortcut is to rank the investments by their BCRs and work down the list, accepting investments until either the money runs out or the BCR drops below 1.0. This suggests that Sullivan should accept projects C, D, and 7/12 of B, for a total NPV of $16,670 [(6,000 + 6,000 + 7/12 × 8,000)]. Only 7/12 of B should be undertaken because the company has only $70,000 remaining after accepting C and D.

Why is it incorrect to rank investments by their NPVs under capital rationing? Because under capital rationing, we are interested in the payoff per dollar invested—the bang per buck—not just the payoff itself. The Sullivan example illustrates the point. Investment A has the largest NPV, equal to $10,000, but it has the smallest NPV per dollar invested. Because investment dollars are limited under capital rationing, we must look at the benefit per dollar invested when ranking investments. This is what the BCR does.

Two other details warrant mention. In the preceding example, the IRR provides the same ranking as the BCR, and although this is usually the case, it is not always so. It turns out that when the two rankings differ, the BCR ranking is the correct one. Why the rankings differ and why the BCR is superior are not worth explaining here. It is sufficient to remember that if you rank by IRR rather than BCR, you might occasionally be in error. A second detail is that when fractional investments are not possible—when it does not make sense for Sullivan Electronics to invest in 7/12 of project B—rankings according to any figure of merit are unreliable, and one must resort to the tedious method of looking at each possible bundle of investments in search of the highest total NPV.

The Problem of Future Opportunities

Implicit in the preceding discussion is the assumption that as long as an investment has a positive NPV, it is better to make the investment than to let the money sit idle. However, under capital rationing, this may not be true. To illustrate, suppose the financial executive of Sullivan Electronics believes that, within six months, company scientists will develop a new product costing $200,000 and having an NPV of $60,000. In this event, the company's best strategy is to forgo all the investments presently under consideration and save its money for the new product.

This example illustrates that investment evaluation under capital rationing involves more than a simple appraisal of current opportunities; it also involves a comparison between current opportunities and future prospects.

The difficulty with this comparison at a practical level is that it is unreasonable to expect a manager to have anything more than a vague impression of what investments are likely to arise in the future. Consequently, it is impossible to decide with any assurance whether it is better to invest in current projects or wait for brighter future opportunities. This means practical investment evaluation under capital rationing necessarily involves a high degree of subjective judgment.

A Decision Tree

Mutually exclusive investment alternatives and capital rationing complicate an already confusing topic. To provide a summary and an overview, Figure 7A.2 presents a capital budgeting decision tree. It indicates the figure or figures of merit that are appropriate under the various conditions discussed in the chapter. For example, following the lowest branch in the tree, we see that when evaluating investments under capital rationing that are independent and can be acquired fractionally, ranking by the BCR is the appropriate technique. To review your understanding of the material, see if you can explain why the recommended figures of merit are appropriate under the various conditions indicated, whereas the others are not.

FIGURE 7A.2   **Capital Budgeting Decision Tree**

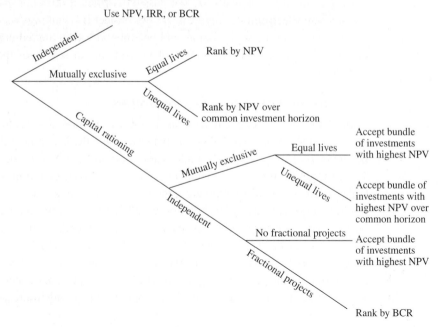

SUMMARY

1. Evaluation of an investment opportunity involves three steps:
   - Estimate relevant cash flows.
   - Calculate a figure of merit.
   - Compare the figure of merit to an acceptance criterion.
2. Money has a time value because
   - Cash deferred imposes an opportunity cost.
   - Inflation reduces purchasing power over time.
   - Risk customarily increases with the futurity of a cash flow.
3. Equivalence
   - Says that a present sum and future cash flows have the same value when the present sum can be invested at the discount rate to replicate the future cash flows.
   - Enables the use of compounding and discounting to eliminate the time dimension from investment analysis.
4. The Net Present Value (NPV)
   - Equals the difference between the present value of an investment's cash inflows and the present value of its outflows.
   - Is a valid figure of investment merit.
   - When positive, indicates the investment should be undertaken.
   - Is an estimate of the expected increase or decrease in wealth accruing to the investor.
   - Provides a practical decision rule for managers seeking to create shareholder value.
5. The Internal Rate of Return (IRR)
   - Is the discount rate at which an investment's NPV equals zero.
   - Is the rate at which money retained in the investment is growing.
   - Is a breakeven rate, meaning that in most instances an investment should be undertaken whenever its IRR exceeds the discount rate, and vice versa.
   - Is a close cousin of the NPV and in most circumstances a valid figure of merit.
6. Estimation of relevant cash flows
   - Is the most difficult task in evaluating investment opportunities.
   - Is guided by two broad principles:
     - The cash flow principle: If money moves, count it, otherwise do not.
     - The with-without principle: All cash flows that differ with or without the investment are relevant, all others are not.

- Presents recurring challenges involving:
  - Annual depreciation: Only relevant to estimate taxes.
  - Working capital and spontaneous sources: Net amount relevant including salvage value.
  - Sunk costs: Not relevant.
  - Allocated costs: Relevant when variable.
  - Cannibalization: Seldom relevant in competitive markets.
  - Excess capacity: Relevant if alternative use now or in future.
  - Financing costs: Relevant but usually captured in discount rate, not cash flows.

ADDITIONAL RESOURCES

Bierman, Harold, and Seymour Smidt. *The Capital Budgeting Decision,* 9th ed. Philadelphia, PA: Taylor & Francis, Inc., 2006. 402 pages.

> The names Bierman and Smidt, both emeritus faculty members at Cornell University, have been synonymous with capital budgeting for many years. This edition is a clear and concise introduction to a complex topic. (See also *Advanced Capital Budgeting Refinements in the Economic Analysis of Investment Projects,* by the same authors. 2007. 392 pages.)

Titman, Sheridan, and John Martin. *Valuation: The Art and Science of Corporate Investment Decisions,* 3rd ed. London: Pearson Education, 2016. 560 pages.

> A great resource on DCF analysis and other topics from a pair of prolific authors in the world of corporate finance.

Financial Calculator Apps

A number of financial calculators are available for iOS, including official versions of the popular Texas Instruments BAII Plus and Hewlett Packard 12C. In Apple's app store, search for "financial calculator." For Android, consider the HP 12C or other independently created financial calculators available at Google Play.

berkshirehathaway.com

More than 20 years of Warren Buffett's legendary letters to shareholders, and an opportunity to purchase a Berkshire Hathaway golf shirt. Check out Buffett's "Owner's Manual," a succinct explanation of Berkshire's broad economic principles of operations. When I grow up, I want to write like Warren Buffett.

PROBLEMS

Answers to odd-numbered problems appear at the end of the book. Answers to even-numbered problems and additional exercises are available in the

Instructor Resources within McGraw-Hill's *Connect* (see the Preface for more information).

1. Answer the following questions assuming the interest rate is 8 percent.

Time Value of Money Problems

a. What is the present value of $1,000 to be received in four years?

b. What is the present value of $1,000 to be received in eight years? Why does the present value fall as the number of years increases?

c. What will be the value in seven years of $12,000 invested today?

d. How much would you pay for the right to receive $5,000 at the end of year 1, $4,000 at the end of year 2, and $8,000 at the end of year 5?

e. How long will it take for a $2,000 investment to double in value?

f. What will be the value in 20 years of $1,000 invested at the end of each year for the next 20 years?

g. A couple wishes to save $250,000 over the next 18 years for their child's college education. What uniform annual amount must they deposit at the end of each year to accomplish their objective?

h. How long must a stream of $600 payments last to justify a purchase price of $7,500? Suppose the stream lasted only five years. How large would the salvage value (liquidating payment) need to be to justify the investment of $7,500?

i. The projected cash flows for an investment appear below. What is the investment's NPV?

Year	0	1	2	3	4	5
Cash flow	−$200	50	75	110	110	80

Rate of Return Problems

j. An investment of $1,300 today returns $61,000 in 50 years. What is the internal rate of return on this investment?

k. An investment costs $900,000 today and promises a single payment of $11.5 million in 22 years. What is the promised rate of return, IRR, on this investment?

l. What return do you earn if you pay $22,470 for a stream of $5,000 payments lasting 10 years? What does it mean if you pay less than $22,470 for the stream? More than $22,470?

m. An investment promises to double your money in five years. What is the promised IRR on the investment?

n. The projected cash flows for an investment appear below. What is the investment's IRR?

Year	0	1	2	3	4	5
Cash flow	−$460	−28	75	160	280	190

    o. In 2013, Picasso's painting *Le Rêve* was sold to hedge-fund manager Steven A. Cohen for $155 million. In 1941, 72 years earlier, the same painting sold for $7,000. Calculate the rate of return on this investment. What does this suggest about the merits of fine art as an investment?

Bank Loan, Bond, and Stock Problems

    p. How much would you pay for a 10-year bond with a par value of $1,000 and a 7 percent coupon rate? Assume interest is paid annually.

    q. How much would you pay for a share of preferred stock paying a $5-per-share annual dividend forever?

    r. A company is planning to set aside money to repay $150 million in bonds that will be coming due in eight years. How much money would the company need to set aside at the end of each year for the next eight years to repay the bonds when they come due? How would your answer change if the money were deposited at the beginning of each year?

    s. An individual wants to borrow $120,000 from a bank and repay it in six equal annual end-of-year payments, including interest. What should the payments be for the bank to earn 8 percent on the loan? Ignore taxes and default risk.

2. Microsoft Corp. reported earnings per share of $1.20 in 2006 and $2.10 in 2016. At what annual rate did earnings per share grow over this period?

3. A developer offers lots for sale at $60,000, $10,000 to be paid at sale and $10,000 to be paid at the end of each of the next five years with "no interest to be charged." In discussing a possible purchase, you find that you can get the same lot for $48,959 cash. You also find that on a time purchase there will be a service charge of $2,000 at the date of purchase to cover legal and handling expenses and the like. Approximately what rate of interest before income taxes will actually be paid if the lot is purchased on this time payment plan?

4. You are looking to purchase a Tesla Model X sport utility vehicle. The price of the vehicle is $93,500. You negotiate a six-year loan, with no money down and no monthly payments during the first year. After the first year, you will pay $1,300 per month for the following five years, with a balloon payment at the end to cover the remaining principal on the loan. The APR on the loan with monthly compounding is 5 percent. What will be the amount of the balloon payment six years from now?

5. A wealthy graduate of a local university wants to establish a scholarship to cover the full cost of one student each year in perpetuity at her university. To adequately prepare for the administration of the scholarship, the university will begin awarding it starting in three years. The estimated full cost of one student this year is $45,000 and is expected to stay constant in real terms in the future. If the scholarship is invested to earn an annual real return of 5 percent, how much must the donor contribute today to fully fund the scholarship?

6. You are selling a product on commission, at the rate of $1,000 per sale. To date, you have spent $800 promoting a particular prospective sale. You are confident you can complete this sale with an added expenditure of some undetermined amount. What is the maximum amount, over and above what you have already spent, that you should be willing to spend to assure the sale?

7. One year ago, Caffe Vita Coffee Roasting Co. purchased three small-batch coffee roasters for $3.3 million. Now in 2018, the company finds that new roasters that offer significant advantages are available. The new roasters can be purchased for $4.5 million, and have no salvage value. Both the new and the old roasters are expected to last until 2028. Management antici-pates that the new roasters will produce a gross margin of $1.2 million a year, so that, using straight-line depreciation, the annual taxable income will be $750,000.

    The current roasters are expected to produce a gross profit of $600,000 a year and, assuming a total economic life of 11 years and straight-line depre-ciation, a profit before tax of $300,000. The current market value of the old roasters is $1.5 million. The company's tax rate is 45 percent, and its minimum acceptable rate of return is 10 percent. Ignoring possible taxes on sale of used equipment and assuming zero salvage values at the end of the roasters' economic lives, should Caffe Vita replace its year-old roasters?

8. Neptune Biometrics, despite its promising technology, is having difficulty generating profits. Having raised $85 million in an initial public offering of its stock early in the year, the company is poised to introduce a new product, an inexpensive fingerprint door lock. If Neptune engages in a pro-motional campaign costing $55 million this year, its annual after-tax cash flow over the next five years will be only $1 million. If it does not under-take the campaign, it expects its after-tax cash flow to be −$15 million annually for the same period. Assuming the company has decided to stay in its chosen business, is this campaign worthwhile when the discount rate is 8 percent? Why or why not?

9. Consider the following investment opportunity:

Initial cost at time 0	$15	million
Annual revenues beginning at time 1	$20	million
Annual operating costs exclusive of depreciation	$13	million
Expected life of investment	5	years
Salvage value after taxes	$ 0	
Annual depreciation for tax purposes	$ 3	million
Tax rate	40%	

What is the rate of return on this investment? Assuming the investor wants to earn at least 10 percent after corporate taxes, is this investment attractive?

10. *This problem tests your understanding of the chapter appendix.* A company is considering the following investment opportunities.

Investment	A	B	C
Initial cost ($ millions)	5.5	3.0	2.0
Expected life	10 yrs	10 yrs	10 yrs
NPV @ 15%	$340,000	$300,000	$200,000
IRR	20%	30%	40%

   a. If the company can raise large amounts of money at an annual cost of 15 percent, and if the investments are independent of one another, which should it undertake?

   b. If the company can raise large amounts of money at an annual cost of 15 percent, and if the investments are mutually exclusive, which should it undertake?

   c. Considering only these three investments, if the company has a fixed capital budget of $5.5 million, and if the investments are independent of one another, which should it undertake?

11. What's wrong with this picture?

   In the following discussion see how many errors you can spot and explain *briefly* why each is an error. *You do not need to correct the error.*

   "Natalie, I think we've got a winner here. Take a look at these numbers!

	($ thousands)				
Year	0	1	2	3 ...	10
Initial cost	−1,000				
Units sold		100	100	100 ...	100
Price/unit		15	15	15 ...	15
Total revenue		1,500	1,500	1,500 ...	1,500
Cost of goods sold		800	800	800 ...	800
Gross profit		700	700	700 ...	700
Operating expenses					
Depreciation		100	100	100 ...	100
Interest expense		100	100	100 ...	100
Income before tax		500	500	500 ...	500
Tax @ 40%		200	200	200 ...	200
Income after tax		300	300	300 ...	300

   "Now, Natalie, here's how I figure it: The boss says our corporate goal should be to increase earnings by at least 15 percent every year, and this project certainly increases earnings. It adds $300,000 to net income after tax every year. My trusty calculator tells me that the rate of return on this project is 30 percent ($300/$1,000), well above our minimum target return of 10 percent. And if you want to use net present value, its NPV discounted at 10 percent is $843.50. So, what do you think, Natalie?"

"Well, David, it looks pretty good, but I do have a few questions."

"Shoot, Natalie."

"OK. What about increases in accounts receivable and stuff like that?"

"Not relevant! We'll get that money back when the project terminates, so it's equivalent to an interest-free loan, which is more of a benefit than a cost."

"But, David, what about extra selling and administrative costs? Haven't you left those out?"

"That's the beauty of this, Natalie. Given the recent recession, I figure we can handle the added business with existing personnel. In fact, one of the virtues of the proposal is that we should be able to retain some people we would otherwise have to terminate."

"Well, you've convinced me, David. Now, I think it will be only fair if the boss puts you in charge of this exciting new project."

12. Read the information regarding a possible new investment available from McGraw-Hill's *Connect* or your course instructor.
    a. Complete the spreadsheet to estimate the project's annual after-tax cash flows.
    b. What is the investment's net present value at a discount rate of 10 percent?
    c. What is the investment's internal rate of return?
    d. How does the internal rate of return change if the discount rate equals 20 percent?
    e. How does the internal rate of return change if the growth rate in EBIT is 8 percent instead of 3 percent?

13. The spreadsheet for this problem provides a brief overview of selected financial functions in Excel and poses several questions regarding mortgage loans requiring monthly payments. The spreadsheet is available for download from McGraw-Hill's *Connect* or your course instructor (see the Preface for more information).

14. This problem asks you to evaluate two mutually exclusive investment alternatives with differing life expectancies under various conditions including capital rationing. Relevant information about the investments

and specific questions are available for download from McGraw-Hill's *Connect* or your course instructor (see the Preface for more information).

15. Waldo Entertainment Products, Inc. is negotiating with Disney for the rights to manufacture and sell superhero-themed toys for a three-year period. At the end of year 3, Waldo plans to liquidate the assets from the project. Additional information is available for download from McGraw-Hill's *Connect* or your course instructor (see the Preface for more information). Given this information, identify the relevant cash flows, then calculate the investment's net present value, benefit-cost ratio, and internal rate of return.

Risk Analysis in Investment Decisions

A man's gotta make at least one bet a day, else he could be walking around lucky and never know it.

Jimmy Jones, horse trainer

Most thoughtful individuals and some investment bankers know that all interesting financial decisions involve risk as well as return. By their nature, business investments require the expenditure of a known sum of money today in anticipation of uncertain future benefits. Consequently, if the discounted cash flow techniques discussed in the last chapter are to be useful in evaluating realistic investments, they must incorporate considerations of risk as well as return. Two such considerations are relevant. At an applied level, risk increases the difficulty of estimating relevant cash flows. More importantly at a conceptual level, risk itself enters as a fundamental determinant of investment value. If two investments promise the same expected return but have differing risks, most of us will prefer the low-risk alternative. In the jargon of economics, we are *risk averse,* and as a result, risk reduces investment value.

Risk aversion among individuals and corporations creates the common pattern of investment risk and return shown in Figure 8.1. The figure shows that for low-risk investments, such as government bonds, expected return is modest, but as risk increases, so too must the anticipated return. I say "must" because the risk-return pattern shown is more than wishful thinking. Unless higher-risk investments promise higher returns, you and I, as risk-averse investors, will not hold them.

This risk-return trade-off is fundamental to much of finance. Over the past five decades, researchers have demonstrated that under idealized conditions, and with risk defined in a specific way, the risk-return trade-off is a straight-line one as depicted in the figure. The line is known as the *market line* and represents the combinations of risk and expected return one can anticipate in a properly functioning economy.

The details of the market line need not detain us here. What is important is the realization that knowledge of an investment's expected return is

FIGURE 8.1   **The Risk-Return Trade-Off**

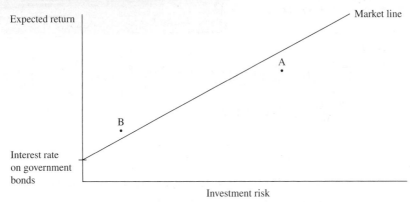

not enough to determine its worth. Instead, investment evaluation is a two-dimensional task involving a balancing of risk against return. The appropriate question when evaluating investment opportunities is not "What's the rate of return?" but "Is the return sufficient to justify the risk?" The investments represented by A and B in Figure 8.1 illustrate this point. Investment A has a higher expected return than B; nonetheless, B is the better investment. Despite its modest return, B lies above the market line, meaning it promises a higher expected return for its risk than available alternatives, whereas investment A lies below the market line, meaning alternative investments promising a higher expected return for the same risk are available.[1]

This chapter examines the incorporation of risk into investment evaluation. Central to our discussion of discounted cash flow techniques in the last chapter was a quantity variously referred to as the interest rate, the discount rate, and the opportunity cost of capital. While stressing that this quantity somehow reflected investment risk and the time value of money, I was purposely vague about its origins. It is time now to correct this omission by explaining how to incorporate investment risk into the discount rate. After defining investment risk in more detail, we will estimate the cost of capital to Hasbro Inc., the company profiled in earlier chapters, and will examine the strengths and weaknesses of the cost of capital as a risk-adjusted discount rate. The chapter concludes with a look at several important pitfalls to avoid when evaluating investment opportunities, and will also cover economic value added, a related

---

[1] Saying the same thing more analytically, we know from our earlier study of financial leverage that owners of asset B need not settle for safe, low returns. Rather, they can use debt financing to lever B's expected return and risk to higher values. In fact, the market line tells us that with just the right amount of debt financing, owners of asset B can attain A's higher expected return, and more, with no greater risk. B is therefore the better investment.

Are You Risk Averse?

Here is a simple test to find out. Which of the following investment opportunities do you prefer?

1. You pay $10,000 today and flip a coin in one year to determine whether you will receive $50,000 or *pay* another $20,000.
2. You pay $10,000 today and receive $15,000 in one year.

If investment 2 sounds better than 1, join the crowd: You are risk averse. Even though both investments cost $10,000 and promise an expected one-year payoff of $15,000, or a 50 percent return, studies indicate that most people, when sober and not in a casino, prefer the certainty of option 2 to the uncertainty of option 1. The presence of risk reduces the value of 1 relative to 2.

For a simple self-test of your risk tolerance from Rutgers University, see **njaes.rutgers. edu/money/riskquiz.**

---

topic in the world of performance appraisal. The appendix considers two logical extensions to the chapter material known as asset betas and adjusted present value analysis, or APV.

You should know at the outset that the topics in this chapter are not simple, for the addition of a whole second dimension to investment analysis in the form of risk introduces a number of complexities and ambiguities. The chapter, therefore, will offer a general road map for how to proceed and an appreciation of available techniques rather than a detailed set of answers. But look on the bright side: If investment decisions were simple, there would be less demand for well-educated managers and aspiring financial writers.

Risk Defined

Speaking broadly, there are two aspects to investment risk: The *dispersion* of an investment's possible returns, and the *correlation* of these returns with those available on other assets. Looking first at dispersion, Figure 8.2 shows the possible rates of return that might be earned on two investments in the form of bell-shaped curves. According to the figure, the expected return on investment A is about 12 percent, while the corresponding figure for investment B is about 20 percent.

Dispersion risk captures the intuitively appealing notion that risk is tied to the range of possible outcomes, or alternatively to the uncertainty surrounding the outcome. Because investment A shows considerable bunching of possible returns about the expected return, its risk is low. Investment B, on the other hand, evidences considerably less clustering, and is thus higher risk. Borrowing from statistics, one way to measure this clustering tendency is to calculate

FIGURE 8.2 **Illustration of Investment Risk: Investment A Has a Lower Expected Return and a Lower Risk than B**

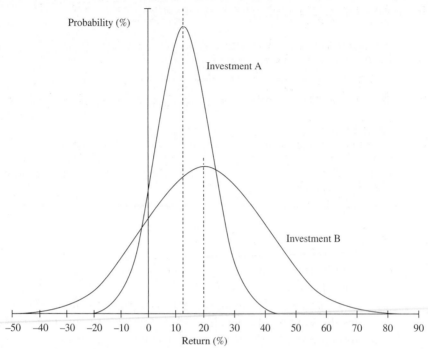

the standard deviation of return. The details of calculating an investment's expected return and standard deviation of return need not concern us here.[2] It is enough to know that risk relates to the dispersion, or uncertainty, in possible outcomes and that techniques exist to measure this dispersion.

[2] An investment's expected return is the probability-weighted average of possible returns. If three returns are possible—8, 12, and 18 percent—and if the chance of each occurring is 40, 30, and 30 percent, respectively, the investment's expected return is

$$\text{Expected return} = 0.40 \times 8\% + 0.30 \times 12\% + 0.30 \times 18\% = 12.2\%$$

The standard deviation of return is the probability-weighted average of the deviations of possible returns from the expected return. To illustrate, the differences between the possible returns and the expected return in our example are (8% − 12.2%), (12% − 12.2%), and (18% − 12.2%). Because some of these differences are positive and others are negative, they would tend to cancel one another out if we added them directly. So we square them to ensure the same sign, calculate the probability-weighted average of the squared deviations, and then find the square root.

$$\text{Standard deviation} = [0.4(8\% - 12.2\%)^2 + 0.3(12\% - 12.2\%)^2 + 0.3(18\% - 12.2\%)^2]^{1/2} = 4.1\%$$

The probability-weighted average difference between the investment's possible returns and its expected return is 4.1 percentage points.

TABLE 8.1 **Diversification Reduces Risk**

Investment	Weather	Probability	Return on Investment	Weighted Outcome
Ice cream stand	Sun	0.50	**60%**	30%
	Rain	0.50	**−20**	−10
				Expected outcome = 20
Umbrella shop	Sun	0.50	**−30**	−15
	Rain	0.50	**50**	25
				Expected outcome = 10
Portfolio:				
1/2 Ice cream stand	Sun	0.50	**15**	7.5
and umbrella shop	Rain	0.50	**15**	7.5
				Expected outcome = 15

Risk and Diversification

Dispersion risk, as just described, is often known as an investment's *total risk,* or more fancifully its Robinson Crusoe risk. It is the risk an owner would face if he were alone on a desert island unable to buy any other assets. The story changes dramatically, however, once the owner is off the desert island and again able to hold a diversified portfolio. For then the risk from holding a given asset is customarily less than the asset's total risk—frequently a lot less. In other words, there is more—or perhaps I should say less—to risk than simply dispersion in possible outcomes.

To see why, Table 8.1 presents information about two very simple risky investments: the purchase of an ice cream stand and an umbrella shop.[3] For simplicity, let's suppose tomorrow's weather will be either rain or sun with equal probability. Purchase of the ice cream stand is clearly a risky undertaking, because the investor stands to make a 60 percent return on his investment if it is sunny tomorrow but lose 20 percent if it rains. The umbrella shop is also risky, because the investor will lose 30 percent if tomorrow is sunny but will make 50 percent if it rains.

Yet despite the fact that these two investments are risky when viewed in isolation, they are not risky when seen as members of a portfolio containing both investments. In a portfolio consisting of half ownership of the ice cream stand and of the umbrella shop, the losses and gains from the two investments

---

[3] I used to think this was a fanciful example until I noticed how quickly street vendors in Washington, D.C., switched between selling soft drinks and umbrellas depending on the weather.

precisely counterbalance one another in each state, so that regardless of tomorrow's weather, the outcome is a certain 15 percent (e.g., if it is sunny tomorrow, the ice cream stand makes 60 percent on half of the portfolio and the umbrella shop loses 30 percent on the other half for a net of 15 percent [$15\% = 0.5 \times 60\% + 0.5 \times -30\%$]). The expected outcome from the portfolio is the average of the expected outcomes from each investment, but the risk of the portfolio is zero. Owning both assets eliminates the dispersion in possible returns. Despite what you may have heard, there really is a free lunch in finance. It is called diversification.

This is an extreme example, but it does illustrate an important fact about risk: When it is possible to own a diversified portfolio, the relevant risk is not the investment's risk in isolation—its Robinson Crusoe risk— but its risk as part of the portfolio. And, as the example demonstrates, the difference between these two perspectives can be substantial.

An asset's risk in isolation is greater than its risk as part of a portfolio whenever the asset's returns and the portfolio's returns are less than perfectly correlated. In this commonplace situation, some of the asset's return variability is offset by variability in the portfolio's returns, and the effective risk borne by the investor declines. Look again at Table 8.1. The return on the ice cream stand is highly variable, but because it hits a trough precisely when the umbrella shop return hits a peak, return variability for the two investments combined disappears. The portfolio will earn 15 percent rain or shine. In other words, when assets are combined in a portfolio, an "averaging out" process occurs that reduces risk.

Because most business investments depend to some extent on the same underlying economic forces, it is unusual to find investment opportunities with perfectly inversely correlated returns as in the ice cream stand–umbrella shop example. However, the described diversification effect still exists. Whenever investment returns, or cash flows, are less than perfectly positively correlated— whenever individual investments are unique in some respects—an investment's risk as part of a portfolio is less than the dispersion of its possible returns.

Saying the same thing more formally, it is possible to partition an investment's total risk into two parts as follows:

$$\text{Total risk} = \text{Systematic risk} + \text{Unsystematic risk}$$

Systematic risk reflects exposure to economywide, or marketwide events, such as interest rate changes and business cycles, and cannot be reduced by diversification. Unsystematic risk, on the other hand, reflects investment-specific events, such as fires and lawsuits, which can be eliminated through diversification. Because savvy shareholders own diversified investment portfolios, only systematic risk is relevant for evaluating investment opportunities. The rest can be diversified away.

FIGURE 8.3   **The Power of Diversification in Common Stock Portfolios**

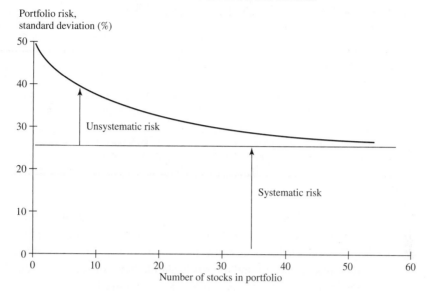

Figure 8.3 demonstrates the power of diversification in common stock port-folios. It shows the relationship between the variability of portfolio returns, as measured by the standard deviation of return, and the number of randomly chosen stocks in the portfolio. Note that variability is high when the number of stocks is low but declines rapidly as the number increases. As the number of stocks in the portfolio grows, the "averaging out" effect takes place, and unsystematic risk declines. Studies suggest that unsystematic risk all but van-ishes when portfolio size exceeds about 50 randomly chosen stocks, and that diversification eliminates approximately one-half of total risk.[4]

Estimating Investment Risk

Having defined risk and risk aversion in at least a general way, let us next consider how we might estimate the amount of risk present in a particular investment opportunity. In some business situations, an investment's risk can be calculated objectively from scientific or historical evidence. This is true, for instance, of oil and gas development wells. Once an exploration company has found a field and mapped out its general configuration, the probability

[4] John Campbell, Martin Lettau, Burton Malkiel, and Yexiao Xu, "Have Individual Stocks Become More Volatile? An Empirical Exploration of Idiosyncratic Risk," *Journal of Finance* 56 (February 2001), pp. 1–43.

Systematic Risk and Conglomerate Diversification

Some executives seize on the idea that diversification reduces risk as a justification for conglomerate diversification. Even when a merger promises no increase in profitability, it is said to be beneficial because the resulting diversification reduces the risk of company cash flows. Because shareholders are risk averse, this reduction in risk is said to increase the value of the firm.

Such reasoning is at best incomplete. If shareholders wanted the risk reduction benefits of such a conglomerate merger, they could achieve them much more simply by just owning shares of the two independent companies in their own portfolios. Shareholders do not depend on company management for such benefits. Executives intent on acquiring other firms must look elsewhere to find a rationale for their actions.

---

that a development well drilled within the boundaries of the field will be commercially successful can be determined with reasonable accuracy.

Sometimes history can be a guide. A company that has opened 1,000 fast-food restaurants around the world should have a good idea about the expected return and risk of opening the 1,001st. Similarly, if you are thinking about buying IBM stock, the historical record of the past variability of annual returns to IBM shareholders is an important starting point when estimating the risk of IBM shares. I will say more about measuring the systematic risk of traded assets, such as IBM shares, a little later.

These are the easy situations. More often, business ventures are one-of-a-kind investments for which the estimation of risk must be largely subjective. When a company is contemplating a new-product investment, for example, there is frequently little technical or historical experience on which to base an estimate of investment risk. In this situation, risk appraisal depends on the perceptions of the managers participating in the decision, their knowledge of the economics of the industry, and their understanding of the investment's ramifications.

Three Techniques for Estimating Investment Risk

Three previously mentioned techniques—sensitivity analysis, scenario analysis, and simulation—are useful for making subjective estimates of investment risk. Although none of the techniques provides an objective measure of investment risk, they all help the executive to think systematically about the sources of risk and their effect on project return. Reviewing briefly, an investment's IRR or NPV depends on a number of uncertain economic factors, such as selling price, quantity sold, useful life, and so on. Sensitivity analysis involves an estimation of how the investment's figure of merit varies with changes in one of these uncertain factors. One commonly used approach is to calculate three returns corresponding to an optimistic, a pessimistic, and a most likely forecast of the uncertain variables. This provides some indication of the range of possible outcomes. Scenario analysis is a modest extension that changes several of the uncertain variables in a mutually consistent way to describe a particular event.

We looked at simulation in some detail in Chapter 3 as a tool for financial planning. Recall that simulation is an extension of sensitivity and scenario analysis in which the analyst assigns a probability distribution to each uncertain factor, specifies any interdependence among the factors, and asks a computer repeatedly to select values for the factors according to their probability of occurring. For each set of values chosen, the computer calculates a particular outcome. The result is a graph, similar to Figure 3.1, plotting project return against frequency of occurrence. The chief benefits of sensitivity analysis, scenario analysis, and simulation are that they force the analyst to think systematically about the individual economic determinants of investment risk, indicate the sensitivity of the investment's return to each of these determinants, and provide information about the range of possible returns.

Including Risk in Investment Evaluation

Once you have an idea of the degree of risk inherent in an investment, the second step is to incorporate this information into your evaluation of the opportunity.

Risk-Adjusted Discount Rates

The most common way to do this is to add an increment to the discount rate; that is, discount the expected value of the risky cash flows at a discount rate that includes a premium for risk. Alternatively, you can compare an investment's IRR, based on expected cash flows, to a required rate of return that again includes a risk premium. The size of the premium naturally increases with the perceived risk of the investment.

To illustrate the use of such risk-adjusted discount rates, consider a $10 million investment promising risky cash flows with an expected value of $2 million annually for 10 years. What is the investment's NPV when the risk-free interest rate is 5 percent and management has decided to use a 7 percent risk premium to compensate for the uncertainty of the cash flows?

A little figure work reveals that at a 12 percent, risk-adjusted discount rate, the investment's NPV is $1.3 million ($11.3 million present value of future cash flows, less $10 million initial cost). The positive NPV indicates that the investment is attractive even after adjusting for risk. An equivalent approach is to calculate the investment's IRR of 15.1 percent and note that it exceeds the 12 percent risk-adjusted rate, again signaling the investment's merit.

Note how the risk-adjusted discount rate reduces the investment's appeal. If the investment were riskless, its NPV at a 5 percent discount rate would be

$5.4 million, but because a higher risk-adjusted rate is deemed appropriate, NPV falls by over $4 million. In essence, management requires an inducement of at least this amount before it is willing to make the investment.

A virtue of risk-adjusted discount rates is that most executives have at least a rough idea of how an investment's required rate of return should vary with risk. Stated differently, they have a basic idea of the position of the market line in Figure 8.1. For instance, they know from the historical data in Table 5.1 of Chapter 5 that over many years, common stocks have yielded an average annual return about 6.2 percentage points higher than the return on government bonds. If the present return on government bonds is 3 percent, it is plausible to expect an investment that is about as risky as common stocks to yield a return of about 9.2 percent. Similarly, executives know that an investment promising a return of 40 percent is attractive unless its risk is extraordinarily high. Granted, such reasoning is imprecise; nonetheless, it does lend some objectivity to risk assessment.

The Cost of Capital

Now that we have introduced risk-adjusted discount rates and illustrated their use, the remaining challenge is to identify the appropriate rate for a specific investment. Do we just add 7 percentage points to the risk-free rate, or is there a more objective process?

There is a more objective process, and it rests on the notion of the *cost of capital.* When creditors and owners invest in a business, they incur opportunity costs equal to the returns they could have earned on alternative, similar-risk investments. Together these opportunity costs define the minimum rate of return the company must earn on existing assets to meet the expectations of its capital providers. This is the firm's cost of capital. If we can estimate this minimum required rate of return, we have an objectively determined risk-adjusted discount rate suitable for evaluating typical, or average risk, investments undertaken by a firm. Rather than relying on managers' "gut feelings" about investment risk, the cost of capital methodology enables us to look to financial markets for valuable information about the appropriate risk-adjusted discount rate.

Moreover, once we know how to estimate one company's cost of capital, we can use the technique to estimate the risk-adjusted discount rate applicable to a wide variety of project risks. The trick is to reason by analogy as follows. If Project A appears to be about as risky as investments undertaken by Company 1, use Company 1's cost of capital as the required return for Project A, or better yet, use an average of the cost of capital to Company 1 and all its industry peers. Thus, if a traditional pharmaceutical company is contemplating an investment in the biotech industry, a suitable required rate of return for the decision is the average cost of capital to existing biotech firms. In the following paragraphs, we define the cost of capital more precisely, estimate Hasbro's cost of capital, and discuss its use as a risk-adjustment vehicle.

The Cost of Capital Defined

Suppose we want to estimate the cost of capital to XYZ Corporation and we have the following information:

	XYZ Liabilities and Owners' Equity	Opportunity Cost of Capital
Debt	$100	10%
Equity	200	20

We will discuss the origins of the opportunity costs of capital a little later. For now, just assume we know that given alternative investment opportunities, creditors expect to earn at least 10 percent on their loans and shareholders expect to earn at least 20 percent on their ownership of XYZ shares. With this information, we need answer only two simple questions to calculate XYZ's cost of capital:

1. *How much money must XYZ earn annually on existing assets to meet the expectations of creditors and owners?*

   The creditors expect a 10 percent return on their $100 loan, or $10. However, because interest payments are tax deductible, the effective after-tax cost to a profitable company with, say, a 50 percent tax rate is only $5. The owners expect 20 percent on their $200 investment, or $40. So in total, XYZ must earn $45 [$45 = (1 − 0.5)(10%)$100 + (20%)$200].

2. *What rate of return must the company earn on existing assets to meet the expectations of creditors and owners?*

   A total of $300 is invested in XYZ on which the company must earn $45, so the required rate of return is 15 percent ($45/$300). This is XYZ's cost of capital.

   Let's repeat the preceding reasoning using symbols. The money XYZ must earn annually on existing capital is

$$(1 - t)K_D D + K_E E$$

where t is the tax rate, K_D is the expected return on debt or the cost of debt, D is the amount of interest-bearing debt in XYZ's capital structure, K_E is the expected return on equity or the cost of equity, and E is the amount of equity in XYZ's capital structure. Similarly, the annual return XYZ must earn on existing capital is

$$K_W = \frac{(1 - t)K_D D + K_E E}{D + E} \qquad (8.1)$$

where K_W is the cost of capital.

From the preceding example,

$$15\% = \frac{(1 - 50\%)\,10\% \times \$100 + 20\% \times \$200}{\$100 + \$200}$$

In words, a company's cost of capital is the cost of the individual sources of capital, weighted by their importance in the firm's capital structure. The subscript W appears in the expression to denote that the cost of capital is a weighted-average cost. This is also why the cost of capital is often denoted by the acronym WACC for weighted-average cost of capital. To demonstrate that K_W is a weighted-average cost, note that one-third of XYZ's capital is debt and two-thirds is equity, so its WACC is one-third the cost of debt plus two-thirds the cost of equity:

$$15\% = (1/3 \times 5\%) + (2/3 \times 20\%)$$

The Cost of Capital and Stock Price

An important tie exists between a company's cost of capital and its stock price. To see the linkage, ask yourself what happens when XYZ Corporation earns a return on existing assets greater than its cost of capital. Because the return to creditors is fixed by contract, the excess return accrues entirely to shareholders. Because the company can earn more than shareholders' opportunity cost of capital, XYZ's stock price will rise as new investors are attracted by the excess return. Conversely, if XYZ earns a return below its cost of capital on existing assets, shareholders will not receive their expected return, and its stock price will fall. The price will continue falling until the prospective return to new buyers again equals equity investors' opportunity cost of capital. Another definition of the cost of capital, therefore, is *the return a firm must earn on existing assets to keep its stock price constant.* Finally, from a shareholder value perspective, we can say that management creates value when it earns returns above the firm's cost of capital and destroys value when it earns returns below this target.

The Cost of Capital for Hasbro Inc.

To use the cost of capital as a risk-adjusted discount rate, we must be able to measure it. This involves assigning values to all of the quantities on the right side of equation 8.1. To illustrate the process, let's estimate Hasbro's cost of capital at year-end 2016.

The Weights

We begin by measuring the weights, D and E. There are two common ways to do this, only one of which is correct: Use the book values of debt and equity appearing on the company's balance sheet, or use the market values. By *market value,* I mean the price of the company's bonds and common shares in

TABLE 8.2   **Book and Market Values of Debt and Equity for Hasbro Inc. (December 31, 2016)**

Source: Data compiled from Hasbro 2016 10-K and from data in the Compustat database.

	Book Value		Market Value	
Source	**Amount ($ millions)**	**Percentage of Total**	**Amount ($ millions)**	**Percentage of Total**
Debt	$1,721	48.0%	$ 1,721	15.1%
Equity	1,863	52.0%	9,685	84.9%
Total	$3,584	100.0%	$11,406	100.0%

securities markets multiplied by the number of each security type outstanding. As Table 8.2 shows, the book values of Hasbro's debt and equity at the end of 2016 were $1,721 million and $1,863 million, respectively. The figure for debt includes only interest-bearing debt because other liabilities are either the result of tax accruals that are subsumed in the estimation of after-tax cash flow (ATCF) or spontaneous sources of cash that are part of working capital in the investment's cash flows. The table also indicates that the market value of Hasbro's debt and equity on the same date were $1,721 million and $9,685 million, respectively.

Consistent with common practice, I have assumed here that the market value of Hasbro's debt equals its book value. This assumption is almost certainly incorrect, but just as certainly the difference between the book and market values of debt is quite small compared to that for equity. The market value of Hasbro's equity is its price per share at year-end of $77.79 times 124.5 million common shares outstanding. The market value of equity exceeds the book value by a ratio of over 5 to 1 because investors are upbeat about the company's future prospects.

To decide whether book weights or market weights are appropriate for measuring the cost of capital, consider the following. Suppose that 10 years ago you invested $20,000 in a portfolio of common stocks that, through no doing of your own, is now worth $50,000. After talking to stockbrokers and investment consultants, you believe a reasonable return on the portfolio, given present market conditions, is 10 percent a year. Would you be satisfied with a 10 percent return on the original $20,000 cost of the portfolio, or would you expect to earn 10 percent on the current $50,000 market value? Obviously, the current market value is relevant for decision making; the original cost is sunk and therefore irrelevant. Similarly, Hasbro's owners and creditors have investments worth $9,685 million and $1,721 million, respectively, on which they expect to earn competitive returns. Thus, the market values of debt and equity are appropriate for measuring the cost of capital.

The Cost of Debt

This is an easy one. Bonds with risk and maturity similar to Hasbro's were yielding a return of approximately 4.9 percent in December 2016, and the company's marginal tax rate is about 35 percent. Consequently, the after-tax cost of debt to Hasbro was 3.2 percent [$(1 - 35\%) \times 4.9\%$]. Some financial neophytes are tempted to use the coupon rate on the debt rather than the prevailing market rate in this calculation. But the coupon rate is, of course, a sunk cost. Moreover, because we want to use the cost of capital to evaluate new investments, we want the cost of new debt.

The Cost of Equity

Estimating the cost of equity is as hard as estimating debt was easy. With debt, or preferred stock, the company promises the holder a specified stream of future payments. Knowing these promised payments and the current price of the security, it is a simple matter to calculate the expected return. This is what we did in the last chapter when we calculated the yield to maturity on a bond. With common stock, the situation is more complex. Because the company makes no promises about future payments to shareholders, there is no simple way to calculate the return expected.

Assume a Perpetuity

One way out of this dilemma recalls the story of the physicist, the chemist, and the economist trapped at the bottom of a 40-foot pit. After failing with a number of schemes based on their knowledge of physics and chemistry to extract themselves from the pit, the two finally turn to the economist in desperation and ask if there isn't anything in his professional training that might help them devise a means of escape. "Why, yes," he replies. "The problem is really quite elementary. Simply assume a ladder." Here our "ladder" is an assumption about the future payments shareholders expect. From this heroic beginning, the problem really does become quite elementary. To illustrate, suppose equity investors expect to receive an annual dividend of $d per share forever. Because we know the current price, *P,* and have assumed a future payment stream, all that remains is to find the discount rate that makes the present value of the payment stream equal the current price. From the last chapter, we know that the present value of such a perpetuity at a discount rate of K_E is

$$P = \frac{d}{K_E}$$

and, solving for the discount rate,

$$K_E = \frac{d}{P}$$

In words, if you are willing to assume investors expect a company's stock to behave like a perpetuity, the cost of equity capital is simply the dividend yield.

Perpetual Growth

A somewhat more plausible assumption is that shareholders expect a per share dividend next year of $d and expect this dividend to grow at the rate of g percent per annum *forever*. Fortunately, it turns out that this cash flow stream also has an unusually simple solution. Without boring you with the arithmetic details, the present value of the assumed payment stream at a discount rate of K_E is

$$P = \frac{d}{K_E - g}$$

and, solving for the discount rate,

$$K_E = \frac{d}{P} + g$$

This equation says that if the perpetual growth assumption is correct, the cost of equity capital equals the company's dividend yield (d/P), plus the growth rate in dividends. This is known as the *perpetual growth equation* for K_E.

The problem with the perpetual growth estimate of K_E is that it is only as good as the assumption on which it is based. For mature companies such as railroads, electric utilities, and steel mills, it may be reasonable to assume that observed growth rates will continue indefinitely. And in these cases, the perpetual growth equation yields a plausible estimate of the cost of equity capital. In all other instances, when it is implausible to think the company can maintain its current rate of growth indefinitely, the equation over-estimates the cost of equity.

Let History Be Your Guide

A second and generally more fruitful approach to estimating the cost of equity capital looks at the determinants of expected returns on risky investments. In general, the expected return on any risky asset is composed of three factors:

$$\begin{array}{c} \text{Expected return} \\ \text{on risky asset} \end{array} = \begin{array}{c} \text{Risk-free} \\ \text{interest rate} \end{array} + \begin{array}{c} \text{Inflation} \\ \text{premium} \end{array} + \begin{array}{c} \text{Risk} \\ \text{premium} \end{array}$$

The equation says that the owner of a risky asset should expect to earn a return from three sources. The first is compensation for the opportunity cost incurred in holding the asset. This is the risk-free interest rate. The second is compensation for the declining purchasing power of the currency over time. This is the inflation premium. The third is compensation for bearing the asset's systematic risk. This is the risk premium. Fortunately, we do not need to treat the first two terms as separate factors because together they equal the expected return on a default-free bond such as a government bond. Because we can readily determine the government bond interest rate, the only challenge is to estimate the risk premium.

When the risky asset is a common stock, it is useful to let history be our guide and recall from Table 5.1 that, on average, over the last century, the annual return on U.S. common stocks has exceeded that on government bonds by 6.2 percentage points. As a reward for bearing the added systematic risk, common stockholders earned a 6.2 percentage point higher annual return than government bondholders. Treating this as a risk premium and adding it to a 2016 long-term government bond rate of 3.0 percent yields an estimate of 9.2 percent as the cost of equity capital for a typical company.

What is the logic of treating the 6.2-percentage-point historical excess return as a risk premium? Essentially, it is that over a long enough time, the return investors receive and what they expect to receive should approximate each other. For example, suppose investors expect a 20-percentage-point excess return on common stocks but the actual return keeps turning out to be 3 percentage points. Then, two things should happen: Investors should lower their expectations, and selling by disappointed investors should increase subsequent realized returns. Eventually expectations and reality should come into rough parity.

A Virtue of Statistics

Many of the concepts in this chapter can be described quite simply with the aid of a little statistics. As already noted, an investment's *total risk* refers to its dispersion in possible returns, commonly represented by the standard deviation of returns, while its *systematic risk* depends on the extent to which the investment's returns correlate with those on a broadly diversified portfolio. We can thus represent the systematic risk of investment j as

$$\text{Systematic risk} = \rho_{jm}\sigma_j$$

where ρ_{jm} is the correlation coefficient between investment j and well-diversified portfolio m, and σ_j is the standard deviation of returns on investment j. The correlation coefficient is, of course, a dimensionless number ranging between $+1$ and -1, with $+1$ characterizing perfectly positively correlated returns and -1 perfectly inversely correlated returns. For most business investments, ρ_{jm} is in the range of 0.5 to 0.8, meaning that 20 to 50 percent of the investment's total risk can be diversified away.

A common stock's *equity beta* equals its systematic risk relative to that of a well-diversified portfolio, or in symbols, stock j's equity beta is

$$\beta_j = \frac{\rho_{jm}\sigma_j}{\rho_{mm}\sigma_m}$$

But because any variable must be perfectly positively correlated with itself, this expression reduces to

$$\beta_j = \frac{\rho_{jm}\sigma_j}{\sigma_m}$$

In addition to representing stock j's equity beta, this expression also equals the slope coefficient of the regression of r_j on r_m, where r_j and r_m are realized returns on stock j and the diversified portfolio, respectively.

FIGURE 8.4   **Hasbro Inc.'s Beta Is the Slope of the Best-Fit Line Below**

Source: Monthly Returns of Hasbro Inc. v. S&P 500, 60 Months through December 2016. Data from Center for Research in Security Prices (CRSP).

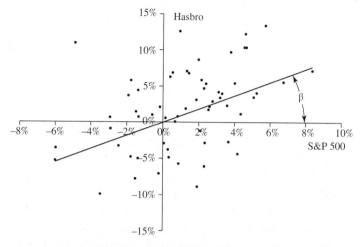

We now have an estimate of the cost of capital to an "average-risk" company, but of course few companies are precisely average-risk. How, then, can we customize our average cost expression to reflect the risk of a specific firm? The answer is to insert a "customization factor," known as the company's *equity beta,* into the expression so that it becomes

$$\frac{\text{Cost of equity}}{\text{capital}} = \frac{\text{Interest rate on}}{\text{government bond}} + \beta_e \left(\frac{\text{Historical excess return}}{\text{on common stocks}} \right)$$

or in symbols,

$$K_E = i_g + \beta_e \times Rp \qquad (8.2)$$

where i_g is a government bond rate, β_e is the equity beta of the target company, and Rp is the excess return on common stocks. You can think of β_e as a scale factor reflecting the systematic risk of a specific company's shares relative to that of an average share. When the stock's systematic risk equals that of an average share, β_e equals 1.0, and the historical risk premium applies directly. But for above-average-risk shares, β_e exceeds 1.0, and the risk premium grows accordingly. Conversely, for below-average-risk shares, β_e is below 1.0, and only a fraction of the historical risk premium applies.

Estimating Beta

But, you might well ask, how do we estimate a company's beta? Actually, it's pretty simple. Figure 8.4 provides everything required to estimate Hasbro's beta. It shows the monthly realized returns on Hasbro's common stock relative to returns on the Standard & Poor's 500 Stock Index over the past 60 months. For example, in October 2014, the S&P index increased 2 percent, while Hasbro's stock rose 5 percent. This return pair constitutes one point on the graph. The S&P 500 index is a broadly diversified portfolio containing many common shares; so its systematic risk is a reasonable surrogate for the systematic risk of an average share, and of the market as a whole. Also appearing in the figure is a best-fit, straight line indicating the average relationship among the paired returns. (If you are familiar with regression analysis, this is a simple regression line.)

The slope of this line is the beta estimate we seek. It measures the sensitivity of Hasbro's equity returns to movements in the S&P index. The indicated slope of 0.81 means that, on average, the return on Hasbro's equity rises or falls 0.81 percent for every one percent change in the index, indicating that Hasbro's equity is lower risk than average. Clearly, if this line were less steeply sloped, Hasbro's stock would be less sensitive to market movements, or alternatively to economywide events, and thus less risky. A more steeply sloped line would imply just the reverse. The fact that all of the return pairs plotted in the figure do not lie precisely on the straight line reflects the importance of unsystematic risk in determining Hasbro's monthly returns. Remember that because unsystematic risk can be eliminated through diversification, it should play no role in determining required returns or prices.

Fortunately, you do not need to worry about calculating betas yourself. Beta risk is so important a factor in security analysis that many financial websites regularly publish the betas of virtually all publicly traded common stocks. Table 8.3 presents recent betas for a representative sample of firms. Observe that beta ranges from a low of 0.04 for Southern Company, an electric utility,

TABLE 8.3 **Representative Company Betas**

Source: Center for Research in Security Prices (CRSP).

Company	Beta	Company	Beta
Advanced Micro Devices	2.57	Dean Foods	0.40
Amazon.com	1.43	Duke Energy	0.11
American Electric Power	0.20	eBay	1.30
American International Group	1.35	Exxon Mobil	0.89
Apple	1.30	Facebook	0.62
AT&T Inc.	0.37	Ford Motor Co.	1.10
Avon Products	2.02	Goldman Sachs	1.61
Baxter International	0.82	H&R Block	0.57
Berkshire Hathaway	0.79	IBM	0.97
Boeing	1.06	Intel	1.06
Caterpillar	1.36	Microsoft	1.13
CBS	1.53	Safeway	0.71
Coca-Cola	0.66	Southern Company	0.04
Costco Wholesale	0.86	Southwest Airlines	0.92
Cummins	1.34	Wells Fargo Bank	0.99

to a high of 2.57 for semiconductor company Advanced Micro Devices. Note, too, that the numbers are intuitively plausible, with high-risk businesses such as some technology companies having high betas, while low-risk companies such as utilities have lower betas.

Inserting Hasbro's estimated equity beta of 0.81 into equation 8.2 yields the following cost of equity capital:

$$K_E = 3.0\% + 0.81 \times 6.2\% = 8.0\%$$

Hasbro's Weighted-Average Cost of Capital

All that remains now is the figure work. Table 8.4 presents my estimate of Hasbro's cost of capital in tabular form. Hasbro's weighted-average cost of capital is 7.3 percent. This means that at year-end 2016, Hasbro needed to earn at least this percentage return on the market value of existing assets to meet the expectations of creditors and shareholders and, by inference, to maintain its stock price. In equation form,

$$K_W = \frac{(1 - 0.35)(4.9\%)(\$1,721 \text{ million}) + (8.0\%)(\$9,685 \text{ million})}{\$1,721 \text{ million} + \$9,685 \text{ million}}$$

$$= 7.3\%$$

Before leaving our discussion of beta, I should mention that while the motivation offered for equation 8.2 has been largely intuitive, the equation actually rests on a solid conceptual foundation known as the Capital Asset Pricing Model, or the CAPM. According to the CAPM, equation 8.2 is nothing less than the equation of the market line shown earlier in Figure 8.1. As such, it describes the equilibrium relationship between the expected return on any risky asset and its systematic risk. Said differently, equation 8.2 defines the minimum acceptable rate of return an investor should demand on any risky asset.

The Cost of Capital in Investment Appraisal

The fact that the cost of capital is the return a company must earn on *existing assets* to meet creditor and shareholder expectations is an interesting detail,

TABLE 8.4   Calculation of Hasbro Inc.'s Weighted-Average Cost of Capital

Source: Yield on debt from Financial Industry Regulatory Authority, Inc.

Source	Amount ($ millions)	Percentage of Total	Cost after Tax	Weighted Cost
Debt	$1,721	15.1%	3.2%	0.5%
Equity	$9,685	84.9%	8.0%	6.8%
			Weighted-Average Cost of Capital =	7.3%

FIGURE 8.5   **An Investment's Risk-Adjusted Discount Rate Increases with Risk**

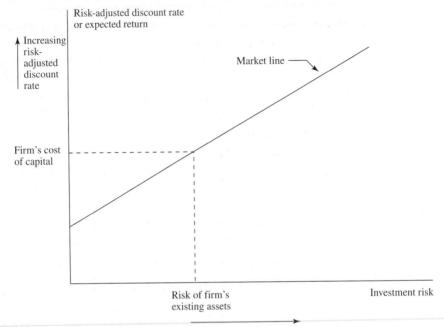

but we are after bigger game here: We want to use the cost of capital as an acceptance criterion for *new investments.*

Are there any problems in applying a concept derived for existing assets to new investments? Not if one critical assumption holds: The new investment must have the same risk existing assets do. If it does, the new investment is essentially a "carbon copy" of existing assets, and the cost of capital is the appropriate risk-adjusted discount rate. If it does not, we must proceed more carefully.

The market line in Figure 8.5 clearly illustrates the importance of the equal-risk assumption. It emphasizes that the rate of return risk-averse individuals anticipate rises with risk. This means, for example, that management should demand a higher expected return when introducing a new product than when replacing aged equipment, because the new product is presumably riskier and therefore warrants a higher return. The figure also shows that a company's cost of capital is but one of many possible risk-adjusted discount rates, the one corresponding to the risk of the firm's existing assets. We conclude that the cost of capital is an appropriate acceptance criterion only when the risk of the new investment equals that of existing assets. For all other investments, the cost of capital is inappropriate. But do not despair, for even when inappropriate itself, the cost of capital concept is central to identifying a correct risk-adjusted rate.

Multiple Hurdle Rates

Companies adjust their hurdle rates for differing investment risks in at least three possible ways. The first two are straightforward extensions of the cost of capital. For large projects, the approach is to identify an industry in which the contemplated investment would be considered average risk, estimate the weighted-average cost of capital for several companies in the industry, and use an average of these estimates as the project's required rate of return. For example, when a pharmaceutical company contemplates a biotechnology investment, a reasonable hurdle rate for the decision is an average of the capital costs to existing biotechnology companies.

A challenge when applying this approach is deciding which companies to include in the sample. The cost of capital to a diversified firm is the weighted average of the capital costs prevailing in each of its businesses. This means that even when a diversified company is a major competitor in the target business, its cost of capital may not accurately reflect the risk of that business. As a result, the best sample candidates are "pure-plays," undiversified firms that compete only in the target business. However, pure-plays are not always available, and in their absence considerable judgment and a certain amount of art must be applied when selecting sample companies and deciding how best to weight their numbers.

A second risk adjustment technique used by multidivision companies is to calculate a separate cost of capital for each division. As just noted, the cost of capital to a multidivision company will be an average of the costs of

---

The Cost of Capital to a Private Company

Two hurdles exist to estimating a private company's cost of capital. The first is conceptual. Some owners of private companies argue that because their company's securities do not trade on public markets, any cost of capital based on these markets is not relevant to them. This reasoning is incorrect. Financial markets define the opportunity costs incurred by all individuals when they make investment decisions regardless of whether those investments are publicly traded or privately held. A private-business owner would obviously be foolish to make a business investment promising a 5 percent return when comparable-risk investments promising 15 percent are available in public markets.

The second hurdle is one of measurement. Without market values for the company's debt and equity and without equity returns on which to base a beta estimate, what do we do? I recommend the strategy described in this section for estimating project and divisional capital costs. Identify one or more public competitors, estimate their capital costs, and use the resulting average to represent the private firm's cost of capital. In instances where the private business has a much different capital structure from the public competitors, it may be necessary to do some further adjusting of the kind described in this chapter's Appendix. When the private firm is much smaller than the public competitors, it may also be appropriate to make an upward adjustment in the cost of capital, amounting to perhaps two percentage points, to reflect the added risks faced by small firms.

capital appropriate to each business line. When such companies use a single, corporatewide cost of capital across all divisions, they risk committing two types of errors. In low-risk divisions, they are inclined to reject some worthwhile, low-risk investments for lack of expected return, while in their high-risk divisions, they are inclined to do just the opposite: accept uneconomic, high-risk investments because of their prospective returns. Over time, such companies find their lower-risk divisions withering for lack of capital, while their higher-risk divisions are force-fed too much capital.[5]

To avoid this dilemma, many multidivision companies use the methods just described to estimate a different hurdle rate for each division. They begin by identifying several primary division competitors—hopefully including a few pure-plays. They then estimate the weighted-average cost of capital of these competitors, and use an average of these numbers as the division's cost of capital.

The third approach is more *ad hoc*. Many companies adjust for differing project risks by defining several risk buckets and assigning a different hurdle rate to each bucket. For example, Hasbro might use the following four buckets.

Type of Investment	Discount Rate (%)
Replacement or repair	5.0
Cost reduction	5.5
Expansion	7.3
New product	12.0

Investments to expand capacity in existing products are essentially carbon-copy investments, so their hurdle rates equal Hasbro's cost of capital. Other types of investments have a higher or lower hurdle rate, depending on their risk relative to expansion investments. Replacement or repair investments are the safest because virtually all of the cash flows are well known from past experience. Cost reduction investments are somewhat riskier, because the magnitude of potential savings is uncertain. New-product investments are the riskiest type of all, because both revenues and costs are uncertain.

Multiple hurdle rates are consistent with risk aversion and with the market line, but the amount by which the hurdle rate should be adjusted for each level of risk is largely arbitrary. Whether the hurdle rate for new product investments should be 3 or 6 percentage points above Hasbro's cost of capital cannot be determined objectively.

---

[5] For more on this problem, see Philipp Kruger, Augustin Landier, and David Thesmar, "The WACC Fallacy: The Real Effects of Using a Unique Discount Rate," *Journal of Finance* 70 (June 2015), pp. 1253–1285.

Four Pitfalls in the Use of Discounted Cash Flow Techniques

You now know the basics of investment appraisal: Estimate the opportunity's annual, expected ATCFs and discount them to the present at a risk-adjusted discount rate appropriate to the risk of the cash flows. When the opportunity is a "carbon-copy" investment, the firm's weighted-average cost of capital is the appropriate discount rate. In other instances, an upward or downward adjustment to the firm's cost of capital is necessary.

In the interest of full disclosure, I will now gingerly mention four pitfalls in the practical application of discounted cash flow techniques. The first two are easily avoided once you are aware of them; the last two highlight important limitations of discounted cash flow techniques as conventionally applied. Collectively, these pitfalls mean you need to master several more topics before attempting to pass as an expert.

The Enterprise Perspective vs. the Equity Perspective

Any corporate investment partially financed with debt can be analyzed from either of two perspectives: that of the company, commonly known as the *enterprise* perspective, or that of its owners, often referred to as the *equity*

The Fallacy of the Marginal Cost of Capital

Some readers, especially engineers, look at equation 8.1 and naively conclude that it is possible to reduce a company's weighted-average cost of capital by using more of the cheap source of financing, debt, and less of the expensive source, equity. In other words, they conclude that increasing leverage will reduce the cost of capital. This reasoning, however, evidences an incomplete understanding of leverage. As we observed in Chapter 6, increasing leverage increases the risk borne by shareholders. Because they are risk averse, shareholders react by demanding a higher return on their investment. Thus, K_E and, to a lesser extent, K_D rise as leverage increases. This means that increasing leverage affects a company's cost of capital in two opposing ways: Increasing use of cheap debt reduces K_W, but the rise in K_E and K_D that accompanies added leverage increases it.

To review this reasoning, ask yourself how you would respond to a subordinate who made the following argument in favor of an investment: "I know the company's cost of capital is 12 percent and the IRR of this carbon-copy investment is only 10 percent. But at the last directors' meeting, we decided to finance this year's investments with new debt. Because new debt has a cost of only about 4 percent after tax, it is clearly in our shareholders' interest to invest 4 percent money to earn a 10 percent return."

The subordinate's reasoning is incorrect. Financing with debt means increasing leverage and increasing K_E. Adding the change in K_E to the 4 percent interest cost means the true *marginal* cost of the debt is well above the interest cost. In fact, it is probably quite close to K_W.

perspective. As the following example demonstrates, these two perspectives are functionally equivalent in the sense that when properly applied they yield the same investment decision—but woe be to him who confuses the two.

Suppose ABC Industries has a capital structure composed of 40 percent debt, costing 5 percent after tax, and 60 percent equity, costing 20 percent. Its WACC is therefore

$$K_W = 5\% \times 0.40 + 20\% \times 0.60 = 14\%$$

The company is considering an average-risk investment costing $100 million and promising an ATCF of $14 million a year in perpetuity. If undertaken, ABC plans to finance the investment with $40 million in new borrowings and $60 million in equity. Should ABC make the investment?

The Enterprise Perspective

The left side of the following diagram shows the investment's cash flows from the enterprise perspective. Applying our now standard approach, the investment is a perpetuity with a 14 percent internal rate of return. Comparing this return to ABC's weighted-average cost of capital, also 14 percent, we conclude that the investment is marginal. Undertaking it will neither create nor destroy shareholder value.

The Equity Perspective

The right side of the diagram shows the same investment from the owners' viewpoint, or the equity perspective. Because $40 million of the initial cost will be financed by debt, the equity outlay is only $60 million. Similarly, because $2 million after-tax must be paid to creditors each year as interest, the residual cash flow to equity will be only $12 million. The investment's internal rate of return from the equity perspective is therefore 20 percent.

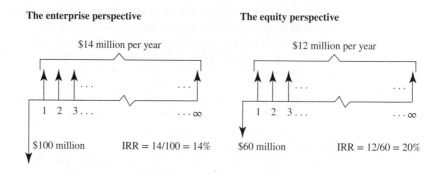

Does the fact that the return is now 20 percent mean the investment is suddenly an attractive one? Clearly, no. Because the equity cash flows are levered, they are riskier than the original cash flows and hence require a higher risk-adjusted discount rate. Indeed, the appropriate acceptance criterion for these equity cash flows is ABC's cost of equity capital, or 20 percent. (Remember, the discount rate should reflect the risk of the cash flows to be discounted.) Comparing the project's 20 percent IRR to equity with ABC's cost of equity, we again conclude that the investment is only marginal.

It is not an accident that the enterprise and equity perspectives yield the same result. Because the weighted-average cost of capital is defined to ensure that each supplier of capital receives a return equal to her opportunity cost, we know that an investment by ABC earning 14 percent, from the enterprise perspective, will earn just enough to service the debt and generate a 20 percent IRR on invested equity. Problems arise only when you mix the two perspectives, using K_E to discount enterprise cash flows or, more commonly, using K_W to discount equity cash flows.

Which perspective is better? Some of my best friends use the equity perspective, but I believe the enterprise perspective is easier to apply in practice. The problem with the equity perspective is that both the IRR to equity and the appropriate risk-adjusted discount rate vary with the amount of leverage used. The IRR to equity on ABC Industries' investment is 20 percent with $40 million of debt financing but jumps to 95 percent with $90 million of debt and rises to infinity with all-debt financing.

The interdependency between the means of financing and the risk-adjusted discount rate is easily handled in a classroom, but when real money is on the line, we often become so enthralled by the return-enhancing aspect of debt that we forget the required rate of return rises as well. Moreover, even when we remember that leverage increases risk as well as return, it is devilishly hard to estimate exactly how much the cost of equity should change with leverage.

Life is short. I recommend you avoid unnecessary complications by using the enterprise perspective whenever possible. Assess the economic merit of the investment without regard to how it will be financed or how you will divvy up the spoils. If the investment meets this fundamental test, you can then turn to the nuances of how best to finance it.

Inflation

The second pitfall involves the improper handling of inflation. Too often, managers ignore inflation when estimating an investment's cash flows but inadvertently include it in their discount rate. The effect of this mismatch is to make companies overly conservative in their investment appraisal, especially with regard to long-lived assets. Table 8.5 illustrates the point. A company with a 15 percent cost of capital is considering a $10 million, carbon-copy investment. The investment has a four-year life and is expected to increase production capacity by 10,000 units annually. Because the product sells for $900, the company estimates that annual revenues will rise $9 million ($900 × 10,000 units),

TABLE 8.5 When Evaluating Investments under Inflation, Always Compare Nominal Cash Flows to a Nominal Discount Rate or Real Cash Flows to a Real Discount Rate ($ millions)

(a) Incorrect Investment Evaluation Comparing Real Cash Flows to a Nominal Discount Rate					
	2016	**2017**	**2018**	**2019**	**2020**
After-tax cash flow	$(10.0)	$3.3	$3.3	$3.3	$3.3
	IRR = 12%				
	$K_W = 15\%$				
	Decision: **Reject**				

(b) Correct Investment Evaluation Comparing Nominal Cash Flows to a Nominal Discount Rate					
	2016	**2017**	**2018**	**2019**	**2020**
After-tax cash flow	$(10.0)	$3.5	$3.6	$3.8	$4.0
	IRR = 18%				
	$K_W = 15\%$				
	Decision: **Accept**				

which, after subtracting production costs, yields an increase in annual after-tax cash flows of $3.3 million. The IRR of the investment is calculated to be 12 percent, which is below the firm's cost of capital.

Did you spot the error? By assuming a constant selling price and constant production costs over four years, management has implicitly estimated real, or constant-dollar, cash flows, whereas the cost of capital as calculated earlier in the chapter is a nominal one. It is nominal because both the cost of debt and the cost of equity include a premium for expected inflation.

The key to capital budgeting under inflation is to always compare like to like. When cash flows are in nominal dollars, use a nominal discount rate. When cash flows are in real, or constant, dollars, use a real discount rate. The bottom portion of Table 8.5 illustrates a proper evaluation of the investment. After including a 5 percent annual increase in selling price and in variable production costs, the expected nominal cash flows from the investment are as shown. As one would expect, the nominal cash flows exceed the constant-dollar cash flows by a growing amount in each year. The IRR of these flows is 18 percent, which now exceeds the firm's cost of capital.[6]

Real Options

The third pitfall involves possible omission of valuable managerial options inherent in many corporate investments. Conventional discounted cash flow

---

[6] An alternative approach would have been to calculate the firm's real cost of capital and compare it to a real IRR. But because this approach is more work and is fraught with potential errors, I recommend working with nominal cash flows and a nominal discount rate instead.

analysis fails to capture these options because it implicitly ignores managerial flexibility—the ability to alter an investment in response to changing circumstances. This omission might be appropriate when dealing with passive stock and bond investments, but can be quite inappropriate when managers are able to make various mid-course corrections. Examples of what are often called *real options* in recognition of their formal equivalence to traded financial options, include

- the option to abandon an investment if cash flows do not meet expectations,

- the option to make follow-on investments if the initial undertaking is successful, and

- the option to reduce uncertainty by deferring investments to a later date.

In each instance, the option gives managers the ability to cherry pick: to act when the odds are in their favor but to walk away when they are not. (The appendix to Chapter 5 provides a brief overview of financial options, and the recommended readings at the end of the chapter offer more rigorous treatments of real options and their valuation.)

Formal real options analysis has been slow to catch on in many businesses, due primarily to its complexity.[7] At a more informal level, however, the realization that many corporate investments contain potentially valuable embedded options has altered the way executives think about these opportunities. An increasingly common item on an analyst's checklist is to identify any real options embedded in a project and to estimate, at least qualitatively, their significance to the business. The next few sections offer an intuitive look at three common real options faced by businesses and illustrate how an understanding of real options can sharpen thinking about corporate investment decisions.

Decision Trees

General Design Corporation is considering investing $85 million to launch a new line of high-speed semiconductors based on an emerging diamond film technology. This is a risky investment. Management thinks the odds of success are only about 50 percent and have decided to apply a risk-adjusted discount rate of 15 percent in their analysis. As shown in Panel (a) of Table 8.6, they estimate that if successful, the present value of expected free cash inflows over the life of the project will total $168 million, while if it is unsuccessful, the same figure will be negative $34 million. Should General Design make the investment?

Panel (a) contains a conventional discounted cash flow analysis of the investment in the form of what is known as a "decision tree," a simple

---

[7] Edward Teach, "Will Real Options Take Root? Why Companies Have Been Slow to Adopt the Valuation Technique," *CFO Magazine,* July 2003, pp. 1–4.

TABLE 8.6   General Designs Diamond Film Project ($ millions)*

(a) Stage 1: Ignoring Option to Abandon, Probability of Success = 50%

Initial cost = $85   Discount rate = 15%

	Present Value		Expected After-Tax Cash Flows			
		1	2	3	4	5
Success	$168	$ 50	$ 50	$ 50	$ 50	$ 50
Failure	$(34)	$ (10)	$ (10)	$ (10)	$ (10)	$ (10)

NPV at 15% = −$18 million (−$18 = 0.50 × $168 −0.50 × $34 − $85)

(b) Stage 1: Including Option to Abandon

Sell plant in year 3 for $50 million

	Present Value		Expected After-Tax Cash Flows			
		1	2	3	4	5
Success	$ 168	$ 50	$ 50	$ 50	$ 50	$ 50
Failure	$ 17	$ (10)	$ (10)	$ 50	$ –	$ –

NPV at 15% = $7 million ($7 = 0.50 × $168 + 0.50 × $17 − $85)

* Totals may not add due to rounding.

graphical technique to portray an uncertain decision. Decision trees are especially useful when the decision involves several interrelated decisions and chance events. Square nodes in the tree represent decisions, while circular nodes denote chance events. Here, there is only one decision: to invest or not, and one chance event: success or failure. Decision trees are drawn from the left, beginning with the most immediate decision and moving to the right along various branches to subsequent chance events, decisions, and outcomes. Analysis of a decision tree, however, moves in the opposite direction—from right to left. Begin at the most distant outcomes, decide what they imply for the most distant decisions, and work progressively back along the branches to the current decision.

The two rightmost outcomes in Panel (a) promise cash flows of $168 million and −$34 million with equal probability, so working to the left along the "success" and "failure" branches, it is easy to calculate that the chance node has an expected value of $67 million ($67 = .50 × $168 − .50 × $34). Combining this expected inflow with the $85 million outlay appearing under the "Invest" branch yields a net present value of −$18 million.

The Option to Abandon

The diamond film project is clearly unacceptable according to conventional analysis. But after reviewing the decision tree for a moment, one General Design executive observes that "this decision tree commits us to manufacturing the new semiconductors, even after we learn the product's a bust. Wouldn't we be smarter in that scenario to just close down the line and sell the plant?" In essence, the executive is suggesting that the conventional analysis in Panel (a) ignores a potentially valuable abandonment option: the right to terminate the project whenever the plant's resale value exceeds the present value of operating cash flows generated by the plant.

Assuming General Design would abandon the project after two years of losses and sell the plant for $50 million, the decision tree in Panel (b) of Table 8.6 adds this abandonment option to the previous tree. Beginning at the right, General Design will clearly want to continue making semiconductors when sales are high, but should abandon the project when sales are low. According to the figures, including the abandonment option increases the project's net present value by $25 million to $7 million (Revised NPV = .50 × $168 + .50 × $17 − $85 = $7). Recognizing that the company has the option to abandon the project when conditions warrant adds $25 million to its value and transforms it from a loser into a winner. The $25 million is the value of the abandonment option and also the amount by which conventional investment analysis understates the project's worth.

Before considering the second type of real option companies frequently encounter, it is appropriate to say a few more words about the strengths and weaknesses of decision trees for analyzing real options. Decision trees are a handy tool for illustrating the compound, contingent nature of many investment decisions, and they help demonstrate how management flexibility can add value to investment opportunities. However, they also suffer from several conspicuous weaknesses. One is that decision trees quickly morph from well-behaved trees into unruly bushes as decisions become more complex and as chance events sprout more possible outcomes. Decision trees are also unable to handle decisions with continuous as opposed to discrete outcomes and when uncertainty resolves gradually over time as opposed to all at once on a specific date. But the most serious weakness is that the solution technique of calculating probability-weighted expected values of distant outcomes and rolling the results back to the present is only approximately correct when valuing real options.[8] Taken together, these observations are a reminder that our discussion here is only an introductory overview, and that rigorous real option analysis requires modeling and valuation techniques that are beyond the scope of this book.

The Option to Grow

A chief attraction of many new-technology investments is that success today creates the option to make highly profitable follow-on investments tomorrow. To illustrate, assume General Design believes initial success in diamond film semiconductors will open the door to a larger stage 2, follow-on investment in two years. If the stage 2 investment were made today, it would be no more likely to succeed than would stage 1; after all, it is the same technology. But, of course, the company does not need to make the stage 2 decision today. It has the option to wait until the initial results from stage 1 are in, and it is able to make a more informed choice based on what it learns in stage 1. The stage 1 investment effectively buys the company an option to grow if future conditions prove attractive.

Problem 17 at the end of this chapter provides the chance to work through an example of General Design's option to grow. With a higher probability of success, it should be no surprise that stage 2 as described in the problem turns out to be much more valuable to the company than stage 1. Just as the option to abandon allows General Design to exit a losing project, the option to grow creates value by allowing General Design to expand when things go well.

The Timing Option

The third common corporate real option is known as a timing option. In addition to passive managers, conventional discounted cash flow analysis also assumes investment decisions are "now or never." Do we make the investment immediately or not at all? Many corporate decisions, however, are of a subtler "now or later" variety. Do we invest today or wait till some more propitious future date? The following is an example of a timing option.

Wind Resources, Inc. (WRI) designs, builds, and sells wind farms to financial investors interested in stable cash flows and lucrative tax shields. Key to the price WRI can charge for a completed wind farm is the long-term contract

---

[8] The problem lies with the risk-adjusted discount rate, which varies in complex ways throughout the tree depending on which options are exercised.

it is able to negotiate with an electric utility to purchase the wind farm's power. The terms of this contract depend, in turn, on the prevailing price of natural gas, the utility's most common alternative energy source. WRI is considering developing an attractive wind farm site it owns in Southern California.

Several company executives recommend immediate development. However, one of the younger managers disagrees and favors waiting for a time. He reasons that natural gas prices might rise in the future, enabling WRI to get a better selling price if it waits. Others sharply disagree, arguing that "gas prices could just as easily go down as up in the future, and anyway, WRI isn't in the business of speculating on natural gas prices." The dissenter responds that there is more involved than just getting lucky on gas prices.

What should WRI do? Consider the choice between developing the site today or in one year. If natural gas prices rise, WRI can develop the wind farm in one year at an even better price than it can get today. If gas prices fall, the company can postpone development at little or no cost until they improve, and if they do not improve, WRI can just walk away. The option to develop in the future if prices move in WRI's favor, but to defer development if they do not, adds value to the project. Note, too, that the option's value rises with uncertainty, so that the wider the dispersion in future natural gas prices, the higher the value of WRI's option to wait. As mentioned in the Appendix to Chapter 5, this is an important characteristic of all options, where value increases with the volatility of the underlying asset. Problem 18 at the end of this chapter enables you to work through an example demonstrating these facts.

The observation that the ability to postpone an investment is valuable raises an obvious question. If WRI should not invest now, when should it invest? When should management quit stalling and build the wind farm? Ironically, the answer to this question in many instances is that the company should wait as long as possible. Because a timing option can only be exercised once and because doing so destroys its value, development should only occur when the resulting gains exceed the value of the option sacrificed. With some opportunities, management may want to invest immediately to take advantage of short-lived profit opportunities, to capture first-mover advantages, or to avoid rising construction costs. But, unless these costs of waiting exceed the value of the option destroyed, it makes sense to wait. In WRI's case, the only significant costs of waiting appear to be the threat of declining government subsidies and of rising construction costs.

In sum, this brief look at real options has demonstrated several important facts:

- Standard DCF analysis of investments containing embedded options systematically understates their value.

- The NPV of such investments equals their NPV ignoring the options, plus the NPV of the options.

- When opportunities contain timing options, it may make sense to defer investment even when the NPV of immediate investment is positive.

- Because option values rise with uncertainty, the incentive to acquire growth options via research and development or other means rises with uncertainty, as does the incentive to delay investing in opportunities containing timing options.

- The logic and vocabulary of real options are increasingly pervading corporate thinking and discussion, even in the absence of rigorous quantitative analysis.

- Smart managers think systematically about the presence of embedded options and assess their value in at least qualitative terms.

- Smart companies realize that embedded options are valuable and work systematically to maintain and acquire them.

The moral should be clear: Failure to appreciate the value of real options embedded in some corporate investment opportunities leads to inaccurate decision making and unnecessary timidity in the face of certain high-risk, high-payoff opportunities.

Excessive Risk Adjustment

Our last pitfall is a subtle one concerning the proper use of risk-adjusted discount rates. Adding an increment to the discount rate to adjust for an investment's risk makes intuitive sense. You need to be aware, however, that as you apply this discount rate to more distant cash flows, the arithmetic of the discounting process compounds the risk adjustment. Table 8.7 illustrates the effect. It shows the present value of $1 in one year and in 10 years, first at a risk-free discount rate of 5 percent and then at a risk-adjusted rate of 10 percent. Comparing these present values, note that addition of the risk premium knocks a modest 4 cents off the value of a dollar in one year but a sizable 23 cents off in 10 years. Clearly, use of a constant risk-adjusted discount rate is appropriate

TABLE 8.7 Use of a Constant Risk-Adjusted Discount Rate Implies that Risk Increases with the Remoteness of a Cash Flow (risk-free rate = 5%; risk-adjusted rate = 10%)

	Present Value of $1	
	Received in 1 Year	Received in 10 Year
Discounted at risk-free rate	$0.95	$0.61
Discounted at risk-adjusted rate	0.91	0.39
Reduction in present value due to risk	$0.04	$0.23

only when the risk of a cash flow grows as the cash flow recedes farther into the future.

For many, if not most, business investments, the assumption that risk increases with the remoteness of a cash flow is quite appropriate, but as we will see by looking again at General Design's diamond film project, this is not always the case.

Recall that General Design is contemplating a possible two-stage investment. The first stage, costing $85 million, is attractive chiefly because it gives management the option to make a much more lucrative follow-on investment. Both stages depend on relatively untested diamond film technology, so the discount rate used throughout the analysis was General Design's hurdle rate for projects of this type: 15 percent.

Given the nature of this investment, many executives would argue that it is entirely appropriate to use this higher risk-adjusted discount rate throughout. But is it really? The investment clearly involves high risk, but because most of the risk will be resolved in the first two years, use of a constant risk-adjusted discount rate is overly conservative.

To see the logic, suppose you are at time 2, stage 1 has been successful, and the company is about to launch stage 2. Because the stage 2 cash flows are now relatively certain, the appropriate discount rate is lower, and the value of the cash flows at time 2 is correspondingly higher. As seen from time 0, the revised NPV for both stages of the General Design project is thus higher than originally calculated. Problem 19 at the end of the chapter works through a specific example.

To recap, whenever you encounter an investment with two or more distinct risk phases, be careful about using a constant risk-adjusted discount rate, for although such investments may be comparatively rare, they are also frequently the type of opportunities companies can ill afford to waste.

Economic Value Added

Many executives and investors use variations of discounted cash flow analysis to evaluate investments. One of the most popular and well-known is Economic Value Added, or EVA. Trademarked by global management consulting firm Stern Value Management, EVA is an example of what is known more broadly as residual income or economic profit. There are subtle, technical differences among these terms, but the main idea is the same.

Having mastered the intricacies of the cost of capital, you will find EVA to be little more than a restatement of what you already know. The central message of this and the preceding chapter has been that an investment creates value for its owners only when its expected return exceeds its cost of capital. In essence, EVA simply extends the cost of capital imperative to performance appraisal.

It says that a company or a business unit creates value for owners only when its operating income exceeds the cost of capital employed. In symbols,

$$EVA = EBIT(1 - t) - K_W C$$

where $EBIT(1 - t)$ is the unit's after-tax operating income, K_W is its WACC, and C is the capital employed by the unit. $K_W C$, then, represents an annual capital charge. The capital-employed variable, C, equals the money invested in the unit over time by creditors and owners. As a first approximation, C is the sum of interest-bearing debt plus the book value of equity or, more generally, all sources of capital to the business on which it must earn a return.[9]

Plugging Hasbro's 2016 numbers into this expression, we find that

$$EVA_{16} = \$807(1 - 22\%) - 7.3\%(\$1,721 + \$1,863)$$
$$= \$368 \text{ million.}$$

Although estimating economic values from accounting data is always problematic, these numbers suggest that Hasbro earned enough in 2016 to cover the cost of capital employed and create $368 million in new value for its owners, an impressive contribution.

EVA and Investment Analysis

An important attribute of economic value added is that the present value of an investment's annual EVA stream equals the investment's NPV. This makes it possible to talk about investment appraisal in terms of EVA rather than NPV—provided, of course, there is something to be gained by doing so. The numerical example in Table 8.8 demonstrates this equality. Part *a* of the table is a conventional NPV analysis of a very simple investment. The investment requires an initial outlay of $100, which will be depreciated on a straight-line basis to zero over four years. Adding depreciation to prospective income after tax and discounting the resulting ATCF at 10 percent yields an NPV of $58.50.

Part *b* of the table presents a discounted EVA treatment of the same investment. To calculate EVA, we need a dollar figure for the annual opportunity cost of capital employed. This equals the percentage cost of capital times the book value of the investment at the beginning of each year. Subtracting this quantity from EBIT after-tax yields annual project EVA, which, discounted at 10 percent, yields a discounted EVA of $58.50—precisely the NPV calculated in part *a*. Thus, another way to evaluate investment opportunities, which is equivalent to NPV analysis, is to calculate the present value of the

---

[9] For details, see G. Bennett Stewart III, *Best-Practice EVA* (New Jersey: John Wiley & Sons, 2013).

TABLE 8.8 Discounting an Investment's Annual EVA Stream Is Equivalent to Calculating the Investment's NPV

(a) Standard NPV Analysis

		Year			
	0	1	2	3	4
Initial investment	−$100.00				
Revenue		$ 80.00	$80.00	$80.00	$80.00
Cash expenses		13.33	13.33	13.33	13.33
Depreciation		25.00	25.00	25.00	25.00
Income before tax		41.67	41.67	41.67	41.67
Tax at 40%		16.67	16.67	16.67	16.67
Income after tax		25.00	25.00	25.00	25.00
Depreciation		25.00	25.00	25.00	25.00
After-tax cash flow	−$100.00	$ 50.00	$50.00	$50.00	$50.00
NPV at 10%	$ 58.50				

(b) Discounted EVA Analysis

		Year			
	0	1	2	3	4
Capital employed		$100.00	$75.00	$50.00	$25.00
K_W		0.10	0.10	0.10	0.10
$K_W \times$ Capital		10.00	7.50	5.00	2.50
$EBIT(1 - t)$		25.00	25.00	25.00	25.00
$- K_W \times$ Capital		10.00	7.50	5.00	2.50
EVA		$ 15.00	$17.50	$20.00	$22.50
EVA discounted at 10%	$ 58.50				

investment's annual EVA. Still to be answered is why one might want to calculate discounted EVA instead of NPV.[10]

EVA's Appeal

If EVA looks vaguely familiar, it should. The fact that capital provided by creditors and owners is costly and this cost is relevant for measuring economic performance has been recognized for many years. Indeed, we made the

[10] Why the equality? The difference between the two approaches lies in the treatment of the initial investment. NPV records the full cost of the investment at time zero. EVA ignores the initial cost but records an annual depreciation charge plus a carrying cost equal to the WACC times the undepreciated asset value. It turns out that the present value of these two annual charges always equals the initial cost of the investment, regardless of the method of depreciation employed. Therefore, the two methods must yield the same result.

point in Chapter 1 when we noted that accounting income overstates true economic income because it ignores the cost of equity. So novelty cannot explain EVA's appeal, nor can EVA's superiority to return on investment, ROI, as a measure of business performance. For the problems with ROI, defined as operating income over operating assets, have also been widely known for a long while.[11] So why the appeal of EVA?

The answer, I think, is that EVA, in its present incarnation, addresses a pervasive business problem, one that has greatly undermined many managers' acceptance of modern finance. EVA's appeal is that it integrates three crucial management functions: capital budgeting, performance appraisal, and incentive compensation. Together these functions are intended to positively influence management behavior, but too often, they work at cross-purposes, giving managers confusing and apparently conflicting signals about what to do. Thus, in the absence of EVA, managers are told to use NPV, IRR, or BCR to analyze investment opportunities, but to look at ROE, ROI, or earnings per share growth when assessing business unit performance. And all the while, the company's incentive compensation plan relies on still other metrics, requires an advanced degree to fully comprehend, and changes more often than the Italian government. Is it any wonder, then, that many operating managers faced with this apparent confusion take none of it very seriously and rely instead on common sense to muddle through?

Contrast this with EVA-based management. The business goal is to create EVA. Capital budgeting decisions are based on discounted EVA at an appropriate cost of capital. Unit EVA, or change in EVA, measures business unit performance, and incentive compensation depends on unit EVA relative to an appropriate target—clean, simple, and straightforward. Consultants Stern Value Management (originally incorporated as Stern Stewart & Co.) have even developed a clever method of distributing a manager's bonus over several periods, known as the bonus bank, that puts middle managers at risk much as though they were owners and also helps to discourage myopic, single-period decision making.[12]

EVA certainly has its own problems, and some of its virtues are more cosmetic than real. But it does address an important barrier to the acceptance of the financial way of thinking in many companies, and for this reason alone deserves our attention.

---

[11] Here is one problem with ROI. Imagine a division with an ROI of only 2 percent and ask what type of investments the division manager is apt to favor. Charged with the task of raising division ROI, the manager will naturally look favorably on any investment promising an ROI above 2 percent regardless of the investment's NPV. Conversely, managers in divisions with high ROIs will be quite conservative in their investment decisions for fear of lowering ROI. A company in which unsuccessful divisions invest aggressively while successful ones invest conservatively is probably not what shareholders want to see.

[12] See G. Bennett Stewart III, *The Quest for Value* (New York: Harper Business, 1991), Chapter 6.

A Cautionary Note

An always present danger when using analytic or numerical techniques in business decision making is that the "hard facts" will assume exaggerated importance compared to more qualitative issues and that the manipulation of these facts will become a substitute for creative effort. It is important to bear in mind that numbers and theories don't get things done; people do. And the best investments will fail unless capable workers are committed to their success. As Barbara Tuchman put it in another context, "In military as in other human affairs will is what makes things happen. There are circumstances that can modify or nullify it, but for offense or defense its presence is essential and its absence fatal."[13]

APPENDIX

Asset Beta and Adjusted Present Value

Most companies have two betas: an observable equity beta, discussed at some length in the chapter, and an unobservable asset beta. Equity beta measures the systematic risk of a company's shares, while asset beta measures the systematic risk of its assets. In rare instances when a company is all-equity financed, the risk of its common stock equals that of its assets, and equity beta equals asset beta. For this reason, asset beta is also commonly referred to as the firm's *unlevered* beta. It is the equity beta a firm would report if it were all-equity financed.

One important use of asset betas is to improve the accuracy by which equity betas are measured. To illustrate, when I estimated Hasbro's equity beta by regressing the company's monthly, realized returns against those of the Standard & Poor's 500 Stock Index, I calculated an equity beta of 0.81, as reported in the chapter. But I also found a standard error of estimate equal to 0.23. Standard error is a statistical indicator of the precision of the beta estimate. As a benchmark, when the deviations of the individual observations from the regression line are distributed in a normal, bell-shaped pattern, we know there is a two-thirds chance that the true slope of the regression line is within plus or minus one standard error of the observed slope. This means we can state with some confidence that Hasbro's equity beta is somewhere in the range of 0.58 to 1.04—not an especially comforting conclusion.

A second important use of asset beta is in conjunction with a net present value technique called *Adjusted Present Value,* or *APV.* Together, asset beta and APV offer a flexible alternative to the standard WACC-based approach

---

[13] Barbara W. Tuchman, *Stilwell and the American Experience in China 1911–1945,* New York: Bantam Books, 1971, 561–62.

to investment appraisal described in the chapter. This alternative is especially attractive when evaluating complex investment opportunities.

Beta and Financial Leverage

Our starting point in the consideration of asset beta and adjusted present value is the effect of financial leverage on equity beta. Recalling our discussion of company financing decisions in Chapter 6, you know that shareholders face two distinct risks: the basic business risk inherent in the markets in which the firm competes, plus the added financial risk created by the use of debt financing. Asset beta measures the business risk, while equity beta reflects the combined effect of business and financial risks. To appreciate the tie between equity beta and financial leverage, recall from Chapter 6 that debt financing increases the dispersion in possible returns to shareholders, which in turn increases the firm's equity beta.

Because most businesses are levered, it is generally impossible to observe asset beta directly. However, with the aid of the following formula, we can easily calculate asset beta given equity beta, and vice versa.[1]

$$\beta_A = \frac{E}{V}\beta_E$$

where β_A is asset beta, β_E is equity beta, and $\frac{E}{V}$ is the equity-to-firm value ratio, measured at market. This equation says that $\beta_A = \beta_E$ when debt is zero and

---

[1] We can express the market value of a levered firm in two ways: as the market value of its debt plus equity, and as the value of the same firm unlevered plus the present value of the tax shields from debt financing. Equating these two expressions,

$$D + E = V_u + tD$$

where D is interest-bearing debt, E is the market value of equity, V_u is the value of the firm without any debt, and t is the marginal tax rate.

An important property of beta is that the beta of a portfolio is the weighted-average of the betas of the individual assets comprising the portfolio. Applying this insight to both sides of the equation above,

$$\frac{D}{D+E}\beta_D + \frac{E}{D+E}\beta_E = \frac{V_u}{V_u + tD}\beta_A + \frac{tD}{V_u + tD}\beta_{ITS}$$

where β_D is the beta of debt, β_E is the beta of equity, β_A is the beta of the unlevered firm, or equivalently, the firm's asset beta, and β_{ITS} is the beta of the firm's interest tax shields.

Assuming for simplicity (1) the firm's debt is risk-free, so $\beta_D = 0$, and (2) the risk of interest tax shields equals the risk of the firm's unlevered asset cash flows, so $\beta_{ITS} = \beta_A$, the above equation simplifies to the equation in the text.

A possible alternative, but to my mind no more plausible, assumption is $\beta_{ITS} = \beta_D = 0$, which yields a more complex expression. For details, see Richard S. Ruback, "Capital Cash Flows: A Simple Approach to Valuing Risky Cash Flows," *Financial Management,* Summer 2002, pp. 85–103.

that β_E rises above β_A by a growing amount as leverage increases. Plugging Hasbro's numbers into the equation, we learn that if the company's equity beta is 0.81, its asset beta must be 0.69 [0.69 = ($9,685/$11,406) × 0.81]. Calculating asset beta from equity beta in this manner is known in the trade as *unlevering* beta, while applying the equation in reverse to calculate equity beta from asset beta is referred to as *relevering* beta.

Using Asset Beta to Estimate Equity Beta

The ability to unlever and relever betas is the key to improving equity beta estimates. Three steps are required:

- Identify industry competitors of the target company, and calculate each competitor's asset beta by unlevering its observed equity beta.

- Average these asset betas, or use their median value, to estimate an industry asset beta.

- Relever this industry asset beta to the target company's capital structure.

The logic of this approach is that firms in the same industry should face the same or similar business risks and should therefore have similar asset betas. Unlevering the observed equity betas removes the differential effects of financial leverage for each company, allowing us to estimate an industry asset beta based on observations from several firms. Then, relevering this asset beta to the target's capital structure produces an equity beta consistent with the target's unique structure. The payoff from this approach is that an equity beta estimate based on data from a number of firms should reduce the unavoidable noise inherent in the conventional, single-firm approach.

Table 8A.1 illustrates the mechanics. It presents an estimate of Hasbro's industry asset beta based on numbers for six competitors of Hasbro's identified in Chapter 2. To avoid giving undue weight to smaller firms, I weighted the firm asset betas by relative market value of equity in calculating the industry figure. The resulting industry asset beta is 0.94. Relevering this industry beta to reflect Hasbro's unique capital structure yields an estimated equity beta of 1.11, about 37 percent above the number reported in the chapter, [1.11 = ($11,406/$9,685) × 0.94]. Whether this number is more accurate, or just different, is difficult to tell.

Asset Beta and Adjusted Present Value

In the standard WACC-based approach to investment appraisal described in the chapter, we ask the weighted average cost of capital to do double duty: to adjust for the risk of the cash flows being discounted, and to capture the tax-shield advantages of the debt financing used by the firm. We reflect these tax

TABLE 8A.1 **Estimate of Industry Asset Beta for Hasbro Inc.**

Source: Data compiled from The Center for Research in Security Prices and Compustat datababases.

Company	Equity Beta	Equity/Firm Value	Asset Beta	Market Value Equity	% of Total Market Value	Weighted- Asset Beta
Activision Blizzard	1.00	85%	0.85	$ 26,837	9%	0.08
Electronic Arts	0.55	95%	0.52	$ 23,766	8%	0.04
JAKKS Pacific	0.75	33%	0.24	$ 103	0%	0.00
Mattel	0.96	80%	0.77	$ 9,423	3%	0.02
Time Warner	1.08	75%	0.81	$ 74,437	25%	0.20
Walt Disney	1.23	89%	1.10	$165,862	55%	0.60
				Industry asset beta		0.94

shield advantages by using the after-tax cost of debt in the weighted-average calculation. In most instances, this creates no problem; however, difficulties can arise when the firm's capital structure is changing over time, or when the project's debt capacity differs from that implicit in the WACC.

In these situations it becomes advantageous to use an APV approach, or what is sometimes called "valuation by parts." First, abstract entirely from anything to do with debt financing by estimating the project's NPV assuming all-equity financing. Then, capture the tax shield effects of debt financing, and any other "side effects," in separate add-on terms. If the sum of these separate present value terms is positive, the opportunity is financially attractive, and vice versa. In symbols,

$$APV = NPV_{\text{all-equity financing}} + PV_{\text{interest tax shields}} + PV_{\text{any other side effects}}$$

At its root, APV is nothing more than a formalization of the idea that when evaluating investment opportunities, the whole should equal the sum of the parts.

Asset beta and APV are ideal partners because asset beta enables us to estimate the appropriate discount rate for valuing investments that are all-equity financed. A moment's review of the WACC equation in the chapter will convince you that in the absence of debt financing, WACC collapses to the cost of equity. The discount rate for evaluating all-equity financed investments is therefore represented by equation 8.2 in the chapter, with β_A replacing β_E.

$$K_A = i_g + \beta_A \times Rp$$

where i_g is a government bond rate, β_A is the investment's asset beta, and Rp is the risk premium, usually approximated by the excess return on common stocks over government bonds.

To illustrate the combined use of APV and asset beta, consider the investment opportunity under review by Delaney Pumps. Delaney Pumps manufactures and distributes an extensive line of agricultural irrigation systems. In recent years, computerized control systems used to automate irrigation and to conserve water have become increasingly important in selling high-end systems. And Delaney management is actively considering investing $160 million to develop a state-of-the-art, computerized controller that promises to leapfrog competition. Development work would be contracted to a software development company on a cost-plus basis. Revenue would come from a new product line featuring the controller and from license fees from selected competitors who elected to include the controller in their products. Projected cash flows for the investment appear in Table 8A.2. The projections extend for only four years because management anticipates that other, more advanced controllers will be available by this time.

Two challenges confronted Delaney management as they began their deliberations. Because the digital controller appeared much riskier than the company's usual capital expenditures, managers were uncomfortable using the company's 10 percent weighted-average cost of capital as the hurdle rate. In addition, Delaney had traditionally financed its business with the goal of maintaining a target times-interest-earned ratio of about 3 to 1. But because this project consisted almost entirely of intangible computer code and because its cash flows were quite uncertain, Delaney's treasurer thought it prudent to target a higher interest coverage of 10 to 1 on this project.

To address these challenges, the treasurer decided to do an APV analysis. Reasoning that the digital controller would probably be an average-risk investment for software companies, she identified five smaller, publicly traded firms specializing in business automation software. She then unlevered the equity betas of these firms and calculated an industry average asset beta equal to 2.41, confirming her intuition that business automation software is indeed a risky business. Combining this asset beta with a 3.0 percent riskless

TABLE 8A.2   Adjusted Present Value Analysis of Automated Irrigation Controller ($ millions)

		Year			
	0	**1**	**2**	**3**	**4**
Earnings before interest and taxes		$50.0	$150.0	$80.0	$30.0
Expected free cash flow	(160.0)	30.0	120.0	60.0	70.0
Interest expense		5.0	15.0	8.0	3.0
Interest tax shield @ 40% tax rate		2.0	6.0	3.2	1.2
Asset beta	2.41				
NPV all-equity	24.6				
PV tax shields	8.6				
APV	**$ 33.2**				

borrowing rate and a 6.2 percent historical risk premium in the earlier equation, she calculated a hurdle rate for unlevered, business automation software investments equal to 17.9 percent ($17.9 = 3.0\% + 2.41 \times 6.2\%$). Using this rate to discount the expected free cash flows in Table 8A.2, she found the project's NPV assuming all-equity financing to be $24.6 million.

The investment's principal side effect was the interest-tax shields it would generate over time. At a target times-interest-earned ratio of 10 to 1 and a 40 percent tax rate, the annual interest expense appearing in the table equals one-tenth of projected EBIT, while the corresponding tax shield is 40 percent of this amount. The discount rate used to calculate the present value of these tax shields should, of course, reflect the risk of the cash flows being discounted. Some executives argue that because interest tax shields are debt-like in terms of risk, they should be discounted at a corporate debt rate. Others maintain that while individual debt contracts may generate predictable cash flows, the total debt a business carries varies with its size and cash flows, in which case a discount rate more like K_A is appropriate. Here, because the tax shields are tied mechanically to operating income, K_A is the proper rate. Discounting at this rate, the tax shields are worth $8.6 million, so the investment's APV is an attractive $33.2 million.

$$APV = NPV_{\text{all-equity financing}} + PV_{\text{interest tax shields}}$$
$$\$33.2 \text{ million} = \$24.6 \text{ million} + \$8.6 \text{ million}$$

Note carefully in this analysis that the treasurer's tax shield calculations had nothing to do with the way Delaney intended to finance the investment and everything to do with how much debt the treasurer believed the project could prudently support. For tactical reasons, companies routinely finance some investments entirely with debt and others entirely with retained profits, but this information is irrelevant to judging an investment's debt capacity and its consequent claim to interest tax shields. To think otherwise would be to commit a variation of the "marginal cost of capital fallacy."

This example deals with a straightforward investment possessing one simple side effect, but I hope it hints at the power of the technique. APV's divide-and-conquer perspective makes it possible to break even very complex problems into a series of tractable, smaller problems, and to solve the complex problem by stringing together solutions to the smaller ones. We can thus analyze a cross-border investment involving several currencies and subsidized financing as the sum of separate NPV calculations for cash flows in each currency translated into the home currency at prevailing exchange rates, plus a separate term capturing the value of the subsidized finance. And we can even apply a separate, customized hurdle rate to each cash flow stream. In a complicated world, APV and its cousin, asset beta, are indeed welcome additions to our tool kit.

SUMMARY

1. An investment's total risk

   - Refers to the range of possible returns.
   - Can be estimated for traded assets as the standard deviation of returns.
   - Can be avoided to some extent by diversifying.

2. Systematic risk

   - Is the part of total risk that cannot be avoided by diversifying.
   - Equals about half of total risk, on average, for stocks.
   - Is the only part of total risk that should affect asset prices and returns.
   - Is positively related to the return demanded by risk-averse investors.
   - Can be estimated as the product of total risk and the correlation coefficient between an asset's returns and those on a well-diversified portfolio.

3. The cost of capital

   - Is a risk-adjusted discount rate.
   - Equals the value-weighted average of the opportunity costs incurred by owners and creditors.
   - Is the return a firm must earn on existing assets to at least maintain stock price.
   - Is relevant for private firms and not-for-profits as well as public firms.
   - Is the appropriate hurdle rate for evaluating carbon copy investments.
   - Can be an appropriate hurdle rate for evaluating non–carbon copy investments when it is the cost of capital of other firms for which the investment *is* a carbon copy.

4. The cost of equity capital

   - Is the opportunity cost incurred by owners.
   - Is the most challenging variable to estimate when measuring a firm's cost of capital.
   - Is best approximated as the sum of an interest rate on a government bond plus a risk premium.
   - Increases with financial leverage.

5. Beta

   - Measures an asset's relative systematic risk.
   - Can be estimated by regressing an asset's periodic realized returns on those of a well-diversified portfolio.
   - When multiplied by the realized excess return on stocks relative to bonds, yields a suitable risk premium for estimating the cost of equity.
   - Increases with financial leverage.

6. Four pitfalls to avoid in discounted cash flow analysis are

   - Confounding an enterprise perspective with an equity perspective.
   - Using a nominal discount rate to value real cash flows, or vice versa.

- Ignoring possibly valuable real options embedded in firm investments.
- Forgetting that a constant discount rate implies risk grows with the futurity of the cash flow.

7. Economic Value Added

- Is a popular measure of firm or division performance.
- Equals a unit's operating income after tax less an annual charge for capital employed.
- Helps unify three apparently disparate topics:
  - Investment evaluation.
  - Performance appraisal.
  - Incentive compensation.

ADDITIONAL RESOURCES

Bernstein, Peter L. *Against the Gods: The Remarkable Story of Risk.* New York: John Wiley and Sons, 1998. 383 pages.

A stimulating history of man's attempt to cope with risk in human affairs from the 13th century to the present. Bernstein does a great job of explaining the principal tools of risk management in nonmathematical terms and putting them in a historical context. Believe it or not, an excellent read. Available in paperback.

Brotherson, W. Todd, Kenneth M. Eades, Robert S. Harris, and Robert C. Higgins. "'Best Practices' in Estimating the Cost of Capital: An Update." *Journal of Applied Finance,* Spring/Summer 2013, pp. 15–33.

A look at the practical challenges of estimating capital costs and how some of America's best companies and investment banks address them.

Copeland, Tom, and Vladimir Antikarov. *Real Options: A Practitioner's Guide,* Revised Edition. New York: Texere, 2003. 384 pages.

A solid, practical introduction to real options with an emphasis on binomial decision trees.

Jacobs, Michael and Anil Shivdasani, "Do You Know Your Cost of Capital?" *Harvard Business Review,* July-August 2012.

A nice discussion of some of the practical challenges that arise when managers try to estimate the WACC. Includes an interactive cost of capital tool. The article is available at **hbr.org/2012/07/do-you-know-your-cost-of-capital.**

Luehrman, Timothy A. "Using APV: A Better Tool for Valuing Operations." *Harvard Business Review,* May–June 1997, pp. 132–154.

A practical introduction to adjusted present value, a simple variant of NPV useful for analyzing complex investments.

Peters, Linda. *Real Options Illustrated*. Springer International Publishing Switzerland, 2016. 107 pages.

> An overview of the real options literature with a more practitioner-oriented approach to the technical details.

finance.yahoo.com; google.com/finance
Two reliable sites to find an estimate of a company's beta. Enter the company's name and find a page with summary statistics, including beta.

pages.stern.nyu.edu/~adamodar/
NYU Professor Aswath Damodaran posts recent estimates of the WACC for various industrial sectors in several regions around the world. Select "Data" then "Current Data." Choose "Risk/Discount Rate" and "Cost of Capital by Industry Sector" to find estimates of the WACC for U.S. industry sectors. Explore the website for a wealth of useful data.

oyc.yale.edu
Free, open-enrollment video courses on financial markets and financial theory by distinguished Yale faculty, including Nobel Prize winner Robert Shiller.

PROBLEMS

Answers to odd-numbered problems appear at the end of the book. Answers to even-numbered problems and additional exercises are available in the Instructor Resources within McGraw-Hill's *Connect* (see the Preface for more information).

1. Is each of the following statements true or false? Explain your answers briefly.
   a. Using the same risk-adjusted discount rate to discount all future cash flows ignores the fact that the more distant cash flows are often riskier than cash flows occurring sooner.
   b. The cost of capital, or WACC, is not the correct discount rate to use for all projects undertaken by a firm.
   c. If you can borrow all of the money you need for a project at 6 percent, the cost of capital for this project is 6 percent.
   d. The best way to estimate the cost of debt capital for a firm is to divide the interest expense on the income statement by the interest-bearing debt on the balance sheet.
   e. One reliable estimate of a privately held firm's equity beta is the average of the equity betas of several publicly held competitors.
   f. Nominal cash flows should always be discounted using a nominal discount rate.

2. The annual standard deviation of return on Stock A's equity is 37 percent and the correlation coefficient of these returns, with those on a well-diversified portfolio, is 0.62. Comparable numbers of Stock B are 34 percent and 0.94. Which stock is riskier? Why?

3. An entrepreneur wants to purchase a particular small business. The asking price is $5 million. He expects to improve the business's operations over a period of five years and sell it at a handsome profit. To help him achieve this goal, a wealthy aunt is willing to loan the entrepreneur $5 million for five years at zero percent interest. Given this loan, what is the lowest rate of return the entrepreneur should be willing to accept on purchase of the business? Why?

4. Your company's weighted-average cost of capital is 11 percent. It is planning to undertake a project with an internal rate of return of 14 percent, but you believe this project is not a wise investment. What logical arguments would you use to convince your boss to forego the project despite its high rate of return? Is it possible that making investments with returns higher than the firm's cost of capital will destroy value? If so, how?

5. ABC Corporation and XYZ Corporation are both bidding for an existing food processing plant located in Monterrey, Mexico. Both firms are highly profitable and have similar debt ratios and costs of debt, but XYZ operates in a more volatile industry than ABC and thus has a higher beta. As ABC and XYZ separately prepare their valuations of the plant, what difference would you expect to see in the appropriate weighted-average cost of capital each firm will use to discount the projected cash flows from the plant?

6. Looking at Figure 8.1, explain why a company should reject investment opportunities lying below the market line and accept those lying above the line.

7. What is the weighted-average cost of capital for SKYE Corporation given the following information?

Equity shares outstanding	1 million
Stock price per share	$30.00
Yield to maturity on debt	7.68%
Book value of interest-bearing debt	$10 million
Coupon interest rate on debt	9%
Interest rate on government bonds	6%
SKYE's equity beta	0.75
Historical excess return on stocks	6.3%
Tax rate	40%

8. You have the following information about Burgundy Basins, a sink manufacturer.

Equity shares outstanding	20 million
Stock price per share	$40.00
Yield to maturity on debt	7.5%
Book value of interest-bearing debt	$320 million
Coupon interest rate on debt	4.8%
Market value of debt	$290 million
Book value of equity	$500 million
Cost of equity capital	14%
Tax rate	35%

Burgundy is contemplating what for the company is an average-risk investment costing $40 million and promising an annual ATCF of $6.4 million in perpetuity.

   a. What is the internal rate of return on the investment?
   b. What is Burgundy's weighted-average cost of capital?
   c. If undertaken, would you expect this investment to benefit shareholders? Why or why not?

9. How will an increase in financial leverage affect a company's cost of equity capital, if at all? How will it affect a company's equity beta?

10. What is the present value of a cash flow stream of $1,000 per year annually for 15 years that then grows at 4 percent per year forever when the discount rate is 13 percent?

11. You are a commercial real estate broker eager to sell an office building. An investor is interested but demands a 20 percent return on her equity investment. The building's selling price is $25 million, and it promises free cash flows of $3 million annually in perpetuity. Interest-only financing is available at 8 percent interest; that is, the debt is outstanding forever and requires no principal payments. The tax rate is 50 percent.

   a. Propose an investment-financing package that meets the investor's return target.
   b. Propose an investment-financing package that meets the investor's target when she demands a 90 percent return on equity.
   c. Why would an investor settle for a 20 percent return on this investment when she can get as high as 90 percent?

12. A security analyst has regressed the monthly returns on Exxon Mobil equity shares over the past five years against those on the Standard & Poor's 500 stock index over the same period. The resulting regression equation is $r_{EM} = 0.02 + 0.65r_{SP}$. Use this equation and any other information you deem appropriate to estimate Exxon Mobil's equity beta.

13. An all-equity financed company has a cost of capital of 10 percent. It owns one asset: a mine capable of generating $100 million in free cash flow every year for five years, at which time it will be abandoned. A buyout firm proposes to purchase the company for $400 million financed with $350 million in debt to be repaid in five, equal, end-of-year payments and carrying an interest rate of 6 percent.

    a. Calculate the annual debt-service payments required on the debt.

    b. Ignoring taxes, estimate the rate of return to the buyout firm on the acquisition after debt service.

    c. Assuming the company's cost of capital is 10 percent, does the buyout look attractive? Why, or why not?

14. The following information is available about an investment opportunity. Investment will occur at year 0 and sales will occur from year 1 to year 8. Use a nominal discount rate, calculated as $i_n = (1 + i_r)(1 + p) - 1$, where i_r is the real discount rate, and p is expected inflation.

Initial cost	$28 million
Unit sales	400,000
Selling price per unit, this year	$60.00
Variable cost per unit, this year	$42.00
Life expectancy	8 years
Salvage value	$0
Depreciation	Straight-line
Tax rate	37%
Real discount rate	10.0%
Inflation rate	0.0%

    a. Prepare a spreadsheet to estimate the project's annual after-tax cash flows.

    b. Calculate the investment's internal rate of return and its net present value assuming zero inflation.

    c. How do the internal rate of return and net present value change when you assume an inflation rate of 8 percent per year in price and variable cost per unit?

    d. How do you explain the fact that inflation causes the internal rate of return to increase and the NPV to decrease?

    e. Does inflation make this investment more attractive or less attractive? Why?

15. The chapter discusses General Design's option to expand its diamond film project.

    a. Is the option a call or a put?

    b. In qualitative terms, what is the option's strike price?

16. Having just returned from a stimulating seminar stressing the virtues of EVA in strategic decision making, the Vice President of Corporate Development for Venture Telecommunications, Inc. asks his assistant to gather data necessary to calculate last year's EVA for two company divisions. The Voice Division is home to the company's traditional businesses, while the Data Division houses the firm's newer initiatives. Voice is much larger than Data, but Data is growing more rapidly.

    The assistant is uncertain about how to best measure the capital devoted to each division but decides to use division assets as reported in the company's annual report. To estimate each division's cost of capital, she uses the median cost of capital of several pure-play competitors of each division. The company's marginal tax rate is 40 percent. The following table contains the information compiled by the assistant.

	($ millions)	
	Voice Division	**Data Division**
Earnings before interest and taxes	$220	$130
Division assets	$1,000	$600
Division cost of capital	10%	15%

    Within minutes of seeing these figures, the VP of Development exclaims "I knew it. The Data Division is bleeding us dry. I'm going to recommend we dump that division immediately!"

    a. Estimate each division's EVA.

    b. Do you agree with the VP of Development? Should the company immediately eliminate the Data Division? Why, or why not?

17. Reconsider General Design's diamond film project from Table 8.6(b). Suppose that General Design now believes it also has an option to grow the project if things go well. Initial success in diamond film semiconductors will open the door to a stage 2, follow-on investment in two years that will be five times as large as the initial stage 1. Stage 2 will be undertaken only if stage 1 is successful, and management believes the chance stage 2 will succeed, given that stage 1 has succeeded, is 90 percent. The discount rate is still 15 percent.

    a. What are the cash flows for the stage 2 investment? What is the present value of the cash flows for the stage 2 investment if it succeeds? If it fails? What is the present value of the initial cost of the stage 2 investment?

    b. If General Design were to evaluate the stage 2 decision today (before learning whether stage 1 is successful), what is its NPV?

    c. Assuming General Design waits to learn whether stage 1 is successful:
       i. What is the NPV today of the stage 2 investment?
      ii. What is total project NPV, incorporating the option to grow?
     iii. What is the value of the option to grow?

18. Consider the problem of Wind Resources (described in the section "The Timing Option" in this chapter). WRI is contemplating developing an attractive wind farm site it owns in southern California. A consultant estimates that at the current natural gas price of 6 cents/kWh (cents per kilowatt hour), immediate development will yield a profit of $10 million. However, natural gas prices are quite volatile. Suppose the price in one year will be either 8 cents/kWh or 4 cents/kWh with equal probability. According to the consultant, WRI's profit will jump to $30 million at a price of 8 cents/kWh and fall to a loss of $10 million at 4 cents/kWh. Because the company won't receive these profits for one year, discount them to the present at a high, risk-adjusted rate of 25 percent. WRI is now considering whether to wait to develop the wind farm.

    a. Draw a decision tree that captures WRI's decision.
    b. What should WRI do? What is the resulting NPV of this project?
    c. What is the value of the option to wait?
    d. Suppose that the change in natural gas prices in one year will be more dramatic than originally envisioned in the problem. In particular, gas prices will either rise to 12 cents/kWh or fall to 2 cents/kWh with equal probability. According to the consultant, WRI's profit will be $60 million at a price of 12 cents/kWh or fall to a loss of $30 million at 2 cents/kWh. What is the new value of the option to wait? How is the value of the option affected by the wider dispersion of natural gas prices?

19. Revisit General Design's option to grow in Problem 17. Suppose you are at time 2, and stage 1 has been successful. Because the stage 2 cash flows are now relatively certain, their discount rate is now 10 percent (which is lower than the discount rate for stage 1).

    a. What is the revised NPV at time 2 of stage 2?
    b. What is the revised total NPV at time 0 for both stages?

20. The spreadsheet for this problem provides key facts and assumptions concerning Montego Company, a producer of recreational equipment. It is available for download from McGraw-Hill's *Connect* or your course instructor (see the Preface for more information). Using this information:

    a. Estimate Montego's cost of equity capital.
    b. Estimate Montego's weighted-average cost of capital. Prepare a table showing the relevant variables.

The following four problems test your understanding of this chapter's Appendix.

21. The spreadsheet for this problem contains information about Kroger Company and four industry competitors in 2017. It is available for download from McGraw-Hill's *Connect* or your course instructor (see the Preface for more information). Using this information:

    a. Estimate the industry asset beta, weighting each competitor by its proportion in the total market value of equity of all four competitors.

    b. Relever the industry asset beta to reflect Kroger's capital structure to estimate an industry-based equity beta for Kroger.

22. A group of investors is intent on purchasing a publicly traded company and wants to estimate the highest price they can reasonably justify paying. The target company's equity beta is 1.20 and its debt-to-firm value ratio, measured using market values, is 60 percent. The investors plan to improve the target's cash flows and sell it for 12 times free cash flow in year five. Projected free cash flows and selling price are as follows.

Year	($ millions)				
	1	2	3	4	5
Free cash flows	$25	$40	$45	$50	$50
Selling price					$600
Total free cash flows	$25	$40	$45	$50	$650

To finance the purchase, the investors have negotiated a $400 million, five-year loan at 8 percent interest to be repaid in five equal payments at the end of each year, plus interest on the declining balance. This will be the only interest-bearing debt outstanding after the acquisition.

Selected Additional Information	
Tax rate	40 percent
Risk-free interest rate	3 percent
Market risk premium	5 percent

   a. Estimate the target firm's asset beta.
   b. Estimate the target's unlevered, or all-equity, cost of capital (K_A).
   c. Estimate the target's all-equity present value.
   d. Estimate the present value of the interest tax shields on the acquisition debt discounted at K_A.
   e. What is the highest price the investors can reasonably justify paying for the target company?
   f. What does your estimated maximum acquisition price in question (e) assume about the costs of financial distress?

23. You are valuing a project for Gila Corp. using the APV method. You already found the net present value of free cash flows from the project (discounted at the appropriate cost of equity) to be $500,000. The only important side effect of financing is the present value of interest tax shields. The project will be partially financed by a constant $1 million in debt over the life of the project, which is three years. Gila's tax rate is 40 percent, and the current interest rate applicable for the project's debt is 8 percent (assume this rate is also appropriate for discounting the interest tax shields). Assuming tax shields are realized at the end of each year, what is the APV of the project?

24. Sinaloa Appliance, Inc., a private firm that manufactures home appliances, has hired you to estimate the company's beta. You have obtained the following equity betas for publicly traded firms that also manufacture home appliances.

| | | ($ millions) | |
| | | | Market Value |
Firm	Beta	Debt	of Equity
iRobot	0.99	$0	$2,740
Middleby's	2.10	732	7,310
National Presto	0.12	0	739
Newell Brands	1.16	11,893	25,770
Whirlpool	1.69	4,470	13,560

a. Estimate an asset beta for Sinaloa Appliance.
b. What concerns, if any, would you have about using the betas of these firms to estimate Sinaloa Appliance's asset beta?

Business Valuation and Corporate Restructuring

To complete our merger negotiations, my attorneys will now mark scent your office.

Fortune

On Monday, June 13, 2016, after four months of confidential negotiations involving at least three bidders, Microsoft Corporation and LinkedIn Corporation announced their intention to merge. At a price of $26.2 billion, Microsoft's friendly takeover of LinkedIn was the sixth-largest technology acquisition in history and by far the largest among Microsoft's some 150 past takeovers. According to Microsoft CEO, Satya Nadella, the merger created a new type of business, which he described euphemistically as ". . . the coming together of the professional network and the professional cloud."[1] With over $100 billion in cash and securities, Microsoft had no trouble financing its all-cash offer, although it was contemplating a new debt issue to ease the burden.

LinkedIn Corporation was the world's largest professional networking company, known by some as the Facebook for professionals. It started in 2003 and went public in 2011 on the New York Stock Exchange. With over 400 million members in more than 200 countries, LinkedIn's principal product was a job search function for individuals and complementary tools for recruiters. In 2015, LinkedIn had revenues of almost $3 billion and a workforce of about 10,000. Like many young Internet companies, LinkedIn was growing rapidly but was only marginally profitable. Microsoft was the world's largest software manufacturer and one of the world's most valuable companies. In 2016, it had 114,000 employees, $85 billion in revenue, almost $17 billion in profits, and a market capitalization of $470 billion. Three-quarters of its profits came from its Windows operating system and Office suite of productivity tools, collectively known to insiders as "the franchise."

---

[1] Christopher Mims, "Why Microsoft Bought LinkedIn," *Wall Street Journal*, June 14, 2016.

Although it will be years before we can say categorically that Microsoft's purchase of LinkedIn was a wise move, some early winners are already apparent. Prominent among them are LinkedIn shareholders who sold their shares for $196, a hefty 50 percent premium to the price immediately before the acquisition was announced. With LinkedIn selling at $131.08 just before the announcement and approximately 134 million shares outstanding, this translates into a gain to shareholders of $8.7 billion ($8.7 billion = [$196 − $131.08] × 134 million). Of this amount, serial-entrepreneur and LinkedIn founder, Reid Hoffman's share was the largest, totaling $941 million. Other clear winners were the bankers and lawyers facilitating the transaction. Estimates are that Microsoft's banker, Morgan Stanley, took home between $10 and $20 million, while Qatalyst Partners and Allen & Company, the two boutique banks representing LinkedIn, pocketed $40 to $45 million. Morgan Stanley stood to earn another $40 to $60 million in fees from the sale of some $15 billion in new debt Microsoft expected to sell to help pay for the acquisition.[2]

The Microsoft buyout of LinkedIn aptly illustrates an important phenomenon in business known broadly as *corporate restructuring*. Guided presumably by the financial principles examined in earlier chapters, senior executives make major, episodic changes in their company's asset mix, capital structure, or ownership composition in pursuit of increased value. In addition to friendly mergers of the Microsoft–LinkedIn variety, corporate restructuring encompasses leverage buyouts, or LBOs, hostile takeovers, purchases or sales of operating divisions, large repurchases of common stock, major changes in financial leverage, spin-offs, and carve-outs. (In a spin-off, the parent company distributes shares of a subsidiary to its stockholders much like a dividend, and the subsidiary becomes an independent company. In a carve-out, the parent sells all or part of the subsidiary to the public for cash.)

The Microsoft–LinkedIn deal and many other restructurings pose several important questions to students of finance, and indeed to all executives. In terms of the LinkedIn takeover, they include the following:

1. What led Microsoft chief executive Satya Nadella to believe that LinkedIn was worth as much as $196 a share?

2. If Mr. Nadella was willing to pay as much as $196 a share for LinkedIn stock, why was the market price immediately prior to the initial bid only $131? Does the stock market misprice companies this drastically, or is something else at work?

3. If LinkedIn stock really was worth $196, why didn't LinkedIn executives, who certainly knew more about their company than Mr. Nadella did,

---

[2] Bob Bryan. "Wall Street Payday: Three Banks Could Reap as Much as $65 Million from Microsoft–LinkedIn Deal," **Businessinsider.com**, June 12, 2016. As estimated by consultants Freeman & Company.

realize this fact and do something to ensure that the value was reflected in LinkedIn's stock price?

4. Ultimately, who should decide the merits of corporate restructurings, management or owners? In the LinkedIn buyout, LinkedIn shareholders voted to approve the deal, but Microsoft shareholders were not asked. More broadly, who really controls today's large corporations, and who should control them? Is it the shareholders who collectively bear the financial risk, or is it the managers who at least nominally work for the shareholders?

This chapter addresses these questions and, in the process, examines the principal financial dimensions of corporate restructuring. We begin by looking at business valuation, a family of techniques for estimating the value of a company or division. We then turn to what is known as "the market for corporate control," where we consider why one company might rationally pay a premium to acquire another and how to estimate an aspiring buyer's maximum acquisition price. Next, we examine three primarily financial motives for business restructuring predicated on the virtues of increased tax shields, enhanced management incentives, and shareholder control of free cash flow. The chapter closes with a brief review of the evidence on the economic merits of mergers and leveraged buyouts and a closer look at the Microsoft–LinkedIn transaction. This chapter's Appendix examines the venture capital method of valuation.

Valuing a Business

Business valuation merits our serious attention because it is the underlying discipline for a wide variety of important financial activities. In addition to their use in structuring mergers and leveraged buyouts, business valuation principles guide security analysts in their search for undervalued stocks. Investment bankers use the same concepts to price initial public stock offerings, and venture capitalists rely on them to evaluate new investment opportunities. Companies intent on repurchasing their stock also frequently use valuation skills to time their purchases. Business valuation principles are even creeping into corporate strategy under the banner of value-based management, a consultant-spawned philosophy urging executives to evaluate alternative business strategies according to their predicted effect on the market value of the firm. It is thus not an exaggeration to say that although the details and the vocabulary differ from one setting to another, the principles of business valuation are integral to much of modern business.

The first step in valuing any business is to decide precisely what is to be valued. This requires answering three basic questions:

- Do we want to value the company's assets or its equity?
- Shall we value the business as a going concern or in liquidation?
- Are we to value a minority interest in the business or controlling interest?

Let us briefly consider each question in turn.

Assets or Equity?

When one company buys another, it can do so by purchasing either the seller's assets or its equity. It might appear that purchasing equity would generally be cheaper, but this is not so. For when a buyer purchases a seller's equity, it must also assume the seller's liabilities. To illustrate, suppose Acquirer Corp. pays $12 billion for the equity of Target Inc. and that Target also has $8 billion of debt outstanding. Because Acquirer must assume the debts of Target, the total purchase price of the acquisition is $20 billion. Although it is all too common to speak of Acquirer paying $12 billion for Target, this is incorrect. The true economic cost of the acquisition to Acquirer's shareholders is $20 billion: $12 billion paid to Target's shareholders, and $8 billion in the form of a legal commitment to honor Target's existing liabilities. The effect on Acquirer's shareholders of assuming Target's debt is the same as paying $20 billion for Target's assets and financing $8 billion of the purchase price with new debt. In both cases, Target's assets need to generate future cash flows worth at least $20 billion, otherwise Acquirer's shareholders will have made a bad investment. Here's a down-home analogy: If you purchased a house for $100,000 cash and assumption of the seller's $400,000 mortgage, you presumably would never say you bought the house for $100,000. You bought it for $500,000 with $100,000 down. Analogously, Acquirer bought Target for $20 billion with $12 billion down.

Most acquisitions involving companies of any size are structured as an equity purchase; so the ultimate objective of the valuation, and the focus of negotiations, is the value of the seller's equity. However, never lose sight of the fact that the true cost of the acquisition to the buyer is the cost of the equity plus the value of all the liabilities assumed.

Dead or Alive?

Companies can generate value for owners in either of two states: in liquidation or as going concerns. *Liquidation value* is the cash generated by terminating a business and selling its assets individually, while *going-concern value* is the present worth of expected future cash flows generated by a business. In most instances, we will naturally be interested in a business's going-concern value.

It will be helpful at this point to define an asset's *fair market value* (*FMV*) as the price at which the asset would trade between two rational individuals, each in command of all of the information necessary to value the asset and neither under any pressure to trade. Usually the FMV of a business is the higher of its liquidation value and its going-concern value. Figure 9.1 illustrates the relationship. When the present value of expected future cash flows is low, the business is worth more dead than alive, and FMV equals the company's liquidation value. At higher levels of expected future cash

FIGURE 9.1 **The Fair Market Value of a Business Is Usually the Higher of Its Liquidation Value and Its Going-Concern Value**

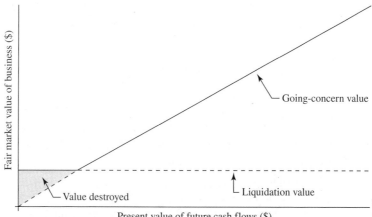

flows, liquidation value becomes increasingly irrelevant, and FMV depends almost entirely on going-concern value. It can also be the case that some of a company's assets, or divisions, are worth more in liquidation, while others are more valuable as going concerns. In this instance, the firm's FMV is a combination of liquidation and going-concern values as they apply to individual assets.

An exception to the general rule that FMV is the higher of a company's liquidation value and going-concern value occurs when the individuals controlling the company—perhaps after reflecting on their alternative employment opportunities and the pleasures afforded by the corporate yacht—choose not to liquidate, even though the business is worth more dead than alive. Then, because minority investors cannot force liquidation, the FMV of a minority interest can fall below the liquidation value. This is represented in the figure by the shaded triangle labeled "value destroyed." Additional latent value exists, but because minority owners cannot get their hands on it, the value has no effect on the price they are willing to pay for the shares. As minority shareholders see it, the individuals controlling the business are destroying value by refusing to liquidate. Later in the chapter, we will consider other instances in which price, as determined by minority investors, does not reflect full value.

When speaking of control, it is important to note that ownership of a company's shares and control of the company are two vastly different things. Unless a shareholder owns or can influence at least 51 percent of a company's voting stock, there is no assurance he or she will have any say at all in company affairs. Moreover, in most large American public companies, no share-holder or cohesive group of shareholders owns enough stock to exercise voting control, and effective control devolves to the board of directors and incumbent management. In these instances, shareholders are just along for the ride.

Minority Interest or Control?

Oscar Wilde once observed that "Economists know the price of everything and the value of nothing." In a very real sense he is correct, because to an economist the value of an asset is nothing more or less than the price at which informed buyers and sellers are willing to trade it. The question of whether an asset has value beyond its selling price is one economists are content to leave to philosophers.

If value is synonymous with selling price, one obvious indicator of the worth of a business is its market value, the aggregate price at which its equity and debt trade in financial markets. Thus, if just before Acquirer Corp.'s take-over of Target Inc., Target had 100 million shares outstanding, each selling for $90, and $8 billion in debt, its market value was $17 billion ($17 billion = $90 × 100 million + $8 billion).

As noted in earlier chapters, the market value of a business is an important indicator of company performance and a central determinant of a company's cost of capital. However, you need to realize that market value measures the worth of the business to *minority* investors. The stock price used to calculate the market value of a business is the price at which small numbers of shares have traded and is thus an unreliable indicator of the price at which a controlling interest might trade. The distinction between minority interest and controlling interest is sharply apparent in LinkedIn's case, where the market value of the firm was only $17.6 billion before Microsoft came along and paid $26.2 billion for the company. Why the difference? Because control enables the holder to change the business any way he likes in pursuit of added profits, a frequently valuable privilege. (More on this point later in the chapter.)

Other instances in which market value is inadequate to the business valuation task include the following: The target is privately held, so market value does not exist. The target's stock trades so infrequently or in such modest volume, that price is not a reliable indicator of value. The target's stock trades actively, but the analyst wants to compare market value to an independent estimate of value in search of mispriced stocks.

In sum, we can say that market value is directly relevant in business valuation only when the goal is to value a minority interest in a public company. In all other instances, market value may provide a useful frame of reference, but cannot by itself answer most interesting valuation questions.

For this, we need to think more carefully about the determinants of business value.

Discounted Cash Flow Valuation

Having examined business valuation in the large, we turn now to the specific task of estimating a company's going-concern value. For simplicity, we will begin by considering the value of a minority interest in a privately held firm.

Absent market prices, the most direct way to estimate going-concern value, if not always the most practical, is to think of the target company as if it were nothing more than a giant capital expenditure opportunity. Just as with any piece of capital equipment, investing in a company requires the expenditure of money today in anticipation of future benefits, and the central issue is whether tomorrow's benefits justify today's costs. As in capital expenditure analysis, we can answer this question by calculating the present value of expected future cash flows accruing to owners and creditors. When this number exceeds the acquisition price, the purchase has a positive net present value and is therefore attractive. Conversely, when the present value of future cash flows is less than the acquisition price, the purchase is unattractive.

In equation form,

$$\text{FMV of firm} = \text{PV (Expected cash flows to owners and creditors)}$$

This formula states that the maximum price one should pay for a business equals the present value of expected future cash flows to capital suppliers discounted at an appropriate risk-adjusted discount rate. Moreover, as in any other application of risk-adjusted discount rates, we know the rate should reflect the risk of the cash flows being discounted. Because the cash flows here are to owners and creditors of the target firm, it follows that the discount rate should be the target company's weighted-average cost of capital.

A legitimate question at this point is: Why waste energy estimating firm value when the ultimate goal of the exercise is usually to value equity? Why not just value the equity directly? The answer is simple once you recall that the value of equity is closely tied to the value of the firm. In equation form, we have our old friend

$$\text{Value of equity} = \text{Value of firm} - \text{Value of debt}$$

To determine the value of a company's equity, therefore, we need only estimate firm value and subtract interest-bearing debt. Moreover, because the market value and the book value of debt are usually about equal to each other, estimating the value of debt amounts to nothing more than grabbing a few numbers off the company's balance sheet.[3] If the fair market value of a business is $4 million and the firm has $1.5 million in debt outstanding, its equity is worth $2.5 million. It's that simple.[4] (We ignore non-interest-bearing debt such as accounts payable and deferred taxes here because they are treated as part of free cash flow, to be described momentarily.)

Free Cash Flow

As in all capital expenditure decisions, the biggest practical challenge in business valuation is estimating the relevant cash flows to be discounted. In Chapter 7, we said the relevant cash flows are the project's annual free cash flows (FCFs), defined as EBIT after tax plus depreciation, less investment. When valuing a company, this translates into the following:

$$\frac{\text{Free}}{\text{cash flow}} = \text{EBIT}(1 - \text{Tax rate}) + \text{Depreciation} - \frac{\text{Capital}}{\text{expenditures}} - \frac{\text{Working capital}}{\text{investments}}$$

where EBIT is earnings before interest and taxes.

The rationale for using free cash flow goes like this. EBIT is the income the company earns without regard to how the business is financed; so EBIT $(1 - \text{Tax rate})$ is income after tax excluding the effects of debt financing. Adding depreciation and any other noncash items yields after-tax cash flow. If management were prepared to run the company into the ground, it could distribute this cash flow to owners and creditors, and that would be the end of it. But in most companies, management retains some or all of this cash flow in the business to pay for new capital expenditures and additions to short-term assets. The annual cash flow available for distribution to owners and creditors is thus operating cash flow after tax less capital expenditures and working capital investments.

The working capital term in this expression can be tricky. Working capital investment equals the increase in current assets necessary to support operations, less any accompanying increases in non-interest-bearing current liabilities, or what I referred to in Chapter 7 as "spontaneous sources." This difference equals the net investment in current assets that must be financed by creditors and owners. A second challenge is how to treat any

---

[3] There are two instances in which the market value and the book value of debt will differ significantly: Default risk has changed significantly since issue, and the debt is fixed rate and market interest rates have changed significantly since issue. In these instances, it pays to estimate the market value of the debt independently.

[4] An alternative approach to equity valuation is to estimate the present value of expected cash flows to equity discounted at the target's cost of equity capital. Executed correctly, this equity approach yields the same answer as the enterprise approach described above; however, I find it more difficult to apply in practice. See the section "The Enterprise Perspective versus the Equity Perspective" in Chapter 8 for details.

excess cash a company accumulates over and above the amount necessary to support operations. My advice is to omit excess cash from the discounted cash flow valuation and treat it as a separate add-on term.

The Terminal Value

We now come to a serious practical problem. Our equation says that the FMV of a business equals the present value of all future free cash flows. Yet because companies typically have an indefinitely long life expectancy, the literal application of this equation would have us estimating free cash flows for perhaps hundreds of years into the far distant future—a clearly unreasonable task.

The standard way around this impasse is to think of the target company's future as composed of two discrete periods. During the first period, of some 5 to 15 years, we presume the company has a unique cash flow pattern and growth trajectory that we seek to capture by estimating individual, annual free cash flows just as the equation suggests. However, by the end of this forecast period, we assume the company has lost its individuality—has grown up, if you will—and become a stable, slow-growth business. From this date forward, we cease worrying about annual cash flows and instead estimate a single *terminal value* representing the worth of all subsequent free cash flows. If the initial forecast period is, say, 10 years, our valuation equation becomes

$$\text{FMV of firm} = \text{PV(FCF years } 1 - 10 + \text{Terminal value at year 10)}$$

Introduction of a terminal value, of course, only trades one problem for another, for now we need to know how to estimate a company's terminal value. I wish I could assure you that financial economists have solved this problem and present a simple, accurate expression for a company's terminal value, but I can't. Instead, the best I can offer are several plausible alternative estimates and some general advice on how to proceed.

Following are five alternative ways to estimate a company's terminal value with accompanying explanatory comments and observations. To use these estimates effectively, note first that no single estimate is always best; rather, each is more or less appropriate depending on circumstances. Thus, liquidation value may be highly relevant when valuing a mining operation with 10 years of reserves but quite irrelevant when valuing a rapidly growing software company. Second, resist the natural temptation to pick what appears to be the best technique for the situation at hand, ignoring all others. Avoid too the simple averaging of several estimates. Instead, calculate a number of terminal value estimates and begin by asking why they differ. In some instances, the differences will be readily explainable; in others, you may find it necessary to revise your assumptions to reconcile the differing values. Then, once you understand why remaining differences exist and feel comfortable with the magnitude of the differences, select a terminal value based on your assessment of the relative merits of each estimate for the target company.

Five Terminal Value Estimates

Liquidation Value   Highly relevant when liquidation at the end of the forecast period is under consideration, liquidation value usually grossly understates a healthy business's terminal value.

Book Value   Popular perhaps among accountants, book value usually yields a quite conservative terminal value estimate.

Warranted Price-to-Earnings Multiple   To implement this approach, multiply the target firm's estimated earnings to common stock at the end of the forecast horizon by a "warranted" price-to-earnings ratio; then add projected interest-bearing liabilities to estimate the firm's terminal value. As a warranted price-to-earnings ratio, consider the multiples of publicly traded firms that you believe represent what the target will become by the end of the forecast period.[5] If, for example, the target company is a startup but you believe it will be representative of other, mature companies in its industry by the end of the forecast period, the industry's current price-to-earnings multiple may be a suitable ratio. Another strategy is to bracket the value by trying multiples of, say, 10 and 20 times. The approach generalizes easily to other "warranted" ratios, such as market value to book value, price to cash flow, or price to sales.

No-Growth Perpetuity   We saw in Chapter 7 that the present value of a no-growth perpetuity is the annual cash flow divided by the discount rate. This suggests the following terminal value estimate:

$$\text{Terminal value of} \atop \text{no-growth firm} = \frac{\text{FCF}_{T+1}}{K_W}$$

where FCF_{T+1} is free cash flow in the first year beyond the forecast horizon, and K_W is the target's weighted-average cost of capital. As further refinement, we might note that when a company is not growing, its capital expenditures should about equal its annual depreciation charges, and its net working capital should neither increase nor decrease over time, both of which imply that free cash flow should simplify to EBIT(1 − Tax rate).

---

[5] For industry price-to-earnings ratios, see **pages.stern.nyu.edu/~adamodar.** Select "Data" and under "Current Data" go to "Multiples."

Because most businesses expand over time, if due only to inflation, many analysts believe this equation understates the terminal value of a typical business. I am more skeptical. For, as noted repeatedly in earlier chapters, growth creates value only when it generates returns above capital costs; and in competitive product markets over the long run, such performance is more the exception than the rule. Hence, even if many companies are capable of expanding, they may be worth no more than their no-growth brethren. The implication is that the no-growth equation is applicable to more firms than might first be supposed. I am also mindful of economist Kenneth Boulding's observation that "Anyone who believes that exponential growth can go on forever in a finite world is either a madman or an economist."

Perpetual Growth   In Chapter 8, we saw that the present value of a perpetually growing stream of cash equals next year's cash flow divided by the difference between the discount rate and the growth rate. Thus, another terminal value estimate is

$$\text{Terminal value of perpetually growth firm} = \frac{\text{FCF}_{T+1}}{K_W - g}$$

where g is the perpetual-growth rate of free cash flow.

A few words of caution are in order about this popular expression. It is a simple arithmetic fact that any business growing faster than the economy *forever* must eventually become the economy. (When I made this point one time at a Microsoft seminar, the immediate response was "Yeah! Yeah! We can do it!") The intended conclusion for mere mortal firms is that the absolute upper limit on g must be the long-run growth rate of the economy, or about 2 to 3 percent a year, plus expected inflation. Moreover, because even inflationary growth invariably requires higher capital expenditures and increases in working capital, free cash flow falls as g rises. This implies that unless this inverse relation is kept in mind, the preceding expression may well overstate a company's terminal value—even when the perpetual growth rate is kept to a low figure.[6]

---

[6] Here is a modestly more complex version of the perpetual-growth expression, to which I am partial:

$$\text{Terminal value} = \frac{\text{EBIT}_{T+1}(1 - \text{Tax rate})(1 - g/r)}{K_W - g}$$

where r is the rate of return on new investment. One virtue of this expression is that growth does not add value unless returns exceed capital cost. To confirm this, set $r = K_W$ and note that the expression collapses to the no-growth equation. A second virtue is that growth is not free, for as growth rises, so must capital expenditures and net working capital. In the equation, higher g reduces the numerator, which is equivalent to reducing free cash flow. See page 29 in the Koller, Goedhart, and Wessels book referenced at the end of this chapter for a demonstration that this expression is mathematically equivalent to the earlier perpetual-growth equation.

The Forecast Horizon

Terminal values of growing businesses can easily exceed 60 percent of firm value, so it goes without saying that proper selection of the forecast horizon and terminal value are critical to the successful application of discounted cash flow approaches to business valuation. Because most tractable terminal value estimates implicitly assume the firm is a mature, slow-growth, or no-growth perpetuity from that date forward, it is important to extend the forecast horizon far enough into the future that this assumption plausibly applies. When valuing a rapidly growing business, this perspective suggests estimating how long the company can be expected to sustain its supernormal growth before reaching maturity and setting the forecast horizon at or beyond this date.

A Numerical Example

Table 9.1 offers a quick look at a discounted cash flow valuation of our friend from earlier chapters: Hasbro Inc. It goes without saying that if I were being

TABLE 9.1 Discounted Cash Flow Valuation of Hasbro Inc. on December 31, 2016[*] ($ millions except per share)

These are our projections; not from annual reports.

	Year					
	2017	**2018**	**2019**	**2020**	**2021**	**2022**
Sales	$5,381	$5,769	$6,184	$6,630	$7,107	
EBIT	861	923	989	1,061	1,137	
Tax at 23.3%	201	215	231	247	265	
Earnings after tax	660	708	759	814	872	
+ Depreciation	172	185	198	212	227	
− Capital expenditures	172	185	198	212	227	
− Increase in working capital	108	115	124	133	142	
Free cash flow	**$553**	**$ 593**	**$ 635**	**$ 681**	**$ 730**	**$748**

PV at 7.3% of FCFs '17–'21	**$2,571**		
Terminal value estimates:		Terminal value in 2021	
Perpetual growth at 2.5% [$FCF_{22}/(K_w - g)$]		$15,589	
Warranted MV firm/Sales in '21 = 3.00 times		21,321	
Projected book value of debt & equity in '21		5,074	
Best guess terminal value		**15,000**	
PV of terminal value	**$10,546**		
Estimated value of firm	**$13,117**		
Value of debt	1,721		
Value of equity	$11,396		
Shares outstanding	124.5 million		
Estimated value per share	**$ 91.54**		

[*] Totals may not add due to rounding.

paid by the hour to value Hasbro and you were being similarly compensated to read about it, we would both proceed much more thoroughly and deliberately. In particular, we would want to know a great deal more about the company's products, markets, and competitors, for a discounted cash flow valuation is only as good as the projections on which it is based. Nonetheless, the table should give you a basic understanding of how to execute a discounted cash flow valuation.

The valuation date is December 31, 2016. The free cash flows appearing in the table are percent-of-sales projections assuming 7.2 percent annual sales growth for the next five years. The percentages used in the forecast are based on careful review of the common-size historical financial statements appearing in Chapter 2, Table 2.3, while the tax rate is Hasbro's average effective rate for the last five years, and the growth rate reflects security analysts' expectations.[7] The present value of these free cash flows discounted at Hasbro's 7.3 percent weighted-average cost of capital, estimated in the last chapter, amounts to $2,571 million.

The valuation considers three terminal value estimates. The first relies on the perpetual-growth equation and assumes that beginning in 2021 Hasbro's free cash flows will commence growing at 2.5 percent a year into the indefinite future. Free cash flow in 2022 will thus be $748 million [$748 = $730 × (1 + .025)]. Plugging these values into the perpetual growth equation, one estimate of Hasbro's terminal value at the end of 2021 is

$$\text{Terminal value} = \frac{\text{FCF in 2022}}{K_W - g} = \frac{\$748 \text{ million}}{0.073 - 0.025} = \$15{,}589 \text{ million}$$

The second terminal value estimate assumes that at the end of the forecast horizon, Hasbro will command a price-to-sales multiple of 3.0 times, a figure reflecting current valuations of comparable firms. I will say more about this multiple a little later. Applying this warranted price-to-sales ratio to Hasbro's sales in 2021 yields a second terminal value estimate:

$$\text{Terminal value} = 3.0 \times \$7{,}107 \text{ million} = \$21{,}321 \text{ million}$$

Finally, I estimate that Hasbro's projected book value of interest-bearing debt and equity in 2021 will be $5,074. This constitutes a third estimate of the company's terminal value, although certainly a low one.

After reflecting on the relative merits of these three estimates, my best guess is that Hasbro will be worth $15,000 million in 2021. Discounting this

---

[7] See **reuters.com/finance/stocks.**

The Problem of Growth and Long Life

In many investment decisions involving long-lived assets, it is common to finesse the problem of forecasting far distant cash flows by ignoring all flows beyond some distant horizon. The justification for this practice is that the present value of far distant cash flows will be quite small. When the cash flow stream is a growing one, however, growth offsets the discounting effect, and even far distant cash flows can contribute significantly to present value. Here is an example.

The present value of $1 a year in perpetuity discounted at 10 percent is $10 ($1/0.10). The present value of $1 a year for 20 years at the same discount rate is $8.51. Hence, ignoring all of the perpetuity cash flows beyond the 20th year reduces the calculated present value by only about 15 percent ($8.51 versus $10.00).

But things change when the income stream is a growing one. Using the perpetual-growth equation, the present value of $1 a year, growing at 6 percent per annum forever, is $25 [$1/(0.10 − 0.06)], while the present value of the same stream for 20 years is only $13.08. Thus, ignoring growing cash flows beyond the 20th year reduces the present value by almost half ($13.08 versus $25.00).

The Sensitivity Problem

At a 10 percent discount rate, the fair market value of a company promising free cash flows next year of $1 million, growing at 5 percent a year forever, is $20 million [$1 million/(0.10 − 0.05)].

Assuming the discount rate and the growth rate could each be in error by as much as 1 percentage point, what are the maximum and minimum possible FMVs for the company? What do you conclude from this?

Answer The maximum is $33.3 million [$1 million/(0.09 − 0.06)], and the minimum is $14.3 million [$1 million/(0.11 − 0.04)]. It is difficult to charge a client very high fees for advising that a business is worth somewhere between $14.3 and $33.3 million.

figure back to 2016 and adding it to the present value of free cash flows in the first five years suggests that Hasbro is worth $13,117 million on December 31, 2016:

$$\text{FMV}_{\text{firm}} = \$2,571 \text{ million} + \$10,546 \text{ million} = \$13,117 \text{ million}$$

The rest is just arithmetic. Hasbro's equity is worth $13,117 million less $1,721 million in interest-bearing debt presently outstanding, or $11,396 million. With 124.5 million shares outstanding, this equates to an estimated price per share of $91.54.

My discounted cash flow valuation thus indicates that Hasbro is worth $91.54 a share, provided the projected free cash flows accurately reflect expected future performance. I take the fact that the company's actual price at the time was $77.79 as evidence that investors were less enthusiastic about the company's prospects than I am.

Problems with Present Value Approaches to Valuation

If you are a little hesitant at this point about your ability to apply these discounted cash flow techniques to anything but simple textbook examples, welcome to the club. While DCF approaches to business valuation are conceptually correct, and even rather elegant, they are devilishly difficult to apply in practice. Valuing a business may be conceptually equivalent to any other capital expenditure decision, but there are several fundamental differences in practice:

1. The typical investment opportunity has a finite—usually brief—life, while the life expectancy of a company is indefinite.

2. The typical investment opportunity promises stable or perhaps declining cash flows over time, while the ability of a company to reinvest earnings customarily produces a growing cash flow.

3. The cash flows from a typical investment belong to the owner, while the cash flows generated by the company go to the owner only when management chooses to distribute them. If management decides to invest in Mexican diamond mines rather than pay dividends, a minority owner can do little other than sell out.

As the problems in the accompanying box illustrate, these practical differences introduce potentially large errors into the valuation process and can make the resulting FMV estimates quite sensitive to small changes in the discount rate and the growth rate employed.

Valuation Based on Comparable Trades

Granting that discounted cash flow approaches to business valuation are conceptually correct but difficult to apply, are there alternatives? One popular technique involves comparing the target company to similar, publicly traded firms. Imagine shopping for a used car. The moment of truth comes when the buyer finds an interesting car, looks at the asking price, and ponders what to offer the dealer. One strategy, analogous to a discounted cash flow approach, is to estimate the value of labor and raw materials in the car, add a markup for overhead and profit, and subtract an amount for depreciation. A more productive approach is comparison shopping: Develop an estimate of fair market value by comparing the subject car to similar autos that have recently sold or are presently available. If three similar-quality 1982 T-Birds have sold recently for $3,000 to $3,500, the buyer has reason to believe the target T-Bird has a similar value. Of course, comparison shopping provides no information about whether 1982 T-Birds are really worth $3,000 to $3,500 in any fundamental sense; it indicates only the going rate. This was amply demonstrated in the dot-com bubble when knowledge that Infospace was fairly priced relative to AOL, Amazon, and Webvan did not prevent Infospace shareholders from losing their shirts when the whole industry cratered. However, in many other instances, knowing relative value is sufficient. (Another tactic recommended by some is to skip the valuation process altogether and proceed directly to bargaining by asking the dealer what he wants for the car and responding, "B———t, I'll give you half of that." This probably works better for cars than for companies, but don't rule it out entirely.)

Use of comparable trades to value businesses requires equal parts art and science. First, it is necessary to decide which publicly traded companies are most similar to the target and then determine what the share prices of the publicly traded companies imply for the FMV of the firm in question. The discounted cash flow valuation equations just considered offer a useful starting point. They suggest that comparable companies should offer similar future cash flow patterns and similar business and financial risks. The risks should be similar so that roughly the same discount rate would apply to all of the firms.

In practice, these guidelines suggest we begin our search for comparable companies by considering firms in the same, or closely related, industries with similar growth prospects and capital structures. With luck, the outcome of this exercise will be several more or less comparable publicly traded companies. Considerable judgment will then be required to decide what the comparable firms as a group imply for the fair market value of the target.

As an illustration, Table 9.2 presents a comparable trades valuation of Hasbro. The valuation date is again December 31, 2016, and the chosen comparable companies are the representative competitors in the toy and gaming industry introduced in Chapter 2. Hasbro competes in multiple lines of business in the toy and gaming area, with special strength in traditional toys. Among the peers introduced in Chapter 2, Mattel (MAT) has the most overlapping business segments, but has been suffering recent financial problems. Hasbro's size puts it among the smaller firms, dwarfed by Disney (DIS) and Time Warner (TWX), but ten-times the size of JAKKS Pacific (JAKK). I dropped Nintendo (NTDOY) from the sample because it was missing so much data.

The first set of numbers in Table 9.2 looks at Hasbro's growth and financial risk relative to peers. The numbers indicate that Hasbro's five-year growth in sales and earnings per share are marginally above the peer group medians. However, security analysts appear less than enthusiastic about Hasbro's future growth prospects, placing the company well below its peers (The website providing these projected growth rates does not indicate what they refer to, or the length of the projection.) Looking at financial leverage,

TABLE 9.2   **Using Comparable Public Companies to Value Hasbro Inc. (December 31, 2016)**

Source: Data compiled from Hasbro, Inc.'s 2012–2016 annual reports and Compustat database.

	Ticker Symbols*							Excluding Hasbro	
	Hasbro	MAT	JAKK	EA	ATVI	DIS	TWX	Median	Mean
Comparison of Hasbro with Comparable Companies:									
Growth Rates, Financial Risks, Size									
5-year growth rate in sales (%)	3.2	(2.7)	0.8	4.1	6.8	6.3	0.2	2.5	2.6
5-year growth rate in EPS (%)	8.8	(15.8)	(24.2)	NM	6.9	17.6	12.8	6.9	(0.5)
Analysts' projected growth (%)**	7.2	13.2	NA	13.1	18.2	9.4	11.5	13.1	13.1
Interest coverage ratio (X)	8.3	5.3	1.4	32.3	6.1	30.3	4.8	5.7	13.4
Total liabilities to assets (%)	63.4	62.9	70.9	51.8	47.7	48.6	63.1	57.4	57.5
Total assets ($ millions)	5,091	6,494	464	7,050	17,452	92,033	65,966	12,251	31,577
Indicators of Value									
Price/earnings (X)		29.7	70.0	17.2	27.9	15.8	19.0	23.4	29.9
MV firm/EBIT(1 – tax rate) (X)		30.0	70.6	17.6	27.5	17.4	19.9	23.7	30.5
MV firm/sales (X)		2.2	0.4	4.8	4.8	3.0	3.4	3.2	3.1
MV equity/BV equity (X)		3.9	0.6	5.9	3.0	3.4	3.1	3.2	3.3
MV firm/BV firm (X)		2.5	0.9	4.6	2.3	2.7	2.0	2.4	2.5

My Estimated Indicators of Value for Hasbro		**Implied Value of Hasbro's Common Stock per Share**
Price/earnings (X)	21.0	$ 93.00 = 21.0 X Net income / # shares
MV firm/EBIT(1 – tax rate) (X)	21.0	$ 91.93 = [21.0 X EBIT(1 – tax rate) – Debt] / # shares
MV firm/sales (X)	3.0	$107.14 = [3.0 X Sales – Debt] / # shares
MV equity/BV equity (X)	4.0	$ 59.85 = [4.0 X BV equity] / # shares
MV firm/BV firm (X)	3.0	$ 72.53 = [3.0 X BV firm – Debt] / # shares
My best guess		$ 90.00
Actual stock price		$ 77.79

* MAT = Mattel, JAKK = JAKKS Pacific, EA = Electronic Arts, ATVI = Activision Blizzard, DIS = Walt Disney, TWX = Time Warner. Nintendo omitted due to missing data.
NM = Not meaningful.
** Mean value of security analysts' long-run growth estimates. Available at **Reuters.com/finance/stocks.** MV = Market value; BV = Book value. Market value of firm is estimated as book value of interest-bearing debt + market value of equity. Earnings are previous 12 months' earnings.

Hasbro appears to be in the middle of the pack in terms of interest coverage and liabilities to assets.

The second set of numbers in the table show five possible indicators of value for the comparable firms. Broadly speaking, each indicator expresses how much investors are paying per dollar of current income, sales, or invested capital for each firm. Thus, the first indicator says that $1.00 of Mattel's (MAT) current income is worth $29.70, while JAKKS Pacific's goes for $70.00. Similarly, the third indicator says that $1.00 of Electronic Arts's (EA) sales costs $4.80, and the last indicator says $1.00 of Time Warner's (TWX) assets, measured at book, costs $2.00. The first and fourth indicators focus on equity value, while the other three concentrate on firm value.

Reflecting on how Hasbro stacks up against its peers in terms of growth and risk, the valuation challenge is to decide what indicators of value are appropriate for Hasbro. The third group of numbers on the lower left contains my necessarily subjective estimates. In coming to these estimates, I considered several factors. First, I customarily believe the first two indicators of value are more reliable than the others because they tie market value to income as opposed to sales or assets. With rare exceptions, investors are interested in a company's income potential when they buy its shares, not its sales or the assets it owns. Asset-based indicators of value are more relevant when liquidation is contemplated. Sales-based ratios tend to be of interest when current earnings are unrepresentative of long-run potential or when investors lose faith in the accuracy of reported earnings. This is not to say that sales are immune to manipulation but only that they are somewhat less manipulable than earnings.

Second, when choosing between indicators focusing on equity value or firm value, I prefer the firm value ratios because they are less affected by the way a business is financed. The problem with the equity approach is that leverage affects a company's price-to-earnings ratio in complex ways, so that, for example, inferring a highly levered firm's price-to-earnings ratio from those of more modestly levered peers can lead to errors.

Third, it makes sense to assign more importance to those indicators of value that are more stable across peer companies. If the calculated value of one indicator was 10.0 for every comparable company, I would deem it a more reliable indicator of value than if it varied from 1.0 to 30.0 from firm to firm. Here, there is considerable variation across all five indicators of value, principally, I think, because JAKKS Pacific is such a pipsqueak and, along with Mattel, has declining earnings.

Fourth, analysts' lack of enthusiasm about Hasbro's growth suggests it may be in the lower half of the indicated valuation range with regard to earnings-based indicators of value. On the other hand, the company's superior asset utilization, as noted in earlier chapters, suggests the reverse for asset-based indicators.

The last set of numbers on the lower right of Table 9.2 presents the price of Hasbro's stock implied by each chosen indicator of value. To the right of each stock price is an equation demonstrating how I translated the chosen indicator into an implied stock price. To illustrate the third equation, I estimated that Hasbro's total firm value should be 3.0 times its sales. Hasbro's sales in 2016 were $5,020 million, so its implied firm value is $15,060 million. Subtracting interest-bearing debt of $1,721 million and dividing by 124.5 million shares yields an estimated stock price of $107.14 a share. The other implied share prices are calculated similarly.

Looking at the resulting five estimates of Hasbro's stock price, note that four are in the $60 to $95 range, with the highest two, those based on earnings, at the upper end of the range. Reflecting on all of these observations, my best guess of a fair price for Hasbro's shares on the valuation date is $90.00 a share, or about $1.50 less than my earlier DCF estimate. Ninety dollars is roughly 16 percent above Hasbro's actual stock price on the valuation date and just outside my usual expectations of +/−15 percent accuracy on such exercises. Two complementary conclusions are possible: (1) valuing common stock, by whatever method, is difficult, and (2) rather than erring on the high side, perhaps my estimate is signaling that Hasbro stock was a buy on the valuation date. Maybe it really was worth $90, and not $78 as the market indicated. Indeed, five days after the valuation date, Hasbro's stock closed at $83.71, and then a month later jumped to $94.31 when analysts expressed enthusiasm about the firm's robust holiday season.

Lack of Marketability

An important difference between owning stock in a publicly traded company and owning stock in a private one is that the publicly traded shares are more liquid; they can be sold quickly for cash without significant loss of value. Because liquidity is a valued attribute of any asset, it is necessary to reduce the FMV of a private company estimated by reference to publicly traded comparable firms. Without boring you with details, a representative lack of marketability discount is on the order of 25 percent.[8] Of course, if the purpose of the valuation is to price an initial public offering of common stock, the shares will soon be liquid, and no discount is required.

A second possible adjustment when using the comparable-trades approach to valuation is a premium for control. Quoted prices for public companies are invariably for a minority interest in the firm, while many valuations involve transactions in which operating control passes from seller to buyer. Because control is valuable, it is necessary in these instances to add a premium to the estimated value of the target firm to reflect the value of control. Estimating the size of this control premium is our next task. But first, I want to call your attention to a close cousin of comparable trades valuation known as comparable *transactions* valuation. The two techniques are identical except that the latter substitutes prices struck in recent corporate acquisitions for publicly quoted stock prices. Transactions prices are obviously much less common than quoted stock prices and are often proprietary. However, in most

---

[8] Shannon P. Pratt, Robert F. Reilly, and Robert P. Schweihs. *Valuing a Business: The Analysis and Appraisal of Closely Held Companies* , 5th ed. (New York: Irwin/McGraw-Hill, 2007).

instances, they are probably a better reflection of the value inherent in an acquisition candidate, and they already contain a premium for control.

The Market for Control

We have noted on several occasions that buying a minority interest in a company differs fundamentally from buying control. With a minority interest, the investor is a passive observer; with control, she has complete freedom to change the way the company does business and perhaps increase its value significantly. Indeed, the two situations are so disparate that it is appropriate to speak of stock as selling in two separate markets: the market in which you and I trade minority claims on future cash flows and the market in which Microsoft and other acquirers trade the right to control the firm. The latter, the *market for control,* involves a two-in-one sale. In addition to claims on future cash flows, the buyer in this market also gains the privilege of structuring the company as he or she wishes. Because shares trading in the two markets are really different assets, they naturally sell at different prices.

The Premium for Control

Figure 9.2 illustrates this two-tier market. From the perspective of minority investors, the fair market value of a company's equity, represented in the figure by m, is the present value of cash flows to equity given current

FIGURE 9.2 **FMV of a Corporation to Investors Seeking Control May Exceed FMV to Minority Investors**

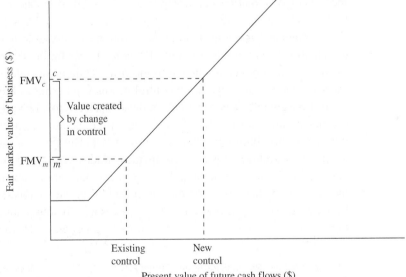

management and strategy. To a corporation or an individual seeking control, however, the FMV is *c,* which may be well above *m.* The difference, $(c - m)$, is the value of control. It is the maximum premium over the minority fair market value an acquirer should pay to gain control. It is also the expected increase in shareholder value created by acquisition. When an acquirer pays FMV_c for a target, all of the increased value will be realized by the seller's shareholders, while at any lower price, part of the increased value will accrue to the acquirer's shareholders as well. FMV_c is therefore the maximum acquisition price a buyer can justify paying. Said differently, it is the price at which the net present value of the acquisition to the buyer is zero.

What Price Control?

There are two ways to determine how large a control premium an acquirer can afford to pay. The brute force approach values the business, first assuming the merger takes place and then assuming it does not. The difference between these values is the maximum premium an acquirer can justify paying. The second, often more practical approach focuses on the anticipated gains from the merger. In equation form,

$$FMV_c = FMV_m + \text{Enhancements}$$

where *c* and *m* again denote controlling and minority interest, respectively. This expression says the value of controlling interest in a business equals the business's FMV under the present stewardship, or what is often called the business's *stand-alone value,* plus whatever enhancements to value the new buyer envisions. If the buyer intends to make no changes in the business now or in the future, the enhancements are zero, and no premium over stand-alone value can be justified. On the other hand, if the buyer believes the merging of two businesses will create vast new profit opportunities, enhancements can be quite large.

Putting a price tag on the value of enhancements resulting from an acquisition is a straightforward undertaking conceptually: Make a detailed list of all the ways the acquisition will increase free cash flows, estimate the magnitude and timing of the cash flows involved, calculate their present values, and sum:

$$\text{Enhancements} = \text{PV(All value-increasing changes due to acquisition)}$$

Controlling Interest in a Publicly Traded Company

An important simplification of our expression for FMV_c is possible when the seller is publicly traded. If we are willing to assume that the preacquisition stock price of the target company reasonably approximates its FMV_m, or at least that we are unable to detect when the approximation is unreasonable, the expression reduces to

$$FMV_c = \text{Market value of business} + \text{Enhancements}$$

where the market value of the business is our old friend the stock market value of equity plus debt. A particular virtue of this formula for valuing acquisition candidates is that it forces attention on the specific improvements anticipated from the acquisition and the maximum price one should pay to get them, a perspective that reduces the possibility that an exuberant buyer will get carried away during spirited bidding and overpay. In other words, it helps to keep animal spirits in check during the negotiation process.

That animal spirits might need an occasional reining in is suggested by Table 9.3. It shows the number of mergers in the United States from 1995 through 2016 and the median premiums paid. Note that the number of acquisitions rose from a cyclical low of about 3,500 in 1995 to what was then an all-time high of over 10,600 in 2006, fell sharply during the recession, only to climb back to new highs in recent years. In addition, the number of big-ticket purchases of more than $1 billion followed a similar pattern, rising to 250 in 2007, falling sharply during the recession, and then rising to new highs.

TABLE 9.3   **Number of Mergers and Median Acquisition Premiums, 1995–2016**

Source: *2017 Mergerstat Review,* FactSet Mergerstat, LLC, Newark, 2017. Factset Mergerstat Global Mergers and Acquisitions Information. Newark, NJ. 800-455-8871, factset.com.

Year	Number of Transactions*	Number over $1 Billion	Median 5-Day Premium (%)**
1995	3,510	74	29.2
1996	5,848	94	27.3
1997	7,800	120	27.5
1998	7,809	158	30.1
1999	9,278	195	34.6
2000	9,566	206	41.1
2001	8,290	121	40.5
2002	7,303	72	34.4
2003	7,983	88	31.6
2004	9,783	134	23.4
2005	10,332	170	24.1
2006	10,660	216	23.1
2007	10,559	250	24.7
2008	7,807	97	36.5
2009	6,796	78	39.8
2010	9,116	153	34.6
2011	9,519	163	37.8
2012	9,610	198	37.1
2013	8,777	172	29.7
2014	11,240	258	28.7
2015	12,012	272	29.6
2016	11,657	284	33.1

* Net number of transactions announced.
** Premiums are based on seller's closing market price five business days before the initial announcement. These calculations exclude negative premiums.

Looking at the acquisition premiums, we see that in every year the median premium paid was in the range of 20 to 40 percent of the seller's share price five days before the announcement. Evidently, acquirers are quite confident of their ability to wring large enhancements out of their acquisitions.

Financial Reasons for Restructuring

We conclude (or at least I conclude) that the best way to value a public company for acquisition purposes is to add the present value of all benefits attributable to the acquisition to the target's current market value. "So," you ask perceptively, "what types of benefits might motivate an acquisition or other form of restructuring?" The list is truly lengthy, ranging from anticipated savings in manufacturing, marketing, distribution, or overhead to better access to financial markets to enhanced investment opportunities. The perceived sources of value vary from merger to merger. So instead of trying to catalog the myriad possible benefits to a restructuring, I will concentrate on three finance-driven potential enhancements that are sufficiently common and controversial to warrant inquiry. I will refer to them as *tax shields, incentive effects,* and *controlling free cash flow.*

Tax Shields

A number of takeovers and restructurings, especially those involving mature, slow-growth businesses, are driven in part by the desire to make more extensive use of interest tax shields. As noted in Chapter 6, the tax deductibility of interest expense reduces a company's tax bill and hence may add to value. A second, more recent tax ploy is known as *inversion.* A U.S. company seeking a lower tax rate and a way to redeploy overseas earnings without triggering

---

Kissing Toads

The Oracle of Omaha, Warren Buffett, attributes corporate executives' willingness to pay large control premiums to three very human factors: an abundance of animal spirits, an unwarranted emphasis on company size as opposed to profitability, and overexposure during youth to "the story in which the imprisoned handsome prince is released from a toad's body by a kiss from a beautiful princess. [From this tale, executives] are certain their managerial kiss will do wonders for the profitability of Company T(arget)." Why else, Buffett asks, would an acquiring company pay a premium to control another business when it could avoid the premium altogether by simply purchasing a minority interest?

"In other words, investors can always buy toads at the going price for toads. If investors instead bankroll princesses who wish to pay double for the right to kiss the toad, those kisses had better pack some real dynamite. We've observed many kisses but very few miracles. Nonetheless, many managerial princesses remain serenely confident about the future potency of their kisses—even after their corporate backyards are knee-deep in unresponsive toads."

Source: Warren Buffett, Berkshire Hathaway, Inc. 1981 annual report.

stiff domestic taxes acquires a firm located in a low-tax country, such as Ireland, and then adopts the target's foreign address and accompanying tax advantages. Before packing, be aware that it is not clear how long Congress will allow this loophole to remain open.

To illustrate the appeal of interest tax shields, consider the following restructuring of Mature Manufacturing, Inc. (2M). Pertinent data for 2M, a publicly traded company, follows.

Mature Manufacturing, Inc. ($ millions)	
Annual EBIT	$25
Market value of equity	200
Interest-bearing debt	0
Tax rate	40%

Global Investing Partners believes 2M's management may be interested in a leveraged buyout (LBO) and has approached it with a proposal to form a new corporation, invariably called NEWCO, to purchase all of 2M's equity in the open market. Because 2M's cash flows are very stable, Global figures it can finance most of the purchase price by borrowing $190 million on a 10-year loan at 10 percent interest. The loan will be interest-only for the first five years. In the longer run, Global believes 2M can easily support annual interest expenses of $10 million. The value of the anticipated interest tax shields to NEWCO, discounted at a 12 percent rate, is as follows:

Year	Interest Expense	Tax Shield at 40% Tax Rate
1	$19.00	$ 7.60
2	19.00	7.60
3	19.00	7.60
4	19.00	7.60
5	19.00	7.60
6	19.00	7.60
7	15.89	6.36
8	12.46	4.98
9	10.00	4.00
10	10.00	4.00
Present value of tax shields years 1—10 at 12%		= $38.87
Present value of tax shields years 10 and beyond at 12%		= 10.73
Total		$49.60 million

Ignoring the increased costs of financial distress that customarily accompany higher financial leverage, these figures suggest that NEWCO can bid up to $249.60 million to purchase Mature Manufacturing, a 25 percent premium over the current market price ($249.60 million = $200 million stand-alone value +$49.60 million of enhancements). Moreover, Global's required equity investment at this price would be only $59.60 million ($249.60 million acquisition price − $190 million in new debt), implying a post acquisition debt-to-assets ratio of 76 percent. LBOs are indeed aptly named.

A final judgment on the value of interest tax shields in leveraged restructurings, of course, rests on a qualitative weighting of the indicated tax savings against the costs of financial distress as discussed in Chapter 6. A reduced tax bill isn't especially attractive when the added debt frightens customers, drives away creditors, and emboldens competitors.

Note that if increased interest tax shields are the objective, an LBO is not the only way to obtain them. 2M can generate much the same effect by simply issuing debt and distributing the proceeds to owners as a large dividend or by a share repurchase. This was Colt Industries' strategy (described in Chapter 6) when it floated a huge debt issue to finance distribution of a special dividend and ended up with $1.6 billion in long-term debt and a negative net worth. But what's to fear from a mountain of debt as long as you have the cash flow to service it? And if you don't, your creditors have so much at stake in your company that they are more likely to behave like partners than police.

Nor must a leveraged buyout necessarily involve a takeover. Many LBOs are initiated by incumbent management who team up with outside investors to purchase all of the company's stock and take it private. (An LBO in which incumbent management takes an active role is known as a management buyout, or MBO.) Management risks its own money in return for a sizable equity position in the restructured company.

Incentive Effects

Tax shield enhancements are clearly just a game: To the extent that shareholders win, "we, the people" (in the form of the U.S. Treasury) lose. If this were the only financial gain to takeovers and restructurings, the phenomena would not command serious public attention. Best that we eliminate the tax benefits and get back to producing goods and services instead of stocks and bonds.

The other two potential enhancements are not so easily dismissed. Both involve free cash flow, and both are premised on the belief that restructuring powerfully affects the performance incentives confronting senior management. To examine the incentive effects of restructuring in more detail, let's return to Mature Manufacturing, Inc.

Before restructuring, the life of a senior manager at Mature Manufacturing, Inc. may well have been an enviable one. With very stable cash flows, a mature business, and no debt, managers had no pressing reason to improve performance. They could pay themselves and their employees generously, make sizable corporate contributions to charity, and, if the president was so inclined, sponsor an Indy race car or a hydroplane. Alternatively, if they wanted 2M to grow, the company could acquire other firms. This might involve some uneconomical investments, but hey—as long as cash flows are strong, almost anything is possible.

Samuel Johnson once observed, "The certainty of hanging in a fortnight focuses the mind wonderfully." Restructuring can have a similar effect, for it fundamentally changes the world of 2M senior executives. Because they probably have invested much of their own resources in the equity of the newly restructured company, their own material well-being is closely tied to that of the business. Moreover, the huge debt service burden restructuring frequently creates forces management to generate healthy cash flows or face bankruptcy—no more "corpocracy" at 2M. The carrot of ownership and the stick of possible financial ruin create significant incentives for management to maximize free cash flow and spend it for the benefit of owners.

Controlling Free Cash Flow

In addition to interest tax shields and incentive effects of high leverage, a third possible enhancement in restructurings rests on the perception that public companies are not always run solely for the benefit of owners. In this view, value can be created by gaining control of such firms and refocusing the business on the single goal of creating shareholder value. Adherents of this view see shareholder–manager relations as an ongoing tug-of-war for control of the firm's free cash flow. When shareholders have the upper hand, companies are run to maximize shareholder value, but when management is in the driver's seat, increasing value is only one of a number of competing corporate goals. After more than 50 years on the losing end of this tug-of-war, the emergence of the hostile raider in the mid-1980s enabled shareholders to gain the ascendancy and force companies to restructure. According to this view, the hostile acquisitions and restructurings during the latter half of the 1980s were a boon not only to shareholders but to the entire economy; for to the extent that shareholders can force management to increase firm value, the economy's resources are allocated more efficiently.

Consistent with this adversarial view of corporate governance, many takeovers and restructurings occur in mature or declining industries. Because investment opportunities in these industries are low, affected businesses often have large free cash flows. At the same time, industry decline creates real concern in the minds of executives about the continued survival of their organization. And although the proper strategy from a purely financial perspective may be to shrink or terminate the business, management often takes another tack. Out of a deep commitment to the business and concern for employees,

Avoiding Dilution in Earnings per Share

An all-too-popular alternative approach to determining how much one company can afford to bid for another looks at the impact of the acquisition on the acquirer's earnings per share (EPS). Popularity is about all this approach has to recommend it, for it grossly oversimplifies the financial effects of an acquisition, and it rests on an inappropriate decision criterion.

Suppose the following data apply to an acquiring firm, A, and its target, T, in an exchange-of-shares merger; that is, A will give T's shareholders newly printed shares of A in exchange for their shares of T.

	Company A	Company T	Merged Company
Earnings ($ millions)	$ 100	$ 20	$130
Number of shares (millions)	20	40	26
Earnings per share	$ 5	$0.50	$ 5 (minimum)
Stock price	$ 70	$ 5	
Market value of equity (millions)	$1,400	$ 200	

The suggested decision criterion is that A should avoid dilution in EPS. If earnings of the merged firm are forecast to be $130 million, the figures above indicate that A can issue as many as 6 million shares without suffering dilution [6 million shares = ($130 million/$5) − 20 million]. At $70 a share, this implies a maximum price of $420 million for T ($70 × 6 million), or a 110 percent premium [(420 − 200)/200]. It also suggests a maximum exchange ratio of 0.15 shares of A for each share of T (6 million/40 million).

The obvious shortcomings of this simplistic approach are, first, that earnings are not the cash flows that determine value and, second, that it is grossly inappropriate to base an acquisition decision on only one year's results. Doing so is comparable to making investments because they promise to increase next year's profits. If T's growth prospects are sufficiently bright, it may be perfectly reasonable to sacrifice near-term EPS in anticipation of long-run gains. This is certainly what Microsoft did in acquiring LinkedIn.

Academics have been stamping on this weed for decades, but it never seems to die. Witness the following from *The Wall Street Journal* announcing the Daimler-Chrysler merger in 1998. "[T]he cross-border union is actually typical of the stock-for-stock deals that have made the 1990s merger boom so fertile: a combination using favorable accounting in which the buyer has a high price-to-earnings ratio that can make a deal 'accretive' because the seller has a low P/E. Chrysler's price-to-earnings ratio has long been around eight times earnings, analysts say, and has only recently crept up to nine times. Daimler's P/E, meanwhile, is more like 20 times profits, giving the buyer the financial firepower to pay 11 to 12 times earnings and still have the transaction 'accretive,' or beneficial to the earnings of the new DaimlerChrysler."* Business valuation is tough in practice, but there is no reason to use flawed techniques just because they are tractable.

*Source: Steven Lipin and Brandon Mitchener, "Daimler-Chrysler Merger to Produce $3 Billion in Savings, Revenue Gains Within 3 to 5 Years," *The Wall Street Journal*, May 8, 1998.

the community, and their own welfare, some managers continue to fight the good fight by reinvesting in the business despite its poor returns, or by entering new businesses despite any convincing reasons to expect success. The purpose of restructuring in these instances is brutally basic: Wrest control of free cash flow away from management and put it in the hands of owners.

How, you might ask, does incumbent management ever gain control of a business in the first place? In theory, managers should be incapable of acting in opposition to owners for at least two reasons. First, if a company operates in highly competitive markets, management has very little discretion; it must maximize value or the firm will be driven from the industry. Second, all corporations have boards of directors with the power to hire and fire management and the responsibility to represent owners' interests.

Theory, however, often differs from reality. Many corporations operate in less than perfectly competitive markets, and corporate boards have not always been an effective, independent shareholder voice. One reason is that most senior executives, usually supported by the courts, believe that a board's primary responsibility is to help incumbent management run the business, not to represent shareholder interests. As a result, boards are often more closely affiliated with management than with owners. Many directors are company insiders; other directors have important ties to the enterprise other than ownership and are more beholden to the chief executive than to shareholders for their seat on the board. Consequently, while such boards may help keep the shelves stocked, they are not about to recommend selling the store.

A second reason directors do not always represent shareholder interests traces to the process by which they are chosen. In the great majority of instances, the proxy materials sent annually to shareholders propose a single, unopposed slate of board candidates nominated by management. And even then, shareholders may not vote against a candidate, but may only withhold approval. The only way disaffected shareholders can contest a board seat is to propose their own candidate and use their own money to campaign against management's choice in a proxy contest. Meanwhile, management is free to use corporate funds to defeat its rivals. Little wonder then that management effectively controls most company boards.

In 2010, following passage of the Dodd–Frank Act, the SEC sought to reduce management control of board elections by forcing companies to accept limited shareholder nominations under certain specified conditions. However, a federal appeals court struck down the controversial regulation before it could be implemented.

The drive for proxy regulations is the product of a long-simmering shareholder rights movement initiated by activist investors. Having tasted the fruits of control in the form of unusually high returns during the hostile takeover era, these investors have found new ways to challenge incumbent managers for free cash flow. Unlike hostile acquirers of the 1980s, the goal of activist investors is not to gain control of a target company, but to browbeat management into actions investors believe will increase shareholder value. These actions usually involve repurchasing shares with excess cash, selling underperforming assets, or putting the company itself up for sale. Many believe activist investing got its start when shareholders grew tired of watching buyout firms make large fortunes executing strategies that incumbent managers could just as easily implement themselves. The goal of activist investors is to provide the requisite motivation. Or in the words of meta-activist Carl Icahn, "We do the job the LBO guys do, but for all the shareholders."

Does activist investing work? Evidence indicates it does. Writing in 2009, April Klein and Emanuel Zur looked at the campaigns of 151 hedge fund activists and 154 other types of activists. Hedge funds are lightly regulated, private equity partnerships that have grown rapidly in the past several decades, to the point where there are now thought to be upward of 8,000 in existence. The authors found that the activist's targets experienced abnormal returns of 5.1 to 10.2 percent, depending on the sample, in the period immediately surrounding public announcement of the activists' intentions and generated additional abnormal returns of 11.4 to 17.8 percent over the following year. They also found that activists were successful 60 to 65 percent of the time in getting incumbent management to acquiesce to their demands. A more recent work comes to a similar conclusion after synthesizing the findings of 73 studies of shareholder activism over 30 years.[10]

As debate topics go, the question of whether management should have broader social responsibilities than simply creating shareholder value is among the more intriguing. Like many important societal questions, however, the issue tends to be resolved more on the basis of power than of logic. Throughout most of the twentieth century, incumbent management retained the power to interpret its responsibilities broadly and to treat shareholders as only one of several constituencies possessing a claim on the corporation. The balance of power shifted abruptly in shareholders' favor during the era of the hostile takeover. Although corporations have largely neutralized the threat of hostile takeover, the rise of the activist shareholder and his ally, the activist board member, suggests that the battle is far from over.

The Empirical Evidence

A final question remains: Do corporate restructurings create value? Do they provide any benefit to society? In the aggregate, the answer is yes. Looking first at mergers, the median five-day acquisition premiums of 20 to 40 percent reported in Table 9.3 leave no doubt that owners of acquired firms benefit

[10] April Klein and Emanuel Zur, "Entrepreneurial Shareholder Activism: Hedge Funds and Other Private Investors," *Journal of Finance*, February 2009, pp. 187–229. See also Mathew R. Denes, Jonathan M. Karpoff, and Victoria B. McWilliams, "Thirty Years of Shareholder Activism: A Survey of Empirical Research," *Journal of Corporate Finance*, March 2016.

handsomely from mergers. Whether the owners of acquiring firms also benefit is more problematic. After reviewing scores of studies completed over the past 30 years, Robert Bruner concludes that, on balance, they do, but that the average gain is small and the range of outcomes is large.[11]

The best early study of whether leveraged buyouts create value is by Steven Kaplan, who examined 48 large management buyouts executed between 1980 and 1986.[12] Looking first at return on operating assets, Kaplan found that relative to overall industry performance, the median buyout firm increased return on operating assets by a healthy 36.1 percent in the two years following the buyout. A similar look at capital expenditures revealed that on an industry-adjusted basis, the typical buyout firm reduced its ratio of capital expenditures to assets by a statistically *in*significant 5.7 percent over the same period. Reflecting both improved operating performance and reduced investment, Kaplan found that the typical buyout firm increased an industry-adjusted measure of free cash flow to total assets an enormous 85.4 percent in the two years following the buyout. Realized returns to investors were equally impressive. Of the 48 firms in his sample, Kaplan was able to find post-buyout valuation data on 25 because they either issued stock to the public, repurchased stock, were liquidated, or were sold. Recognizing that these 25 may be the cream of the crop, he nonetheless observed impressive performance. The median, market-adjusted return to all sources of capital over the 2.6 years from the buyout date to the valuation date was 28 percent. Moreover, the median internal rate of return to equity on these firms was a staggering 785.6 percent, demonstrating yet again the power of extensive debt financing when things go well.

A subsequent study indicates that although the eye-popping numbers observed by Kaplan two decades earlier had diminished substantially, LBOs were still generating superior performance.[13] Looking at 94 LBOs between 1990 and 2006, the authors found median market and risk-adjusted returns to total capital of 40.9 percent, which they attributed in roughly equal measure to improved operating performance, increased industry valuation multiples, and tax benefits from greater financial leverage. Interestingly, the study observes that the greatest improvement in operating performance occurred when the buyout firm replaced the CEO soon after the purchase and when financial leverage was high. Evidently, aggressive oversight and the discipline of heavy debt service obligations really do focus management's attention.

[11] Robert F. Bruner, Applied Mergers & Acquisitions (New Jersey: John Wiley & Sons, 2004), Chapter 3.
[12] Steven Kaplan, "The Effects of Management Buyouts on Operating Performance and Value," *Journal of Financial Economics*, October 1989, pp. 217–254.
[13] Shourun Guo, Edith S. Hotchkiss, and Weihong Song, "Do Buyouts (Still) Create Value?" *Journal of Finance*, April 2011, pp. 479–518.

On balance, the evidence suggests that financial restructurings are not just tax gimmicks. Rather, the increased managerial incentives that often accompany such transactions appear strong enough to stimulate meaningful improvements in operating performance and in shareholder value.[14] Beyond explaining why buyout firms have become so popular, this evidence also poses a stark challenge to those who argue that management alone should control America's corporations.

The LinkedIn Buyout

Microsoft's buyout of LinkedIn should no longer hold much mystery. LinkedIn's $131 pre-merger stock price was its value to minority investors given LinkedIn's potential as a stand-alone entity under the direction of incumbent management, while the $196 price paid by Microsoft included a sizable premium for control. Clearly, neither price was necessarily incorrect or irrational. Although we might wonder whether Microsoft paid too much or too little for LinkedIn, I can assure you that having paid an estimated $50 to $65 million in combined investment advisory fees, Microsoft and LinkedIn had numerous valuation studies of the type described here supporting the acquisition pricing. Whether the assumptions and forecasts underlying those studies were accurate remains to be seen.

A cynic might say that Microsoft's acquisition of LinkedIn was nothing more than a classic example of buying growth. Microsoft had dominated the personal computer software market for years, but the market was rapidly maturing, and Microsoft risked becoming the next Hewlett Packard or IBM. LinkedIn didn't make much money, but was growing 20–40 percent a year, and Microsoft, with plenty of cash, hoped to catch a bit of lightning. A more realistic interpretation of Microsoft's merger motives would note that LinkedIn wasn't just any bolt of lightning. It had over 400 million professional members who were prime customers for Microsoft's software products, it was a natural customer for Microsoft's Azure cloud platform, it offered massive amounts of customer data supportive of Microsoft's artificial intelligence initiative, and as a Silicon Valley stalwart, it helped strengthen Microsoft's ties to the heart of the Valley. It was no coincidence that Reid Hoffman, LinkedIn's founder and a prominent industry player, joined Microsoft's board shortly after the merger. A more imaginative interpretation of Microsoft's intentions would go even further saying that by combining software design, cloud computing, and professional networking in one organization, the merger created a unique new vehicle for innovation of a yet unknown kind.

[14] For a thorough review of corporate restructurings, see Espen B. Eckbo and Karin S. Thorburn, "Corporate Restructuring: Breakups and LBOs," *Handbook of Corporate Finance: Empirical Corporate Finance* , Vol. 2, Chapter 16, 2008, pp. 431–496. See also Robert S. Harris, Tim Jenkinson, and Steven N. Kaplan, " Private Equity Performance: What Do We Know?" *Journal of Finance* , September 2014, pp. 1851–1882.

Like many young technology companies, LinkedIn's biggest attraction to investors was growth. If LinkedIn grew rapidly, investors were willing to overlook its lack of earnings. But then in February 2016, LinkedIn's stock price fell 40 percent in a single day in reaction to a management forecast of weaker-than-expected revenue growth. It was probably no coincidence that LinkedIn and Microsoft began serious merger discussions at just about this time. From a high of $225 a share before the weak earnings forecast, LinkedIn's stock price continued to fall to just over $100 as merger negotiations continued. Apparently, cash in hand, especially at a 50 percent premium, began to look better to LinkedIn owners than prospects in professional networking as a stand-alone business. To make matters worse, LinkedIn had always been an aggressive user of stock-based compensation to attract and retain top talent. This had worked well for years, but as the company's stock price cratered, dragging employee wealth down with it, concern about the company's ability to retain newly demoralized employees began to mount. Better perhaps to lock in a decent price of $196 a share than to risk further deterioration.

Microsoft's only difficulty during negotiations was dealing with Salesforce.com, a growing power in cloud-based business applications. Once close friends who twice considered merging, Microsoft and Salesforce became direct, and apparently bitter, competitors in pursuit of LinkedIn. LinkedIn began negotiations by talking to as many as three suitors, including Salesforce, but within a brief time, and after receiving best offers from each suitor, decided to narrow its focus exclusively to Microsoft. Consistent with standard practice, LinkedIn wanted to attempt an agreement with Microsoft, on the understanding that negotiations would be reopened if this proved impossible. Despite this rebuff, Salesforce refused to admit defeat and repeatedly sweetened its supposedly best offer, ultimately forcing Microsoft to boost its bid an estimated $5 billion before LinkedIn's board felt it could legally accept Microsoft's number. Then, immediately after the merger announcement, Marc Benioff, Salesforce's CEO, asserted that Salesforce would have paid "much more" than Microsoft's successful bid if it had just been given a chance, implying that Microsoft and LinkedIn had colluded to exclude his firm from negotiations. And to really cinch its Poor Loser crown, Salesforce then complained to regulators in the U.S. and Europe that the combination should be blocked, or at least restricted, on antitrust grounds. In the words of Salesforce's chief legal officer, Burke Norton, "Given Microsoft's history and existing monopolies, it is sometimes necessary for antitrust enforcement agencies to intervene to ensure that Microsoft is operating in a manner that promotes competition, rather than stifles it."[15]

Although little has come of Salesforce's pique, it is probably safe to speculate that the two companies will not soon be talking merger again.

[15] Nick Wingfield and Katie Benner, "How LinkedIn Drove a Wedge Between Microsoft and Salesforce," *New York Times*, November 5, 2016.

APPENDIX

The Venture Capital Method of Valuation

Venture capitalists are the carrier pilots of corporate finance. They make high-risk, high-return investments in new or early-stage companies thought capable of growing rapidly into sizable enterprises. Their investment horizon is typically five or six years, at which time they expect to cash out as the target company goes public or sells out to a competitor. To manage risk, venture capitalists typically make staged investments in which the company must meet a stated business milestone before qualifying for the next financing round. Venture capitalists often specialize in a particular financing round, such as startup, early stage, or mezzanine. The mezzanine round is the company's last private financing round prior to going public, or merging. In most instances, the risk to new investors and, hence, the return demanded, diminishes from one financing round to the next.

The standard discounted cash flow valuation technique discussed in the chapter is ill-suited to venture investing for several reasons. First, the cash infusions from venture investors are intended to cover near-term, negative free cash flows, so projecting and discounting annual free cash flows is not relevant. Second and more fundamentally, the standard approach to business valuation does not gracefully accommodate multiple financing rounds at different required rates of return.

Rather than use the standard approach, venture capitalists employ a specialized discounted cash flow technique that is better suited to their needs. Our purpose here is to illustrate the venture capital method of valuation, to indicate the level of target returns used in the industry, and to offer several explanations of why these targets appear so outlandishly high. We begin with a simple example of a company in need of only one financing round. We then build on this example to consider a more realistic situation involving multiple financing rounds.

The Venture Capital Method—One Financing Round

Jerry Cross and Greg Robinson, two veteran computer programmers, have what they believe is a pathbreaking idea for a new product. Soon after incorporating as ZMW Enterprises and arbitrarily awarding themselves 2,000,000 shares of common stock, Cross and Robinson prepared a detailed business plan and began talking to venture capitalists about funding their company. The business plan envisions an immediate $6 million venture capital investment, profits of $5 million in year 5, and rapid growth thereafter. The plan indicates that

$6 million will be sufficient to commence operations and to cover all anticipated cash needs until the company begins generating positive cash flows in year 5.

After hearing the entrepreneurs' pitch, a senior partner at Touchstone Ventures, a local venture capital company, expressed interest in financing ZMW but demanded 3.393 million shares in return for his firm's $6 million investment. He also mentioned in passing that his offer implied a pre-money valuation for ZMW of $3.537 million and a post-money value of $9.537 million. Determined not to be intimidated, Greg Robinson challenged the venture capitalist to justify his numbers, hoping in the process to learn what he meant by pre- and post-money.

Panel A of Table 9A.1 presents a valuation of ZMW using the venture capital method. Three steps are involved.

1. Estimate ZMW's value at some future date, often based on a conventional comparable trades or comparable transactions analysis.

2. Discount this future value to the present at the venture capitalist's target internal rate of return.

3. Divide the venture capitalist's investment by ZMW's present value to calculate the venture capitalist's required percentage ownership.

TABLE 9.A1 The Venture Capital Method of Valuation

Panel A: One Financing Round						
Facts and Assumptions (000 omitted)						
Net income year 5	$ 5,000					
Price-to-earnings ratio in year 5	20					
Investment required at time 0	$ 6,000					
Touchstone Ventures' target rate of return	60%					
Time 0 shares outstanding	2,000					
Cash Flow and Valuation						
Year	**0**	**1**	**2**	**3**	**4**	**5**
Investment	$ 6,000					
ZMW value in year 5						$100,000
PV at time 0 of year 5 value discounted at 60%	$ 9,537					
Time 5 Touchstone ownership to earn target return	**62.9%**					
Shares purchased by Touchstone[1]	3,393					
Price per share	$ 1.77					
Pre-money value of ZMW	$ 3,537					
Post-money value of ZMW	$ 9,537					

Panel B: Two Financing Rounds

Facts and Assumptions (000 omitted)

Net income year 5	$ 5,000
Price-to-earnings ratio in year 5	20
Investment required at time 0	$ 6,000
Investment required at time 2	$ 4,000
Touchstone Ventures' target rate of return	60%
Second-round investor's target rate of return	40%
Time 0 shares outstanding	2,000

Cash Flow and Valuation

Year	0	1	2	3	4	5
Investment	$ 6,000		$ 4,000			
Terminal value year 5						$100,000
Second-Round Investor						
PV at time 2 of year 5 value discounted at 40%			$36,443			
Time 5 ownership to earn target return			11.0%			
Touchstone Ventures						
PV at time 0 of year 5 value discounted at 60%	$ 9,537					
Time 5 Touchstone ownership to earn target return	62.9%					
Retention ratio[2]	89.0%					
Time 0 Touchstone ownership to earn target return	70.7%					
Shares purchased by Touchstone[1]	4,819					
Price per share	$ 1.24					
Pre-money value of ZMW	$ 2,490					
Post-money value of ZMW	$ 8,490					
Second-Round Investor						
Shares purchased by second round investor[1]			841			
Price per share			$ 4.76			
Pre-money value of ZMW			$32,443			
Post-money value of ZMW			$36,443			

[1] If x equals the number of shares purchased by new investors, y is the number of shares currently outstanding, and p is the percentage of the firm purchased by new investors, then $x/(y + x) = p$, and $x = py/(1 - p)$.

[2] Retention ratio = $(1 -$ second round investor's percentage ownership$) = (1 - 11.0\%)$.

As shown in Panel A, Touchstone accepted the entrepreneurs' projection that ZMW would earn $5 million in year 5. They then multiplied this amount by a "warranted" price-to-earnings ratio of 20 to calculate a firm value of $100 million. The price-to-earnings ratio used here typically reflects the multiples implied by other recent venture financings or the multiples presently commanded by public companies in the same or related industries.

Discounting the year 5 value to the present at Touchstone's 60 percent target rate of return yields a present value for ZMW of $9.537 million [$9.537 million = $100 million/$(1 + 0.60)^5$]. This, in turn, implies a percentage ownership for Touchstone of 62.9 percent. The logic here is that if the company is worth $9.537 million after the investment, and if Touchstone contributes $6 million to this total, its fractional ownership should be $6 million/$9.537 million, or 62.9 percent. To confirm this logic, note that if ZMW is worth $100 million in five years, Touchstone's 62.9 percent ownership will be worth $62.9 million, which translates into an internal rate of return of precisely 60 percent on a $6 million investment.

The rest is just algebra. If Touchstone is to own 62.9 percent of ZMW and the company presently has 2 million shares outstanding, Touchstone needs to receive 3.393 million new shares [62.9% = 3.393/(2 + 3.393)], which, in turn, implies a per share price of $1.77 ($6 million/3.393 million shares). ZMW's estimated value before Touchstone's investment, or its pre-money value, is, thus, $3.537 million ($1.77 per share × 2 million shares), and its value after the investment, or its post-money value, is $9.537 million (1.77 per share × 5.393 million shares).

Cross and Robinson are likely to be of two minds about this valuation: flabbergasted that Touchstone would demand a 60 percent return when all they do is put up money, but pleased to learn that Touchstone apparently puts a $3.537 million price tag on their idea.

The Venture Capital Method—Multiple Financing Rounds

The venture capital method is easy to apply when there is only one financing round prior to the valuation date. Things get more complicated, and more realistic, when there are multiple rounds. To illustrate, let's change the ZMW example by supposing that Cross and Robinson's business plan calls for two financing rounds: the original $6 million at time 0, plus a second investment of $4 million at time 2. Because ZMW will be a functioning company at time 2, it is reasonable to suppose that second-round investors will demand a lower rate of return. Based on Touchstone's experience, let us assume that second-round investors will demand "only" 40 percent.[1] Reworking the earlier figures, as shown in Panel B of Table 9A.1, Touchstone will now demand 4.819 million shares, or 70.7 percent ownership, in return for their $6 million investment.

To arrive at these figures, note that each subsequent financing round will dilute Touchstone's investment. Therefore, owning 62.9 percent of ZMW today, as in our first example, will no longer be adequate. To capture the effect of dilution imposed by subsequent financing rounds, it is necessary to apply the logic described earlier recursively to each financing round, beginning with the most distant. Panel B shows that at a discount rate of 40 percent, the time 2 value of ZMW to a new investor will be $36.443 million, so round 2 investors will demand 11.0 percent of the company for their $4 million investment (11.0% = $4 million/$36.443 million).

Once we know this number, we are ready to calculate Touchstone's initial ownership. We know that Touchstone wants 62.9 percent of ZMW in year 5 and that round 2 dilution makes it necessary to gross this number up by some amount. To determine how much, we divide 62.9 percent by what is known as a *retention ratio*. Here, the retention ratio turns out to be 0.89, so Touchstone's current ownership must be 70.7 percent (70.7% = 62.9%/0.89). The logic of the retention ratio goes like this. If y represents Touchstone's initial ownership, then $y - 0.11y = 0.629$, so $y = 0.629/(1 - 0.11) = 70.7\%$. The quantity in parentheses is the retention ratio.

Extending this reasoning to an arbitrary number of financing rounds, the retention ratio for the ith financing round is

$$R_i = (1 - d_{i+1})(1 - d_{i+2}) \ldots (1 - d_n),$$

where d_{i+1} is the percentage ownership given to the ith + 1 round investors, and n is the total number of subsequent financing rounds. With only one subsequent financing round, Touchstone's retention ratio is $(1 - 0.11) = 0.89$. The need to work recursively from the most distant financing round to the

---

[1] How can Series B investors be satisfied with 40 percent a year for the last three years of their investment, while Series A investors demand a target return of 60 percent per year over their full investment horizon (which includes these last three years)? Notice that these are average returns (or more formally, IRRs). One scenario consistent with the expectations of both Series A and Series B investors is that the entrepreneurs deliver an average return of 95.5 percent per year for the first two years, and 40 percent per year for the last three years. This pattern would satisfy the requirements of a 60 percent annual return for the Series A investors [$(1 + 0.60)^5 = (1 + .955)^2 \times (1 + 0.40)^3$] and the 40 percent return for Series B. This pattern is also intuitively reasonable, if we imagine that the company becomes less risky as it grows.

present should now be clear. Because the retention ratio for each round depends on dilution created by all subsequent rounds, it is impossible to calculate the initial percentage ownership of early-round investors without knowing that of all later rounds.

Once we know the percentage ownership at each financing round, it is easy to calculate stock prices as well as pre- and post-money values. As noted in Panel B, ZMW's pre-money value at time 0 is $2.49 million, while the same quantity at time 2 is $32.443 million. The corresponding share prices are $1.24 and $4.76, respectively.

Table 9A.2 confirms the validity of the venture capital method. It shows the resulting cash flows to Touchstone Ventures, the second-round investor, and the founding entrepreneurs—assuming that ZMW can achieve its business plan. Observe that these cash flows yield precisely the target rates of return demanded by the venture capitalists. Note too that although the entrepreneurs lose majority control of their company, the prospect of owning shares worth $26.109 million in five years should provide some consolation.

Why Do Venture Capitalists Demand Such High Returns?

To begin, it is important to understand that the sky-high target returns demanded by venture capitalists do not come close to approximating the realized returns they actually earn. Although estimating realized returns in venture capital is difficult for a number of reasons, the best current estimates suggest that after adjusting for differences in investment risk and liquidity, realized returns in venture

TABLE 9A.2 Prospective Returns to Investors in ZMW ($ thousands)

	Year					
	0	**1**	**2**	**3**	**4**	**5**
Touchstone Ventures						
Free cash flows	$(6,000)	0	0	0	0	$ 62,915
Internal rate of return	**60%**					
Second round investor						
Free cash flows			$(4,000)	0	0	$ 10,976
Internal rate of return			**40%**			
Entrepreneurs' cash flows						
Value of idea	$(2,490)	0	0	0	0	$ 26,109
Internal rate of return	**60%**					
Total						$100,000

capital do not differ systematically from comparable stock market returns.[2] They might be consistently better for some leading venture firms and for the industry as a whole in some years, but the figures do not suggest that venture capitalists are systematically gouging the entrepreneurs with whom they partner.

Why then are target returns so high? There are at least four possible explanations. First, venture investing is a very risky business, and high risk invariably commands high return. When venture investors must screen as many as 100 proposals for each investment made, and when they earn real money on only 1 or 2 investments in 10, target rates must be high to compensate for the many disappointments. Second, high target rates have history on their side. They have been consistent over the years with adequate deal flow and, as just noted, the realized returns earned using these high targets have been sufficient to attract new investment capital. Third, venture capitalists argue that they provide much more than money when they invest and that they deserve compensation for these ancillary services. Rather than bill directly for their counsel, connections, and occasional outright direction, venture capitalists bundle their fees into the required target return.

Finally, high target returns may be a natural outgrowth of the dynamic between venture capitalist and entrepreneur. Venture capitalists consistently maintain that the business plans crossing their desks are overly optimistic. It is not so much that the numbers in the plan are unobtainable, but rather that the plan ignores the myriad ways in which a startup business can fail. So instead of representing the expected outcome, the plan is essentially a best-case scenario. When presented with such projections, the venture capitalist has two choices: Try to argue the entrepreneur down to more reasonable numbers, or accept the entrepreneur's numbers at face value and discount them at an inflated target rate.

Two forces favor the "inflated target" strategy. For psychological reasons, the venture capitalist would prefer that the entrepreneur strive to meet his optimistic plan rather than settle for a lower, albeit more realistic, objective. Moreover, for practical reasons, the venture capitalist will find it difficult to convince the entrepreneur—who typically knows more about the business than the venture capitalist—that his plan is overly optimistic. Better to concede gracefully on the business plan, and recoup by demanding a high target return. This might suggest a war of escalating projections in which entrepreneurs progressively ratchet up their forecasts to counteract venture capitalists' artificially high rates, while venture investors progressively raise their target rates to offset entrepreneurs' increasingly implausible projections. However, this is unlikely to occur. Venture capitalists are expert at ferreting out overblown forecasts, so unless the entrepreneur truly believes her numbers, she has little chance of convincing venture capitalists of their plausibility.

---

[2] Steven Kaplan and Josh Lerner, "It Ain't Broke: The Past, Present, and Future of Venture Capital," *Journal of Applied Corporate Finance* , Spring 2010, pp. 36–47.

SUMMARY

1. Valuing a business
   - Is the art of pricing all or part of a business.
   - Is the central discipline underlying all corporate restructurings, including:
     – Leveraged buyouts, acquisitions, large stock repurchases, sale or purchase of a division, recapitalizations, spin-offs, and carve-outs.
   - Begins by answering three questions:
     – Value a firm's assets or its equity?
     – Value the business dead or alive?
     – Value a minority interest or control?

2. Discounted cash flow valuation
   - Views a business as if it were a large capital expenditure opportunity.
   - Estimates the present value of a target's free cash flows discounted at its weighted-average cost of capital.
   - Presents two major challenges:
     – Estimating a forecast horizon when the target can be treated as mature.
     – Estimating a terminal value applicable at the forecast horizon, possibly based on liquidation value, book value, a warranted price-to-earnings multiple, a no-growth perpetuity, or a perpetually growing cash flow.

3. Comparable trades valuation
   - Infers value from the prices at which comparable public firms trade.
   - Requires identifying suitable indicators of value such as
     – Price to earnings.
     – Price to sales.
     – Price to book value.
   - May require a discount for lack of marketability, or a premium for control.
   - Is a close cousin to comparable transactions valuation.

4. The premium for control
   - Is the excess above a firm's stand-alone value paid by an acquirer.
   - Should not exceed the present value of all enhancements anticipated by the buyer.
   - May include the value of three possible financial enhancements:
     – Increased tax shields.
     – Improved incentives from new ownership.
     – Shareholders wresting control of free cash flow from managers.

5. Empirical evidence indicates that (on average)
   - Acquisitions create shareholder value.
   - Shareholders of selling firms receive premiums of 20–40 percent.

- Shareholders of buying firms earn little or no premiums.
- Leveraged buyouts lead to improvements in operating performance and attractive returns to buyers.

ADDITIONAL RESOURCES

Brotherson, Todd, Kenneth Eades, Robert Harris, and Robert Higgins. "Company Valuation in Mergers and Acquisitions: How is Discounted Cash Flow Applied by Leading Practitioners?" *Journal of Applied Finance,* Vol. 24, No. 2, 2014, pp. 43–51.

   Based on interviews with major investment banks, the authors find considerable alignment among advisors, academics, and practitioners on the use of discounted cash flow techniques as applied to business valuation.

Bruner, Robert F. *Applied Mergers and Acquisitions.* New York: John Wiley & Sons, 2004. 1,029 pages.

   A hefty book written to bridge the gap between theory and practice. Topics range from strategy and the origination of merger proposals through valuations and accounting to post-merger integration.

Gaughan, Patrick A. *Mergers, Acquisitions, and Corporate Restructurings.* 6th ed. New York: John Wiley & Sons, 2015. 688 pages.

   A balanced look at corporate acquisitions and restructurings. Less technical and broader in scope than the Koller book. Includes a historical overview, as well as accounting and legal dimensions of the topic.

Kaplan, Steven N., and Richard S. Ruback. "The Valuation of Cash Flow Forecasts: An Empirical Analysis." *Journal of Finance,* September 1995, pp. 1059–1093.

   Empirical support for the discounted cash flow approach to business valuation. The authors compare present values of projected cash flows to subsequent market values of 51 highly levered transactions between 1983 and 1989. Discounted cash flow valuations are within 10 percent, on average, of market values. The DCF valuations prove at least as accurate as those based on comparable trades.

Koller, Tim, Marc Goedhart, and David Wessels. *Valuation: Measuring and Managing the Value of Companies.* 6th ed. New York: John Wiley & Sons, 2015. 848 pages.

   Written by two McKinsey & Company consultants and an academic, this is a practical, how-to discussion of business valuation. You can spend $60,000 and let McKinsey do a valuation for you or spend about $50 for the paperback edition of this book and learn how to do it yourself.

uValue Mobile

Created by professors Aswath Damodaran at NYU and Anant Sundaram at Dartmouth, this app helps you value companies using various methods, including WACC and APV. Also includes tools for valuing bonds and calculating the cost of capital, among others. Available for iOS (search Apple's app store for "uValue Mobile").

valuepro.net

A free discounted cash flow valuation model based on 20 input variables. Enter a stock ticker symbol and Valuepro performs a DCF valuation of the business based on current estimates of the 20 variables. Change any of the variables and see how the estimated stock price changes. Created by three faculty members at Penn State. Check out how overpriced your stocks really are.

khanacademy.org

For brief, easy-to-follow tutorials on mergers and acquisitions, select Economics and finance > Stocks and bonds > Mergers and acquisitions. Also available as a free app for iOS or Android.

ecorner.stanford.edu

Sponsored by the Stanford Technology Ventures Program, this site contains hundreds of podcasts and videos by such luminaries as Mark Zuckerberg, founder of Facebook, and Reid Hoffman, founder of LinkedIn. Topics include finance and venture capital, opportunity recognition, and marketing and sales.

PROBLEMS

Answers to odd-numbered problems appear at the end of the book. Answers to even-numbered problems and additional exercises are available in the Instructor Resources within McGraw-Hill's *Connect* (see the Preface for more information).

1. Is each of the following statements true or false? Explain your answers briefly.
   a. On average, acquisitions destroy shareholder value.
   b. A discounted cash flow valuation of a target company discounts the target's estimated free cash flows at the acquirer's cost of capital.
   c. An acquirer should be willing to pay a higher control premium for a well-managed company than a poorly managed one.
   d. The liquidation value of a company's shares always places a floor under its stock price.
   e. An unusually low stock price in managements' eyes encourages management to take the company private in a management buyout.

2. Calculate free cash flow for 2017 for Monarch Textiles, Inc., based on the financial information that follows. Assume that all current liabilities are non-interest-bearing liabilities and that no fixed assets were sold or disposed of during 2017.

Monarch Textiles, Inc. ($ thousands)				
Income statement		**Selected balance sheet items**		
	2017		**2016**	**2017**
Sales	1,100	Current assets	300	400
Cost of sales	700	Net fixed assets	100	200
Operating expenses	100			
Depreciation	50	Current liabilities	200	280
Interest expense	50			
Earnings before taxes	200			
Tax	80			
Net income	120			

3. In July 2007, News Corp. entered into an agreement to purchase all of the outstanding shares of Dow Jones and Company for $60 per share. Immediately prior to the News Corp. bid, the shares of Dow Jones traded at $33 per share. The number of outstanding shares at the time of the announcement was 82 million. The book value of interest-bearing liabilities on the balance sheet of Dow Jones was $1.46 billion.

   a. Estimate the cost of this acquisition to the shareholders of News Corp.

   b. What value did News Corp. place on the control of Dow Jones and Company?

4. The following table shows the projected free cash flows of an acquisition target. The potential acquirer wants to estimate its maximum acquisition price at an 8 percent discount rate and a terminal value in year 5 based on the perpetual growth equation with a 4 percent perpetual growth rate.

Year	1	2	3	4	5
Free cash flow	−800	−400	0	200	700

   a. Estimate the target's maximum acquisition price.

   b. Estimate the target's maximum acquisition price when the discount rate is 7 percent and the perpetual growth rate is 5 percent.

   c. Considering your answers to parts (a) and (b) of this question, what is the percentage change in the maximum acquisition price when the discount rate is reduced one percentage point and the perpetual growth rate is increased one percentage point?

5. A recent income statement for Rainier Printing is shown next.

Net sales	$10,000
Cost of sales	6,500
Gross profit	3,500
Operating expense	1,200
Depreciation expense	600
Operating income	1,700
Interest expense	300
Income before tax	1,400
Tax	420
Income after tax	$ 980

Calculate Rainier's free cash flow in this year, assuming it spent $630 on new capital equipment and increased current assets net of non-interest-bearing current liabilities by $450.

6. A sporting goods manufacturer has decided to expand into a related business. Management estimates that to build and staff a facility of the desired size and to attain capacity operations would cost $450 million in present value terms. Alternatively, the company could acquire an existing firm or division with the desired capacity. One such opportunity is a division of another company. The book value of the division's assets is $250 million and its earnings before interest and tax are presently $50 million. Publicly traded comparable companies are selling in a narrow range around 12 times current earnings. These companies have book value debt-to-asset ratios averaging 40 percent with an average interest rate of 10 percent.

a. Using a tax rate of 34 percent, estimate the minimum price the owner of the division should consider for its sale.
b. What is the maximum price the acquirer should be willing to pay?
c. Does it appear that an acquisition is feasible? Why or why not?
d. Would a 25 percent increase in stock prices to an industry average price-to-earnings ratio of 15 change your answer to (c)? Why or why not?
e. Referring to the $450 million price tag as the replacement value of the division, what would you predict would happen to acquisition activity when market values of companies and divisions rise above their replacement values?

7. Flatbush Shipyards is a no-growth company expected to pay a $12-per-share annual dividend into the distant future. Its cost of equity capital is 15 percent. The new president abhors the no-growth image and proposes to halve next year's dividend to $6 per share and use the savings to acquire another firm. The president maintains that this strategy will boost sales, earnings, and assets. Moreover, he is confident that after the acquisition, dividends in year 2 and beyond can be increased to $12.75 per share.

    a. Do you agree that the acquisition will likely increase sales, earnings, and assets?

    b. Estimate the per share value of Flatbush's stock immediately prior to the president's proposal.

    c. Estimate the per share value immediately after the proposal has been announced.

    d. As an owner of Flatbush, would you support the president's proposal? Why or why not?

8. a. What does it mean when a company's free cash flow is negative in one or more years?

    b. Do negative values of free cash flow in any way alter or invalidate the notion that a company's fair market value equals the present value of its free cash flows discounted at the company's weighted-average cost of capital?

    c. Suppose a company's free cash flows were expected to be negative in all future periods. Can you conceive of any reasons for buying the company's stock?

9. Procureps, Inc. (P) is considering two possible acquisitions, neither of which promises any enhancements or synergistic benefits. V1 is a poorly performing firm in a declining industry with a price-to-earnings ratio of 8 times. V2 is a high-growth technology company with a price-to-earnings ratio of 35 times. Procureps is interested in making any acquisition that increases its current earnings per share. All of Procureps's acquisitions are exchange-of-share mergers.

    a. Calculate the maximum percentage premium Procureps can afford to pay for V1 and V2 by replacing the question marks in the following table.

    b. What do your answers to part (a) suggest about the wisdom of using "avoid dilution in earnings per share" as a criterion in merger analysis?

Company	P	V1	P + V1	V2	P + V2
Earnings after tax ($ millions)	2	1	3	1	3
Price-to-earnings ratio (X)	30	8		35	
Market value of equity ($ millions)	?	?		?	
Number of equity shares (millions)	1	1	?	1	?
Earnings per share ($)	2	1	2	1	2
Price per share ($)	?	?		?	
Maximum new shares issued (millions)		?		?	
Value of new shares issued ($ millions)		?		?	
Maximum acquisition premium (%)		?		?	

10. Stryker Corporation is a leading medical technology company head-quartered in Kalamazoo, Michigan, that trades on the New York Stock Exchange. Use the following information on Stryker and seven other similar companies (indicated by their ticker symbols) to value Stryker's common stock as of December 31, 2013.

Stryker Corp. ($ millions)	
Sales	9,021
Net income	1,616
Number of common shares (millions)	378
Earnings before interest and tax	2,163
Tax rate	22.3%
Book value of equity	9,047
Book value interest-bearing debt	2,764

	Stryker	BAX	BDX	COV	MDT	SNN	STJ	ZMH
Comparison of Stryker with comparable companies:								
5-year growth rate in sales (%)	6.1	4.3	2.4	0.6	4.2	2.7	4.7	2.9
5-year growth rate in EPS (%)	8.4	3.0	0.9	3.5	11.6	7.7	17.8	4.5
Analysts' projected growth (%)	9.1	8.0	9.0	NA	6.6	9.9	10.7	8.4
Interest coverage ratio (X)	15.6	12.2	7.8	10.8	12.0	81.2	10.7	15.0
Total liabilities to assets (%)	42.5	67.2	58.5	53.6	46.4	30.5	57.0	34.2
Total assets ($ millions)	15,743	25,869	12,035	19,619	37,231	5,819	10,248	9,581
Indicators of Value								
Price/earnings (X)	17.8	18.8	23.1	20.3	15.8	23.2	24.6	20.8
MV firm/EBIT(1−Tax rate) (X)	18.5	21.7	23.9	20.5	17.7	23.5	28.1	21.5
MV firm/sales (X)	3.5	3.1	3.1	3.5	4.1	3.0	3.9	3.8
MV equity/BV equity (X)	3.1	4.5	4.2	3.3	2.9	3.2	4.1	2.5
MV firm/BV firm (X)	2.0	1.8	2.1	1.8	1.8	2.3	2.1	1.8

MV = Market value; BV = Book value. Market value is estimated as book value of interest-bearing debt + market value of equity. Earnings are fiscal-year earnings.

11. The following is a four-year forecast for Torino Marine.

Year	2018	2019	2020	2021
Free cash flow ($ millions)	−52	76	92	112

a. Estimate the fair market value of Torino Marine at the end of 2017. Assume that after 2021, earnings before interest and tax will remain constant at $200 million, depreciation will equal capital expenditures in each year, and working capital will not change. Torino Marine's weighted-average cost of capital is 11 percent and its tax rate is 40 percent.

b. Estimate the fair market value per share of Torino Marine's equity at the end of 2017 if the company has 40 million shares outstanding and the market value of its interest-bearing liabilities on the valuation date equals $250 million.

c. Now let's try a different terminal value. Estimate the fair market value of Torino Marine's equity per share at the end of 2017 under the following assumptions:

1. Free cash flows in years 2018 through 2021 remain as above.
2. EBIT in year 2021 is $200 million, and then grows at 5 percent per year forever.
3. To support the perpetual growth in EBIT, capital expenditures in year 2022 exceed depreciation by $30 million, and this difference grows 5 percent per year forever.
4. Similarly, working capital investments are $15 million in 2022, and this amount grows 5 percent per year forever.

d. Lastly, let's try a third terminal value. Estimate the fair market value of Torino Marine's equity per share at the end of 2017 under the following assumptions:

1. Free cash flows in years 2018 through 2021 remain as above. EBIT in year 2021 will be $200 million.
2. At year-end 2021, Torino Marine has reached maturity, and its equity sells for a "typical" multiple of year 2021 net income. Use 12 as a typical multiple.
3. At year-end 2021, Torino Marine has $250 million of interest-bearing liabilities outstanding at an average interest rate of 10 percent.

The following three problems test your knowledge of this chapter's Appendix.

12. A venture capital company buys 400,000 shares of a start-up's stock for $5 million. If the company has 1.6 million shares outstanding prior to the purchase, what is the company's pre-money value? What is its post-money value?

13. New ventures commonly set aside 10 to 20 percent of company shares at the valuation date for employee bonuses and stock options. Modify the valuation of ZMW Enterprises in Panel B of Table 9A.1 to include an employee set aside equal to 20 percent of the company in year 5. Specifically, calculate Touchstone's required percentage ownership at time 0 under these revised conditions. Assume as before that Touchstone and the second-round venture capital company continue to target returns of 60 percent and 40 percent, respectively.

14. Using the following information, please answer the questions about Sure-lock Homes, a start-up company. In your analysis, assume the valuation date is the end of year 6, projected earnings in year 6 will be $12 million,

and an appropriate price-to-earnings ratio for valuing these earnings is 20 times.

Financing Round	Amount in millions	Year	Required Return
1	$ 6	0	60%
2	8	2	40%
3	12	4	30%

In addition, the company wants to reserve 15 percent of the shares outstanding at time 6 for employee bonuses and options.

a. What percentage ownership at time 0 should round 1 investors demand for their $6 million investment?

b. If Surelock presently has 1 million shares outstanding, how many shares should round 1 investors demand at time 0?

c. What is the implied price per share of Surelock stock at time 0?

d. What is Surelock's pre-money value at time 0? What is its post-money value?

15. The spreadsheet available for download from McGraw-Hill's *Connect* or your course instructor (see the Preface for more information) contains information concerning the potential acquisition of Fractal Antenna Systems, Inc. by Integrated Communications Ltd. After reviewing this information, answer the questions appearing with the problem.

16. The spreadsheet available for download from McGraw-Hill's *Connect* or your course instructor (see the Preface for more information) presents information concerning Harley-Davidson and five of its peers. Use the given information to estimate the value of Harley-Davidson.

GLOSSARY

A

accelerated depreciation   Any *depreciation*[1] that produces larger deductions for depreciation in the early years of a project's life.

acceptance criterion   Any minimum standard of performance in investment analysis (cf. *hurdle rate*).

accounting income   An economic agent's *realized income* as shown on financial statements (cf. *economic income*).

accounting rate of return   A figure of investment merit, defined as average annual cash inflow divided by total cash outflow (cf. *internal rate of return*).

accounts payable (payables, trade payables)   Money owed to suppliers. Obligations due to trade suppliers within one year.

accounts receivable (receivables, trade credit)   Money owed by customers.

accrual accounting   A method of accounting in which *revenue* is recognized when earned and expenses are recognized when incurred without regard to the timing of cash receipts and expenditures (cf. *cash accounting*).

accrued liabilities   *Other liabilities.* A catchall accounting term referring to a collection of unpaid expenses that are individually too small to warrant a separate line on the balance sheet.

acid test (quick ratio)   A measure of *liquidity,* defined as *current assets* less inventories divided by *current liabilities.*

activist investor   A professional investor, not a company insider, who seeks to initiate significant corporate actions to improve her investment returns.

adjusted present value (APV)   *Net present value* of an asset if financed entirely by equity plus the present value of any side effects, such as interest tax shields.

---

[1] Words in italics are defined elsewhere in the glossary.

after-tax cash flow   Total cash generated by an investment annually, defined as profit after tax plus depreciation or, equivalently, operating income after tax plus the tax rate times depreciation.

allocated costs   Costs systematically assigned or distributed among products, departments, or other elements.

amortization   The provision for the gradual elimination of an asset or a liability by regular payments or charges. Often synonymous with depreciation.

annuity   A level stream of cash flows for a limited number of years (cf. *perpetuity*).

asset   Anything with value in exchange.

asset turnover ratio   A broad measure of asset efficiency, defined as net sales divided by total assets.

B

bankruptcy   A legal condition in which an entity receives court protection from its creditors. Bankruptcy can result in *liquidation* or reorganization.

bearer securities   Any securities that are not registered on the books of the issuing corporation. Payments are made to whoever presents the appropriate coupon. Bearer securities facilitate tax avoidance.

benefit-cost ratio   *Profitability index.*

β-risk (systematic risk, nondiversifiable risk)   Risk that cannot be diversified away.

bond   Long-term publicly issued debt.

bond rating   An appraisal by a recognized financial organization of the soundness of a *bond* as an investment.

book value   The value at which an item is reported in financial statements (cf. *market value*).

book value of equity   The value of *owners' equity* as shown on the company's balance sheet (cf. *market value of equity*).

breakeven analysis   Analysis of the level of sales at which a firm or product will just break even.

breakup value   The value one could realize by dividing a multibusiness company into a number of separate enterprises and disposing of each individually.

business risk   Risk due to uncertainty about investment outlays, operating cash flows, and salvage values without regard to how investments are financed (cf. *financial risk*).

C

call option   Option to buy an asset at a specified exercise price on or before a specified maturity date (cf. *put option*).

call provision   Provision describing terms under which a bond issuer may redeem the bond in whole or in part prior to maturity.

cannibalization   In corporate investing, an investment that attracts cash flows from existing products or services.

capital   The amount invested in a venture (cf. *capitalization*).

capital budget   List of planned investment projects.

capital consumption adjustment   Adjustment to historical-cost depreciation to correct for understatement during inflation.

capital in excess of par value (paid in surplus, additional paid in capital)   Cash contributed by shareholders over and above par value of shares issued. The sum of common stock and capital in excess of par value is the total amount paid for common shares.

capital rationing   Fixed limit on capital that forces the company to choose among worthwhile projects.

capital structure   The composition of the liabilities side of a company's balance sheet. The mix of funding sources a company uses to finance its operations.

capitalization   The sum of all long-term sources of financing to the firm or, equivalently, total assets less current liabilities.

cash   Any immediately negotiable medium of exchange.

cash accounting   A method of accounting in which changes in the condition of an organization are recognized only in response to the payment or receipt of cash (cf. *accrual accounting*).

cash budget   A plan or projection of cash receipts and disbursements for a given period of time (cf. *cash flow forecast, cash flow statement, pro forma forecast*).

cash conversion cycle (CCC)   A measure of the length of time cash is tied up in *working capital*. It is defined as *days inventory outstanding* plus *collection period* minus *payables period*.

cash cow   Company or product that generates more cash than can be productively reinvested.

cash flow   The amount of cash generated or consumed by an activity over a certain period of time.

cash flow forecast   A financial forecast in the form of a *sources and uses statement*.

cash flow from operating activities   Cash generated or consumed by the productive activities of a firm over a period of time; defined as profit after tax plus *noncash charges* minus noncash receipts plus or minus changes in *current assets* and *current liabilities*.

cash flow principle   Principle of investment evaluation stating that only actual movements of cash are relevant and should be listed on the date they move.

cash flow-production cycle   The periodic transformation of cash through *working capital* and fixed assets back to cash.

cash flow statement   A report of the sources of cash to a business and the uses to which the cash was put over an accounting period.

certainty-equivalent   A guaranteed amount of money that a decision maker would trade for an uncertain cash flow.

close off the top   Financial jargon meaning to foreclose the possibility of additional debt financing.

collection period   A ratio measure of control of *accounts receivable,* defined as accounts receivable divided by credit sales per day.

common shares   *Common stock.*

common-size financial statements   Device used to compare financial statements, frequently of companies of disparate size, whereby all the balance sheet entries are divided by total assets and all the income statement entries are divided by net sales.

common stock (common shares)   Securities representing an ownership interest in a firm. Also, on the balance sheet, the total par value of common shares issued.

comparable trades valuation   A valuation technique that relies on prices of shares trading on financial markets and representing small, minority interests.

comparable transactions valuation   A valuation technique that relies on prices of shares determined in acquisitions and representing controlling interest of the companies sold.

comparables   A method for estimating the *fair market value* of a closely held business by comparing it to one or more comparable, publicly traded firms.

compounding   The growth of a sum of money over time through the reinvestment of interest earned to earn more interest (cf. *discounting*).

comprehensive income (loss)   An obscure, technical accounting term equaling net income plus changes in the unrealized value of securities held for resale, foreign currency translation adjustments, minimum required pension liability adjustments, and certain futures contracts qualifying as hedges.

conglomerate diversification   Ownership of operations in a number of functionally unrelated business activities.

constant-dollar accounting   System of inflation accounting in which historical cost items are restated to adjust for changes in the general purchasing power of the currency (cf. *current-dollar accounting*).

constant purchasing power   The amount of a currency required over time to purchase a stable basket of physical assets.

consumer price index (CPI)   An index measure of the price level equal to the sum of prices of a number of commodities purchased by consumers weighted by the proportion each represents in a typical consumer's budget.

contribution to fixed cost and profits   The excess of *revenue* over *variable costs*.

control ratio   Ratio indicating management's control of a particular current asset or liability.

conversion ratio   Number of shares for which a *convertible security* may be exchanged.

conversion value   Market value of shares an investor would own if he or she converted one convertible security.

convertible security   Financial security that can be exchanged at the holder's option for another security or asset.

corporate restructuring   Any major episodic change in a company's capital or ownership structure.

correlation coefficient   Measure of the degree of comovement of two variables.

cost of capital (opportunity cost of capital, hurdle rate, weighted-average cost of capital)   Return on new, average-risk investment that a company must expect to maintain share price. A weighted average of the cost to the firm of individual sources of capital.

cost of debt   *Yield to maturity* on debt; frequently after tax, in which event it is 1 minus the tax rate times the yield to maturity.

cost of equity   Return equity investors expect to earn by holding shares in a company. The expected return forgone by equity investors in the next best equal-risk opportunity.

cost of goods sold (cost of sales)   The sum of all costs required to acquire and prepare goods for sale.

coupon rate   The interest rate specified on interest coupons attached to bonds. Annual interest received equals coupon rate times the *par value* of the bond.

covenant (protective covenant)   Provision in a debt agreement requiring the borrower to do, or not do, something.

coverage ratio   Measure of financial leverage relating annual operating income to annual burden of debt (cf. *times-interest-earned ratio, times-burden-covered ratio*).

crowdfunding   Raising money for a venture by pooling small contributions from many investors, usually through the Internet.

cumulative preferred stock   *Preferred stock* containing the requirement that any unpaid preferred dividends accumulate and be paid in full before common dividends may be distributed.

currency swap A contract in which one party pays principal and interest in one currency in exchange for principal and interest in another currency.

current asset Any asset that will turn into cash within one year.

current-dollar accounting System of inflation accounting in which historical-cost items are restated to adjust for changes in the price of a specific item (cf. *constant-dollar accounting*).

current liability Any liability that is payable within one year.

current portion of long-term debt That portion of long-term debt that is payable within one year.

current ratio A measure of *liquidity*, defined as current assets divided by current liabilities.

D

days inventory outstanding A ratio measure of control of *inventory*, defined as inventory divided by *cost of goods sold* per day.

days' sales in cash A measure of management's control of cash balances, defined as cash divided by sales per day.

debt (liability) An obligation to pay cash or other goods or to provide services to another.

debt capacity The total amount of debt a company can prudently support given its earnings expectations and equity base.

debt-to-assets ratio A measure of *financial leverage*, defined as debt divided by total assets (cf. *debt-to-equity ratio*).

debt-to-equity ratio A measure of *financial leverage*, defined as debt divided by shareholders' equity.

default To fail to make a payment when due.

default premium The increased return on a security required to compensate investors for the risk that the company will default on its obligation.

deferred income taxes A recognized obligation to pay income taxes in the future.

deferred tax liability An estimated amount of future income taxes that may become payable from income already earned but not yet recognized for tax reporting purposes.

delayed call Provision in a security that gives the issuer the right to call the issue, but only after a period of time has elapsed (cf. *call provision*).

depreciation The reduction in the value of a long-lived asset from use or obsolescence. The decline is recognized in accounting by a periodic allocation of the original cost of the asset to current operations (cf. *accelerated depreciation*).

derivative A financial instrument such as an option, forward contract, or swap, whose value depends upon the value of some other asset.

dilution The reduction in any per share item (such as earnings per share or book value per share) due to an increase in the number of shares outstanding either through a new issue or the conversion of outstanding securities.

discount rate Interest rate used to calculate the *present value* of future cash flows.

discounted cash flow The method of evaluating long-term projects that explicitly takes into account the time value of money.

discounted cash flow rate of return *Internal rate of return.*

discounting Process of finding the present value of future cash flows (cf. *compounding*).

diversifiable risk That risk that is eliminated when an asset is added to a diversified portfolio (cf. *β-risk*).

diversification The process of investing in a number of different assets.

dividend payout ratio A measure of the level of dividends distributed, defined as dividends divided by earnings.

Dodd–Frank Act A set of U.S. regulations enacted in 2010 with the intent of reducing risk in the financial system.

E

earnings (income, net income, net profit, profit) The excess of revenues over all related expenses for a given period.

earnings per share (EPS)   A measure of each common share's claim on earnings, defined as earnings available for common divided by the number of common shares outstanding.

earnings yield   *Earnings per share* divided by stock price.

EBIT   Abbreviation for earnings before interest and taxes.

economic income   The amount an economic agent could spend during a period of time without affecting his or her wealth (cf. *accounting income*).

economic value added   A business's or a business unit's operating income after tax less a charge for the opportunity cost of capital employed.

efficient market   A market in which asset prices instantaneously reflect new information.

enterprise value   The *present value* of projected cash flows to *equity* and to creditors discounted by the *weighted-average cost of capital*.

equity (owners' equity, net worth, shareholders' equity)   Ownership interests of common and preferred stockholders in a company. On a balance sheet, equity equals total assets less all liabilities.

equity value   The *present value* of projected cash flows to *equity* discounted by the *cost of equity*.

equivalence   Equality of value of two cash flows occurring at different times if the cash flow occurring sooner can be converted into the later cash flow by investing it at the prevailing interest rate.

equivalent annual cost or benefit   The *annuity* having the same time-adjusted value as a given stream of cash inflows and outflows.

Eurodollar   Originally a U.S. dollar in Europe, now any currency outside the control of its issuing monetary authority. The Eurodollar market is any market in which transactions in such currencies are executed.

expected return   Average of possible returns weighted by their probability.

F

fair market value (FMV) (intrinsic value)   An idealized *market value* defined as the price at which

an asset would trade between two rational individuals, each in command of all of the information necessary to value the asset and neither under any pressure to trade.

figure of merit   A number summarizing the investment worth of a project.

Financial Accounting Standards Board (FASB)   Official rulemaking body in the U.S. accounting profession.

financial asset   Legal claim to future cash payments.

financial flexibility   The ability to raise sufficient capital to meet company needs under a wide variety of future contingencies.

financial leverage   Use of debt to increase the expected return and the risk to equity (cf. *operating leverage*).

first-in, first-out (FIFO)   A method of inventory accounting in which the oldest item in inventory is assumed to be sold first (cf. *last-in, first-out*).

Fisher effect   Proposition that the nominal rate of interest should approximately equal the real rate of interest plus a premium for expected inflation (cf. *real amount, nominal amount*).

fixed cost   Any cost that does not vary over the observation period with changes in volume.

fixed-income security   Any security that promises an unvarying payment stream to holders over its life.

forcing conversion   Strategy in which a company forces owners of a convertible security to convert by calling the security at a time when its call price is below its conversion value (cf. *call provision, convertible security*).

foreign exchange exposure   The risk that an unexpected change in exchange rates will impose a loss of some kind on the exposed party. With **transaction exposure,** the loss is to reported income; with **accounting exposure,** the loss is to net worth; and with **economic exposure,** the loss is to the market value of the entity.

forward contract   A contract in which the price is set today for a trade occurring at a specified future date.

forward market   A market in which prices are determined for trade at a specified future date.

free cash flow   The *cash flow* available to a company after financing all worthwhile investments; defined as operating income after tax plus depreciation less investment. The presence of large free cash flows is said to be attractive to a corporate raider.

frozen convertible (hung convertible)   *Convertible security* that has been outstanding for several years and whose holders cannot be forced to convert because its *conversion value* is below its call price (cf. *forcing conversion*).

funds   Any means of payment. Along with cash flow, "funds" is one of the most frequently misused words in finance.

futures contract   A standardized, exchange-traded contract in which the price is set today for a trade occurring at a specified future date.

G

gains to net debtors   Increase in debtor's wealth due to a decline in the purchasing power of liabilities.

general creditor   Unsecured creditor.

going-concern value   The *present value* of a business's expected future *free cash flows*. The going-concern value of *equity* is the present value of cash flows to equity, while the going-concern value of the firm is the present value of cash flows to all providers of capital.

goodwill   Excess of purchase price over fair market value of net assets acquired in a merger or acquisition.

gross margin percentage   Revenue minus cost of goods sold divided by revenue.

growth options   Value-creating opportunities in which the firm has not yet invested.

H

hedge   A strategy to offset investment risk. A perfect hedge is one that eliminates all possibility of gain or loss due to future movements of the hedged variable.

historical-cost depreciation   *Depreciation* based on the amount originally paid for the asset.

hurdle rate   Minimum acceptable rate of return on an investment (cf. *acceptance criterion, cost of capital*).

I

income   *Earnings.*

income statement (profit and loss statement)   A report of a company's revenues, associated expenses, and resulting *income* for a period of time.

inflation premium   The increased return on a security required to compensate investors for expected inflation.

insolvency   A debtor's inability to pay his debts.

interest rate swap   A contract in which one party pays a fixed rate of interest on a specified amount of principal in exchange for a floating rate of interest on the principal.

internal rate of return (IRR)   *Discount rate* at which a project's *net present value* equals zero. Rate at which funds left in a project are *compounding* (cf. *rate of return*).

internal sources   Cash available to a company from *cash flow from operations.*

International Financial Reporting Standards (IFRS)   A set of accounting rules being progressively adopted around the world, intended to make financial statements reliable and comparable across countries.

inventories   Raw materials and items available for sale or in the process of being made ready for sale. For financial institutions: securities bought and held for resale.

inventory turnover ratio   A measure of management's control of its investment in inventory, defined as *cost of goods sold* divided by ending inventory, or something similar.

inventory valuation adjustment   Adjustment to historical-cost financial statements to correct for the possible understatement of inventory and *cost of goods sold* during inflation.

inversion   A tax ploy in which a company lowers its tax rate by acquiring a firm in a low-tax environment and moving its country of incorporation to that of the acquired firm. Not popular with the federal government.

investment bank   A financial institution specializing in the original sale and subsequent trading of company securities.

investment value   Value of a *convertible security* based solely on its characteristics as a fixed-income security and ignoring the value of the conversion feature.

investments   The company's ownership interest in the net assets of unconsolidated subsidiaries and affiliates.

J

junk bond   Any *bond* rated below investment grade.

L

last-in, first-out (LIFO)   A method of inventory accounting in which the newest item in inventory is assumed to be sold first (cf. *first-in, first-out*).

lemons problem   When sellers know more about an asset than buyers, buyers won't pay more than an average price for the asset. Sellers with above average assets will withdraw from the market, causing asset quality and bid prices to fall.

leveraged buyout (LBO)   Purchase of a company financed in large part by company borrowings.

leveraged recapitalization   An episodic change in capital structure or ownership composition involving substantial debt financing.

liability   An obligation to pay an amount or perform a service.

liquid asset   Any asset that can be quickly converted to cash without significant loss of value.

liquidation   The process of closing down a company, selling its assets, paying off its creditors, and distributing any remaining cash to owners.

liquidation value   The cash generated by terminating a business and selling its assets individually. The liquidation value of equity is the proceeds of the asset sale less all company liabilities.

liquidity   The extent to which a company has assets that are readily available to meet obligations (cf. *acid test, current ratio*).

liquidity ratio   Any ratio used to estimate a company's *liquidity* (cf. *acid test, current ratio*).

long-term debt   Interest-bearing debt obligations due more than one year from the company's balance sheet date.

M

mark-to-market accounting   The practice of adjusting the carrying value of traded assets and liabilities appearing on a business's balance sheet to their recent market values.

market for control   The active, competitive trading of controlling interests in corporations, effected by the purchase or sale of sizable blocks of common stock.

market line (security market line)   Line representing the relationship between *expected return* and *β-risk*.

market value   The price at which an item can be sold (cf. *book value*).

market value of equity   The price per share of a company's *common stock* times the number of shares of common stock outstanding (cf. *book value of equity*).

market value of firm   The market value of *equity* plus the market value of the firm's debt.

marketable securities   Securities that are easily convertible to cash.

monetary asset   Any asset having a value defined in units of currency. Cash and accounts receivable are monetary assets; inventories and plant and equipment are physical assets.

multiple hurdle rates   Use of different *hurdle rates* for new investments to reflect differing levels of risk.

mutually exclusive alternatives   Two projects that accomplish the same objective so that only one will be undertaken.

N

net income   *Earnings.*

net monetary creditor   Economic agent having *monetary assets* in excess of *liabilities.*

net monetary debtor   Economic agent having *monetary assets* less than *liabilities.*

net present value (NPV)   *Present value* of cash inflows less present value of cash outflows. The increase in wealth accruing to an investor when he or she undertakes an investment.

net profit   *Earnings.*

net sales   Total sales revenue less certain offsetting items such as returns and allowances and sales discounts.

net worth   *Equity,* shareholders' equity.

nominal amount   Any quantity not adjusted for changes in the purchasing power of the currency due to inflation (cf. *real amount*).

noncash charge   An expense recorded by an accountant that is not matched by a cash outflow during the accounting period.

nondiversifiable risk   *β-risk, systematic risk.*

notes payable   The total amount of interest-bearing short-term obligations.

O

operating cycle   A measure of the length of time cash is tied up in *working capital.* It is defined as *days inventory outstanding* plus *collection period.*

operating leverage   Fixed operating costs that tend to increase the variation in profits (cf. *financial leverage*).

opportunity cost   Income forgone by an investor when he or she chooses one action over another. Expected income on the next best alternative.

opportunity cost of capital   *Cost of capital.*

option   See *call option, put option.*

option premium   The amount paid per unit by an option buyer to the option seller for an option contract.

other assets   A catchall accounting term referring to a collection of assets that are individually too small to warrant a separate line on the balance sheet.

other expenses   A catchall accounting term referring to a collection of expenses that are individually too small to warrant a separate line on the income statement.

over-the-counter (OTC) market   Informal market in which securities not listed on organized exchanges trade.

owners' equity   *Equity.*

P

paid-in capital   That portion of *shareholders' equity* that has been paid in directly, as opposed to earned profits retained in the business.

par value   An arbitrary value set as the face amount of a security. Bondholders receive par value for their bonds on maturity.

payables period   A measure of a company's use of trade credit financing, defined as accounts payable divided by purchases per day.

payback period   A crude figure of investment merit and a better measure of investment risk, defined as the time an investor must wait to recoup his or her initial investment.

peer-to-peer lending   Online marketplaces that match lenders to borrowers without using a bank as an intermediary.

perpetual-growth equation   An equation representing the *present value* of a *perpetuity* growing at the rate of *g* percent per annum. Defined as next year's receipts divided by the difference between the *discount rate* and *g*.

perpetuity   An *annuity* that lasts forever.

plug   Jargon for the unknown quantity in a pro forma forecast.

portfolio   Holdings of a diverse group of assets by an individual or a company.

position diagram   A graph relating the value of an investment position on the vertical axis to the price of an underlying asset on the horizontal axis.

post-money value   A company's equity value implied by the price per share an investor pays, after investing (cf. *pre-money value*).

preferred stock   A class of stock, usually fixed-income, that carries some form of preference to income or assets over *common stock* (cf. *cumulative preferred stock*).

premium for control   The premium over and above the existing *market value* of a company's *equity* that an acquirer is willing to pay to gain control of the company.

pre-money value   A company's equity value implied by the price per share an investor agrees to pay prior to investing (cf. *post-money value*).

prepaid income taxes   A prepayment of taxes treated as an asset until taxes become due.

present value   The present worth of a future sum of money.

price-to-earnings ratio (P/E ratio)   Amount investors are willing to pay for $1 of a firm's current earnings. Price per share divided by earnings per share over the most recent 12 months.

principal   The original, or face, amount of a loan. Interest is earned on the principal.

private placement   The raising of capital for a business through the sale of securities to a limited number of well-informed investors rather than through a public offering.

pro forma statement   A financial statement prepared on the basis of some assumed future events.

profit center   An organizational unit within a company that produces revenue and for which a profit can be calculated.

profit margin   The proportion of each sales dollar that filters down to *income,* defined as income divided by *net sales.*

profitability index (benefit-cost ratio)   A figure of investment merit, defined as the *present value* of cash inflows divided by the present value of cash outflows.

profits   *Earnings.*

property, plant, and equipment   The cost of tangible fixed property used in the production of revenue.

protective covenant   *Covenant.*

provision for income taxes   Taxes due for the year based on reported income. Often differs from taxes paid, which are based on separate tax accounting rules.

public issue (public offering)   Newly issued securities sold directly to the public (cf. *private placement*).

purchasing power parity   A theory stating that foreign exchange rates should adjust so that, in equilibrium, commodities in different countries cost the same amount when prices are expressed in the same currency.

put option   Option to sell an asset at a specified exercise price on or before a specified maturity date (cf. *call option*).

Q

quick ratio   *Acid test.*

R

range of earnings chart   Graph relating *return on equity* (*ROE*) or *earnings per share* (*EPS*) to earnings before interest and taxes (EBIT) under alternative financing options.

rate of return   Yield obtainable on an asset.

ratio analysis   Analysis of financial statements by means of ratios.

real amount   Any quantity that has been adjusted for changes in the purchasing power of the currency due to inflation (cf. *nominal amount*).

realized income   The earning of income related to a transaction as distinguished from a paper gain.

residual income security   A security that has last claim on company income. Usually the beneficiary of company growth.

residual profits   An alternative to *return on investment* as a measure of *profit center* performance, defined as *income* less the annual cost of the capital employed by the profit center.

retained earnings (earned surplus)   The amount of earnings retained and reinvested in a business and not distributed to stockholders as dividends.

return on assets (ROA)   A measure of the productivity of assets, defined as *income* divided by total assets. A superior but less common definition includes interest expense and preferred dividends in the numerator.

return on equity (ROE)   A measure of the productivity or efficiency with which shareholders' equity is employed, defined as *income* divided by *equity.*

return on invested capital (ROIC) A fundamental measure of the earning power of a company that is unaffected by the way the company is financed. It is equal to earnings before interest and tax times 1 minus the tax rate, all divided by *debt* plus *equity.*

return on investment (ROI) The productivity of an investment or a profit center, defined as *income* divided by *book value* of investment or *profit center* (cf. *return on assets*).

revenues *Sales.*

rights of absolute priority Specification in bankruptcy law stating that each class of claimants with a prior claim on assets in liquidation will be paid off in full before any junior claimants receive anything.

risk-adjusted discount rate (cost of capital, hurdle rate) A *discount rate* that includes a premium for risk.

risk aversion An unwillingness to bear risk without compensation of some form.

risk-free interest rate The interest rate prevailing on a default-free bond in the absence of inflation.

risk premium The increased return on a security required to compensate investors for the risk borne.

S

sales (revenue) The inflow of resources to a business for a period from sale of goods or provision of services (cf. *net sales*).

Sarbanes–Oxley Act A U.S. law enacted in 2002 with the intent of reducing corporate financial fraud.

secured creditor A creditor whose obligation is backed by the pledge of some asset. In liquidation, the secured creditor receives the cash from the sale of the pledged asset to the extent of his or her loan.

Securities and Exchange Commission (SEC) Federal government agency that regulates securities markets.

selling, general, and administrative expenses All expenses of operation not directly related to product production incurred in the generation of operating income.

semistrong-form efficient market A market in which prices instantaneously reflect all publicly available information.

senior creditor Any creditor with a claim on income or assets prior to that of *general creditors.*

sensitivity analysis Analysis of the effect on a plan or forecast of a change in one of the input variables.

shareholders' equity *Equity, net worth.*

shelf registration SEC program under which a company can file a general-purpose prospectus describing its possible financing plans for up to two years. This eliminates time lags for new public security issues.

simulation (Monte Carlo simulation) Computer-based extension of *sensitivity analysis* that calculates the probability distribution of a forecast outcome.

sinking fund A fund of cash set aside for the payment of a future obligation. A bond sinking fund is a payment of cash to creditors.

solvency The state of being able to pay debts as they come due.

sources and uses statement A document showing where a company got its cash and where it spent the cash over a specific period of time. It is constructed by segregating all the changes in balance sheet accounts into those that provided cash and those that consumed cash.

spontaneous sources of cash Those liabilities, such as accounts payable and accrued wages, that arise automatically, without negotiation, in the course of doing business.

spot market A market in which prices are determined for immediate trade.

spread Investment banker jargon for the difference between the issue price of a new security and the net to the company.

standard deviation of return A measure of variability. The square root of the mean squared deviation from the *expected return.*

statement of changes in financial position A financial statement showing the sources and uses of working capital for the period.

stock *Common stock.*

stock option A contractual privilege sometimes provided to company officers giving the holder the right to purchase a specified number of shares at a specified price within a stated period of time.

strike price (exercise price)   The fixed price for which a stock can be purchased in a call contract or sold in a put contract (cf. *call option, put option*).

strong-form efficient market   A market in which prices instantaneously reflect all information, public or private.

subordinated creditor   A creditor who holds a debenture having a lower chance of payment than other liabilities of the firm.

sunk cost   A previous outlay that cannot be changed by any current or future action.

sustainable growth rate   The rate of increase in sales a company can attain without changing its profit margin, assets-to-sales ratio, debt-to-equity ratio, or dividend payout ratio. The rate of growth a company can finance without excessive borrowing or issuing new stock.

T

tax shield   The reduction in a company's tax bill caused by an increase in a tax-deductible expense, usually depreciation or interest. The magnitude of the tax shield equals the tax rate times the increase in the expense.

times burden covered   A *coverage ratio* measure of *financial leverage,* defined as earnings before interest and taxes divided by interest expense plus principal payments grossed up to their before-tax equivalents.

times interest earned   A *coverage ratio* measure of *financial leverage,* defined as earnings before interest and taxes divided by interest expense.

total capital   All long-term sources of financing to a business.

total enterprise value (TEV)   *Market value of the firm.* The market value of equity plus the market value of debt.

trade payables   *Accounts payable.*

transfer price   An internal price at which units of the same company trade goods or services among themselves.

treasury stock   The value of a company's common stock that has been repurchased. Treasury shares neither receive dividends nor vote.

U

underwriting syndicate   A group of *investment banks* that band together for a brief time to guarantee a specified price to a company for newly issued securities.

unrealized income   Earned income for which there is no confirming transaction. A paper gain.

V

variable cost   Any expense that varies with sales over the observation period.

volatility   The standard deviation of the return on an asset. A measure of asset risk.

W

warrant   A security issued by a company granting the right to purchase shares of another security of the company at a specified price and for a stated time.

weak-form efficient market   A market in which prices instantaneously reflect information about past prices.

weighted-average cost of capital   *Cost of capital.*

with-without principle   Principle defining those cash flows that are relevant to an investment decision. It states that if there are two worlds, one with the investment and one without it, all cash flows that differ in these two worlds are relevant and all cash flows that are the same are irrelevant.

working capital (net working capital)   The excess of current assets over current liabilities.

working capital cycle   The periodic transformation of cash through current assets and current liabilities and back to cash (cf. *cash flow-production cycle*).

Y

yield to maturity   The *internal rate of return* on a bond when held to maturity.

Suggested Answers to Odd-Numbered Problems

Chapter 1

1. a. It means that the company's operating activities consumed cash. A combination of two things can cause this: operating losses, and increases in accounts receivable and inventories. Operating losses can obviously be dangerous. Rising receivables and inventories need not be dangerous provided they are growing in step with sales, and provided the company is able to finance the cash shortfalls. Rising receivables and inventories relative to sales suggests slackening management control of important operating assets, a potential danger.

   b. This means that the company's investing activities consumed cash, that the company purchased more property, plant, equipment, or marketable securities than it disposed of during the year. For most growing, stable companies, cash flows from investing activities are negative as firms build production capacity and replace used equipment. Positive cash flows from investing activities can signal problems, suggesting the firm has no attractive investment opportunities or that it might be liquidating productive assets due to financial difficulties.

   c. Negative cash flows from financing activities means that the firm is paying out more money to investors (in the form of debt principal repayment, interest payments, dividends, and share repurchases) than it is raising from investors. Usually, negative cash flows from financing activities are associated with mature companies generating more than enough cash from operations to fund future activities. It is not necessarily bad news. Conversely, early-stage firms, rapidly growing firms, and those in financial distress typically have positive cash flows from financing activities.

3. a. False. Shareholders' equity is on the liabilities side of the balance sheet. It represents owners' claims on company assets. Or said differently, the money contributed by owners and supplemented by retained profits has already been spent to acquire company assets.

   b. False. Book value of equity is simply the "plug" number that makes the book value of assets equal the sum of the book value of liabilities and the book value of equity. If the book value of liabilities is greater than the book value of assets, then (by definition) book value of equity must be negative. This does not automatically spell bankruptcy. Bankruptcy occurs when a firm cannot pay its bills in a timely manner and creditors force it to seek, or it voluntarily seeks, court protection.

c. False. Earnings are allocated to either dividends or retained earnings after net income is calculated. Increasing the dividend will reduce retained earnings, but will not affect net income.

d. True. By comparing a balance sheet from the beginning of 2017 (year-end 2016) with a balance sheet from the end of 2017, it is possible to construct a sources and uses statement for 2017.

e. False. Goodwill arises when one firm acquires another at a price above its book value. For example, if one firm acquires another for $10 million in cash but the target has a book value of only $8 million, the accountants record a $10 million reduction in the acquirer's cash, an $8 million increase in assets, and a $2 million increase in goodwill to balance the accounts.

f. False. It's just the reverse. As an asset account decreases, cash is made available for other uses. Thus, decreases in assets are sources of cash. In order to decrease a liability account, the firm must use cash to lower the liability. Thus, decreases in liability accounts are uses of cash.

g. False. It is typical, but not always the case, that a company's market value of equity exceeds its book value of equity. For example, if a company's business strategy is outdated and its assets are obsolete, it may well have a market value of equity below book value.

5. Because the accountant's primary goal is to measure earnings, not cash generated, she sees earnings as a fundamental indicator of viability, not cash generation. A more balanced perspective is that, over the long run, successful companies must be both profitable and solvent; that is, they must be profitable and have cash in the bank to pay their bills when due. This means you should pay attention to both earnings and cash flows.

7. The General Secretary has confused accounting profits with economic profits. Earning $300 million on a $7.5 billion equity investment is a return of only 4 percent. This is poor performance and is too low for the company to continue attracting new investment necessary for growth. The company is certainly not covering its cost of equity.

9. Acadia, Inc. generated $480,000 of cash during 2016. The $500,000 net income ignores the fact that accounts receivable rose $150,000, a use of cash. It also treats $130,000 depreciation as an expense, whereas it is a non-cash charge. The $25,000 increase in market value of assets adds to the market value of the business, but is not a cash flow. Here are the figures:

Accounting income	$500,000
Depreciation (a non-cash charge)	+ $130,000
Increase in accounts receivable	− $150,000
Cash generated	$480,000

11. a. In 2017, company sales were $782 million, but accounts receivable rose $30 million, meaning the company received only $752 million in cash. (This ignores possible changes in bad debt reserves.) Letting bop stand for beginning of period, and eop for end of period, the relevant equation is

$$\text{Accounts receivable}_{eop} = \text{Accounts receivable}_{bop}$$
$$+ \text{Sales} - \text{Collections}$$
$$\text{Collections} = \text{Sales} - \text{Change in}$$
$$\text{accounts receivable}$$
$$\$752 \text{ million} = \$782 \text{ million} - \$30 \text{ million}$$

b. During 2017, the company sold $502 million of merchandise at cost, but finished goods inventory fell $10 million, indicating that the company produced only $492 million of merchandise. The equation is

$$\text{Inventory}_{eop} = \text{Inventory}_{bop} + \text{Production} - \text{Cost of sales}$$
$$\text{Production} = \text{Cost of sales} + \text{Change in inventory}$$
$$\$492 \text{ million} = \$502 \text{ million} - \$10 \text{ million}$$

c. Net fixed assets rose $78 million, depreciation reduced net fixed assets $61 million, so capital expenditures must have been $139 million (ignoring asset sales or write-offs).

$$\text{Net fixed assets}_{eop} = \text{Net fixed assets}_{bop} + \text{Capital expenditures}$$
$$- \text{Depreciation}$$
$$\text{Capital expenditures} = \text{Change in net fixed assets} + \text{Depreciation}$$
$$\$139 \text{ million} = \$78 \text{ million} + \$61 \text{ million}$$

d. There are two ways to derive cash flow from operations. If there were no financing cash flows for the year, then changes in the year-end cash balance must be due to cash flows from operations and investing activities. The capital expenditures of $139 million represent the investing cash flows of the firm. Thus, we can use the change in the cash balance from 2016 to 2017 ($49 million) and the cash flows from investing to obtain cash flow from operations.

$$\text{Change in cash balance} = \text{CF from ops} + \text{CF from investing}$$
$$+ \text{CF from financing}$$
$$\$49 \text{ million} = \text{CF from ops} + (-\$139 \text{ million}) + 0$$
$$\text{CF from operations} = \$49 + \$139 = \$188 \text{ million}$$

Alternatively, you can calculate the cash flow from operations from the items in the table. Begin with net income, remove any non-cash items (such as depreciation), and add any cash transactions that are not captured by the income statement (such as changes to working capital accounts). We can see that accounts receivable increased by $30 million, finished goods inventory decreased by $10 million, and accounts payable increased by $5 million. Depreciation was $61 million.

$$CF \text{ from operations} = \text{Net income} - \text{increase in acct. receivable}$$
$$+ \text{ decrease in inventory} + \text{increase in}$$
$$\text{acct. payable} + \text{depreciation}$$
$$CF \text{ from operations} = 142 - 30 + 10 + 5 + 61 = \$188 \text{ million}$$

13. a. Stock price per share = $90 billion/1.5 billion shares = $60 per share. Book value per share = $6 billion/1.5 billion shares = $4 per share.

b. Starbucks would pay $60 per share for the 25 million shares it repurchases. This reduces the book value of equity by $1.5 billion. Assuming all else remains the same, the new book value would be $4.5 billion.

c. Because nothing else has changed, investors do not change their perceptions of the firm, and there are no taxes or transaction costs, the market value should fall by exactly the amount of the cash paid in the transaction. The new market value should be $88.5 billion. Another way to think about the question is to note that repurchase of the shares will reduce cash by $1.5 billion or increase liabilities by the same amount if they finance the repurchase with debt. Either way, the firm is worth $1.5 billion less to owners after the repurchase, or $88.5 billion. With 1.475 billion shares outstanding after repurchase, the price per share remains $60 ($88.5 billion/1.475 billion shares). (In practice, share repurchases often have a positive price effect at the time of announcement. There are several explanations for this effect, some of which we will cover in later chapters.)

d. Shares outstanding increase by 25 million shares. At $60 per share, Starbucks would raise $1.5 billion. Assuming all else remains the same, the new book value of equity will be $7.5 billion ($6 billion + $1.5 billion).

e. Due to the same reasoning as in part (c), the market value should rise by $1.5 billion. In essence, the sale raises company cash by $1.5 billion, increasing the value of the firm by just this amount. The new market value should be $91.5 billion. The price per share should remain $60 ($91.5 billion/1.525 billion shares). (In practice, such equity sales often cause investors to be less optimistic about the firm's future performance and thus generate negative price effects at the time of announcement. We will discuss this topic more in Chapter 6.)

Chapter 2

1. The CEO is correct that ROE is the product of profit margin, asset turnover, and financial leverage, but an increase in prices will not necessarily increase ROE because increased prices will likely reduce sales. If operating costs are fixed, the profit margin could actually fall when prices rise. Even if operating costs are variable, a decrease in sales will reduce the asset turnover, and thus reduce ROE. It is uncertain whether the effect of the increase in profit margin on ROE will outweigh the effect of the decrease in asset turnover. When thinking about the levers of performance, it is important to remember that changes in company strategy can affect multiple levers, often in different directions.

3. a. True. Let L = liabilities, E = equity, and A = assets. Does $A/E = 1 + L/E$? Does $A/E = (E + L)/E$? Yes.

   b. True. The numerators of the two ratios are identical. ROA can exceed ROE only if assets are less than equity, which implies that liabilities would have to be negative.

   c. False. A payables period longer than the collection period would be nice because trade credit would finance accounts receivable. However, payables periods and collections periods are typically determined by industry practice and the relative bargaining power of the firms involved; depending on a company's circumstances, it may have to gracefully put up with a collection period longer than its payables period.

   d. True. The two ratios are the same except that inventory, which is never negative, is subtracted from the numerator to calculate the acid test.

   e. True. Decomposing ROE shows that a higher asset turnover ratio increases ROE. Thus, a firm wants to maximize asset turnover (all else being equal, of course).

   f. False. Earnings yields and price-to-earnings ratios are the inverse of one another. If two firms have identical earnings yields, they will have identical price-to-earnings ratios.

   g. False. Ignoring taxes and transactions costs, unrealized gains can always be realized by the act of selling, so they must be worth as much as a comparable amount of realized gains.

5. a.

	Year 1	Year 2
Current ratio	9.70	2.80
Quick ratio	9.61	2.31

Amberjack's short-run liquidity has deteriorated considerably, but from a high initial base.

b.

	Year 1	Year 2
Collection period (days)	28.3	28.1
Inventory turnover (X)	38.5	4.7
Payables period (days)	42.3	24.3
Days' sales in cash	919.3	243.7
Gross margin	8%	25%
Profit margin	−57%	−88%

c. The company lost money in both years, more in the second year than the first. Cash flow from operations is negative in both years—but has improved. Liquidity has fallen and the inventory turnover is down sharply. The more than 10-fold increase in inventory suggests that Amberjack was either wildly optimistic about potential sales or completely lost control of its inventory. A third possibility is that the company is building inventory in anticipation of a major sales increase next year. In any case, the inventory investment warrants close scrutiny. In general, these numbers look like those of an unstable, startup operation.

7. a.

	Atlantic Corp.	Pacific Corp.
ROE	28.1%	56.9%
ROA	21.3%	11.3%
ROIC	22.5%	15.2%

b. Pacific's higher ROE is a natural reflection of its higher financial leverage. It does not mean that Pacific is the better company.

c. This is also due to Pacific's higher leverage. ROA penalizes levered companies by comparing the net income available to equity to the capital provided by owners *and* creditors. It does not mean that Pacific is a worse company than Atlantic.

d. ROIC abstracts from differences in leverage to provide a direct comparison of the earning power of the two companies' assets. On this metric, Atlantic is the superior performer, although both percentages are quite attractive. Before drawing any firm conclusions, however, it is important to ask how the business risks faced by the companies compare and whether the observed ratios reflect long-run capabilities or transitory events.

9. Collection period = Accounts receivable/Credit sales per day
Credit sales = 0.75 × $420 million = $315 million

Accounts receivable = Collection period × Credit sales per day
= 55 × $315 million/365 = $47.5 million.

Inventory turnover = COGS/Ending inventory
COGS = Sales × (1 − Gross margin) = $420 million
× (1 − 0.40) = $252 million

Inventory = COGS/Inventory turnover
= $252 million/8 = $31.5 million

Payables period = Accounts payable / Purchases per day
(Because information is not available on Purchases, use COGS.)

Accounts payable = Payables period × COGS per day
= 40 × $252 million/365 = $27.6 million

11. Sales = (Cash/Days' sales in cash) × 365 = (1,100,000/34) × 365
= $11,808,824

Accounts receivable = Collection period × Credit sales per day
= Collection period × (Sales/365)
= 71 × 11,808,824/365 = $2,297,059

Cost of goods sold = Inventory turnover × Ending inventory
= 5 × 1,900,000 = $9,500,000

Accounts payable = Payables period × (Cost of goods sold/365)
= 36 × 9,500,000/365 = $936,986

Total liabilities = Assets × Liabilities to assets
= 8,000,000 × 0.75 = $6,000,000

Shareholders' equity = Total assets − Total liabilities
= 8,000,000 − 6,000,000 = $2,000,000

Current liabilities = Current assets/Current ratio
= 5,297,059/2.6 = $2,037,330

Assets	
Current assets:	
Cash	$1,100,000
Accounts receivable	2,297,059
Inventory	1,900,000
Total current assets	5,297,059
Net fixed assets	2,702,941
Total assets	8,000,000
Liabilities and shareholders' equity	
Current liabilities:	
Accounts payable	936,986
Short-term debt	1,100,344
Total current liabilities	2,037,330
Long-term debt	3,962,670
Shareholders' equity	2,000,000
Total liabilities and equity	$8,000,000

13. a. Days inventory outstanding = Inventory/(Cost of goods sold/365)

   Toyota: 18,342/(201,125/365) = 33.3 days

   Apple: 2,132/(131,376/365) = 5.9 days

   Collection period = Accounts receivable/(Sales/365)

   Toyota: 83,027/(252,708/365) = 119.9 days

   Apple: 29,299/(215,369/365) = 49.7 days

   Operating cycle = Days inventory outstanding + Collection period

   Toyota: 33.3 + 119.9 = 153.2 days

   Apple: 5.9 + 49.7 = 55.6 days

   On average, it takes Toyota 153 days from the time it acquires raw materials inventory until the time it collects payment for its finished product. The comparable time for Apple is only 56 days.

   b. Payables period = Accounts payable/(Cost of goods sold/365)

   Toyota: 48,570/(201,125/365) = 88.1 days

   Apple: 59,321/(131,376/365) = 164.8 days

   Cash conversion cycle = Operating cycle – Payables period

   Toyota: 153.2 – 88.1 = 65.1 days

   Apple: 55.6 – 164.8 = –109.2 days

On average, it takes Toyota 65 days from the time it pays for inventory until the time it collects payment for its finished product. Toyota needs financing to cover this period of time from when cash is paid out until it is received. The comparable number for Apple is *negative* 109 days, meaning that, on average, it receives payment for finished product well before it pays for its inventory.

c. Having a negative cash conversion cycle is rare, and it is a great financial advantage for Apple, because it does not need financing to cover its inventory. In fact, Apple's fast collection time and slow payment time result in a source of financing for the company. However, the possible disadvantages of having a short (or negative) cash conversion cycle are the risk of inventory shortfalls from having too little inventory on hand, the risk of driving away customers from demanding payment so quickly, and the risk of alienating suppliers from taking so long to pay for goods.

15. Suggested answers to *Connect* problems are available from McGraw-Hill's *Connect* or your course instructor (see the Preface for more information).

Chapter 3

1. A negative value implies that the company has excess cash above its desired minimum. You can confirm this on the balance sheet by setting the external financing requirement to zero and adding the figure for external financing required to cash. You will find that assets equal liabilities plus owners' equity in this circumstance; in other words, the balance sheet balances.

3. This would tell me I had erred in constructing one or both of the forecasts. Using the same assumptions and avoiding accounting and arithmetic errors, the estimated external financing required should equal the estimated cash surplus or deficit for the same date.

5. a. Net fixed assets$_{2018}$ = Net fixed assets$_{2017}$ + Capital expenditures$_{2018}$ − Depreciation$_{2018}$

   Net fixed assets$_{2018}$ = 2,000 + 500 − 260

   Net fixed assets$_{2018}$ = 2,240

   b. Equity$_{2018}$ = Equity$_{2017}$ + Net income$_{2018}$(1 − Payout ratio)

   Equity$_{2018}$ = 2,950 + 156(0.5)

   Equity$_{2018}$ = 3,028

   c. Total assets$_{2018}$ = Current assets$_{2018}$ + Net fixed assets$_{2018}$

   Total assets$_{2018}$ = 2,750 + 2,240 = 4,990

   Total liabilities and equity$_{2018}$ = Current liabilities$_{2018}$ + Bank loan$_{2018}$ + Equity$_{2018}$

   Total liabilities and equity$_{2018}$ = 1,155 + 500 + 3,028 = 4,683

   External funding required = 4,990 − 4,683 = 307

7. The company needs a certain level of cash in order to operate efficiently. Operating cash flows can be volatile and difficult to predict from day to day. Companies rely on a cash cushion to cover periodic cash flow imbalances. The amount of cushion depends on many things, including the volatility of the cash flows and the availability of other sources of liquidity, such as unused bank credit lines. While one might argue that the company could get by with less than 18 days' sales in cash as implied in the forecast, this figure is a good bit less than the recent median for nonfinancial firms in the S&P 500 of about 40 days.

9. Pro forma forecast for R&E Supplies 2019:

Income Statement Forecast	
Net sales	$33,496
Cost of goods sold	28,807
Gross profit	4,689
General, selling, and administrative expense	3,685
Interest expense	327
Earnings before tax	678
Tax	305
Earnings after tax	373
Dividends paid	187
Additions to retained earnings	$ 187
Balance Sheet Forecast	
Current assets	$ 9,714
Net fixed assets	270
Total assets	9,984
Current liabilities	4,823
Long-term debt	560
Equity	1,995
Total liabilities & shareholders' equity	$ 7,378
External Financing Required	$ 2,606

a. Projected external financing required in 2019 is $2.606 million, over $1 million more than in 2018. R&E Supplies needs to get off this treadmill as soon as possible.

b. External financing required falls to $2.416 million, down 7.3 percent.

c. External financing required rises to $2.977 million, up 14.2 percent in this recession scenario.

11.

Westmark Industrial, Inc. Income Statement
January 1, 2018–March 31, 2018 ($ thousands)

Net sales	$1,080
Cost of sales	540
Gross profit	540
Selling and administrative expense	540
Interest	90
Depreciation	30
Net profit before tax	(120)
Tax at 33%	(40)
Net profit after tax	(80)
Dividends	300
Additions to retained earnings	$ (380)

Balance Sheet March 31, 2018 ($ thousands)

Assets	
Cash	$ 150
Accounts receivable	192
Inventory	1,800
Total current assets	2,142
Gross fixed assets	900
– Accumulated depreciation	180
Net fixed assets	720
Total assets	$2,862
Liabilities	
Bank loan	**$1,362**
Accounts payable	240
Miscellaneous accruals	60
Current portion long-term debt	0
Taxes payable	80
Total current liabilities	1,742
Long-term debt	990
Shareholders' equity	130
Total liabilities & equity	$2,862

Comments:

Inventory is estimated as follows:

Beginning inventory Jan. 1	$1,800
+ 1st quarter purchases	540
– 1st quarter cost of goods sold	540
Ending inventory March 31	$1,800

Taxes payable are estimated as follows:

Taxes payable Dec. 31, 2017	$ 300
– payments	180
+ 1st quarter taxes accrued	−40
Taxes payable March 31	$ 80

a. Estimated external financing needed on March 31: $1,362,000.

b. Yes, they are the same. If they weren't, it would indicate I had made a mistake or used different assumptions for the two forecasts.

c. Yes, the pro forma forecasts can be analyzed in the usual manner to assess the firm's financial health.

d. They say little about financing needs at any time other than the forecast date.

13. a. Negative numbers for taxes mean the company's tax liability will fall by this amount. If the company does not have an accrued tax liability but has paid taxes in the recent past, it can file for a rebate of past taxes paid.

b. Cash balances exceed the minimum required level because the company has excess cash in these quarters. Cash balances are determined in these periods by first noting that external financing required is negative when cash is set at the minimum level. External financing required is then set to zero and cash becomes the balancing item equating assets to liabilities and owners' equity.

c. When greater than zero, external financing required becomes the balancing item equating assets to liabilities and owners' equity.

d. The company should easily be able to borrow the money. The amounts required are less than one-quarter of accounts receivable in each quarter.

15. Suggested answers to *Connect* problems are available from McGraw-Hill's *Connect* or your course instructor (see the Preface for more information).

17. Suggested answers to *Connect* problems are available from McGraw-Hill's *Connect* or your course instructor (see the Preface for more information).

Chapter 4

1. This statement is incorrect and evidences a basic misunderstanding of the chapter. A correct statement would be "An important top-management job is to anticipate differences between their company's actual and sustainable growth rates and to have a plan in place to prudently manage these differences." Constraining a rapidly growing company's actual growth rate to approximate its sustainable rate risks needlessly sacrificing valuable growth, while boosting the growth rate of a slow-growth business risks promoting value-destroying growth.

3. a. False. In addition to issuing new equity, companies can grow at rates above their current sustainable rate by increasing any of the four ratios comprising the sustainable growth rate: their profit margin, asset turnover, financial leverage, or retention ratio. The problem is that there are limits to a company's ability to increase these ratios.

b. False. Glamorous companies such as Twitter with an exciting story to tell can raise equity despite operating losses. More traditional companies have much more difficulty.

c. True. Repurchases reduce the number of shares outstanding, which contributes to increasing earnings per share. At the same time, the money used to repurchase the shares has a cost, which reduces earnings and tends to reduce earnings per share. In most instances, the former outweighs the latter and earnings per share rise when shares are repurchased.

d. True. Survey evidence suggests that most managers, most of the time, believe their shares are undervalued. Repurchasing undervalued stock is a productive use of company resources benefiting remaining shareholders.

e. False. A major theme of this chapter has been that slow-growth companies have subtle and often more serious growth management problems than their rapidly growing neighbors.

f. False. Good growth yielding returns above cost increases stock price. Bad growth at returns below cost destroys value and will reduce stock price sooner or later.

5. In most years since 1985, net equity issuance has been negative, meaning U.S. corporations have retired more shares measured in terms of value than they have issued. In aggregate, then, new equity has been a use of capital to U.S. corporations, not a source. (At the same time, Figure 4.6 illustrates that new equity has been an important source to a certain subset of companies characterized primarily by high growth.)

7. a. Medifast's sustainable growth rates are

	2006	2007	2008	2009	2010
Sustainable growth rate (%)	12.4	23.8	14.0	17.5	30.0

For example, in 2006 $g* = 6.0\% \times 99.5\% \times 1.3 \times 1.6 = 12.4\%$

b. Medifast's actual growth rate exceeded its sustainable growth rate by a wide margin in every year except 2008. The company was growing at a rate well above its sustainable growth rate. Its challenge was how to manage this growth without growing broke.

c. Between 2006 and 2010, Medifast increased every ratio except leverage, especially its asset turnover. Had Medifast not improved its operating performance, as reflected in profit margin and asset turnover, the financial leverage required to generate the company's sustainable growth rate would have been about four times as high as observed.

9. a. Jos. A. Bank's sustainable growth rates are

	2006	2007	2008	2009	2010
Sustainable growth rate (%)	28.4	24.4	22.3	21.9	22.1

For example, in 2010 $g* = 10.0\% \times 100.0\% \times 1.3 \times 1.7 = 22.1\%$

b. Jos. A. Bank does have a sustainable growth problem. Its actual growth rate is much lower than its sustainable growth rate.

c. Jos. A. Bank used excess cash to reduce financial leverage, and this helps to reduce the sustainable growth rate. The steady decline in asset turnover helps to decrease the sustainable growth rate as well, but it also signals a potentially troubling decrease in efficiency. Despite the decreases in these ratios, the spread between the sustainable growth rate and the actual growth rate is still substantial in 2010.

11. Suggested answers to *Connect* problems are available from McGraw-Hill's *Connect* or your course instructor (see the Preface for more information).

13. Suggested answers to *Connect* problems are available from McGraw-Hill's *Connect* or your course instructor (see the Preface for more information).

Chapter 5

1. Common stocks are riskier than U.S. government bonds. Risk-averse investors demand higher returns on common stocks than government bonds as compensation for the added risk. If returns on government bonds were, on average, as high as those on common stocks, prices of government bonds would rise and prices of common stocks would fall as investors fled to the safer but equally promising bonds. This would result in lower expected returns on bonds for new investors and higher expected returns on stocks until the trade-off of risk for return reappeared.

3. The value of shareholdings owned is most important to the investor. A company can arbitrarily change its stock price, and the number of shares outstanding, by splitting its stock. The stock price and the number of shares owned are of interest only to the extent that they help the investor calculate more meaningful dollar ownership numbers.

5. a. The holding period return is −4.76 percent [($60 − $110)/$1,050].

b. The bond's price might have fallen because investor perceptions of its risk rose or because interest rates rose. The price of a bond is the present value of future cash receipts. As interest rates rise, the present value of future cash flows falls, as does the price of the bond. See Chapter 7 for details.

7. a.

Stock price	$75.00
− 8% underpricing	6.00
Issue price	69.00
− 7% spread	4.83
Net to company	$64.17

Number of shares = $500 million/$64.17 = 7.79 million

b. Investment bankers' revenue = $4.83 × 7.79 million = $37.63 million

c. Underpricing is not a cash flow. It is, however, an opportunity cost to current owners because it means that more shares must be sold to raise $500 million, and each existing share will represent a smaller owner- ship interest in the company. P.S. Opportunity costs are just as real as cash flow costs.

9. While intriguing, this is not evidence of market inefficiency. Think of flipping a coin and trying to get "heads." If skill is involved, you would expect to get heads more than 50 percent of the time. But if coin-flipping is just luck, you would only get heads, on average, half of the time. Thus, if mutual fund returns were random, you would expect to see about half of all mutual funds outperform the market each year. Of these "winning" mutual funds, about half would again outperform the market in the sub- sequent year (in coin-flipping terms, when you flip heads, the next flip will result in heads approximately half of the time). After five years, you would expect that roughly 1/32 of the original sample of mutual funds would have outperformed the market each year [$(1/2)^5 = 1/32$]. When you start with 5,600 mutual funds, one would expect that, if no skill is involved, about 175 would have outperformed the market each year for five years (5,600/32 = 175). Given that only 104 have done so, it seems that luck (and not skill) is the likely cause of their success.

11. a. Suppose Liquid Force shares sell for $40 and it has announced a $6 per share dividend. Buy Liquid Force stock immediately prior to the announced dividend date for $40, receive the $6 dividend, and imme- diately sell the stock for $37. You invest $40, and immediately after the sale have $43 in cash. Easy money.

b. Liquid Force's stock price would rise prior to the dividend and fall more when the dividend is paid. As more and more investors pursue this strategy, the price drop will become larger and larger until the decline equals the dividend, ignoring any taxes or transaction costs.

c. Suppose Liquid Force stock sells for $40 before the dividend and the dividend is $6. You want to sell Liquid Force's stock short. Borrow Liquid Force stock from a shareholder and sell it immediately prior to the dividend for $40, pay the $6 dividend to the person from whom you borrowed the stock, and buy the stock for $28. Cover the short sale by returning the stock to the lender. You invest $34 ($28 + $6) and, immediately after the transaction, you have $40 cash. Again, easy money.

d. Liquid Force's stock price would fall prior to the dividend and fall less when the dividend is paid. As more and more investors pursue this strategy, the price drop will equal the dividend (in the absence of transaction costs and taxes).

e. Such trading guarantees that the stock price will drop by an amount equal to the dividend payment.

f. Ignoring taxes and transactions costs, a $1 increase in dividends results in a $1 decline in stock price, and thus a $1 reduction in capital appreciation. Rational investors are indifferent to whether they receive their return as dividends or price appreciation, so increasing the dividend cannot benefit investors.

13. The observed financing pattern can be attributed to several causes. First, there are significant fixed costs in selling bonds that make it uneconomical to raise the modest sums usually sought by small firms. Second, small firms, especially privately held small firms, face information asymmetry problems. Most investors know comparatively little about small firms and have little incentive to spend the resources necessary to learn more. This creates a market niche for local banks that are often familiar with local borrowers via other business relations and community activities. The banks are able to capitalize on this information advantage by charging a premium over public market interest rates. A danger to banks is that this information advantage appears to be dwindling over time as information technology improves.

15. The table below shows Yosemite's net interest payments for years 1 through 3. Negative signs indicate cash flows paid by Yosemite and positive signs indicate cash flows received by Yosemite, all in dollars. Note that Yosemite ends up paying an effective floating rate and that it benefits when LIBOR falls.

Year	LIBOR	Outstanding debt payment	Fixed leg of swap	Floating leg of swap	Net payment
0	5.1%				
1	4.7%	−500,000	+480,000	−510,000	−530,000
2	4.4%	−500,000	+480,000	−470,000	−490,000
3		−500,000	+480,000	−440,000	−460,000

17. The analogy is an appropriate one. Think of equity as a call option on the company's assets with a strike price equal to the value of debt outstanding. When the value of company assets is very low, equity holders' call option is out of the money. If they wish, they can walk away, leaving their option unexercised and firm assets in the hands of creditors. When the value of company assets exceeds the value of debt, the owners' call option is in the money. They can exercise their option by paying the value of the debt to creditors and owning the assets free and clear. The value of equity relative to the value of the firm looks like the payoff diagram for a call option.

Chapter 6

1. Public utilities have very stable cash flows. Few of us turn off our lights or take cold showers during recessions. Stable cash flows are just what are needed to support large interest obligations. In addition, utilities have large investments in land and fixed assets, excellent sources of loan collateral.

   Information technology companies, on the other hand, have highly uncertain cash flows, the kind ill-suited to servicing interest obligations. Many also aspire to rapid growth, meaning that maintaining the flexibility necessary to assure access to financial markets is important. They are thus wary of "closing off the top" by borrowing aggressively.

3. Because all firms face business risk, company EBIT varies over time. Debt is a fixed income security, meaning interest expense does not vary with EBIT. As a result, all of the variability in EBIT is borne by equity investors, who hold a residual income security. As leverage increases, the same variability in EBIT is borne by a smaller equity investment, causing variability per dollar invested to rise. This results in increased volatility in shareholder returns—or increased risk. Also, as evident from the range of earnings chart, leverage increases the slope of the line relating EBIT to ROE, and the steeper the slope, the greater the variability in EPS, and ROE, for any given variability in EBIT.

5. a. There are several reasons. First, companies with promising investment opportunities typically have valuable intangible assets whose value would decline sharply if the company got into financial difficulty; that is, the resale value of their assets is low. Second, it is important for such companies to maintain the financial flexibility that comes with a conservative capital structure to assure funding for future investment opportunities. They are making money on the asset side of the business and are thus ill-advised to do anything on the liability side to jeopardize future investments.

b. Most would follow this recommendation if they could, but lack of sufficient operating cash flow and the inability to raise additional equity force many small businesses into an extensive reliance on debt financing. For these companies, it is either grow with debt or do not grow. Also, many entrepreneurs view debt as a way to stretch their limited equity to gain control over more assets. In essence, they like playing with someone else's chips.

7. a. EBIT = Income before tax + Interest expense = $42/(1 - 0.3) + 10$

   $= \$70$

   Interest expense $= 10 + 0.04(50) = \$12$

   Times interest earned $= 70/12 = 5.8$ times

b. Times burden covered = EBIT/[Interest expense + Principal payment/(1 − Tax rate)]

   $= 70/[12 + 20/(1 - 0.3)] = 1.7$ times

c. EPS $= (70 - 12)(1 - 0.3)/20 = \$2.03$

d. Times interest earned $= 70/10 = 7.0$ times

   Times burden covered $= 70/[10 + 15/(1 - 0.3)] = 2.2$ times

   EPS $= (70 - 10)(1 - 0.3)/(20 + 2) = \$1.91$

9. a. An increase in the interest rate would lower the debt financing line in the range of earnings chart. This would reduce the EPS advantage of the increased leverage, or increase the disadvantage if EBIT is below the crossover point. It would also increase the crossover EBIT. Both changes would reduce the attractiveness of increased financial leverage.

b. An increased stock price would reduce the number of shares the company would need to sell to raise targeted funds. This would increase EPS at all EBIT levels under the equity financing alternative, making increased leverage less attractive. Said differently, a higher stock price would raise the equity financing line at all EBIT values, making debt financing less attractive relative to equity financing.

c. The range of earnings chart will be unchanged, but increased uncertainty will increase the probability that EBIT will fall below the crossover point. Such increased business risk will make debt financing riskier and hence less attractive.

d. Increased common dividends will not affect the range of earnings chart. The increased dividends will require paying out a greater proportion of earnings per share under both options. But because there are more shares outstanding with the equity issue, the higher dividend will make a debt issue relatively more attractive.

e. An increase in the amount of debt already outstanding will increase interest expense and lower EPS under both options. This will lower both lines in the range of earnings chart by the same amount, but will not affect the attractiveness of the one option relative to the other, at least as far as the range of earnings chart is concerned. Interest coverage obviously falls as existing debt rises, which makes additional debt financing riskier and thus less attractive.

11. a. Each year, sources of cash must equal uses. Sources are earnings plus new borrowing. Uses are investment and dividends. So, each year, the following equation applies: $E + 1.2(E - D) = I + D$, where E is earnings, 1.2 is the target debt-to-equity ratio, D is dividends, and I is investment. [The target debt-to-equity ratio is Debt $= 1.2 \times$ Equity. Annual additions to equity = Retained profits = $E - D$. Annual new borrowing thus equals $1.2(E - D)$.] Solving for D, $D = E - I/2.2$. The following table presents the resulting annual dividend and payout ratio.

b. Summing dividends and dividing by total earnings, the stable payout ratio is \$219/\$930 = 24 percent. Substituting this into the sources and uses equation, $E + 1.2(E - 0.24E) = I + 0.24E + CM$, where CM is the change in the marketable securities portfolio. Solving for CM, $CM = 1.67E - I$. The resulting values for CM and the year-end marketable securities portfolio appear in the following table. (Had I carried out the calculations with more accuracy, the ending marketable securities would have equaled the beginning value: \$200.)

	($ millions)				
Year	1	2	3	4	5
Dividends	20	−6	34	71	100
Payout ratio (%)	20	−5	20	31	33
Stable payout ratio (%)	24	24	24	24	24
Stable dividend	24	31	41	55	72
Change in marketable securities	−8	−83	−16	34	61
Marketable securities	192	109	93	127	188

c. The company can do any or some combination of the following: reduce marketable securities, increase leverage, sell new equity, cut dividends.

d. The pecking-order theory predicts a company will favor internal financing sources over external, and among external sources it will favor lower risk assets, such as bonds, over equity. The options are ranked according to the pecking order as they appear in the answer to part (c). Although cutting dividends is technically an internal source of financing, the adverse signaling associated with cutting dividends when the firm has a history of stable dividends is so strong I expect firms would list it behind selling new equity in their pecking order. Feel free to ignore cutting dividends in grading your answer to this question.

e. The pecking-order theory follows from the desire to avoid negative signaling (or lemon) effects of new equity issues, supplemented by the desire to maintain access to financial markets. If these goals are important to managers, they will naturally follow the pecking order.

13. The annual interest tax shield is the annual interest expense times the tax rate. In Haverhill's case, this is $6\% \times \$5$ million $\times 35\% = \$105{,}000$.

15. Suggested answers to *Connect* problems are available from McGraw-Hill's *Connect* or your course instructor (see the Preface for more information).

Chapter 7

1. a. PV = $735.03. The Excel formula to solve the problem is given by:

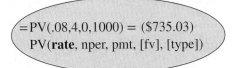

=PV(.08,4,0,1000) = ($735.03)
PV(**rate**, nper, pmt, [fv], [type])

The problem can also be solved using a financial calculator as follows:

Input:	4	8	?	0	1,000
	n	i	PV	PMT	FV

Output: −735.03

Note: The following answers will present only the Excel method, but in each case the problem can be solved equally well with a financial calculator.

b. PV = $540.27. The present value is less because the present sum has more time to grow into $1,000.

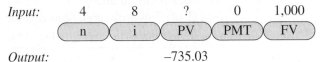

=PV(.08,8,0,1000) = ($540.27)
PV(**rate**, nper, pmt, [fv], [type])

c. FV = $20,565.89

=FV(.08,7,0,-12000) = $20,565.89
FV(**rate**, nper, pmt, [pv], [type])

d. PV = $13,503.65

=NPV(.08,5000,4000,0,0,8000) = 13,503.65
   NPV(**rate**, value1, [value2],...)

e. Nine years

=NPER(.08,0,– 2000,4000) = 9.01
   NPER(**rate**, pmt, pv, [fv], [type])

f. FV = $45,761.96

=FV(.08,20,-1000) = $45,761.96
   FV(**rate**, nper, pmt, [pv], [type])

g. PMT = $6,675.52

=PMT(.08,18,0,250000) = ($6,675.52)
   PMT(**rate**, nper, pv, [fv], [type])

h. If the stream lasted forever, PV = 600/0.08 = $7,500.00. Hence, the stream must be a perpetuity. If the stream lasted only five years, the salvage value would have to be $7,500. This is the amount required to be invested at 8 percent to generate $600 per year in perpetuity from year 5 on.

i. NPV = $133.22

=NPV(.08,50,75,110,110,80) – 200 = $133.22
   NPV(**rate**, value1, [value2],...)

Rate of Return Problems

j. IRR = 8%

=RATE(50,0,–1300,61000) = 8.00%
   RATE(**nper**, pmt, pv, [fv], [type], [guess])

k. IRR = 12.28%

> =RATE(22,0,–900000,11500000) = 12.28%
> RATE(**nper**, pmt, pv, [fv], [type], [guess])

l. IRR = 18%. Paying less than $22,470 implies an IRR greater than 18 percent, and vice versa.

> =RATE(10,5000,–22470) = 18.00%
> RATE(**nper**, pmt, pv, [fv], [type], [guess])

m. IRR = 14.87%. Assume you invest $1 today and receive $2 in 5 years. (Any other amount for which double is received in 5 years will give the same answer.)

> =RATE(5,0,–1,2) = 14.87%
> RATE(**nper**, pmt, pv, [fv], [type], [guess])

n. IRR = 10.36%. First, enter the investment cash flows in row 1, columns A through F on your spreadsheet.

> =IRR(A1:F1) = 10.36%
> IRR(**values**, [guess])

o. IRR = 14.9%. (Note that Excel requires you to enter a guess for this particular problem in order to solve it.) Once again, we see the power of compound interest. This does not suggest that investing in fine art is especially attractive. It ignores the costs of maintaining, insuring, and protecting a valuable painting, and the return on a Picasso can be expected to be much higher than the return on a typical fine art investment.

> =RATE(72,0,–7000,155000000,,.15) = 14.9%
> RATE(**nper**, pmt, pv, [fv], [type], [guess])

Bank Loan, Bond, and Stock Problems

p. PV = $932.90

> = PV(.08,10,70,1000) = ($932.90)
> PV(**rate**, nper, pmt, [fv], [type])

q. PV = 5/0.08 = $62.50

r. PMT = $14.1 million

> = PMT(.08,8,0,150) = ($14.10)
> PMT(**rate**, nper, pv, [fv], [type])

If the money is deposited at the beginning of each year, set the "type" equal to one for beginning-of-year payments. The answer is $13.06 million.

> = PMT(.08,8,0,150,1) = ($13.06)
> PMT(**rate**, nper, pv, [fv], [type])

s. PMT = $25,958

> = PMT(.08,6,120000) = ($25,958)
> PMT(**rate**, nper, pv, [fv], [type])

3. The effective interest rate on the time purchase plan is the discount rate that makes the seller indifferent to a cash sale for $48,959 and a time payment sale for $10,000 now and $10,000 for each of the next five years plus $2,000 fees. Subtracting the initial $12,000 (fees and first payment) from $48,959, the remaining annual payments would have to have a present value of $36,959. The interest rate at which the present value of a $10,000 annual payment for 5 years equals $36,969 is 11 percent.

> = RATE(5,10000,–36959) = 11.00%
> RATE(**nper**, pmt, pv, [fv], [type], [guess])

5. The present value of a constant stream of cash flows one year before the first cash flow can be determined using the perpetuity formula. The present value of the scholarship fund at time 2 is PV = $45,000/0.05 = $900,000. In order to have $900,000 in the scholarship fund in 2 years, it would be necessary to contribute $816,327 today.

$$= PV(.05,2,0,900000) = (\$816,327)$$
$$PV(\textbf{rate}, nper, pmt, [fv], [type])$$

7. This is a straightforward replacement problem.

	Old Roasters	New Roasters
Gross profit	$600,000	$1,200,000
– Depreciation	300,000	450,000
Profit before tax	300,000	750,000
Tax at 45%	135,000	338,000
Profit after tax	165,000	412,000
+ Depreciation	300,000	450,000
After-tax cash flow	$ 465,000	$ 862,000

If the company keeps the old roasters, NPV = $2.857 million.

$$= PV(.1,10,465) = (\$2,857)$$
$$PV(\textbf{rate}, nper, pmt, [fv], [type])$$

The present value of the after-tax cash flows from the new roasters is $5,297 million. If they sell the old roasters and buy the new ones, NPV = −4.500 + 1.500 + 5.297 = $2.297 million. Therefore, keep the old roasters.

$$= PV(.1,10,862) = (\$5,297)$$
$$PV(\textbf{rate}, nper, pmt, [fv], [type])$$

Alternatively, one can look at the difference in cash flows between the two alternatives. This amounts to analyzing the *incremental* cash flows. Subtracting the old roasters' cash flows from the new roasters' cash flows, where NPV = −3.000 + 2.439 = −0.561 million, indicates that spending an incremental $3 million to buy the new roasters is not attractive. It should not surprise you to learn that this NPV equals the difference in the NPVs of the two options. That is, −0.561 million = $2.297 million − $2.857 million. The IRR of the incremental cash flows is 5.4 percent, which because it is below 10 percent again indicates the incremental investment is unwarranted.

$$= PV(.1, 10, 397) = (\$2,439)$$
$$PV(\textbf{rate}, \text{nper}, \text{pmt}, [\text{fv}], [\text{type}])$$

9. The after-tax flows from the investment are:

Year	0	1	2	3	4	5
Initial cost	$15,000					
Revenue		$20,000	$20,000	$20,000	$20,000	$20,000
Operating expense		13,000	13,000	13,000	13,000	13,000
Depreciation		3,000	3,000	3,000	3,000	3,000
Income before tax		4,000	4,000	4,000	4,000	4,000
Tax @ 40%		1,600	1,600	1,600	1,600	1,600
Income after tax		2,400	2,400	2,400	2,400	2,400
+ Depreciation		3,000	3,000	3,000	3,000	3,000
After-tax cash flow	$(15,000)	$ 5,400	$ 5,400	$ 5,400	$ 5,400	$ 5,400

The investment is quite attractive. Its internal rate of return is 23.4 percent, well above the minimum target of 10 percent.

$$= RATE(5, 5400, -15000) = 23.4\%$$
$$RATE(\textbf{nper}, \text{pmt}, \text{pv}, [\text{fv}], [\text{type}], [\text{guess}])$$

11. What's wrong with this picture?

a. Add back depreciation to calculate after-tax cash flow. We are interested in the cash generated by the project, not the accounting profits. Using a salvage value less than initial cost captures the reality of depreciation. To also subtract an annual amount would be double-counting.

b. Do not subtract interest expense. The opportunity cost of money invested is captured in the discount rate. To also subtract financing costs would again be double-counting. More broadly, you should separate the investment and the financing decision whenever possible. If you must mix the two, it is possible to analyze the project from a purely equity perspective, but then you must also subtract principal payments to determine cash flows to equity. As we will see in the next chapter, this equity perspective can be tricky to apply in practice.

c. A 15 percent annual growth in earnings is not an appropriate corporate goal because it is not necessarily consistent with increasing shareholder value, or anyone else's value for that matter. Accounting numbers can easily be manipulated to create apparent growth even when none exists. Blind pursuit of growth biases management in favor of retaining income to invest in even very low return projects because they generate growth while dividends do not. The appropriate corporate objective is to create shareholder value, to undertake projects promising a positive NPV.

d. Thirty percent is the accounting rate of return, not the correct internal rate of return.

e. Increases in accounts receivable and "stuff like that" are relevant. True, much of the investment in working capital is recovered at the end of the project's life, but because money has a time value, the present value of the recovered working capital investment is less than the original outlay, and thus constitutes a relevant cash flow.

f. Extra selling and administrative costs are relevant if they are incremental to the project. Remember the with-without principle. If surplus employees would be laid off in the absence of this project, retaining them to work on this project generates incremental costs. If surplus employees would be retained and remain idle in the absence of this project, the costs would exist even without this project and would thus be irrelevant. The former situation appears more likely. I agree with Natalie: Dump David as rapidly as possible.

13. Suggested answers to *Connect* problems are available from McGraw-Hill's *Connect* or your course instructor (see the Preface for more information).

15. Suggested answers to *Connect* problems are available from McGraw-Hill's *Connect* or your course instructor (see the Preface for more information).

Chapter 8

1. a. False. Future cash flows are discounted more than near cash flows for risk because the discount rate in the denominator is raised to a higher power. A constant discount rate assumes risk increases at a constant geometric rate as the cash flow recedes in time.

b. True. The WACC is the appropriate discount rate to use for projects that have the same risk as existing assets of the firm. If a project is either safer (riskier) than average, it should be evaluated at a discount rate below (above) the firm's WACC.

c. False. This is yet another example of the marginal cost of capital fallacy. A company may be able to borrow the entire cost of a project. However, this does not imply that the cost of capital for the investment equals the borrowing rate. Increasing leverage increases the risks borne by shareholders, which increases the cost of equity capital. Alternatively, the discount rate for an investment is an opportunity cost reflecting the return available on same-risk investments elsewhere in the economy; it is not the cost of any particular funding source.

d. False. Interest expense reflects the coupon rate on debt outstanding when payments were made. There are several reasons interest expense/end-of-period debt outstanding may be a poor estimate of a firm's cost of debt. First, the amount of debt outstanding may vary over time, so the end-of-period debt does not equal the debt outstanding when payments were made. Second, we want the cost of new debt, and interest expense/end-of-period debt outstanding is a historical number. If market interest rates, or the company's creditworthiness, have changed since existing debt was issued, the historical cost will differ from the cost of new debt. Third, debt coupon rates may not equal the full return expected by the lender.

An extreme example is zero-coupon debt where all of the return is in the form of price appreciation. The cost of debt is best approximated by the yield to maturity on the existing debt; this is the rate of return investors demand today on new debt.

e. False. A firm's equity beta depends on two factors: the business risk of the firm and the financial risk imposed by the firm's capital structure. While firms in the same industry should have similar business risks, there is no guarantee that the firms will have similar financial risk.

f. True. The key to capital budgeting under inflation is to always compare like to like. When cash flows are nominal, use a nominal discount rate. If cash flows are real, use a real discount rate.

3. The lowest rate of return the entrepreneur should be willing to accept has nothing to do with the presence of an interest-free loan. The lowest acceptable rate is the rate the entrepreneur could expect to earn on the next best alternative investment at the same risk. The cost of capital is an opportunity cost determined by the attractiveness of alternative investment opportunities.

5. The WACC should be based on the risk of the project being considered, not of the firm doing the valuation. Both firms should use a beta for the cost of equity that reflects the risk in food processing, regardless of the volatility of their own industries. So no difference should be expected in the appropriate WACC each firm would use.

7. Equation 8.1 is used to calculate the weighted-average cost of capital:

$$K_W = \frac{(1 - t)K_D D + K_E E}{D + E}$$

In the case of SKYE Corporation, D is the book value of debt because the market value of debt is unknown ($10 million). E is the market value of equity, given by the stock price times the number of shares outstanding (30×1 million = $30 million). K_D is the yield to maturity on SKYE's debt (7.68%). Finally, K_E is found using Equation 8.2: $K_E = 6\%$ + 0.75(6.3%) = 10.7%. Putting all this together gives SKYE's weighted-average cost of capital as 9.2%, as shown below.

$$K_W = \frac{(1 - 0.4)(7.68\%)10 + (10.7\%)30}{10 + 30} = 9.2\%$$

9. Increasing financial leverage increases the risk borne by equity investors and hence increases the cost of equity capital. The company's equity beta will rise as well. Indeed, the rising equity beta causes the cost of equity to rise. Figure 6.1 shows the relationship graphically.

11. a. IRR of perpetuity = Annual receipt/Initial investment. We want IRR = 20% = ($3 million − (1 − 0.50)8%X)/($25 million − X), where X = Required loan. Here, X = $12.5 million. So the investor can pay $25 million for the property financed with a $12.5 million loan and earn an expected 20 percent return on her investment.

   b. 90% = ($3 million − (1 − 0.50)8%X)/($25 million − X). X = $22.67 million. All she needs to do is borrow $22.67 million of the required $25 million investment.

   c. Make certain you understand this answer. It's important. An investor would settle for a lower return because it takes less debt financing to achieve it. Leverage increases expected return to equity but also the risk to equity. Indeed, if the investor can borrow at 8 percent on her own, the broker is not making this investment any more attractive by borrowing more to increase the return to equity. See Chapter 6.

13. a. The annual debt service payment = $83.09 million. [$83.09 = PMT (.06,5,350)].

   b. The equity investor invests $50 million at time 0 and receives $16.91 million annually for five years ($100 − $83.09 = $16.91). The internal rate of return on this cash flow is 20.5 percent.

   c. This is a poor investment. Discounting the company's free cash flows at its cost of capital, its enterprise value is only $379.08 million. Buying the company for $400 million implies a negative NPV of −$20.92 million. (If the problem had not instructed us to ignore taxes, an additional source of value would be the present value of interest tax shields. But that term is not relevant here.) A 20.5 percent return to equity looks attractive, but this is just leverage talking. The return to equity is not sufficient to justify the risk borne. The investment is below the market line.

15. a. It is a call option. It gives General Design the option to "purchase" the expansion.

b. The strike price is the price at which General Design can purchase the expansion.

17. In addition to the discussion below, see the suggested answers available from McGraw-Hill's *Connect* or your course instructor (see the Preface for more information).

a. Stage 2 is identical to stage 1, but five times as large. The investment will take place 2 years from today and cost $425 million ($85 × 5). The following table summarizes expected future cash flows if the project succeeds and if it fails. Cash flows are all five times larger than the stage 1 analysis in Table 8.6(b) and delayed two years to reflect the later starting date of stage 2. If the project fails, cash flows reflect the option to abandon and earn five times the sales proceeds for the plant.

	Expected After-Tax Cash Flows ($ millions)							
	Present Value	1	2	3	4	5	6	7
Success	$634	0	0	250	250	250	250	250
Failure	$63	0	0	(50)	(50)	(50)	0	0

The present value of the future payoffs to the project is $634 million if it succeeds, and $63 million if it fails. The present value of the initial investment is $321 million [$321 = 425/(1 + 0.15)^2].

b. If General Design were to evaluate stage 2 before learning whether this technology is successful, the probability of success would still be the same as for stage 1 at 50 percent. The stage 2 decision is parallel to stage 1, so General Design would again abandon the project if it fails. The decision tree (for stage 2 only) is:

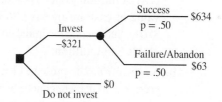

The present value of the expected cash flows for stage 2 therefore equals $348 and, after subtracting the present value of the cost of the stage 2 investment ($321), the NPV of stage 2 is $27 million ($27 = 0.50 × $634 + 0.50 × $63 − $321).

c. i. If General Design waits to learn whether stage 1 is successful, the full decision tree for both stages is:

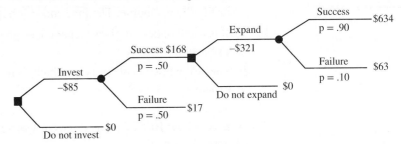

The main differences relative to part (b) are that stage 2 will only be undertaken if stage 1 is successful, and the probability of success for stage 2 is now 0.90.

The present value of the expected cash flows for stage 2 equals $577 and, after subtracting the present value of the cost of the stage 2 investment ($321), the NPV of stage 2 is $256 million ($256 = 0.90 × $634 + 0.10 × $63 − $321).

ii. Recognizing that there is only a 50 percent chance the stage 2 investment will ever be made, its expected NPV is $128 million ($128 = 0.50 × $256). Adding this figure to the $7 million NPV from stage 1 generates a combined NPV for both stages of $135 million.

iii. Explicit consideration of the option to expand adds $128 million ($128 million = $135 million − $7 million) to an already attractive project.

19. In addition to the discussion below, see the suggested answers available from McGraw-Hill's *Connect* or your course instructor (see the Preface for more information).

a. The present value of "success" cash flows at time 2 discounted at 10 percent is $948. The corresponding figure for "failure" cash flows is $101 million. At a 90 percent chance of success, the expected present value of cash inflows is $863 million ($863 = 0.90 × $948 + 0.10 × $101). Subtracting the initial cost of $425 million (already in year 2 dollars) yields $438 million.

b. As seen from the present, General Design's decision to invest in stage 1 gives it a 50 percent chance at a follow-on investment worth $438 million in two years. Because the next two years are higher risk, it makes sense to value stage 2 today by discounting this sum to the present at the original 15 percent discount rate, for a present value of $331 [$331 = $438/(1 + 0.15)^2]. Applying a 50 percent probability, the revised stage 2 NPV today is $166 million ($166 = $331 × 0.5).

Adding this to the original stage 1 NPV of $7 million [Table 8.6(b)] produces a revised total NPV for both stages equal to $173 million, $38 million higher than the value of the project using the constant 15 percent discount rate throughout (from Problem 17).

21. Suggested answers to *Connect* problems are available from McGraw-Hill's *Connect* or your course instructor (see the Preface for more information).

23. The annual interest tax shield is the interest expense times the tax rate ($1,000,000 $\times$ 0.08 $\times$ 0.4 = $32,000). The present value of the tax shields is found by summing the discounted annual tax shield for each of the three years [$32,000/1.08 + $32,000/(1.08^2) + $32,000/(1.08^3) = $82,467]. Then, the APV is the sum of the NPV of the free cash flows ($500,000) and the present value of the tax shields, or $582,467.

Chapter 9

1. a. False. Taking into account the gains to stockholders of both the acquiring firm and the target firm, acquisitions create value, on average, but virtually all of it accrues to selling shareholders.

   b. False. A discounted cash flow valuation of a target company discounts the target's estimated free cash flows at the *target's* cost of capital. The basic principle is: The discount rate should reflect the risk of the cash flows discounted. Here, the risk of the cash flows discounted is that of the target.

   c. False. Acquirers make money by buying poorly run companies and improving their performance. When a company is well run, the likeliwhood of materially improving performance is small, and the control premium should be correspondingly modest.

   d. False. The liquidation decision is in the hands of controlling shareholders—or if ownership is widely dispersed, incumbent management. These parties are under no obligation to liquidate, even when the firm is worth more dead than alive. If controlling parties are optimistic about the firm's prospects or if they are receiving large non-pecuniary firm rewards, they may elect to continue operations even when others believe the firm is worth more in liquidation.

   e. True. Say a company's stock price is $30, while management believes it is worth $80. Buying an $80 asset for $30—usually with the financial help of a buyout firm—has got to be an attractive investment. It can also create a major conflict of interest as management realizes they can get an even better price if they run down the company before buying it.

3. a. The value of the bid to News Corp.'s shareholders is the value of the assets acquired in the merger. This includes the value of the equity acquired plus the liabilities assumed by the buyer. The estimated cost

of the acquisition was thus ($60 × 82 million shares) + $1.46 billion = $6.38 billion. This is an estimate because the book value of Dow Jones' debt only approximates the market value, although the approximation is probably reasonably close.

b. The value of control is the difference between the bid price per share and the price per share immediately prior to the bid, times the number of shares outstanding, or $2.21 billion ([$60 – $33] × 82 million shares).

5. Free cash flow = EBIT(1 – Tax rate) + Depreciation – Fixed

investment – Working capital investment

EBIT = Income before tax + Interest = 1,400 + 300

= 1,700

Tax rate = 420/1,400 = 0.30

Free cash flow = 1,700(1 – 0.30) + 600 – 630 – 450 = $710

7. a. Any time one company acquires another, its sales and assets increase. Further, if the acquired company's earnings exceed the interest cost of any debt issued in the acquisition, earnings will increase as well. This is no surprise.

b. Value per share before proposal = $12/0.15 = $80

c. Value per share after proposal = $6/(1 + 0.15) + ($12.75/0.15)/(1 + 0.15) = $79.13

d. Clearly, owners of Flatbush should oppose the president's plan. It may result in a larger company, but it will destroy shareholder value; that is, the stock price will fall under the plan. The problem with the president's plan is that it takes money with an opportunity cost of 15 percent to owners and invests it in a venture yielding only 12.5 percent ($0.75 per year added dividend in perpetuity for a $6 investment yields 12.5 percent return).

9. a.

Company	P	V1	P + V1	V2	P + V2
Earnings after tax ($ millions)	2	1	3	1	3
Price-to-earnings ratio (X)	30	8		35	
Market value of equity ($ millions)	60	8		35	
Number of equity shares (millions)	1	1	1.5	1	1.5
Earnings per share ($)	2	1	2	1	2
Price per share ($)	60	8		35	
Maximum new shares issued (millions)		0.5		0.5	
Value of new shares issued ($ millions)		30		30	
Maximum acquisition premium (%)		275%		–14%	

b. This problem illustrates why concern with earnings per share dilution or accretion is shortsighted. Here, Procureps is tempted to pay a huge premium to buy V1 but is disinclined to even look at V2. Yet V2 is the exciting firm with future potential.

11. a. FMV = PV{FCF, 2018–2021} + PV{Terminal value}. PV{FCF, 2018–2021} = \$155.9 million. Terminal value = EBIT(1 − Tax rate)/0.11 = \$120/0.11 = \$1,090.9 million. PV{Terminal value} = \$1,090.9 million/$(1 + 0.11)^4$ = \$718.6 million. Summing, FMV = \$874.5 million.

   b. FMV of equity = (\$874.5 − \$250)/40 = \$15.61 per share.

   c. Terminal value = FCF in 2022/(0.11 − 0.05). FCF in 2022 = \$200(1.05) (1 − 0.40) − 30 − 15 = \$81. So terminal value = \$81/(0.11 − 0.05) = \$1,350. Present value of terminal value = \$889.3. FMV of company = \$155.9 + \$889.3 = \$1,045.2 million. FMV of equity per share = (\$1,045.2 − \$250)/40 = \$19.88

   d. Terminal value = Value of equity + Value of interest-bearing liabilities. Value of equity = 12 × Net income in 2021 = 12 × (200 − 0.10 × 250) (1 − 0.40) = \$1,260 million. Terminal value = \$1,260 million + \$250 million = \$1,510. Present value of terminal value = \$994.7. Therefore, FMV of company on valuation date = \$155.8 + \$994.7 = \$1,150.5 million. Value per share = (\$1,150.5 million − \$250 million)/40 = \$22.51.

13.

Employee ownership at time 5		20.0%
Round 2 VC's ownership at time 5		11.0%
Round 2 VC's retention ratio	= (1 − 0.20)	0.80
Round 2 VC's ownership at time 2	= 0.11/0.80	13.8%
Touchstone ownership at time 5		62.9%
Touchstone retention ratio	= (1 − 0.20)(1 − 0.138)	0.69
Touchstone ownership at time 0	= 0.629/0.69	91.2%

Confirmation of answer

Let X equal total shares outstanding at time 5 and recall that the founders own 2 million shares. Then, $0.20X + 0.11X + 0.629X + 2$ million $= X$

Total shares at time 5		32.79 million
Touchstone ownership at time 5	= 0.629 × 32.79	20.62 million
Price per share at time 5	= \$100 million/32.79	\$3.05
Value of Touchstone shares at time 5	= 20.62 million × \$3.05	\$62.9 million
IRR to Touchstone	See Table 9.A2	60%
Round 2 VC's ownership at 5	= 0.11 × 32.79	3.61 million
Value of Round 2 VC's shares at time 5	= 3.61 million × \$3.05	\$11.0 million
IRR to Round 2 VC	See Table 9.A2	40%
Value of options	= 20% × \$100 million	\$20 million
Value of founders' ownership	= 2 million × \$3.05	\$6.1 million

Note that the founders effectively pay for the employee options. Touchstone and the second round VC still get their target returns of 60 percent and 40 percent, respectively, while the value of the founders' time 5 ownership falls from \$26.1 million (see Table 9.A2) to \$6.1 million, with the missing \$20 million going to employee options.

15. Suggested answers to *Connect* problems are available from McGraw-Hill's *Connect* or your course instructor (see the Preface for more information).

Index

Financial statements
  analysis, and performance evaluation
    (*See* Financial performance)
  balance sheet, 6–12
  cash flow cycle, 3–6
  cash flow statement, 6, 18–22
  common-size, 65, 66
  economic income *vs.* accounting income, 26–27
  importance of, 5
  imputed costs, 27–30
  income statement, 6, 12–15
  market value *vs.* book value, 22–26
  ties among, 9
  and value problem, 22–30
Financing activities, 9, 22
Financing costs, 267–269
Financing decisions, 193–194. *See also* Cost of
    capital; Debt financing; Return on equity
    (ROE); Sustainable growth
  borrowing
    bankruptcy costs, 209–211
    irrelevance, 206–208
    tax benefits, 208
  capital rationing, 256–257, 270, 274–275
    unequal lives, 271–274
  cash flows and, 208
  financial leverage, 195–198
    and earnings, 203–206
    effects on business, 199–206
    and risk, 201–203
  and growth, 219–222
  Higgins 5-Factor Model, 208–219
    distress costs, 208–213
    flexibility, 213–215
    management incentives, 218–219
    market signaling, 215–218
    tax benefits, 208
  maturity structure, 222–223
Fixed assets, 5
  depreciation of, 13
  turnover, 47
Fixed-income security, 143

Flexibility, financing decisions, 213–215
Floating-rate debt, 145
FMV. *See* Fair market value (FMV)
Ford, 67
Forecast horizon, 348
Forecasting. *See* Financial forecasting
Foreign bonds, 145
Foreign exchange futures, 175
Forward contracts
  hedging with, 172–173
  types of, 174–175
Forward markets, 172
Fox, Justin, 186
Free cash flow (FCF), 21, 260–261
  business valuation, 344–345
  controlling, 362–365
Fridson, Martin S., 70
Friedlob, George T., 31
Futures contracts, 173–174
  types of, 174–175
Futures exchange, 173

G

Gaughan, Patrick A., 377
General creditors, 146
General Motors, 158, 162
Genomic Devices, 159
Gladwell, Malcolm, 158
Goedhart, Marc, 377
"Go-for-broke" problem, 212
Going-concern value, 340
Good growth, 126
Goodman, Jordan Elliot, 31
Goodwill, 25–26, 26n
Graham, John R., 132n
Grantham, Jeremy, 169n
Grossing up, 50
Gross margin, 41–42
Growth
  balanced, 115–116
  buying, and slow-growth problem, 127–128